# Fictional Discourse and the Law



Drawing on insights from literary theory and analytical philosophy, this book analyzes the intersection of law and literature from the distinct and unique perspective of fictional discourse.

Pursuing an empirical approach, using examples that range from Victorian literature to the current judicial treatment of rap music, the volume challenges the prevailing fact–fiction dichotomy in legal theory and practice by providing a better understanding of the peculiarities of legal fictionality, while also contributing further material to fictional theory's endeavor to find a transdisciplinary valid criterion for a definition of fictional discourse. Following the basic presumptions of the early law-as-literature movement, past approaches have mainly focused on textuality and narrativity as the common denominators of law and literature, and have largely ignored the topic of fictionality. This volume provides a much needed analysis of this gap.

The book will be of interest to scholars of legal theory, jurisprudence and legal writing, along with scholars and students of literature and the humanities.

**Hans Jochen Lind** (Ph.D. Yale University) is a Lecturer and, since 2003, Attorney-at-Law. He teaches German Literature, Theatre Studies and Media Studies at Yale University and at Vienna University's Institute for Theatre, Film and Media Studies. He was a Fulbright Scholar (2004–2005) and a Giamatti Fellow at Yale University (2005–2006), and later acted as coordinator of the Yale Whitney Humanities Center's working group "Fictionality – Interdisciplinary Approaches. Law – Literature – Science" (2010–2013). Legal clerking included the 5th Civil Chamber of Appeal (Law Clerk to Presiding Judge Basel).

# Fictional Discourse and the Law

Edited by Hans J. Lind

Routledge
Taylor & Francis Group
a GlassHouse book

First published 2020
by Routledge
2 Park Square, Milton Park, Abingdon, Oxon OX14 4RN

and by Routledge
605 Third Avenue, New York, NY 10017

First issued in paperback 2021

*Routledge is an imprint of the Taylor & Francis Group, an informa business*

A Glasshouse book



*British Library Cataloguing-in-Publication Data*
A catalogue record for this book is available from the British Library

*Library of Congress Cataloging-in-Publication Data*
A catalog record has been requested for this book

ISBN 13: 978-1-03-223668-1 (pbk)
ISBN 13: 978-1-138-60475-9 (hbk)

Typeset in Galliard
by Integra Software Services Pvt. Ltd.

# Contents


*Acknowledgements* viii
*List of contributors* ix

**PART I**
**From narrative to fiction in legal theory and practice** **1**

1 Theorizing fictional discourse: Toward a reassessment of the fact–fiction dichotomy in legal theory and practice 3
HANS J. LIND

**PART 2**
**The ubiquity of fictional discourse in legal theory and practice** **65**

2.1 Fictions of constitutional privacy: Toward a linguistic subject 67
CYNTHIA A. MERRILL

2.2 Adultery, criminality and the fiction of the king's body 84
ERIN SHELEY

2.3 Memory, history, and forgetting: *Shelby County, Alabama v. Holder* 92
LAURA CISNEROS

2.4 Boilerplate: Deconstructing the fiction of contract 105
TAL KASTNER

**PART 3**
**A matter of evidence? Fact and fiction in the courtroom** **115**

3.1 Dying declarations 117
PETER BROOKS

3.2 Rap as courtroom reality 124
HANS J. LIND

3.3 Fiction as courtroom fact? Exploration accounts as evidence in aboriginal rights and title litigation 138
LUIS CAMPOS

**PART 4**
**Fictional discourse as law's mirror and cradle: Metafictional qualities of law in literature** **153**

4.1 "A fearful and wonderful institution": Representing law in sensation novels 155
SARA MURPHY

4.2 Fictions of corporate intention: The epistemological problem of the good corporation 163
LISA SIRAGANIAN

4.3 Remedial fictions: The novelization of habeas corpus and the history of human rights 175
SARAH WINTER

**PART 5**
**Fictional discourse and the law: A theoretical perspective** **189**

5.1 Legal fictions and legal fabrication 191
SIMON STERN

5.2 Linguistic fictions and legal rule 200
HANS J. LIND

5.3 Cognitive fictionalizing and legal legitimacy 235
KAREN PETROSKI

5.4 Law as authoritative fiction 252
ANDREI MARMOR

*Index* 269

# Acknowledgements

I would like to express my deep gratitude to all those who made this project possible with their valued contributions and support. In particular, I want to thank Prof. Caleb Smith of the Yale Department of English for the vigorous assistance he provided, and Prof. Gary Tomlinson and the Yale Whitney Humanities Center both for funding the working group that resulted in this book and for providing the venue and support for the group's concluding symposium. My grateful thanks are also extended to Prof. Peter Brooks, who not only founded the center but also enriched our group with his contribution, and to Yale's Office of the Provost for additional financial support at a later stage of the project. Special thanks goes to Dr. Ursula Stelzenmüller and Anu Nijhawan for their insightful comments on the manuscript, and to Dr. Colin Perrin, Nicola Sharpe, and Naomi Hill for their valuable support during the publication process.

This book is dedicated to my father, Dr. Dr.-Ing. Günter Lind.

# Contributors

**Peter Brooks** (Ph.D. Harvard) is Sterling Professor Emeritus of Comparative Literature at Yale University and Andrew W. Mellon Scholar in the Department of Comparative Literature and the Center for Human Values at Princeton University. He has published on narrative and narrative theory, on the 19th- and 20th-century novel and, more recently, on the interrelations of law and literature. He is the author of several books, including *Enigmas of Identity* (Princeton UP, 2011), *Henry James Goes to Paris* (Princeton UP, 2007), *Realist Vision* (Yale UP, 2005), *Troubling Confessions: Speaking Guilt in Law and Literature* (Chicago UP, 2000), *Psychoanalysis and Storytelling* (Oxford UP, 1994), *Body Work* (Harvard UP, 1993), *Reading for the Plot* (NY, 1984), *The Melodramatic Imagination* (Yale UP, 1976) and *The Novel of Worldliness* (Princeton UP 1969). He also co-edited *The Humanities and Public Life* (Fordham UP, 2014), *Whose Freud?* (Yale UP, 2000) and *Law's Stories* (Yale UP, 1996).

**Luis Campos** (S.J.D. Toronto U) is Assistant Professor of Law, University of New Brunswick.

**Laura Cisneros** (J.D. Loyola U) is Professor of Law and Faculty Director, Honors Lawyering Program at Golden Gate University School of Law and has numerous publications in constitutional law and theory.

**Tal Kastner** (J.D. Yale Law School, Ph.D. Princeton) is a Postdoctoral Fellow of Law and Interdisciplinary Studies at Cardozo Law School and an Adjunct Professor at Baruch College. Publications incluce "'Bartleby': A Story of Boilerplate" (*Law and Literature*) and "The Persisting Ideal of Agreement in an Age of Boilerplate" (*Law & Social Inquiry*). She most recently contributed to *The Routledge Research Companion to Law and Humanities in Nineteenth-Century America.*

**Andrei Marmor** (Ph.D. Oxford, J.D. Tel Aviv U) is Professor of Philosophy and Law at Cornell University. His most recent books include *Social Conventions: From Language to Law* (Princeton UP, 2009), *Philosophy of Law* (Princeton UP, 2011) and *The Language of Law* (Oxford UP, 2014).

Marmor is the founding editor of the *Journal of Ethics and Social Philosophy*, and the editor of several important volumes in legal philosophy, including, most recently, *The Philosophical Foundations of Language in the Law* (with Scott Soames, Oxford UP 2011), and *The Routlege Companion to Philosophy of Law*.

**Cynthia Merrill** (J.D. Yale Law School, Ph.D. University of Washington) is Research Scholar at the UCLA Center for the Study of Women and Lecturer in Law at UCLA Law. She served as Editor, Senior Editor and Submissions Editor of the *Yale Law Journal* and as Articles Editor of the *Yale Journal of Law and Humanities*.

**Sara Murphy** (Ph.D. NYU) is Clinical Associate Professor at NYU. Recent work has appeared in *Law and Literature* and *Law, Culture and the Humanities, Hypatia; Signs: Journal of Women in Culture and Society; Philosophy & Social Criticism; Studies in Law, Politics and Society; The Oxford Encyclopedia of Women in World History; Feminists Contest Politics and Philosophy;* as well as several forthcoming essay collections.

**Karen Petroski** (JD Berkeley, Ph.D. Columbia) is Professor of Law at Saint Louis University. She has published on law and fiction, most recently in *Legal Fictions in Theory and Practice* (Springer, 2015) and in *The Nature of Legal Interpretation: What Jurists Can Learn from Linguistics and Philosophy* (Chicago UP, 2017). Her most recent book, *Fiction and the Language of Law,* appeared with Routledge in 2019.

**Erin Sheley** (J.D. Harvard Law School, Ph.D. George Washington U) is Associate Professor of Law, University of Oklahoma College of Law. She has also served as an Olin-Searle Fellow at Georgetown University Law Center. Select publications include articles in the *Indiana Law Journal*; *BYU Law Review*; *Law and Literature; Law, Culture, and the Humanities*; and *Impassioned Jurisprudence: Law, Literature, and Emotion, 1600–1800* (Bucknell UP 2015).

**Lisa Siraganian** (Ph.D. Johns Hopkins U) is Associate Professor and Chair of the Department of Comparative Thought and Literature at Johns Hopkins University. She is the author of *Modernism's Other Work: The Art Object's Political Life* (Oxford UP, 2012), shortlisted for the Modernist Studies Association Book Prize (2013). She recently won a Harvard University Andrew W. Mellon New Directions Fellowship.

**Simon Stern** (Ph.D. Berkeley, J.D. Yale) is Professor of Law and English and Co-Director, Center for Innovation Law & Policy at the University of Toronto. He is General Editor for *Law and Literature* (Taylor & Francis), Co-Editor (with Robert Spoo) of Oxford UP's *Law and Literature* series, Co-Editor (with Maksymilian Del Mar & Bernadette Meyler) of *The Oxford Handbook of Law and Humanities* (2019), and has also edited the *Routledge Research Companion to Law and Humanities in Nineteenth-Century America*. For Oxford UP, he has edited *Blackstone's Commentaries on the*

*Laws of England*, and is currently editing *The Oxford Handbook of Law and Humanities.*

**Sarah Winter** (Ph.D. Yale), is Professor of English at the University of Connecticut and Director of the UConn Human Rights Institute. Her recent articles on human rights and literature appear in *Comparative Literature Studies, NOVEL*, the MLA volume *Teaching Human Rights in Literary and Cultural Studies* and the *Routledge Companion to Literature and Human Rights*. She is the author of *The Pleasures of Memory: Learning to Read with Charles Dickens* (Fordham UP, 2011) and *Freud and the Institution of Psychoanalytic Knowledge* (Stanford UP, 1999)

Part 1

# From narrative to fiction in legal theory and practice

Chapter 1

# Theorizing fictional discourse

## Toward a reassessment of the fact–fiction dichotomy in legal theory and practice

*Hans J. Lind*


I. From narrative to fiction in legal theory and practice 3
II. The basis of the fact–fiction dichotomy 6
III. Truth and fiction reconsidered 11
IV. Fictional discourse and fictional theory 18
V. Speech act approaches to fictionality 25
VI. Mapping the conceptual network: Family resemblance, prototype theory and the problem of non-hierarchical taxonomies 32


### I From narrative to fiction in legal theory and practice

At a recent workshop at London's King's College debating the future of the Law and Literature enterprise, where I was invited to present on translation approaches in legal hermeneutics, I was not surprised that, when the movement's history was addressed, rhetorical criticism, hermeneutical criticism and narrative criticism of law were the most important phases of the endeavor recounted. It surely cannot be disputed that rhetoricity, textuality and narrativity were key criteria that served in reconciling literary criticism and law as disciplines, and there are certainly some other aspects to be added.[1] It was also generally agreed that there was still significant room for further exploration: law and the image, law and affect, law and media, and law and performance were some of the propositions, mirroring the suggestions of a recent volume on law and literature and its future perspectives.[2] I regret, however, that an issue dear to me was not mentioned: the question of fictionality within legal discourse. It is well known that there are some obstacles in approaching law from the perspective of its literariness, with literary theory itself – not without reason – having struggled to reach an agreement on the establishment of a sufficient criterion for literature,[3] although, regarding legal literariness, some overlap with issues already comprehensively discussed certainly exists, as textuality and narrativity were long held to also be key constituents of literature. The question of fictionality, on the other hand, controversially debated as a criterion of literariness,[4] seems a more straightforward one when it comes to legal fictionality. Indeed, in the history of legal theory and practice, a substantial number of authors have already addressed the issue. The discussion on legal fictionality, however, usually stays confined within the disciplinary borders, rarely reaching out to involve literary criticism, or the other proponent in nowadays' debate on fictionality, analytic philosophy. Within its disciplinary confines, there furthermore has been an unfortunate tendency to see fictionality as an issue best eliminated.

It is especially the practice of the so-called "legal fictions", dating back to Roman law, which has been subject to a harsh criticism throughout the ages. "[T]hat a son killed in battle is supposed to live forever for the benefit of his parents; and that [...] captives, when freed from bondage, were held to have never been prisoners, and such as died in captivity were supposed to have died in their own country" are Blackstone's examples of fictions already "adopted and encouraged in Roman law".[5] That "[f]ictions permeate archaic procedure" can be further demonstrated by a number of examples: a foreigner could sue under the fiction of citizenship, the purchaser of an insolvent estate could sue on a fiction that he was heir,[6] and a fictitious sale could not only be used to substitute a will, but could also serve in the emancipation of a son *in potestas*, as well as "to enable a woman to get rid of a guardian".[7] And it is the practice of procedural fictions to which our present vocabulary stills owes the names of "John Doe" and "Richard Roe".[8]

In his 1910 publication *The Nature and Sources of the Law*, John Gray does not fail to mention two "absurd" examples:

> The most grotesque of these fictions was that by which, for the purpose of giving a remedy in England for a wrong done in the Mediterranean, it was alleged that the Island of Minorca was at London, in the parish of St. Mary Le Bow in the Ward of Cheap; and yet, perhaps, the palm must be given to that fiction of the United States Federal Courts that all the stockholders in a corporation are citizens of the State which incorporates it.[9]

"In a discipline primarily concerned with issues of fact and responsibility, the notion of a legal fiction should seem an anathema, or at the very least, the ill-suited means to promote a just result", a scholarly essay recently stated,[10] mirroring Hans Kelsen's 1919 dictum that "in the realm of science [...] a fiction can be nothing but an impermissible, fully useless, and solely harmful lapse".[11] In *Jurisprudence*, Roscoe Pound characterized legal fictions as rudiments of legal past, which were proper at the time, and should even be considered as "the first agency through which the traditional element of a legal system is enabled to grow", but which shall be overcome in a mature system of law.[12] John Gray, while assuming that some types of fictions do serve a legitimate purpose,[13] follows Henry Maine in the conviction that fictions can quickly exhaust their purpose: [14]

> Fictions are scaffolding, – useful, almost necessary, in construction, – but, after the building is erected, serving only to obscure it.[15]

While Ernst Zitelmann compares legal fictions to the veil of Isis, which was only required for those eyes not yet strong enough to gaze at the truth,[16] in his 1865 treatise on law, Rudolf von Jhering characterized legal fictions as "white lies" and "crutches"[17] that, at a certain stage of the evolution of law, need to be overcome:

> Every fiction should serve the [legal] science as a reminder to rid itself from it, since with every fiction, it admits to an imperfect solution of a problem.[18]

Drawing on Bouvier's understanding of legal fictionality as denial of "plain matters of fact", a scholar in the 1910 *Michigan Law Review* explains:

> In the age of fact, fancy is at a discount. Consequently legal fictions, which required the play of some fancy in their beginning, have fallen not only into disuse but also into disfavor.[19]

Similar attitudes are threaded throughout the history of the discipline, with Jeremy Bentham having arguably formulated the harshest criticism of the "pestilential breath of fiction",[20] an "opiate"[21] and "syphilis" which "runs in every vein, and carries into every part of the system" of English Law.[22] It is not counterfactuality *per se*, but the stain of weakness and illegitimacy that Bentham denounces in this context:

> A fiction of law may be defined a willful falsehood, having for its object the stealing legislative power by and for hands which could not, or durst not, openly claim it.[23]

Within the long history of legal fictionality, Bentham's harsh criticism belongs to the "newer" voices, however, since in Philippe de Renusson's treatise on law, published in 1733, attacks on legal fictionality were already considered to be commonplace.[24]

In light of the above criticism, it must be surprising that legal fictions nevertheless have been and still are ubiquitous, and the reason for this for sure is their well-proven expediency. Blackstone already noted that legal fictions, "though at first [...] may startle the student", will inevitably be found "highly beneficial and useful",[25] Jhering listed legal fictions as effective "means of legal economy",[26] and Kuntze even called them the "nourishment" that fueled the constantly growing "organism" of law.[27] For Henry Maine,[28] legal fictions were "invaluable expedients for overcoming the rigidity of law," which do not only aim at securing that rules are "judicially administrable", but furthermore ensure the "acceptability of a decision" within a general public.[29]

Maine's contemporary Oskar Bülow has also commented on legal fictions, now as a "psychological technique" that enhances the vividness of intellectual conception and facilitated the intellectual permeation of abstract messages,[30] and Lon Fuller later lists the function of "keeping the law persuasive".[31] But not only functionalist considerations seem to lie at the root of legal fictionality as a long institutionalized practice. Despite being a critic of contemporary legal fictionality, Jhering refers to legal fictions as "law's rococo style",[32] and in 1840, a writer muses:

> [I]t is always a matter of extreme delight and refreshment to turn to those exquisite fictions which both adorn and simplify our law – mingling utility with sweetness, and tending to the noblest end to which poetry can devote itself [...].[33]

The theoretical heyday of the treatment of legal fictions stretched from the beginning of the 19th century to the first third of the 20th century, with Victorian literature[34] having led to a knowledge of "those especially pampered children of the Law"[35] among the more general public. Early on, scholars debated the issue within a more theoretical framework, such as Bentham, Maine, Gray, Pound and Fuller in the English-speaking world, and Demelius, Jhering, Tourtoulon, Bülow, Vaihinger, Kelsen, Lecocq, Mallachow and Münzer on the European continent.[36] Arguably, also the law and literature enterprise of the late 20th century has contributed its part, leading to a renewed interested in the topic since the 1980s, adding to corporate personhood as the most prominent legal fiction a number of "newer" types. While "ejectment",[37] the "fiction of survival"[38] and "constructive possession"[39] had a long tradition of use,[40] and were not only generally agreed to be fictions, but were also rarely confused with facts, newer fictions are said to operate more covertly.[41] Often there is a certain overlap with legal conceptualizations, idealizations and illusions, as the concept of the "legal person",[42] the idealization of "reasonable man"[43] or the illusion of an "original public meaning" in constitutional law[44] illustrates. Also, not only do judges use the device, but so do legislators, as a number of provisions in US tax law well demonstrate.[45]

## II The basis of the fact–fiction dichotomy

Within the long treatment of legal fictionality, a clear hierarchy has been established. That fiction feigns as real what is unreal ("*fictio fingit vera esse ea, quae vera non sunt*")[46] is a definition of legal fictionality most scholars agree on, and the traditional understanding of the relation between fact and fiction is clearly hierarchical, since fiction has also long been said to yield to truth: "*fictio cedit veritati*".[47] Such hierarchy must even be strengthened when the sole possibility of factuality is postulated to unconditionally triumph over fiction: "*fictio cessat ubi veritas locum habere potest*" – fiction yields where truth can have a place.[48]

The passages quoted above, however, also demonstrate a common denominator in the treatment of legal fictionality: legal fictions are presumed to be untrue and thus irreducibly tied to the criterion of truth, rendering a classical understanding of counterfactuality the key criterion: *fictio est contra veritatem, sed pro veritate habetur.*[49] Correspondingly, Baldus de Ubaldis stated for the field of law:

> [F]iction is an assumption contrary to truth in a matter known with certainty; and it is to be noted that wherever something can be said properly to be asserted, or properly to exist, there is truth; and where something cannot be said properly to be asserted, or properly to exist, there is fiction.[50]

The latter premise is mirrored in many definitions of legal fiction, both old and new. In England, in his characterization of legal fiction as "willful falsehood" and "a false assertion of the privileged kind, which, though acknowledged to be false, is at the same time, argued from and acted upon, as if true",[51] Bentham can recur on a commonplace definition of legal fictionality, for example as propagated by Henry Finch, who in his 1613/1625 treatise[52] understands legal fiction as a "construction [...] when the law construes a thing otherwise than it is in truth".[53] On the continent, Renusson invokes the postglossators' definition,[54] and De Tourtoulon can state in the same tradition that, regarding legal fictions, "non-existence" is considered equal to "existence" – and that it is in fact the "equality between the true and the false which gives the fiction its particular character".[55]

Legal dictionaries have subsequently perpetuated this view. The third edition of *Ballantine's Law Dictionary* still defines "legal fiction" as "a contrived condition or situation", and centers on counterfactuality as the key criterion:

> A [legal] fiction is a rule of law which assumes as true, and will not allow to be disproved, something which is false, but not impossible.[56]

The 2012 *Wolters Kluwer Bouvier Law Dictionary Desk Edition* reads:

> FICTION OF LAW. The assumption that a certain thing is true, and which gives to a person or thing, a quality which is not natural to it, and establishes, consequently, a certain disposition, which, without the fiction, would be repugnant to reason and to truth. It is an order of things which does not exist, but which the law prescribes or authorizes; it differs from presumption, because it establishes as true, something which is false. [...]. A factual assumption [...] which is not based on reality.

Even the most current edition[57] of *Black's Law Dictionary* characterizes a "fiction of law" as a "rule of law which assumes as true, and will not allow to be disproved, something which is false".

Most scholars have equally centered on the question of classical counterfactuality, among them Lon Fuller, perhaps the best-known theorist of legal fictionality of the early 20th century in the English-speaking world. In his first 1930 essay on legal fictionality, Fuller defines legal fictions as "either a statement propounded with a complete or partial consciousness of its falsity, or (2) a false statement having utility".[58] Consequently, Fuller can maintain that "[a] statement must be false before it can be a fiction".[59] Just how long such understanding has been perpetuated is shown by a 2015 essay, where it is stated: "Fictions are, by definition, false, and thus a legal fiction is a legal falsehood."[60]

There were (and are), of course, notable exceptions to the rule. Some scholars claim that the question of legal fictionality does not or should not involve matters of fact, or that the true–false dichotomy is at least misleading when assessing legal fictionality. Within the earlier scholarship, Demelius,[61] Lecocq,[62] Somlò[63] and Kelsen[64] are most noteworthy here; of the newer scholarship, Ross (1969),[65] Samek (1981),[66] Campbell (1983),[67] Birks (1986), [68] Soifer (1986)[69] and, most recently, Petroski,[70] Stern[71] and Lind[72] in Del Mar's 2015 volume,[73] as well as Marmor, Petroski, Stern and Lind in Part 5 of this volume. Alf Ross has categorically rejected a definition based on the criterion of counterfactualty[74] and has proposed an alternate treatment of legal fictionality based on speech act theory instead.[75] Robert Samek has suggested that fictions "have their own reality" – and that instead of contrasting fiction with truth, we should "concentrate on what the two have in common".[76] Kenneth Campbell has renewed the focus on the preservative function of legal fictions,[77] seeing "a tension between two classifications of fact"[78] as constitutive for legal fictionality. Aviam Soifer has pointed to the fact that, in a "post-realist world", "legal fictions are not some small, awkward patch but rather the whole seemless cloth of law".[79] A more recent essay claims that legal fictions are in fact true, at least in the "the linguistic jural systems within which they originate and are used", understanding an "intersystemic conflict" as constitutive of legal fictionality.[80] While Karen Petroski, in light of discourse analysis, has further developed Fuller's notion of an interdependence of fictionality and the development and boundaries of the legal vocabulary by reopening the inquiry into "what makes a legal 'fact'", and subsequently into "the relationship of such 'facts' to other aspects of legal discourse", thereby shifting the focus more to the aspect of linguistic "communities of convention and practice",[81] Simon Stern has analyzed legal fictionality in terms of narrative and imaginative engagement, building on Ross's insight that certain legal fictions "differ from literary fictions in possessing no appeal to imagination".[82] In "Literary and Legal Fictions,"[83] Stern maintains that legal fiction should be identified with a distinct narrative structure, and that contrary both to literary fictionality and legal fictionality in general,[84] in terms of its constraint[85] "generative potential", legal fictions in particular are "singularly immune to the logic of plot".[86] In Chapter 5.1 of this volume, Stern in fact theorizes that legal fictions achieve "in legal thought, what metafiction achieves in the literary realm". Andrei Marmor also questions if truth can be the adequate criterion for fictionality (Chapter 5.4 of this volume). Using David Lewis's idea of prefixed contexts, Marmor claims that legal and literary discourse were, in fact, not distinct in terms of fictionality, but only in terms of authority. Both in a 2011 essay[87] and in Chapter 5.2 of this book, I propose a different point of departure for a general definition of fictionality, based on institutional practices. I theorize (pp. 200, 219–23) that the characteristics of a legal fiction lie in the particularity that, within an institutionalized practice of language use, a linguistic convention is openly suspended. Thus explicitly establishing a divergent denotative practice of use, which operates under the overt condition that the superordinate practice remains untouched in terms of authority, such merely relative institution can be meaningfully talked about and referred to without alluding to any notion of counterfactuality – and is applicable both in realist and nominalist systems. That the common focus on the criterion of counterfactuality could already have early been avoided is furthermore shown by those current approaches which define legal fictionality, in the tradition of Henry Maine,[88] not by its form, but by its intended aim instead. By using a solely functional criterion here, the pitfalls of counterfactuality are elegantly evaded.

In contrast, however, the majority of scholars still seem to adhere explicitly or tacitly to the basic presumptions of the classical dichotomy when dealing with legal fictions – as shown in a 2014 essay, which openly shares Bentham's conviction that "legal fictions propagate so many untruths in the practice of law" and consequently characterizes legal fictions as "practical – but untrue".[89] Some recent scholarship distinguishes "classical" from "new legal fictions", which supposedly are "not acknowledged to be false, or in some cases [...] are not in fact demonstrably false", and which are held to contain types that "do not have a clear measure of truth or falsity".[90] Baker, in a lecture published in 2001, differentiates "factual fictions" from fictions where "the evidence was partly fictionalized", though proof itself was provided by "real eye-witnesses", and from "linguistic fictions" (e.g. statutory fictions, where a "rule of law [...] seems to conflict with reality").[91] Not only are some of the examples Baker cites claimed to be "not exactly false",[92] but Baker also correctly subsumes that the "line between a fiction and the expansion of a legal concept or term of art may be a fine one"[93] – and thus reiterates Fuller's and Jhering's remarks on a possible relativity of what is factual and what is fictional.[94] Even within this newer scholarship, however, there is a clear tendency to mark non-counterfactual fictions wrongfully labelled as "fictions". Accordingly, Knauer subsumes that a large part of these newer forms should not be called fictions, but should instead be labelled legal "mistakes" or "lies"[95] – the former to be the case with "empirical legal errors", the latter with "discredited legal regimes" and "statutory schemes".[96] Baker categorically excludes statutory fictions from the label of "fiction", since "[r]ules of law cannot be false in the factual sense", and claims that such deeming provisions though they "are often said to be fictions[,] [t]hey are not really so."[97] In a Kelsenian notion, Baker also adds, that, in general, legal metaphors should not be confused with reality – and that a contradiction to reality is not possible in this domain.[98] Accordingly, the basic premise of this scholarship is still the referential axiom: "Before we can speak of fictions, we must be able to identify the truth",[99] an essay on new types of fiction concludes. Comparably, in Campbell's essay, the fact–fiction dichotomy continues to be upheld, since it is presumed that legal fiction "arises from the content of the rule being false when regarded as a question of fact according to non-legal classifications".[100]

Other scholars have propagated a mixed approach, openly or covertly blending a formalistic definition with a functionalistic one. Although Harmon in a 1990 essay (that also reiterates well the history of legal fictionality) acknowledges that there is little agreement on what a legal fiction is, when it comes to statements that are not strictly counterfactual, she, in practice, nevertheless implicitly propagates a notion of reasonable correspondence as criterion,[101] while at the same time focusing on Maine's criterion of utility. In the context of counterfactual fictions, Harmon even deviates from Fuller's view on linguistic relativity with respect to legal fictionality: "Without limitations set on the use of false statements, we run the risk of linguistic anarchy", the essay reads, and continues: "There is only so much falsity we can bear."[102] MacLean in his 1999 essay manages to avoid the question of truth by adopting Jhering's[103] formal understanding of dogmatic fictions as the "operation" to "extend to B a rule of law which applies to A by saying 'B shall be deemed to be A'".[104] He, at the same time, however, assumes legal fictions to have a particular relation "both to words and things", insofar as "they can only be known by means of the former, and stand in contradistinction to the latter".[105] Such mixed, and sometimes even methodically inconsistent approaches were present as early as the turn of the last century, as Miller's 1910 categorization, which fuses functionalist and counterfactual notions, demonstrates:

> A legal fiction is probably best defined as "a legal assumption of an innocent and beneficial character, made to advance the interest of justice". [...] Generally fictions may be classed as of three kinds: first – positive, when a fact which does not exist is assumed; second – negative, when a fact which does exist is ignored; third – by relation, when the act of one person is taken as that of another; or when an act at one time is treated as if performed at a different time or place; or when an act in relation to a certain thing is treated as if in relation to another thing.[106]

In fact, Jhering in his 1865 approach already explicitly mixes criteria of form and function when stating that a legal fiction's "characteristics" were to be found in "the form in which it conveys, and its reason for doing so".[107] Further, when Fuller treats the "death" of a fiction, it becomes evident that, in his definition, both falsity and functionality are necessary criteria for legal fictionality: A legal fiction ceases to be a fiction, first when it becomes "true" due to a change in language conventions (e.g. semantical extension),[108] and second, if it "becomes dangerous and loses its utility",[109] rendering a change in its merely perceived truth value (as a question of utility) equal to a change in its actual truth value (as a question of referential adequacy).

Conversely, not all scholars that categorically uphold truth-oriented definitions postulate counterfactuality as criterion, but already accept the possibility of counterfactuality as sufficient instead – and by this effectively void the classical distinction between presumptions and fictions, which reads: *Nam fingit esse, quod vere non est, quae sane fictio esso non potest nostro in casu, in quo no est certum.*[110] Following *New Hampshire Strafford Bank v. Cornell* and *Hibbert v. Smith*, both *Ballantine's* and *Black's Law Dictionary* (2nd edition) define legal fiction as "an assumption or supposition of law that something which is or may be false is true." That the requirement of falsity has been loosened here[111] should, however, not be overestimated. Since a number of legal fictions served the purpose of facilitating a decision in cases where proof is impossible[112] or was excluded for reasons of justice or equity, the above non-parsimonious definitions rather reflect a practical demand, instead of providing evidence for a theoretical reassessment of fictionality as such. Responding to the latter need, a loosened criterion of counterfactuality was already in use during the 19th century, as a 1858 *Imperial Dictionary* entry demonstrates: "A 'Fiction in Law' is an assumption of a thing made for the purpose of justice, though the same thing could not be proven and may be literally untrue."[113]

## III Truth and fiction reconsidered

With the above definitions either including the criterion of truth, or its opposition, falsity, and usually understanding truth as correspondence, it might seem that law's treatment of the issue dissociates not only from what fictional theory has elaborated during the 20th century, but also from science's and philosophy's discoveries – especially in the fields of epistemology and the philosophy of language. Bentham, as propagated by Ogden, had long held that every complex discourse in language was in a way fictional, as it is irreducibly bound to concepts (understood as fictitious entities which have no direct correspondence in the real world).[114] Bentham elaborates:

> By ficticious entities are here meant, not any of those which will be presented by the name of fabulous, i.e. imaginary persons [...] but such as quality – property (in the sense in which it is nearly synonymous to quality) [...] Incorrect as it would be if the entities in question were considered as being, in point of reality, upon a footing with real entities as

> above distinguished, the supposition of a sort of verbal reality, so to speak, as belonging to these ficticious entities is a supposition without which the matter of language could never have been formed, nor between man and man any converse carried on other than such as hath place between brute and brute.[115]

Although the problem of qualities in particular, and of abstractions in general, dates back to Greek antiquity, and has been revisited on a regular basis during the centuries, the claim it culminated in, was, in its radicalism, left for the 20th century to be fully grasped. Already with both philosophy and the sciences questioning the idea of truth as correspondence, either in the old understanding of an adequacy of intellect and reality (*veritas adaequatio intellectus ad rem/veritas adaequatio rei et intellectus*), or in the newer form of an adequacy of propositions of language and reality, a number of different perspectives on the issue of truth and its criteria have emerged. Lon Fuller must at first appear contradictory in his statements on legal fictionality, when he, on the one hand, insists on a definition of fiction as "untrue", while, on the other, assumes that legal fictionality is bound to the current conventions of language use, and thus what qualifies as fiction is in a certain way relative:

> [T]he inaccuracy of a statement must be judged with reference to the standards of language usage.[116]

Corresponding well to the latter, on the occasion of the "action of trover", where "the defendant is alleged to have found a chattel he may really have taken by force", Fuller writes:

> These statements are felt as fictions. Is this because there is any inherent reason why the words used could not acquire a special sense which would make them true? Could not "finding" mean, in a legal sense, taking? [...]. Neither of these things are impossible. But the fact simply is, that these possible changings have not occurred. Since they have not, these statements remain fictions.[117]

Fuller's contradiction is, however, only ostensible, and can be explained by a novel understanding of truth, which leads Fuller to acknowledge that what is fact or fiction is rather a result of a conventionalized practice – and thus could be subject to change over time. Accordingly, Fuller concludes:

> A fiction dies when a compensatory change takes place in the meaning of the words or phrases involved, which operates to bridge the gap that previously existed between the fiction and reality. This is a process that is going on all the time [...] Of course this process is not confined to the law – it takes place in the whole of our language.[118]

As for many of his contemporaries, Fuller's dawning understanding of a constructedness not only of language but also of reality is, however, paired with moderate realist tendencies, upholding the belief that finding an approximation to reality in our representations of the world was possible.[119] Correspondingly, instead of abandoning the idea of adequacy, Fuller formulates:

> No statement is an entirely adequate expression of reality, but we reserve the label "false" for those statements involving an inadequacy that is outstanding or unusual. The truth of a statement is, then, a question of degree.[120]

In a similar fashion, in *La fiction juridique* (1935), Dekkers defines legal fiction in terms of category misplacement – and thus of language.[121] Dekkers's criterion of unsuitability is, however, not merely a question of ad-rem adequacy, but instead highlights the question of functional inappropriateness of category reasoning and practice. By doing so, both Dekkers's and Fuller's moderate constructivist positions, however, already point towards a more radical constructivism. Such is no coincidence. Fuller follows German philosopher Hans Vaihinger in his treatment of fictionality, whose monograph *Philosophy of the As If* (Berlin, 1911) was introduced into the current debate in 1924 via an English translation by Charles Kay Ogden, unsurprisingly also the author of *Bentham's Theory of Fictions*.[122] Vaihinger uses the topic of legal fictionality to elaborate a functionalistic theory of knowledge in general, which shares many of the pragmatists' convictions. In *The Philosophy of the As If*, it is maintained that all our concepts and theories are "false", if truth is understood as adequacy. In order to successfully cope with the world, our concepts and theories can, however, be made more "useful", with truth correctly understood to be nothing but "the most expedient error".[123] Though still having considerable realist rudiments,[124] which also extend to Fuller's treatment of the issue, Vaihinger's claims can already be read as a prefiguration of an up-to-date understanding of truth as viability, as currently propagated by Ernst von Glasersfeld.[125] Other contemporary legal authors also seem to have understood the precarious status of truth both outside and within the legal discourse, an example being de Tourtoulon, who states in his 1908 treatise on law:[126]

> In order to understand, man needs intellectual stability, and stability cannot be achieved but at the expense of truth. The truth is a perpetual oscillation; its mobility, its variety is disconcerting. We cannot grasp it, without falsifying it.[127]

Despite the legal debate around Vaihinger, to which Fuller contributed in his third essay (1931) on legal fictionality,[128] a closer examination of the legal discussion in the first part of the 20th century also shows that a certain conservatism prevented newer ideas from other disciplines from entering the broad legal discussion – and it also seems that the Benthamism perpetuated by Ogden played its part in delaying innovation. In his 1933 review of Ogden's monograph, Felix Cohen elaborates:

> Unfortunately, however, the traditional English insularity in law and philosophy circumscribes the scope of Mr. Ogden's efforts. The discussion of functionalism and operationalism in philosophy is carried on with complete disregard of the work of Rudolf Carnap, Charles S. Peirce, John Dewey, and C. I. Lewis, and with only the most perfunctory reference to Ludwig Wittgenstein.[129]

The renewed treatment of legal fictions seems not to have increased significantly in complexity in the last two decades of the 20th century and the first decade of the 21st century either,[130] despite the critical re-readings of Bentham[131] noticed also by legal scholars,[132] and the rapid development of the discussion of fictional discourse in both analytic philosophy and literary theory. As long as literary and philosophical definitions of fictions were tied to simple notions of truth, the definition of fiction in both disciplines necessarily mirrored the above accounts of fictionality in law – and the changes in understandings of truth were necessarily represented both in legal and in fictional theory. Sheppard's account of fictionality shows this common aspect of both disciplines, parsimoniously defining "fiction" as "[a]nything pretended or invented but presented as true".[133] Correspondingly, his dictionary entry does not fail to mention that such understanding is not limited to the field of law, but considered transdisciplinarily valid, mirroring Bentham's understanding of "poetry and truth" as a "natural opposition", with the poet characterized as "always in need of something false", performing the act of pretence that "his foundations [were] laid in truth": [134]

> Fiction, in the law, is essentially as it is in literature, an invention or artifice presented as if it might be true, though with the intention by its inventor or creator that those who rely on it treat it simultaneously as if it were true while knowing that it is not.[135]

Although the notion of a constitutive tension between belief and disbelief has lately been revived both in analytic philosophy and literary theory,[136] the assumption that literary and legal fictionality could be as easily equated is, however, not an insight to be taken for granted. While in legal discourse, the issue was confined to the question of mere counterfactuality, much of the early and mid-18th-century discussion of literary fiction instead grappled with the distinction between higher (universal) truth and particular truth, reviving the Aristotelian understanding of the higher truthfulness of poetry that is opposed to the contingent and thus inferior status of the mere factual discourse of historiography[137] – and was therefore rather concentrated on the question of mimesis as verisimilitude, with its essential criterion being probability, not correspondence.[138] That artefacts refer to a "higher" or "universal" truth, while their constituents (entities or propositions) were at the same time false or feigned, since they clearly deviated from the factual world, was not understood as a contradiction here, but rather as an axiomatic presupposition of poetics. The subsequent century, however, led to a number of changes. Harsh oppositions between idealist, realist and later naturalist notions, and the growing awareness of the artificiality of memory[139] were only the onset of a fundamental revision of the nature of poetics that also led to a surprising convergence in the treatment of fictionality in both disciplines. It is no coincidence, therefore, that, when it comes to the issue of fictionality, a convergence of literature and law can be monitored again over the 19th century. The combination of a re-emergent consciousness of the inevitable fictionality of language of certain complexity (Bentham) and the awareness fostered both in philosophy and science that the models and descriptions of the world are far from adequate not only added a further complication but also paved the way for Vaihinger's aforementioned account of legal fictionality.

It is especially the debate on truth in this context that should be illuminating for the question of legal fictionality. While scholars such as Moritz Schlick[140] still propagated some form of correspondence at the turn of the century, Francis Herbert Bradley in his two 1909 essays "Truth and Coherence" and "Coherence and Contradiction" claimed the criterion of truth to be that a proposition does not stand in conflict with other propositions within the "system".[141] Also, Vaihinger's notion of truth as the most expedient error is mirrored in William James's understanding of truth:[142]

> Ideas [...] become true just in so far as they help us to get into satisfactory relations with other parts of our experience";[143]
>
> "The true", to put it very briefly, is only the expedient in the way of our thinking, just as "the right" is only the expedient in the way of our behaving.[144]

Vaihinger accordingly subsumes:

> It is a mistake to assume that an objective truth can be found, or an absolute measure of knowledge or agency; the higher life is based on noble deceits [...] As error, fiction and truth are closely related theoretically, so are they practically.[145]

It is well known that theories on truth have diverged much further later. Pierce's notion of truth as general consensus was not only continued by John Dewey,[146] but continues to be present in more recent theories – such as Habermas's discursive understanding of truth as "the potential assent of all others",[147] or the Erlangen School's criterion of "interpersonal verification".[148] As did Francis Herbert Bradley before him, Otto Neurath revised the neo-Hegelian ideal of truth as coherence in light of modern epistemology, attributing truth with a notion of relativity: Understanding "science as a system of propositions", the decisive criterion for truth is merely whether a proposition can be integrated into the predominant system without contradictions. Falseness is then of relative nature only, and can be remedied by adapting the system as a whole. Neurath formulates:

> Each new proposition will be confronted with the totality of [past] propositions which are in agreement with each other. Correct [true] is called a proposition if it can be integrated. What cannot be integrated will be rejected as incorrect. Instead of rejecting the incorrect proposition [...] the entire propositional system can be modified until the new proposition can be integrated.[149]

Neurath's approach was not only successfully continued by Rescher, who stipulated three necessary criteria for coherence ("comprehensiveness", "consistency" and "cohesiveness"),[150] but is mirrored in Fuller's treatment of legal fictionality.[151] Both Fuller and Neurath also seem to agree on the fact that although truth is nothing but relative to an already established system, a certain conservatism of mind will make Neurath's second possibility (changing the system) less likely.[152]

In a similar manner, Richard Rorty has repeatedly pointed out that truth is a construct, and locates the reason for this within language as a system:

> [T]here is no way to think about either the world or our purposes except by using our language.[153]

> [S]ince vocabularies are made by human beings, so are truths. [154]

Rorty's assessment culminates in a parallelism of the essences of truth and language based on a causality of one for the other: "truth was made rather than found" since "languages are made rather than found".[155] Also, while semantic theories of truth in the tradition of Tarski have occupied a considerable part of the debate, poststructuralist thinkers (from Foucault to Derrida)[156] have fruitfully renewed the interest in a critical assessment of what truth is. Foucault states:

> Each society has its regime of truth, its "general politics" of truth: that is, the types of discourse which it accepts and makes function as true; the mechanisms and instances which enable one to distinguish true and false statements, the means by which each is sanctioned; the techniques and procedures accorded value in the acquisition of truth; the status of those who are charged with saying what counts as true.[157]

More recently, one particular aspect of such regime has further been investigated: that truth might not only be the product of a specific discursive practice alone, but of a specific "apparatus" or "deployment" *(dispositif)*, understood as a heterogeneous network of discursive and non-discursive elements.[158] The cross-dissemination from other disciplines is equally noteworthy, especially newer insights in narratology. By questioning the distinction between historical and fictional narrative, a considerable number of authors, among them Hayden White and Paul Ricoeur, have challenged our notion of what historical truth consists in if truth depends on narrative representation.[159] Narratology has also added another helpful distinction to the equation: while "fictitiousness", as pertaining to level of *histoire*, is understood to be tied to the question of truth (however revised), some authors claim that, in contrast, "fictionality" is a sole question of the narratological *discours*.[160]

Of the aforementioned, already the earlier developments are important for the treatment of legal fictions, since they led to a revision of the understanding of the nature of language in general, and the concept of truth in particular – and thereby laid the foundation of much of the 20th century's theoretical approaches to the phenomenon of fictionality. It is evident that changes in its underlying understanding of truth cannot leave unchanged a concept of fiction that is based on the criterion of falseness or counterfactuality: though modifications of the understanding of what truth is do not necessarily call for an abolishment of counterfactuality as the criterion of fictionality, they at least call for a reassessment of what counterfactuality exactly means. The latter is especially relevant if the criterion of falseness continues to be upheld: a new pluralism of truth then necessarily results in a plurality of concepts of fictional discourse if tied to the criteria of counterfactuality. Historically, the growing insight that our scientific models of the world are constructions, and therefore might differ from other "fictions" only in degree[161] and not in nature, also called for the establishment of a new criterion that could distinguish fictional discourse from a mere constructivist (pan-)fictionalism[162] – a problem a number of scholars attempted to solve by challenging the validity of truth as a criterion of fictionality in general. It is evident that the field of law cannot be an exception here, since it operates within the conceptual sphere of language. Another claim raised in the 20th century's treatment of the question of truth might also be of relevance for the question of legal fictionality: the position that different discourses might require different criteria of truth, leading to a theory of truth as plural and discourse-relative.[163] Foucault himself has commented on the question of truth in law, claiming that in the legal field, truth in the referential sense was early replaced by a formalized "verbal game".[164]

It seems, however, that once the above historical developments had gathered their first momentum, the treatment of issues of fictionality in and outside law dissociated again. While both philosophy and literary theory were deeply invested in theorizing the issue of fictionality during the second half of the 20th century, legal scholarship on fictionality mainly stayed confined to the boundaries that were established until the late 1930s, with a few newer exceptions that also addressed the pragmatist considerations of truth within a legal framework and their consequences for legal fictionality.[165] Surprisingly, this was even the case despite the emergence of Critical Legal Studies and the incorporation of poststructuralist ideas into legal theory by Balkin, Cornell, Desan, Frug, Peller, Kennedy and others.[166]

I will speak colloquially of "fictional theory" in the remaining part of this chapter to refer to a plurality of approaches, as the sum of disparate attempts to theorize fictional discourse both in analytic philosophy and literary theory. This is, however, for reasons of economy of argument only. I am well aware that no homogenous movement exists here, and that to sum the complex approaches under one header to a certain degree violates the approaches' integrity – the latter especially being the case with a number of scholars within literary theory clearly opposing any attempts towards a transdisciplinary valid definition of fictionality.[167] As a heuristic means, however, the improper label "fictional theory" will allow me to juxtapose approaches which aim at establishing inter- or transdisciplinary criteria of fictional discourse on the one hand, and the particularly different treatment of fictionality in the history of legal theory and practice on the other.

## IV Fictional discourse and fictional theory

As already stated, the majority of approaches on legal fictionality have drawn on counterfactuality as criterion, and consequently tied the question of truth to the criterion of reference. These two interrelated questions also constitute an important issue within fictional theory. Fictional theory, however, dissociates from the legal treatment of fictionality by proposing an alternative to the traditional opinion that fictional discourse needs be understood as a false proposition, by reassessing both the necessity and the consequences of reference as criterion. Regarding reference, two main perspectives are usually taken: first, that fictional discourse is discourse that refers to fictional entities, and second, that fictional discourse is non-referential discourse. At first sight, the former notion of fictionality seems to be identical with the classical notion, as present in the definition of "fiction" in *Ballentines' Laws Dictionary* – which, in its failure to provide a parsimonious definition, mirrors the aforementioned dissociation between legal and extralegal understandings of fictionality:

> Fiction. In the sense of a fiction of law, a contrived condition or situation […] As a literary work, a novel, a portrayal with imaginary characters.[168]

Since it has been argued that any reference to non-existing objects is necessarily a false proposition, the 19th century and early 20th century's treatment of literary fictionality could still closely mirror law's truth–false dichotomy:[169] Bertrand Russell held that in Shakespeare's *Hamlet* "[t]he propositions in the play are false because there was no such man" – and, by doing so, shared Bentham's account of fictionality as discourse that assumes something to exist which in fact doesn't – and thus is literally false.[170] In the history of fictional theory, however, the criterion of referentiality has strongly been contested – but nevertheless stayed an issue of debate throughout the whole 20th century, although the referential criterion has consecutively been modified.[171] In *Of Mind and Other Matters* (1984), while agreeing with a modern notion of a conflicting plurality of truth by assuming that there was "no such thing as the actual world", but that there were "many worlds if any",[172] Nelson Goodman assumes the classical standpoint: "All fiction is literal, literary falsehood."[173] Accordingly, he rejects the idea of fiction as referring to fictional entities, or even to a fictional world:[174]

> [M]ost fictions seem to be about fictive persons, things, and even events or about imaginary and even impossible beings and entities. Works of fiction, we often hear, are about fictive worlds. But strictly speaking, fiction cannot be about anything nonactual, since there is nothing nonactual [...][175]

Goodman's notion is based on a common belief also upheld by Searle: being able to refer to fictional entities would presuppose that fictional entities exist[176] – thus fictional statements, as referring to non-existing entities, are necessarily false statements.

It consequently seems that only the second perspective (the "no assertion view")[177] could serve as an alternative to the classical understanding of fictionality. Proponents of the no-assertion view usually assume the following:

> In fictional discourse the speaker does not claim that his referring expressions have referents. He speaks *as if* the referring expressions had referents. [...] In fictional discourse, the rule of reference is out of place.[178]

Accordingly, for Gottfried Gabriel, fictional discourse can also be defined as being denotationless:

> In fictional discourse the speaker does not claim that the predicative expressions used at the subject place have denotations; he only speaks *as if* these expressions have denotations.[179]

While Gabriel, for the sake of a parsimonious definition of fictional discourse, has avoided the referential paradigm,[180] a relevant number of scholars have instead upheld the criterion of reference, while at the same time deviating from the classical understanding that fictional discourse is false discourse. The latter debate seems to partially mirror the medieval debate on the ontological status of universals. Accordingly, while some scholars understand fictional objects as abstract, man-made objects, Platonist ideas have also found their way into the debate. Wolterstorff claims a fictional character is a subtype of persons that differs from other persons only in terms of properties, and since properties are said to exist independently from fictional discourse, fictitious characters are supposed to be rather selected than made.[181] Meinongian positions (as those of Terence Parsons and Richard Routley) even assume the possibility of reference without existence in the strict sense of the word – understanding fictional discourse as a discourse involving non-existing but possible entities being referred to.[182] While these objects, from an ontological perspective, are said to be non-existent ("nicht-existierend"), they are, however, understood to subsist ("bestehen"),[183] thus allowing them to have metaphysical properties, with one categorical exception, though: the property of existence.[184] Terence Parsons has elaborated a Meinongian theory[185] applicable also in the case of literary fiction.[186] Graham Priest propagates a theory of a "supervenience of the fictional on the real", assuming that "the nonexistent can be meaningfully be talked about, referred to or quantified over in our world 'supervenes' on the actions of the relevant existents in that world in particular" once they are created.[187] Martinich and Stroll assert that propositions containing a fictitious name or entity are possible in cases where an institutionalized praxis exists that is linked to a fictional name used, allowing the possibility of reference even in the case of non-existence.[188] Certain proponents of possibilism even go further by claiming a certain form of existence for things that do not exist, but that are possible. Erich Rast writes:

> According to possibilism in its classical form, the things that have actuality or existence form only a proper subset of the things that are *tout court.* What is actual exists, and what is non-actual but only possible does not exist, yet could exist. This is another way of saying that objects that do not actually exist may still exist in various other ways.[189]

A number of scholars even assume that fictional discourse refers not only to non-existent entities but to non-existent but possible worlds.[190] Such idea of fictional worlds, clearly rejected by Gabriel[191] and Goodman ("There are no fictive worlds"),[192] is maintained by scholars of different provenience, as the wide application of possible world theory on the question of fictional narrative illustrates (Eco,[193] Doležel,[194] Pavel,[195] Ryan[196]).

Both perspectives, however, allow truth values to be attributed to fictional discourse. While Goodman revives the non-referential Aristotelian notion of a higher truth of literature despite its literal falsity ("While all fiction is literally false, some is metaphorically true"),[197] a number of scholars have assessed the truth values of propositions within fictional discourse, partly even maintaining that fictional statements can be true in a referential sense – among them David Lewis, Terence Parsons and Gregory Currie. Presuming a "fictional operator",[198] Rast propagates an idea that is already present in

David Lewis's theory, one of the first proponents of an elaborated account of fictional worlds,[199] who, as an alternative to Meinongianism, proposed three provisional definitions of fictional truth (termed "Analysis 0", "Analysis 1" and "Analysis 2"):

(1) "A sentence of the form 'In fiction f, Ø' is true iff Ø is true at every world where f is told as known fact'"[200]
(2) "A sentence of the form 'In the fiction f, Ø' is non-vacuously true iff some world where f is told as a known fact and Ø is true differs less from our actual world, on balance, than does any world where f is told as known fact and Ø is not true. It is vacuously true iff there are no possible worlds where f is told as known fact"[201]
(3) "A sentence of the form 'In the fiction f, Ø' is non-vacuously true iff, whenever w is one of the collective believes worlds of the community of origin of f, then some world where f is told as known fact and Ø is true differs less from the world w, on balance, than does any world where f is told as known fact and Ø is not true. It is vacuously true iff there are no possible worlds where f is told as known fact."[202]

Lewis consequently claims that "truth in fiction is the joint product of two sources: the explicit content of the fiction, and a background consisting either of the facts about our world (Analysis 1) or our beliefs overt in the community of origin (Analysis 2)".[203] According to Lewis, fictional propositions not only can have truth values, but can be true precisely because a fictional proposition is usually a truncated assertion that involves a "fictional operator". Such assertions are presupposed to always have the logical form of "In fiction f, Ø".

Even non-referential views, as Gabriel's theory shows, have found a way to attribute truth values to statements containing fictitious elements, by assuming in the semantics of fiction a "non-ontological conception of sense (intension)".[204]

For the treatment of legal fictionality, the above-mentioned perspectives are evidently of use. Bentham's claim of the irreducible fictional nature of any discourse as bound to abstractions (qua fictional entities), which is also found in a modified form in the early ideas of a panfictionality of the legal conceptual system (Tourtoulon, Vaihinger, Lecocq),[205] would make much of legal discourse fictional – and thus is comparable to the issue of a supposed panfictionality both in philosophy and literary theory.[206] It is evident that a theory which categorizes the majority of propositions in language as fictional might not serve well as a heuristic means – or in the words of Fuller: "If everything is 'fiction', then the meaning of the word has been lost, and 'as if' has become simply 'is'",[207] with the consequence that the "utility" of the category "fiction" will become "utterly destroyed".[208] Contemporary approaches in analytic philosophy and literary theory, which have tackled this particular problem by establishing more differentiating criteria in order to make the distinction operable again, could also help to shed a more differentiated light on the legal field.

Furthermore, it is not only the parallelism between fictional theory and the Kelsenian notions of legal language understood as referring to legal concepts as non-actual entities, that might prove the endeavor useful (and can consequently be found in a 2001 publication on legal fictions),[209] but also the fact that a number of the aforementioned approaches within fictional theory in general offer an escape to the usual dichotomous treatment of legal fictionality. A consideration of the above should make clear that at least a revision of the classical criterion of falsity is long overdue – and that a number of persisting claims on legal fictionality (e.g. that legal fictions were "unlike literary fictions in that they do not relate to verisimilitude in the same way", since they had no 'similitude' with real things") are too simplistic in their approach.[210]

The fruitfulness of a reassessment of legal fictionality based on a fictional theory is also supported by the fact that a newer concept of legal fictionality already mentioned (the suggestion that legal fictions are in fact true "within the linguistic jural system within which they originate and are used")[211] is nothing but a covert paraphrase of Lewis's account of fictionality (the proposition that a fictional proposition not only can have truth values, but can be true precisely because a fictional proposition is usually a truncated assertion that involves the unsaid fictional operator "In fiction f, Ø").

Even the understanding of fictional discourse as referring to fictional entities or fictional worlds could find a valid application in legal discourse, and this in two regards. On the one hand, both the idea of a realism of legal concepts (e.g. Gray's question if corporations are "real or fictitious entities"[212]), which would make legal concepts in general rather found than made, and the ideal of a parallel universe of legal concepts and relations, have been invoked in civil law countries already in early times, the latter both with Platonic and non-Platonic connotations (e.g. Jhering's metaphor of a "heaven of legal concepts"[213] and Kelsen's observation that "[i]n the imagination of the lawyer, the person – the physical as well as the corporate – lives as a creature independently existing from the legal order").[214] Kuntze in his 1856 monograph even opposes three realms – the sensible world, the legal world and the realm of legal fictions.[215] Krückmann (1909/1919) claims, that due to particularities of the concept of causality, in law, an inevitable dissociation between reality and the legal realm necessarily occurs, and that due to this, for example in criminal law, never a "real" committer is to be found, but only the "legal" committer – and that law treats the "legal" committer "as if" he was the "real" committer.[216]

While newer voices have reiterated the latter topic,[217] a closer examination of Kelsen would already have provided valuable insights into this matter. Although Kelsen has just received new attention in the English-speaking world due to a translation of his 1919 essay "On a Theory of Legal Fictions", an idea Kelsen raises in this essay has nevertheless been neglected by this most recent scholarship: Kelsen in fact suggested a "modification"[218] of Vaihinger's definition of fictionality, which, in light of fictional theory, could be of interest for a revised approach on legal fictionality in general. Readings of Kelsen's 1919 essay that assume that Kelsen unconditionally rejected legal fictionality often forget that the essay mainly counters the application of Vaihinger's epistemological theory to the field of law, demonstrating that due to the combination of the criteria Vaihinger stipulates (overt counterfactual assumption that is provisional/expedient), legal fictions do not qualify as fictions in a Vaihingerian sense. In his 1911 habilitation, however, which appeared as a second, amended edition in 1924 (and thus did not abandon the 1911 position on fictionality, as his 1919 essay might suggest), Kelsen does not reject legal fictionality per se, but only a classical notion of fictionality that propagates realist notions by confusing the realms of nature and of law/ethics:

> Not because a [legal] fiction is something feigned, [...] but because, and only insofar as it claims to contain something "being" ("ein Seiendes"), every fiction needs to be rejected. [...] What needs to be rejected [...] is the methodological error, that in a concept, which has not been abstracted from the world of the "being", something "being" is nevertheless searched for, [...] though the latter is only a figment [...] of the wish of an "ought-not to be" ("Nicht-Sein Sollen").[219]

When treating dogmatic and judicial fictions, Kelsen then raises an interesting point about how fictionality could in fact be thought in the realm of law, leading to an "extended understanding of fiction"[220] – and by doing so anticipates the arguments of some more recent voices in scholarship: legal fiction defined as a contradiction with respect to a referential system alternate to the real world. According to Kelsen, this referential system is the "legal order", which he also characterizes as an artificial "reality" or "world" that needs to be distinguished from the "natural reality" (the "reality of the senses"),[221] and that has its own factuality,[222] with the consequence that legal discourse would have its own truth values, independent from the "real world".[223] That in his 1919 essay Kelsen nevertheless claims that legal fictions are not "fictions" seems to be primarily based on two of Kelsen's presuppositions. First, Kelsen treats fictionality in the context of Vaihinger's definition, requiring counterfactuality and expediency[224] – and while statutory fictions are found to lack in counterfactuality, both dogmatic and judicial fictions are considered not to be expedient,[225] with the consequence that legal fictions could at the very most appear as "pseudo-fictions".[226] Second, Kelsen nevertheless seems to presume a referential contradiction to be a necessary condition for fictionality, and therefore demands a proposition which is assertive[227] – though it is unclear if Kelsen himself agrees with Vaihinger's other criteria for "real" fictionality.[228] To decide the latter, however, would be crucial, for in his 1919 essay, though rejecting statutory fictions for the reason of not being assertive ("the law affirmeth nothing, [...] it commands"),[229] some legal fictions are in fact both considered to be assertive and to contain a referential contradiction – and are only rejected by Kelsen for lack of the criterion of expedience Vaihinger prescribed.[230] With fictional theory having in fact fundamentally challenged the classical criterion of counterfactuality, and, as we will see later in the chapter, with certain proponents of speech act theory contesting Kelsen's premise that fictionality presumes an assertion, these changes would now allow the full scope of legal fictions to be reassessed in light of Kelsen's aforementioned "extended" definition.

Also, it is not only the idea of an alternate reality that has long been present in a number of legal approaches, thereby establishing a competing reference system for truth claims, but also many of the assumptions of possible world theory. Both in the law of tort and in contract law, counterfactual considerations are commonplace – and could be best described in terms of the construction of an alternate possible universe that differs from reality only on a very restricted factual basis. "Factual causation" is often considered to be the basis for liability, both criminal and civil,[231] and when it comes to determining factual causation, the hypothetical "but for" test is usually cited as criterion: "[A]n event X causes an event Y if, but for X, Y would not have occurred."[232] To rethink how the world would now be in absence (or counterfactual presence) of a past event X is also required in the calculation of damages to be paid – for example, in order to account for "lost profits".[233] In other branches of law, the questions of hypothetical gains or losses are also commonplace – for example, in tax law.[234] It is, however, procedural law, where a parallel world of legal factuality (which might be substantially deviating from the actual world) is created on a daily basis – with the consequence that the truth value of propositions pertaining to such legal discourse could be assessed in a manner parallel to how possible world theory is used by fictional theory to assess alternate worlds of facts (Lewis, Beardsley, Reicher). Not only were a substantial number of the "classical" fictions in fact procedural fictions, but also a number of provisions and principles of nowadays' procedural law either force the participants to disregard facts or might even require them to assume a factual basis as legally relevant which deviates considerably from the real world. The doctrine of estoppel, which "prevents a party from asserting a position in one legal proceeding that directly contradicts a position taken by that same party in an earlier proceeding",[235] can, for example, lead to a dissociation of factual and legal reality. But not only in civil procedure might certain evidence be excluded: in criminal cases, a jury might be asked to also "disregard" certain facts despite them being true. Such deviation from reality can even be cemented, perpetuating an alternate version of reality that is also binding for future recipients: *res judicate pro veritate accipitur.*[236]

But also from another perspective, the question of fictional reference could be valuable for the question of legal fictionality. It has been suggested by Simon Stern (Chapter 5.1 of this volume) that legal fictionality might be comparable to metafiction in literature. Having once established such a hypothesis, fictional theory's treatment of the question of truth and falseness pertaining to metafiction[237] might be apt to provide valuable insights.

Last but not least, the discussion of fictionality within fictionality theory could be fruitful for another aspect of the legal debate: legal and literary fictions both have factual effect in the "real" world in question of knowledge,[238] action and status. Niklas Luhmann has already extensively treated the effect of fictional literature on social practices,[239] and comparably, in Chapter 4.2 of this volume, Sarah Winter investigates the effects of fictional literature within the history of codification of human rights.

## V Speech act approaches to fictionality

Another important angle fictional theory provides to the issue of legal fictionality is a performative approach to the issue. Gregory Currie has objected to Lewis's account of fictionality that fictional worlds and possible worlds were not to be confused:

> [F]ictional worlds, if there are any, cannot be assimilated to possible worlds [...] Possible worlds are determinate with respect to truth, every proposition is either true or false in a possible world. They are consistent; nothing logically impossible is true in a possible world. But fictional worlds are always indeterminate and sometimes inconsistent [...] The failure to assimilate fictional worlds to possible worlds shows why we cannot explain truth in fiction as truth in a possible world.

Currie maintains that although Lewis's treatment could lead to correct results, it nevertheless is based on the wrong presumptions.[240] In "On Being Fictional", Currie even concludes that the truth status of fictional discourse is fundamentally different from factual discourse, since fictional truth or falseness can in fact be a question of degree.[241] The reason for Currie's rejection of Lewis's claim, however, is a fundamentally different approach to fictional discourse, which is shared by a number of scholars. Such an approach operates under the assumption that fictional discourse might not be assertive at all. Scholars that base their theory of fictionality on speech act theory in brief propagate that the illocutionary act performed by the speaker when speaking is as important as the locutionary act (propositional content). In the context of the question of fictionality, the illocutionary act is even said to be the relevant part of an utterance. John Searle has proposed a theory of fictionality based on such a premise, assuming that in fictional discourse, an assertive speech act is not performed, but instead, such an assertion is only pretended – making the criterion of pretence the key notion of fictionality. Though having the same propositional content as an assertion, fictional discourse is said to fail in complying with some of the basic rules of assertive discourse.[242] Searle's characterization of fictional pretence is surprisingly close to the criteria that have been established in the context of Vaihinger's theory. Fictional pretence means:

> to engage in a performance which is *as if* [...] *without any intent to deceive.*[243]

Gottfried Gabriel and Monroe Beardsley also follow Searle's idea that fictional discourse consists in acting *as if* one was making an assertion. According to Gabriel,

> the speaker speaks as if he were performing a particular kind of speech act, but in fact is not performing this particular kind of speech act at all.[244]

In a similar way, Beardsley defines fictional discourse as

> discourse in which there is a make-belief illocutionary action, but in fact no such action is performed.[245]

He, however, slightly deviates from Searle by not using pretence, but "representation" as the criterion: "Fiction [...] is the representation, not the performance, of illocutionary action".[246]

For Beardsley, it is nevertheless also Searle's (and thus Austin's) criterion of a non-fulfilment of semantic or pragmatic requirements that turns an assertion or any other type of illocutionary act into a representation:

> When a text is produced that could be used to perform an illocutionary action of some recognizable kind, and enough of the requisite conditions are present or presupposed to permit the kind to be recognized – but not enough for such an action actually to occur – then we have a representation.[247]

In order to distinguish fictional discourse from lies and deceit, Beardsley also requires the non-compliance to be overt. The demand that fictional discourse is an overt deviation from semantic or pragmatic rules at the same time functions as a guarantee for the success of fictional utterances:

> It is only necessary to make clear that one or more of the requisite conditions is lacking, while at the same time inviting the receiver (hearer or reader) to make-believe that they are also present, in order to convert a genuine illocutionary action into a fictive one.[248]

Although Searle's account has been criticized by scholars such as Richard Rorty, Thomas Pavel and Nicholas Wolterstorff, a substantial number of scholars currently propagate speech act approaches to fictionality, among them even Searle's critic Wolterstorff. Wolterstorff admits that Searle was correct in approaching the issue from the perspective of illocution, and thus engages in a performative understanding of the issue, but argues that he was wrong in assuming that in fictional discourse an illocutionary act is only pretended:

> As I see it, fictional world-projection is the doing of something by means of inscribing words under certain conditions, not merely the inscribing of words under certain conditions. And I am myself inclined to think that the "doing" in question in fact is an illocutionary action – something like inviting to suppose, or inviting to consider.[249]

Maria Reicher comparably assumes that fictional discourse always performs the illocutionary act to devise a fictional world,[250] and in "What is fiction?", Gregory Currie maintains that in fictional discourse a "genuine illocutionary act"[251] is being performed, that, though not assertive, is well "on a par with assertion".[252] Although he agrees with Searle that the intention of the speaker determines whether a speech act is fictional or not ("The illocutionary act is a function of the speaker's intention"[253]), Currie weakens the requirement of intentionality (and consequently of overtness) by accepting "secondary fiction" where the intent of the author is misunderstood or neglected by the audience.[254] Currie, however, has subsequently modified his theory[255] – and his approach shares some traits with another performative understanding of fictionality, as propagated by Kendall Walton. For Walton, fictionality is reduced to the functional misappropriation of an object that, contrary to its ordinary usage, is now used as prop in a make-believe game.[256] Walton's theory is claimed to better provide a general criterion of fictionality, since it can also account for fictionality in non-verbal media, and has been well received in the current debate. However, it has also been harshly criticized,[257] in part precisely because of its broadness which also guarantees its transmedial application.[258] Literary critics have particularly pitted against Walton's approach. This, however, does not mean that literary criticism is fundamentally opposed to speech act approaches (or performative approaches in general). The contrary is actually the case. Independent of analytic philosophy, Gerard Genette[259] and Dorrit Cohn[260] have also tied the issue of fictionality to questions of speech, understanding the dissociation of author and speaker as the key criterion for fictionality. It is surely no coincidence here that the foundations of this approach were laid in the founding era of speech act theory, with Wolfgang Kayser's 1958 essay "Who Narrates a Novel?"[261] and Käte Hamburger's 1957 monograph *The Logic of Literature*.[262] Also, Searle's claim that, in literary fiction in general, an author is pretending to narrate,[263] and that in first-person narrative in particular, he is even pretending to be the (main) character making assertions,[264] clearly bridges the above gap. The theory of Hamburger is, however, complicated in this regard, since, though focusing on a certain type of literary speech,[265] it also needs to be understood as an opposition both against speech act theory approaches[266] and Vaihinger's theory of an “as if”.[267] But not only literary theory's distinction between narrator and author is in accord with speech act theory. Especially continental European literary theorists have derived a fundamental distinction from a speech-act-oriented perspective: the distinction between “fictive” and “fictional”. While the fictitiousness of the material of a story is regarded as a question on the level of the story (Genette's *histoire*) and thus can be traditionally approached using the criterion of truth, fictionality is instead understood to be a question of illocution, and thus solely to be decided on the level of *discours*,[268] possibly rendering the criterion of truth irrelevant.[269]

Despite the differences between the latter theories of fictionality, and the evident inapplicability of some of literary theory's conceptions of fictional discourse on phenomena outside the literary field, it is evident that the above approaches have in common that they call for a reassessment of the classical understanding of the relation of fictional discourse to truth. If Searle is right that fictional discourse can neither be true nor false, since only real and not pretended assertions can have truth values, fictional discourse at least can no longer be defined as counterfactual discourse. The latter claim already has well-known precursors. In *The Defence of Poesy*, Philip Sidney already stated: “Now for the poet, he nothing affirms and therefore never lies, for, as I take it, to lie is to affirm that to be true which is false”.[270] Correspondingly, according to Bentham, the poet “pretends” that “his foundations [were] laid in truth”.[271] However, even under the presupposition of speech act theory, it is generally agreed that at least metafictional propositions can well have truth values. Some scholars even maintain a hybrid view: while the speaker of fictional discourse does not claim that his utterances are true, the utterances can, however, nevertheless be accidentally true. Beardsley positions himself clearly regarding the question of truth in fiction by characterizing fiction as a discourse “in which the report-sentences are not asserted, while these sentences may still be true or false.”[272] Currie reaches a similar conclusion, claiming that a discourse can be fictional “though entirely true”,[273] although such truth is completely “accidental”[274] – and thus not a valid criterion for fictionality. Currie correspondingly warns not to confuse the question of truth with the question fictionality:

> [T]he distinction […] between factional and fictional statements is not the same as the distinction between false and true statements. Nor is it the distinction between what the author (and readers) acknowledge as factual and what they do not so acknowledge.[275]

We do not, however, need to assume Currie's or Beardsley's position to understand that a certain schizophrenia is possible in or even constitutive for fictional discourse: Lewis's theory already allowed for a dissociation of the truth values of fictional discourse and its propositional content. While it is assumed by Lewis that "at our world" fictional discourse is only pretence, and thus fictional names are "denotationless", within the fictional universe the same discourse even needs to be understood as an assertion:

> The worlds we should consider, I suggest, are the worlds where the fiction is told, but as known fact rather as fiction. The act of storytelling occurs, just as it does here, at our world; but there it is what here it falsely purports to be: truth-telling about a matter whereof the teller has knowledge.[276]

Also Gabriel, though following Searle in clearly rejecting the notion of truth values of fictional discourse, nevertheless upholds that, since fictional discourse "may 'create' fictive worlds", "the fictional utterance is true (or false) [...] in the corresponding fictional world".[277] Currie and others, however, have maintained that while truth in fiction might exist, "truth-in-fiction" was not "truth" in the conventional sense,[278] and have consequently questioned whether Lewis's possible-world-theory-oriented definition of fictional truth can actually serve its purpose. In *The Nature of Fiction*, Currie has linked fictional truth with the criterion of belief instead.[279] He, however, revoked this claim seven years later in "On Being Fictional".[280]

Richard Gale seems to aim at a compromise in this matter instead:

> Sentences in fictive utterances when construed non-contextually might be true or false or lacking in truth values. The fictive stance, not a theory of presupposition or assertion, determines how they are to be taken. Truth and falsity are indifferent to what it is possible to imagine, entertain or make-belief. Some sentences – notably those containing fictional singular terms – have no truth-values on a non-contextual construal but construed in context perform the function of characterizing objects and states of affaires whose very nature is determined by the descriptive content of the utterances themselves.[281]

Given the above, it should become obvious that the theory of legal fictionality could well profit from these more reflected approaches on fictionality. While some of the concepts of fictionality that originated within literary theory evidently cannot be applied to legal fictionality without modification (e.g. the criterion of a dissociation between author and narrator), others are easily applied. The reassessment of both the criteria of truth in general and fictionality in particular is evidentially relevant here, in light of the unreflected dichotomous understanding of fictionality as counterfactual discourse that still lingers in legal thought. The question of applicability is not as simple with speech act approaches, however. Though, early on, Alf Ross proposed a definition of legal fictionality that shares a striking similarity with speech act approaches, claiming that in legal fictional discourse, a proposition "is only posed, not affirmed",[282] and characterizing judiciary fictions "make-belief actions" that do not require counterfactuality,[283] a theory of speech acts might at first sight rather deepen the gap between legal and literary fictionality.[284] Despite the fact that speech act analysis has long found its application in legal theory,[285] a transfer of this approach to legal studies might prove problematic when it comes to the question of legal fictions. Legal and fictional discourse seem to differ considerably in the quality of their illocutionary performances – at least if literary discourse is taken as the paradigm of fictional discourse. While legal scholars have long stipulated that legal norms, without exception, have to be understood as a certain type of illocutions, namely commands (directives),[286] in contrast, at least in the field of literature, the participants of fictional discourse are rarely embedded in a comparable authoritative framework, and the speech acts pertaining to it might also be of a different type. Under this presupposition, the inevitable question must be if fictional discourse can play any relevant role in the legal field. For Bouvier, it is evident that, due to the authoritative character of law, legal fictionality is not impossible, but unnecessary – and has to be regarded as an alien element within the legal system.[287] In a comparable manner, in Chapter 5.4 of this volume, Andrei Mamor has identified the criterion of authority as the differentiating criterion between the legal and the literary field.

On closer examination, however, the opposition might not be as polar anymore. At least in the one case of legal fictionalizing that Bouvier would accept as legitimate but unnecessary (the case of statutory fictions, which are not based on the lack of authority),[288] an imperative has already been construed by the early scholarship: the command to feign or to regard/to treat "as well"/"as if" (Bülow, Kelsen, Kluckmann).[289] But also in general, the gap might not be as gaping. From the perspective of legal fictionality, at least some legal fictions clearly bear the surface structure of assertions, and not of commands. From the perspective of literary fiction, a convergence towards the legal realm of authority can also be monitored, since "fiction" as an institutionalized cultural practice within literature and the arts well prescribes a certain stance of reception, or at least strongly suggests one. To imagine as instructed; to treat as if; to suspend disbelief; to refrain from performing a reality test: these are only some of the commands identified by scholars that fictional discourse might entail. The conventions of interaction between producer and recipient of a literary work, early paraphrased as a - "contract",[290] might not be equivalent in authority to contractual relation as established in the legal realm, but the term used surely is also more than a mere metaphor. In film theory, Christian Metz and Jean Louis Baudry have investigated the cultural practice of fictional film reception as a prescriptive "apparatus" – and in this process unveiled a substantial amount of cultural conventions and rules that lead to a certain prescribed receptive stance of the audience.[291] Correspondingly, Walton's approach to fictionality not only contains an invitation to imagine a certain event, but instead has been considered as mandatory, a peculiarity that Matravers has also commented on:

> [A] proposition is fictional if there is a mandate to imagine it. [...] There are many propositions that are part of the content of fictional works that the reader is mandated to believe rather than make-belief.[292]

Newer voices, such as Richard Gerrig,[293] have inverted Coleridge's dictum of a "suspension of disbelief" as part of the mutually binding framework of fiction. Assuming that, in daily life, belief is rather the rule than the exception, the fictional stance is instead said to be characterized by its opposite, the "construction of disbelief".[294]

For the field of literature, the proponents of the Constance School early on highlighted in their version(s) of a reader-response theory (Jauß in a 1967 publication, Iser in his 1970, 1972 and 1976 monographs) that while the author often only invites, he sometimes might also clearly demand a certain activity of reception. "Receptional prescriptions",[295] "receptional directives"[296] or "appellative structures"[297] are terms used for those instances where a text prescribes a certain action or attitude to the reader[298] (as opposed to the more usual mere "receptional invitations").[299] Iser claims that although the meaning of a text is always a co-product of reader and author (understanding the text rather as a score that leaves the recipient enough indeterminateness to be filled in by his knowledge, personal history and his conscious and unconscious wishes and needs), there are nevertheless signposts and structural orientation which are prescriptive and thus demand with a certain authorial authority that the reader follow. Though, contrary to the legal field, the adherence to such rules is usually not secured by pain of penalties, few readers will, for example, ignore the paratextual command of a book labelled "novel" and read it as a factual account instead, though the latter might, of course, happen by accident, a problem literature theory also has been grappling with.[300] Equally, despite many innovations in modern and postmodern theatre and other performative arts, spectators of a play continue to have the tendency of refraining from dialogue with the actors on stage (even if ostensibly addressed), and much less will they storm on stage in order to fight the villain and free the imprisoned maiden.[301] In short, the institutionalized cultural practice of literary fiction, like the legal realm, is characterized as being part of an authoritative framework – and the difference between the two frameworks might not be a difference in nature here, but rather in degree. Searle's assessment is noteworthy here: that regarding the typology of speech acts, between an invitation and a command, the difference is of the latter sort (not of category, but of degree), since both are in fact "directives".[302]

Especially one strain of fictional theory has investigated this notion more extensively. Although Kendall Walton's treatment of fictionality shares with speech act approaches that it is based on the idea of a performative understanding of fictionality, it has, however, considerably shifted away from the idea of a speaker's intention as the criterion of fictionality (as propagated by Searle). Since the intention of an original communicator (e.g. an author) is irrelevant in Kendall's account of fictionality (which focuses on the mere fact that a prop is used in a game of make-believe, as part of an established "institution"[303]), fictionality is fairly reduced to the practical question of receptive stance.[304] The problems raised by such a position (questions of truth, reference, etc.) are, however, not different in essence from the above already treated – and as many speech act theorists claim, fictionality needs to be understood not as a syntactical or semantic question, but as a purely pragmatic one, anyway. In literary theory, the idea has been fruitfully extended to an institutional theory of fiction, claiming that fictional discourse functions within an institutionalized framework that also institutionalizes rules both of production and/or reception. Peter Lamarque and Stein Olson have characterized such an institutionalized practice as "constituted by a set of conventions and concepts which both regulate and define the actions involved in the practice".[305] "Institution" is then circumscribed as "a rule-governed practice which makes possible certain (institutionalized) actions which are defined by the rules of the practice and which could not exist as such without those rules".[306]

The advantage of a theory of fictional discourse as institutionalized practice is that it can account for degrees and differences, since the participants of an institution may to a greater or lesser degree obey the norms. The rules, even if not followed, are nevertheless indispensable, for, as a framework, they constitute a necessary condition of fictional discourse as a practice. Some of these rules were already present in this chapter, such as Lewis's principles; others spring from possible world approaches, as the principle of minimal departure.[307] Although institutional-practice theories were formulated for and developed specifically within a theory of literature, art or media – and therefore rather dissociate from the more common definitions of analytic philosophy – the idea to also understand legal fiction as an institutionalized practice seems fruitful, especially since the use of legal language is already part of an institutionalized practice of language use. Within this different framework, a number of Fuller's questions – for example, as to whether fictionality requires overtness and thus presumes consciousness[308] – can also be more adequately assessed.

## VI Mapping the conceptual network: Family resemblance, prototype theory and the problem of hierarchical taxonomies

Although the disparity of approaches to fiction within fictional theory is primarily based on different methodological presuppositions, the historic discourse on legal fictionality is less homogenous than one would initially expect, but for different reasons. Although the notion of counterfactuality is present in the majority of approaches, at its edges the definition field has in fact always been heterogeneous. "What is a legal fiction?" Louise Harmon writes in a 1990 essay, and continues: "[n]one of the participants in the historical debate could agree. The problem was one of scope: what should be included in the definition."[309]

Within the scope of fictional theory in analytic philosophy and literary theory, the disagreement on whether it is possible to bring into accord different communicative artefacts or propositions coherently and without contradiction – and to subsume them under one parsimonious definition – has led to the suggestion that fictional discourse was better to be approached from the idea of "family resemblance". In his *Philosophical Investigations* (published posthumously in 1953), Wittgenstein assumes that concepts exist that cannot sufficiently be captured by a taxonomical classification centering on criteria common to all category members, but instead have to be understood only as "a complicated network of similarities, overlapping and crisscrossing".[310] "Family resemblance" is the term Wittgenstein chose to explicate a category where the "phenomena have no one thing in common which makes us use the same word for all", although "they are related to one another" – but "in many different ways".[311] Linked to this idea is the more modern notion of prototype semantics that certain categories are not defined "on the basis of their sharing of a set of common, defining features",[312] but instead by their similarity to a prototype. Within prototype semantics, the definition of such a "prototype" considerably varies. From an ontological perspective, a prototype can either be understood as "the abstract representation of a category" – and thus as a non-existing idealization – or as the (existing) member of a category "to which subjects compare items when judging category membership"[313] and is usually conflated with the "best example" or the "clearest case".[314] Rosch has particularly stressed the cognitive and genetic peculiarity of prototypes, as "perceptually salient points in the domain (around which categories form)". From this cognitive perspective, not the statistical average might be relevant, but the "'default' category member", as the member "that is activated in the absence of more specific information".[315] Correspondingly, according to Coleman and Cay, prototypical categorical reasoning "associate[s] a word or phrase with a prelinguistic, cognitive scheme or image".[316] Our preference for prototypicality when it comes to natural category establishment and reasoning is explained both by factors of conditioning (prototypes are those examples encountered most frequently) and cognitive efficiency (prototypes maximize the distinctiveness of a category vi-à-vis its neighboring, contrasting categories).[317] With Wittgenstein's idea of family resemblance, prototype semantics shares a number of similarities. As in the *Philosophical Investigations*, cluster categories are defined as "networks of overlapping attributes" that have no defining feature common to all category members.[318] Scholars also disagree whether a certain "gestalt" view is decisive for both "family resemblance" and "prototypicality".[319] For Mervis and

Ross, family resemblance and prototypicality are furthermore interwoven: not only are categories understood in the sense of a network of overlapping attributes (only), but a clear correlation between prototypicality and family resemblance has been suggested. Here, a prototype is described as "having less family resemblance with members of other categories", while in the center of the semantic space the greatest family resemblance is said to be observed. The latter view also allows for degrees, since the "distance of the items from the origin of the space is determined by their degree of family resemblance":[320]

> Although family resemblance was defined in terms of discrete features no one of which was common to all category members, [...] the property of the centrality of items in the semantic field was still interpretable; that is, degree of family resemblance was highly predictive of centrality in a semantic space defined by global similarity ratings of the items in category.[321]

The idea of "family resemblance" as a new form of category reasoning has rapidly found an application within the arts. Morris Weitz has used Wittgenstein's idea of a cluster definition[322] in his inquiry on the nature of art.[323] Gerard Genette applied the idea in *Fiction and Diction* to characterize literature.[324] Charles L. Stevenson used it to discern the characteristics of a poem.[325] And the idea has subsequently also been applied to different literary genre.

In "Literary Theory and its Discontents", John Searle has explicitly invoked the notion of family resemblance in the context of the debate on fictionality:

> [T]he distinction between literal and metaphorical, serious or nonserious, fiction and nonfiction, and yes, even true and false, admit of degrees, and all apply more or less. It is, in short, generally accepted that many, perhaps most, concepts do not have sharp boundaries [...]. Indeed, in addition to examinations of the problem of vagueness, there have been quite extensive discussions of family resemblance [...][326]

Consequently, in fictional theory, the apparent disagreement of scholars regarding a necessary or even sufficient criterion for fictionality could be alternatively approached not by asking for the common elements to all cases, but instead by uncovering the network of overlapping traits. Also, the methodically more developed field of prototype semantics might be applicable both to legal and literary fictionality.[327] Prototype semantics would especially allow the question if counterfactual discourse was to be understood as the "prototype" or "clearest example" of fictional discourse, which "most strongly reflect[s] the attribute structure of the category as a whole", even though counterfactuality cannot be considered as a common attribute to all members of the semantic field of fictionality (anymore) – or if counterfactuality instead is merely correlative, and maybe even only an accidental trait of some members of the fictional discourse family.[328]

Although family resemblance has recently been criticized as applied to literary fictionality,[329] from a heuristic perspective it seems a promising starting point for a volume on legal fictionality that aims at approaching the issue of fictionality not from a dogmatic but from a particularly empirical perspective. Dogmatic approaches inevitably share the danger of circularity, since they work with a preselection of cases or examples that are usually chosen because they comply with certain dogmatic presuppositions – and in the case of legal fictionality, are thus often selected on the prejudice of already knowing what legal fictionality consists of. The latter is most evident in the treatment of statutory fictions (often found as deeming provisions, e.g. in US tax law), which a considerable number of scholars would see incorrectly labelled as "fictions".[330] As I will attempt to show in Chapter 5.2 of this volume, despite their disputed status, statutory fictions can well shed a light on the question of the nature of fictionality in general, and should therefore not be excluded prematurely.

To avoid the dogmatic fallacies often involved when constructing a conceptual taxonomy, this volume has also selected its examples with a certain arbitrariness: some sprung from the sessions and conferences of the group I have coordinated for three years at Yale University's Whitney Humanities Center ("Fictionality: Law, Literature, Science"), others from my previous participation in a postdoctoral research group at Berlin's Freie Universität. I have nevertheless tried to mirror the complex semantical network of category members (or, metaphorically speaking, the "gestalt" of the semantic field associated with legal fictionality) by selecting examples from different areas of the semantic field. However, the limited space available imposed some unfortunate restrictions on this volume, and, apart from some very standard examples, I therefore rather chose examples that have not yet been extensively treated.

It is also important to stress that this volume does not presume legal fictionality to be a Wittgensteinian cluster concept based on family resemblance. Instead, I want to proceed with caution in this matter, since cluster definitions are often prematurely used in cases where a common criterion can only be carved out with utmost difficulty, even though such a criterion might actually exist and a critical feature approach would have instead been the adequate proceeding. Cluster representations, however, have particular heuristic value in cases where it is unclear if a common denominator can be found, because they are useful irrespective of whether the cluster hypothesis is later proven correct, or not. While, in the latter case, the choice of this volume to represent fictional discourse rather as a disparate field or overlapping network of category members would be the only way of doing justice to its internal structure, in the former case, the field established in this volume can at least provide a basis (and thus a heuristic means) for a reassessment of legal fictional discourse – and thereby could consequently serve as the basis of a later taxonomical categorization in the sense of a critical feature approach. In this regard, this volume thus only aims at providing the first step of a reassessment of legal fictionality. Due to this approach, the volume will also refrain from a simplistic conclusion. Instead, a final part (Chapters 5.1–5.4) of diverging theoretical approaches to legal fictionality that open rather than conclude the question will mark the end of this volume. In light of the fact that the debate on fictionality within analytic philosophy and literary theory failed to reach a consensus even after decades of critical inquiry, it would be presumptuous to assume that one volume alone could map the whole network, or that it could even provide legal discourse with a satisfying criterion of fictionality. To avoid a mere parataxis of approaches, however, the essays of Part 5 will add a theoretical perspective by again reassessing the question of legal fictionality from differing methodological angles. Furthermore, not only are a number of phenotypes of fictionality to be established in the first three parts of this volume, but a reversal of perspective will be taken, when, in Part 4, legal fictionality is to be assessed as represented within the fictional framework of literary fiction, presupposing that a metafictional perspective can provide additional insights on the matter. By mapping the field of legal fictional discourse, this volume, however, also has a second aim. With a few notable exceptions (such as Hans Vaihinger's early treatment), legal fictionality has been excluded from the debate on a transdisciplinary valid definition of fictional discourse, and therefore has not played any relevant role both within analytic philosophy and literary theory – presumably because it has not been considered a particularly "good example" of fictional discourse, least of all its prototype. This volume hopes to provide fictional theory with new material by demonstrating the diversity of forms of fictionality within the legal discourse – and thereby aims at convincing fictional theory to reconsider the past exclusion of the legal field from its debate.

## Notes

1 Gyora Binder and Robert Weisberg, *Literary Criticism of Law* (Princeton: Princeton UP, 2000).
2 Elisabeth Anker and Bernadette Meyler, *New Directions in Law and Literature* (Oxford UP, 2017).
3 On literariness cf. the 1973 fall issue of *New Literary History* (Vol. 5, No. 1: What Is Literature?) with essays by Todorov, Ricoeur, Fish and Kernan, and the 2007 winter issue (Vol. 38, No. 1: What Is Literature Now?) with essays by Culler, Todorov and Gans. See also the essays of Sparshott, Wellek, Hirsch, Davenport, McFadden and Altieri in: *What is Literature?*, ed. Paul Hernadi (Bloomington: Indiana UP, 1978).
4 That it is necessary to distinguish fictionality and literariness seems to be majorly accepted – cf. John Searle (John Searle, "The Logical Status of Fictional Discourse", *New Literary History* 6, No. 2 (1975), 319) and Tzvetan Todorov, the latter claiming fictionality is neither a necessary nor a sufficient condition of literature (Monroe Beardsley, "Aesthetic Intentions and Fictive Illocutions", in: Hernadi, *What is Literature?*, 172). A similar debate pertains to the relation of narrative both to fictionality and literariness.
5 William Blackstone, *The Oxford Edition of Blackstone's Commentaries on the Laws of England*, ed. T. Gallanis (Oxford: Oxford UP, 2016), 3: 72.

6 Roscoe Pound, *Jurisprudence* (St. Paul, MN: West, 1959), 451.
7 Ibid. p. 455.
8 John Chipman Gray, *The Nature and Sources of The Law* (New York: Columbia UP, 1909), 33. In Roman law, "Numerius Negidius" and "Aulus Agerius" were commonly used as fictional parties.
9 Ibid.
10 Nancy Knauer, "Legal Fictions and Juristic Truth", *St. Thomas Law Review* 23, 88.
11 Hans Kelsen, "Zur Theorie der juristischen Fiktionen. Mit besonderer Berücksichtigung von Hans Vaihingers Philosophie des Als Ob", *Annalen der Philosophie und philosophischen Kritik* 1 (1919), 632 (my translation). As both Kelsen's essay and his 1911 habilitation show, Kelsen's rejection of legal fictionality (with the exception of statutory fictions, which Kelsen does not see as counterfactual) is rather based on the dangerous illusionary effects legal fictions entail (cf. infra notes 64 and 218). Knauer seems to aim at a similar notion, discrediting only a certain type of newer "fictions" (see e.g. Knauer, "Legal Fictions", 94).
12 Pound, *Jurisprudence*, 3: 459, 466. In his 1922 *Introduction to the Philosophy of Law* (New Haven, Yale UP, 1930), 114, however, Pound writes: "In other words, a more subtle fiction does for the maturity of law what is done for the strict law by its relatively crude procedural fictions."
13 Gray, *Sources of Law*, 30.
14 Henry Maine: *Ancient Law. Its Connection with the Early History of Society, and Its Relation to Modern Ideas* (London: John Murray, 1861), 26; The same argument was already propagated by Renusson in 1733: Philippe de Renusson, *Traité des propres réels, reputez réels et conventionnels* (Paris: Pierre Armand, 1733), 438–9, Maine, however, also maintains that, for contemporary law, it would be "unworthy of us to effect an admittedly beneficial object by so rude a device as a legal fiction" (p. 27).
15 Henry Maine, quoted by Gray (Gray, *Ancient Law*, 35).
16 Ernst Zitelmann, *Begriff und Wesen der sogenannten juristischen Personen* (Leipzig: Duncker und Humblot,1873), 114 (my free translation).
17 Rudolph von Jhering, *Geist des römischen Rechts auf den verschiedenen Stufen seiner Entwicklung* (Leipzig: Breitkopf und Härtel, 1852–1869), 3: 260–1: "technische Nothlügen", ibid.
18 Ibid. (my free translation).
19 Sidney T. Miller, "The Reasons for Some Legal Fictions", *Michigan Law Review* 8, No. 8 (June 1910), 623–36.
20 Jeremy Bentham, *A Fragment on Government*, ed. J.H. Burns and H.L.A. Hart (Cambridge: Cambridge UP, 1988), 21.
21 Bentham, *Government*, 51; Bentham uses the term again in context of the fiction of the social contract.
22 Jeremy Bentham, *The Works of Jeremy Bentham, published under the Superintendence of his Executor, John Bowring* (Edinburgh: William Tait, 1838–1843), Vol. 5, 92.
23 Bentham, *Government*, 117.
24 Renusson, *Traité*, 438; Renusson, however, also understands fictions as a necessary and suitable remedy against the rigidities of law, 439.
25 Blackstone, *Commentaries*, 28.
26 Jhering, Geist, 3: 260–1.
27 Johannes Kuntze, *Die Obligation und die Singularsuccession des römischen und heutigen Rechts* (Leipzig: Hermann Mendelsohn, 1856), 399.
28 As a necessary practice that does "not offend the superstitious disrelish for change which is always present", Henry Maine, *Ancient Law* (Cambridge and New York: Cambridge UP, 2012 [1861]), 26; cited by Aviam Soifer, "Reviewing Legal Fictions", *Georgia Law Review* 20 (1986), 876.

29 Peter Smith, "New Legal Fictions". *Georgetown Law Journal* 95 (2007), 1478–9.
30 Oskar Bülow, "Civilprozessualische Fiktionen und Wahrheiten", *Archiv für die civilistische Praxis* 62 (1879), 6.
31 Lon Fuller, *Legal Fictions* (Stanford: Stanford UP, 1967), 26.
32 Rudolf Jhering, *Geist*, 2: 299.
33 *The American Jurist and Law Magazine*, Vol. 25 (April 1841), 69 [reprint of an article of the *Monthly Law Magazine*, December 1840].
34 See: Marjorie Stone, "Dickens, Bentham, and the Fictions of the Law: A Victorian Controversy and Its Consequences", *Victorian Studies* 29, No. 1 (Autumn, 1985), 125–54.
35 Cf. Miller, "Legal Fictions", 623–36.
36 Pound also mentions Austin's *Jurisprudence* (5th ed. 1885, p. 609–11) and § 150 of Phelps' *Juridical Equity* (1894) as relevant places of discussion (Pound, *Jurisprudence*, 449); their contribution is, however, limited – and mainly sums arguments already present within the debate.
37 "[T]he action of ejectment was devised to meet the case of a lessee who had been evicted but could not bring a real action because he did not have an estate of freehold" (Pound, *Jurisprudence*, 435). In order to secure the recovery of possession of land – and to avoid a trial by battle – a fictitious lessee in a supposed lease had to be created, cf. "Ejectment" in: *Black's Law Dictionary*, ed. Bryan Garner, 6th edition (St.Paul, MN: West Group, 1990), 516.
38 Supra note 5.
39 "Constructive (possession) is a legal fiction or principle to which the courts will resort when a fact or a condition does not have the character assigned to it in its own essential nature but is vested with such a character in consequence of the way it is regarded by a rule of policy of law." Frank Emerson Clark, *A Treatise on the Law of Surveying and Boundaries* (Indianapolis: The Bobbs-Merrill Company, 1922), § 22.09; on the newer discussion cf. Elspeth Reid and Eric Descheemaeker, eds, *Consequences of Possession* (Edinburgh: Edinburgh UP, 2014), especially: Simon Douglas: "Is Possession Factual or Legal", 77–94; and: Lena Kunz: "*Processio civilissima* in Spanish and German Law. Possession between Fact and Fiction", 141–70.
40 For the long history of legal fictions in Roman and common law, see: Gustav Demelius, *Die Rechtsfiktion in ihrer geschichtlichen und dogmatischen Bedeutung* (Weimar: Hermann Boehlau, 1858); Gray, *Sources*, 30–62; Pound, Jurisprudence, 449–67; and Ian Maclean, "Legal Fictions and Fictional Entities in Renaissance Jurisprudence", *Legal History* 20 (1999), 1–24.
41 Peter Smith, "New Legal Fictions". *Georgetown Law Journal* 95 (2007), 1465.
42 Ngaire Naffine, "Legal Persons as Abstractions: The Extrapolation of Persons from the Male Case." In: *Legal Personhood: Animals, Artificial Intelligence and the Unborn*, ed. Visa A.J. Kurki and Tomasz Pietrzykowski (New York: Springer, 2017), 15; [anon.], "What We Talk about When We Talk about Persons: The Language of a Legal Fiction", *Harvard Law Review* 114, No. 6 (2001), 1745–68. It is for sure no coincidence that Gray's lengthy excursion on legal fictionality (Gray, *Sources*, 30–62) is a part of his chapter on legal personhood (Chapter 2). Kelsen also elaborates on the issue: "If [...] the legal subject, the physical as well as the juridical was nothing but a personification of a complex of norms, with the aim of simplification and illustration, [...] then the idea of a person, as it is common in modern jurisprudence was a typical example of those fictions [...] Vaihinger has examined [...]", Kelsen, "Theorie", 633–4 (my translation). Also Ross comments on the issue: Ross, *Legal Fictions*, 220.
43 Rant Reichmann, "Law's affective thickets?" In: Anker, *New Directions*, 112.

44 I have commented on the issue of "original public meaning" as a counterfactual construction in a co-authored paper with Christina Mulligan, Michael Douma and Brian Quinn ("Founding-Era Translations of the United States Constitution", *Constitutional Commentary* 31, No. 1 (2016). 1–53). A summary and theoretical reassessment of the results is currently being prepared, and will soon appear as: Hans Lind, Christina Mulligan, Michael Douma and Brian Quinn, "Translation Approaches in Constitutional Hermeneutics", *The International Journal for the Semiotics of Law* (Special Issue "Situating Jurilinguistics across Cultures using Translation and Discourse Approaches", Springer: 2020). Jack Balkin also concluded from our work that the notion of an "original public meaning" is nothing other than a "theoretical construction" (Jack Balkin, "The Construction of Original Public Meaning", *Constitutional Commentary* 31 (2016), 72, 78). Smith even calls this highly problematic premise of originalism a "new legal fiction" (Smith, "New Legal Fictions", 1464).

45 Knauer mentions Section 7872 of the Internal Revenue Code (Knauer, *Legal Fictions*, 87). The treatment of deeming provisions as "fictions" is, however, disputed (cf. my Chapter 5.2 of this volume).

46 Anaclet Reiffenstuel, *Ius Canonicum universum, clara method iuxta titulus quinque librorum. Tomus Primus.* (Monachij (=Munich): Joannis Hermmanni, 1702), 121.

47 A common principle of Roman law, cf. e.g. Samuel v. Cocceji, *Ius civile controversum* (Francofurti & Lipsiae [Frankfurt & Leipzig]: Weidmanns Erben, 1740), 470, in the context of the vindication against the *possessor bonae fidei.*

48 (My very literal translation); or: "Et ubi veritas locum habere potest, cessat fictio": Simon Vaz Barbosa, *Prinzipia et Loci Communies seu Regulae tam decisionum, quam Argumentorum U.J. cum plenissima Doctorum allegatione collecta* (Trajecti ad Rhenum [=Utrecht], 1651).

49 Renusson lists Bartolus de Saxoferrato as a source for this dictum: Renusson, *Traité des propres réels*, 439.

50 Cited by Kurt Eggert, "Deference and Fiction: Reforming Chevron's Legal Fictions After King v. Burwell", *Nebraska Law Review* 95 (2016), 761.

51 Bentham, *Works*, XVII, p. 77.

52 Henry Finch, *Law, Or, a Discourse Thereof*; the first English edition appeared in 1625, it was, however, preceded by a French edition (London: 1613) titled: *Nomotexnia; Cestascavoir, Un Description del Common Leys D'angleterre Solonque les Rules Del Art.*

53 Henry Finch, *Law, Or, a Discourse Thereof: In Four Books* (London: Henry Lintot & J. Shuckburg: 1759), 2:66.

54 Renusson, *Traité des propres réels*, 439; he also reiterates Pontanus' defninition: «fictio, dit-il, est Juris dispositio super re certa contra veritatem quae est possibilis & pro veritate habetur», ibid.

55 (My translation), the complete passage reads: «Donc la « non existence » équivaut à l'« existence » comme dans toute fiction. […] Car c'est ce rapport d'égalité établi entre le vrai et le faux qui donne à la fiction son caractère spécial.»: Pierre de Tourtoulon, *Les Principes philosophiques de L'histoire du Droit* (Lausanne/Paris: Librairie Payot, 1908–1919), 463.

56 John Ballantine, *A Law Dictionary* (Indianapolis: The Bobbs-Merrill Company: 1969), 458.

57 10th edition, ed. Bryan Garner (St. Paul, MN: Thomson Reuters, 2014).

58 Fuller, *Legal Fictions*, 9.

59 Op. cit., 11.

60 Frederick Schauer, "Legal Fictions Revisited", in: *Legal Fictions in Theory and Practice*, ed. William Twining & Maksymilian Del Mar (Cham: Springer, 2015),

113–29, though Schauer admits "a complex relation between legal truth and truth *simpliciter*", 114.

61 Demelius, *Rechtsfiktion*, S. 39.

62 Lecocq most strongly attacks the notion of counterfactuality in the case of "retroactive fictions": Lucien Lecocq, *De la Fiction comme Procede Juridique* (Paris: Arthur Rousseau, 1914), 23; 87. It is unclear, however, if according to Lecocq, this "fiction" would not better be called fiction, cf. 88, 71 ("la rétroactivité de la loi n'est pas une fiction").

63 Felix Somlò, *Juristische Grundlehre* (Leipzig: Felix Meiner, 1917).

64 In his "Theory of Legal Fictions", Kelsen maintains that the paradigm of legal fictions was not counterfactual, but that instead it bears no relation to reality whatsoever. Cf. p. 639, where Kelsen formulates, that, in the case of statutory fictions, a contradiction to reality is literally impossible (cf. also Chapter 5.2). However, Kelsen's notion of the "epistemological fiction" in law is still based on a "contradiction", though not on "reality", but with its "object", Kelsen, "Theorie", 633. Kelsen already laid out the basis of most of his claims on legal fictionality in: Hans Kelsen, *Hauptprobleme der Staatsrechtslehre, entwickelt aus der Lehre vom Rechtssatze* (Tübingen: Mohr, 1911).

65 Alf Ross, "Legal Fictions", in: *Law, Reason and Justice: Essays in Legal Philosophy*, ed. Graham Hughes (New York: New York UP, 1969), 217–34.

66 Robert Samek, "Fictions and the Law", *University of Toronto Law Journal* 31 (1982), 290.

67 Kenneth Campbell, "Fuller on Legal Fictions", *Law & Philosophy* 2 (1983), 338.

68 Peter Birks, "Fictions ancient and modern", in: *The Legal Mind: Essays for Tony Honoré*, ed. Neil MacCormick and Peter Birks (Oxford: Clarendon, 1986), 83–101.

69 Aviam Soifer, "Reviewing Legal Fictions", *Georgia Law Review* 20 (1986), 871–915.

70 Karen Petroski, "Legal Fictions and the Limits of Legal Language", in: *Legal Fictions in Theory and Practice*, ed. Maksymilian Del Mar and William Twining (Cham: Springer, 2015), 131–56; see also: Karen Petroski, *Fiction and the Languages of Law: Understanding Contemporary Legal Discourse* (New York: Routledge, 2018).

71 Simon Stern, "Legal Fictions and Exclusionary Rules", in: Del Mar, *Legal Fictions*, 157–73; Stern also contributed an Essay on the topic in Elisabeth Anker's and Bernadette Mayler's volume: Simon Stern, "Legal and Literary Fictions", in: *New Directions in Law and Literature*, ed. Elizabeth Anker and Bernadette Mayler (Oxford: Oxford UP, 2017), 313–26.

72 Douglas Lind, "The Pragmatic Value of Legal Fictions", in: Del Mar, *Legal Fictions*, 83–107.

73 Del Mar, Maksymilian and William Twining, ed., *Legal Fictions in Theory and Practice* (Cham: Springer, 2015).

74 Ross, "Legal Fictions", 223–4: "[T]he prevalent definition of fictions as a consciously false assumption is contradictory and therefore has no reference", 224.

75 Ross, "Legal Fictions", 223–33. Ross seems to tacitly follow Kelsen in his assessment that only "dogmatic fictions" might quality as counterfactual statements – and consequently categorically rejects a definition based on the latter criterion. In *Directives and Norms* (Routledge & Kegan Paul, 1968), Ross in contrast negates any notion of fictionality both for statutory fictions and judiciary fictions with respect to the immediate propositions involved. For the case of judiciary fictions, he, however, identifies an act of clear pretense: "When a new law is in fact created by the judge, he pretends in his acts […] that the law is unchanged. […] Such make-belief actions (which are of course false statements) are in social life quite common" (p. 32).

76 Samek, "Fictions", 281.
77 Campbell, "Fuller on Fictions", 365.
78 Ibid.
79 Soifer, "Reviewing Legal Fictions", *Georgia Law Review* 20 (1986), 873.
80 Lind, op. cit. Douglas Lind, however, also states on p. 93 that a legal fiction "would be a false proposition if asserted under different techniques of usage in a belief system or realm of reality outside law".
81 Petroski, "Fictions", 136.
82 Ross, "Legal Fictions", 229.
83 Simon Stern, "Legal and Literary Fictions" in: *New Directions in Law and Literature*, ed. Elizabeth Anker and Bernadette Meyler (Oxford UP, 2017), 313–26. Available at SSRN: https://ssrn.com/abstract=2425999. Please note that the page-numbers of the SSRN version are different from the printed book. I will use the SSRN numbering in this chapter.
84 Stern, "Legal and Literary Fictions", SSRN 12.
85 Stern, "Exclusionary Rule", 170.
86 Stern approaches legal fictionality in terms of their "distinct narrative structure" (SSRN 9), its "latent narrative potential" – meaning whether they "hold the seed of a plot" – and comes to the conclusion that if legal fictions "display a generative potential that invites analogy to literary fictions, that kinship owes more to the way in which both fictional modes solicit a particular kind of attention, than a shared ability to spin out narrative arrays" (SSRN 4).
87 Hans J. Lind, "Fictio Legis. Zu einer allgemeinen Fiktionstheorie", in *Formen der Fiktion*, ed. Remigius Bunia (Munich: Wilhelm Fink, forthcoming). The status of the German publication is unclear, though, since the volume was originally scheduled to already appear in 2015.
88 Henry Sumner Maine has defined legal fiction functionally as an "assumption that conceals, or affects to conceal, the fact that a rule has undergone alteration, its letter remaining unchanged, its operation being modified": Henry Maine, *Ancient Law. Its Connection with the Early History of Society, and Its Relation to Modern Ideas* (London: John Murray, 1861), 26–7.
89 Alina Ng Boyte, "The Conceits of Our Legal Imagination: Legal Fictions and the Concept of Deemed Authorship", *New York University Journal of Legislation & Public Policy* 17 (2014), 707–8.
90 Knauer, "Legal Fictions", 88.
91 Baker, *Law's Two Bodies*, 39.
92 Ibid.
93 Op. cit., 42.
94 Infra notes 116–20 (and accompanying text) as well as Chapter 5.2, notes 145–8 and 159–60.
95 Knauer, "Legal Fictions", 119 ("empirical errors are mistakes, not fictions"); 120: "at some point the fiction can become a lie".
96 Op. cit., 89, 94, 96, 108, 119–20.
97 Baker, *Law*, 44.
98 Baker, *Law*, 45–6.
99 Knauer, "Fictions", 88.
100 Campbell, "Fuller on Fictions", 359.
101 Louise Harmon, "Falling off the Vine: Legal Fictions and the Doctrine of Substituted Judgment", *Yale Law Journal* 100 (1990), 1–71. On p. 63 e.g. it is written: "The first pretense of Lord Eldon's legal fiction, that the idiot has the capacity to possess intentional states, flies in the face of reason."
102 Harmon, "Falling", 59.

103 Jhering, however, only uses this model for the class of "dogmatic fictions".
104 Ian Maclean, "Legal Fictions and Fictional Entities in Renaissance Jurisprudence", *The Journal of Legal History* 20 (1999), 1, following, *Lectures on Jurisprudence* (ed. J.A. Jolowicz), 365–6.
105 Maclean, Fictions, 1; though it needs to be noted that "contradistinction" is not congruent with "contradiction". McLean's dictum of "contradistinction" even applies to those fictions that are not used "conterfactually", but are applied in order to "construct meaning", p. 11.
106 Miller, "The Reasons for Some Legal Fictions", 623–5.
107 Jhering, *Geist*, 289 (my translation); it seems, however, that the more important criterion for Jhering is function, not form.
108 Thus if the meaning of a term has considerably extended or if the metaphorical meaning has become the literal meaning: Fuller, *Legal Fictions*, 11–23.
109 Fuller, *Legal Fictions*, 10–11.
110 The classical distinction assumes that presumptions require that things are uncertain, whereas fictions require counterfactuality – and thus certainty. Correspondingly, Reiffenstuel explicates: "In quibus Fictio juris differat a Praesumptione juris? [...] Fictio juris assumitur in casu certo contra veritatem; nam Fictio fingit vera esse ea, quae vera non sunt: Praesumptio autem assumitur in caso dubio secundum verisimilem veritatem; nam Praesumptio est super eo, quod est dubium, & incertum, colligendo ex indiciis ita esse, quod caeteroquin est dubium, & incertum": Anaclet Reiffenstuel, *Ius Canonicum universum, clara method iuxta titulus quinque librorum. Tomus Primus.* (Monachij (=Munich): Joannis Hermmanni, 1702), 121. Renusson gives a comparable distinction between the fiction and presumption: Renusson, Traité des propres réels, 439. Hans Kelsen, however, has objected that fictions differ from presumptions in nature, and not only in degree of certainty: Kelsen, "Fiktionen", 640. Cf. Chapter 5.2 note 11 and 56.
111 "May be false" instead of "is false" in the first two definitions; improbability instead of impossibility in the third definition.
112 Eggert, "Deference", 765.
113 Cited by Stone, "Dickens", 127.
114 For a full account of "Bentham's Theory of Fiction" (Ogden), which is closely tied to his theory of language, see Philip Schofield's chapter on the issue ("Real and Ficticious Entities") in his monograph *Utility and Democracy: The Political Thought of Jeremy Bentham* (Oxford: Oxford UP, 2006). Cf. Nomi Stolzenberg, "Bentham's Theory of Fictions – A Curious Double Language", *Cardozo Studies in Law and Literature* 11, No. 2 (winter 1999), 223–62; Michael Quinn: "Fuller on Legal Fictions. A Benthamian Perspective" in: Del Mar, *Legal Fictions*, 55–82; Emmanuelle De Champs, "The Place of Jeremy Bentham's Theory of Fictions in Eighteenth-Century Linguistic Thought", *Journal of Bentham Studies* 2 (1999). Available from: www.uclpress.co.uk/pages/journal-of-bentham-studies [Accessed 3 Feb 2018]; Charles Ogden, *Bentham's Theory of Fictions* (New York: Harcourt, Brace & Co., 1932).
115 Bentham, *Works*, 8:126.
116 Fuller, *Legal Fictions*, 11–12.
117 Fuller, *Legal Fictions*, 12.
118 Fuller, *Legal Fictions*, 14–15.
119 Cf. Albert Einstein and Leopold Infeld: *The Evolution of Physics: The Growth of Ideas from Early Concepts to Relativity and Quanta* (Cambridge: Cambridge UP, 1938), 296.
120 Fuller, *Legal Fictions*, 10.

121 René Dekkers, *La fiction juridique: étude de droit romain et de droit comparé* (Paris: Sirey, 1935), 250.
122 Ogden, op. cit.
123 Hans Vaihinger: *Die Philosophie des Als Ob. System der theoretischen, praktischen und religiösen Fiktionen der Menschheit auf Grund eines idealistischen Positivismus. Mit einem Anhang über Kant und Nietzsche* (Berlin: Reuther & Reichard, 1911), 143: "'Wahrheit' [...] nur der zweckmäßigste Irrtum". Although with Ogden's translation, an English edition is available which was even endorsed by Vaihinger, I nevertheless decided to use the German (second) edition, since Ogden's translation is not always reliable, and has also been considerably shortened.
124 Vaihinger, *Die Philosophie*, 216.
125 Ernst von Glasersfeld, "An Interpretation of Piaget's Constructivism", *Revue Internationale de Philosophie* 36, No. 142/143, 612–35; Ernst von Glasersfeld, *Radical Constructivism. A Way of Knowing and Learning* (London: Falmer, 1995), Ernst v. Glasersfeld and Paul Cobb: *Knowledge as Environmental Fit, Man-Environment-Systems*, 1983; Cf. Paul Feyerabend, "Realism and Instrumentalism: Comments on the logic of factual support", in M.A. Bunge, ed., *The Critical Approach to Science and Philosophy* (London: The Free Press, 1964).
126 The book was translated into English in 1922.
127 Tourtoulon, *Principes*, 460 (my translation).
128 Lon Fuller, "Legal Fictions", *Illinois Law Review* 1931, 877–910.
129 Felix Cohen, Review of "Bentham's Theory of Fictions by C.K. Ogden" and "The Theory of Legislation by Jeremy Bentham", *Yale Law Review* 42, No. 7 (1933), 1149–52.
130 A list of articles can be found at: Eggert: "Deference and Fiction", 754 (notes 289–302).
131 Cf. supra note 114.
132 Nomi Stolzenberg and Philip Schofield are the scholars cited the most by legal scholars in this context – see also supra note 114.
133 *The Wolters Kluwer Bouvier Law Dictionary Desk Edition* (2012), lemma "Fiction (Fictitious)".
134 Cited by Ogden, *Bentham's Theory of Fiction*, xciii. Bentham furthermore adds: "the ornament of his superstructures are fictions".
135 *The Wolters Kluwer Bouvier Law Dictionary Desk Edition* (2012), lemma "Fiction (Fictitious)".
136 With Aleida Assmann and Kendall Walton, two proponents of very different approaches to fictionality have recently again pondered on this particular dialectics of fictionality. Cf. Aleida Assmann, *Die Legitimität der Fiktion: ein Beitrag zur Geschichte der literarischen Kommunikation* (München: Wilhelm Fink, 1980); id., "Fiktion als Differenz", *Poetica* 21 (1989), 239–60; cf. Kendall Walton, "Appreciating Fiction: Suspending Disbelief Or Pretending Belief?", *Dispositio* 5, No. 13/14 (Invierno-Primavera 1980), 1–18; Christian Metz has treated the issue for the domain of fictional film, cf. infra note 291.
137 Whether Aristoteles was seriously invested in the dichotomy he propagated in Chapter 9 of his "Poetics", or whether the claim was only rhetorical has, however, lately been questioned, cf. Thornton Lockwood, "Aristotle on the (alleged) inferiority of history to poetry", in *Reading Aristotle: Argument and Exposition*, ed. William Wians and Ron Polansky (Leiden, Boston: Brill, 2017), 315–33.
138 Alexander Gottlieb Baumgarten's work is particularly instructive here, since the criterion of possibility is key to his understanding of poetry as necessarily "heterocosmic" – and also explains why in his 1935 dissertation (*"Meditationes philosophicae de nonnullis ad poema pertinentibus"*), utopic literature is harshly rejected as genre,

cf. Alexander Gottlieb Baumgarten, *Reflections on Poetry*, transl. Karl Aschenbrenner and William B. Holther (Berkeley: University of California Press, 1954). But also the Leibniz-Wolffian school in general, with its extensions in Gottsched, is interesting in this regard.

139 J.W. v. Goethe has much theorized on the issue in his autobiography *Dichtung und Wahrheit*, written between 1808 and 1831, cf. Johann Wolfgang von Goethe, *Truth and Poetry: From My Own Life*, transl. John Oxenford (Cambridge/New York: Cambridge UP, 2013 [1848]) [reprint]. A newer translation has chosen an alternate title well representing the content: *Autobiography: Truth and Fiction Relating to My Life*.

140 Moritz Schlick, "Das Wesen der Wahrheit nach der modernen Logik", *Vierteljahrsschrift für wissenschaftliche Philosophie und Soziologie* 34 (1910), 386–477; id., "Die Grenze der naturwissenschaftlichen und philosophischen Begriffsbildung", *Vierteljahrsschrift für wissenschaftliche Philosophie und Soziologie* 34 (1910), 121–42.

141 Cf. Francis Bradley, *Essays on Truth and Reality* (Oxford: Clarendon University Press, 1914), 202–18 and 219–44.

142 William James, *Pragmatism* (Cambridge, MA; London: Harvard UP, 1975 [1907]); id., "Pragmatism's Conception of Truth", *The Journal of Philosophy, Psychology and Scientific Methods* 4, No. 6 (March 14, 1907), 141–55; id., *The Meaning of Truth* (Cambridge, MA: Harvard UP, 1975 [1909]); found at: Hookway, Christopher, "Pragmatism", *The Stanford Encyclopedia of Philosophy* (Summer 2016 Edition), ed. Edward N. Zalta, https://plato.stanford.edu/archives/sum2016/entries/pragmatism, last accessed 02/27/2019.

143 James, *Pragmatism*, 34.

144 James, *Pragmatism*, 106; id., "Pragmatism's Conception of Truth", 151.

145 Vaihinger, *Die Philosophie*, 143 (my translation).

146 "The best definition of *truth* from the logical standpoint which is known to me is that by Peirce": John Dewey, *Logic: The Theory of Inquiry* (New York: Holt, 1938), cited in: Donald Davidson, "The Structure and Content of Truth", *The Journal of Philosophy* 87, No. 6 (June 1990), 279–328; Pierce, however, also draws on expediency: *The Collected Papers of Charles Sanders Peirce*, edited by Charles Hartshorne and Paul Weiss, Volumes 5–6: *Pragmatism and Pragmatism/Scientific Metaphysics* (Cambridge, MA: Harvard UP, 1974), 232.

147 Jürgen Habermas, *On the Pragmatics of Social Interaction*, transl. Barbara Fultner (Cambridge: Polity Press, 2003); id., "Wahrheitstheorien", in *Wirklichkeit und Reflexion. Walter Schulz zum 60. Geburtstag*, ed. Helmut Fahrenbach (Pfullingen: Neske, 1973), 211–265; Habermas, however, considerably modified his theory later, reviving realist notions, see: Jürgen Habermas, *Truth and Justification*, transl. B. Fultner (Cambridge, MA: MIT Press, 2003). See also: Philip Pettit, "Habermas on Truth and Justice", *Royal Institute of Philosophy Lectures* 14 (1982), 207–28.

148 *Logische Propädeutik: Vorschule des vernünftigen Redens*, ed. Wilhelm Kamlah and Paul Lorenzen, (Stuttgart: Metzler, 2016), 121 (Chapter 4 §1).

149 Otto Neurath, "Soziologie im Physikalismus", *Erkenntnis* Vol. 2 (1931), 403.

150 Nicholas Rescher, *The Coherence Theory of Truth* (Oxford: Clarendon Press: 1973), 169–73.

151 Fuller, *Legal Fictions*, 11–12.

152 Neurath writes that the latter "is a decision commonly not easily made", Neurath, *Physikalismus*, 403; Fuller also acknowledges the relativity, but more neutrally concludes that "these possible changes in meaning have not occurred", Fuller p. 12.

153 Richard Rorty, *Consequences of Pragmatism: Essays, 1972–1980* (Minneapolis: University of Minnesota Press, 1982), xix.

154 Richard Rorty, *Contingency, Irony, and Solidarity* (Cambridge: Cambridge UP, 1989), 21.
155 Op. cit., 3, 4, 5, 7, 8.
156 Cf. Michel Foucault, "Truth and Power", in: *Contemporary Sociological Theory*, ed. Craig J. Calhoun (Blackwell, 2007 [1977]), 201–8). Derrida has also contributed to the debate on truth, cf. Christopher Norris, "Truth in Derrida," in *Companion to Derrida* ed. Zeynep Direk and Leonard Lawlor (Hoboken, NJ: Wiley Blackwell, 2015), 23–41; Ralph Shain: Derrida on Truth, *Philosophical Forum* 49, No. 2, 193–213; Michael Payne, "The survival of truth after Derrida", *Cultural Values* 4 (2000) Issue 1, 127-143
157 Foucault, "Truth and Power", 307.
158 Cf. Michel Foucault, *Power/Knowledge: Selected Interviews and Other Writings, 1972–1977* (Brighton, Sussex: Harvester Press, 1980), 194.
159 Hayden White, *Methahistory. The Historical Imagination in Nineteenth-Century Europe* (Baltimore: Johns Hopkins UP, 1973), especially pp. 6, 49–51, 103, 339; 375; id., "The History–Fiction Divide". *Holocaust Studies* 20 (2014), No. 1–2, 17–34; "Historical Pluralism", *Critical Inquiry* 12, No. 3 (Spring, 1986), 480–93; "The Value of Narrativity in the Representation of Reality", *Critical Inquiry* 7, No. 1, On Narrative (Autumn 1980), 5–27. Paul Ricoeur has monitored an "interweaving of history and fiction" where fiction serves historiography and vice versa: Paul Ricoeur, *Temps et Récit* (Paris: Seuil, 1985), 3:264.
160 Cf. infra note 268 and accompanying text.
161 Fuller, *Legal Fictions*, 10.
162 I do not want to imply that constructivism and fictionalism were congruent. I rather want to point out that, as Vaihinger demonstrates, the question of epistemological construction was early associated with the label of "fiction". For factionalist approaches in general cf. Emily Caddick Bourne, "Fictionalism", *Analysis* 73 (2013), Issue 1, 147–62.
163 Especially within the arts, a number of notable scholars have renounced a transmedial or interdisciplinary valid criterion of fictionality, cf. infra note 166.
164 Michel Foucault, "Truth and Juridical Forms", in: *Power. The Essential Works of Michel Foucault 1954–1984*, ed. James Faubion (New York: New Press, 2000), 31–45.
165 Douglas Lind is probably the most recent example in this context.
166 Cf. on this topic: Binder, *Criticism*, 378–461; Jack Balkin, "Deconstructive Practice and Legal Theory", *Yale Law Journal* 96 (1987), 743; Drucilla Cornell, *The Philosophy of the Limit* (New York: Routledge, Chapman & Hall, 1992).
167 For the latter, cf. Marie-Laure Ryan, "Fiction, Cognition and Non-Verbal Media", *in Intermediality and Storytelling*, ed. Marie-Laure Ryan and Marina Grishakova (Berlin and New York: De Gruyter, 2010). The other extreme is Walsh who propagates a rhetorical concept of fiction. Cf. Richard Walsh, *The Rhetoric of Fictionality* (Columbus: Ohio State UP, 2007), 1–7.
168 James Ballentine, *A Law Dictionary* (Rochester, NY: Lawyers Co-operative Pub. Co., 1969).
169 "Reference is needed for utterances which have truth values", Gabriel, "Fiction", 251.
170 In Bentham's case: abstract concepts of language, cf. supra notes 114 and 115.
171 Cf. Reference and "About" in: Lamarque and Olsen, *Truth, Fiction and Literature*, 107–37; On the general question of modification (not only pertaining to reference) cf. Richard van Oort, "Three Models of Fiction: The Logical, the Phenomenological, and the Anthropological (Searle, Ingarden, Gans)", *New Literary History* 29 (1998), 439–65, especially p. 454 (on Ingarden).

172 "[…] when I add that neither is there any such thing as the actual world. Since there are conflicting truth, there are many worlds, if any, but no such thing as *the* world", Nelson Goodman, "Fiction for Five Fingers", *Philosophy and Literature* 6 (1982), 162–4.
173 Bertrand Russel: *An Inquiry into Meaning and Truth* (London: Pelican Books, 1962), 277; Nelson Goodman: *Of Mind and Other Matters* (Cambridge, MA: Harvard UP, 1984). Both quoted in Lamarque, op. cit., 53.
174 "There are no fictional worlds", Goodman, "Five Fingers", 163.
175 Ibid.
176 John Searle, *Speech Acts: An Essay in the Philosophy of Language* (Cambridge: Cambridge UP, 1969), 77; Gabriel formulates: "To maintain that fictional discourse is about fictive entities is to say that there are fictive entities." Gottfried Gabriel, "Fiction – a semantic approach", *Poetics* 8 (1979), 255.
177 As it will be shown later in this volume, a number of prominent scholars follow the non-assertion view, the majority adhering to speech act approaches, such as Searle, Beardsley, Currie, Wolterstorff and Walton. In Germany, Gabriel has mainly propagated this idea of Analytical Philosophy and elaborated a theory of fictional speech acts: Gottfried Gabriel, *Fiktion und Wahrheit: Eine semantische Theorie der Literatur* (Stuttgart: Frommann Und Holzboog, 1975). Given the lack of an English translation, I will use three shorter English essays of his in this chapter: "Fiction – a semantic approach", *Poetics* 8 (1979), 245–55); "Fiction and truth reconsidered", *Poetics* 11 (1982), 541–51) and: "Fictional Objects? A 'Fregean' Response to Terence Parsons", *Modern Logic* 3, No. 4 (October 1993), 367–75.
178 Gabriel, "Semantic Approach", 347.
179 Gabriel, "Semantic Approach", 248; Bruck has criticized Gabriel's claim, maintaining that while it was true that in fictional texts the rules of reference were suspended, this was not true for the rules of predication: Jan Bruck, "Zum Begriff literarischer Fiktion", *Zeitschrift für gemanistische Linguistik* 6 (1978), 283.
180 Gabriel, "Semantic Approach", 205. In "Fictional Objects", Gabriel suggest a "way of 'getting around' fictive objects" based on a "Frege-Wittgenstein approach"(Gabriel, "Fictional Objects", 396).
181 Nicholas Wolterstorff, "Characters and their names", *Poetics* 8, No. 1–2 (April 1979), 101–27, cited by Jan C. Werner, "Fiktion, Wahrheit, Referenz", in *Fiktionalität. Ein interdisziplinäres Handbuch*, ed. Tobias Klauk and Tilmann Köppe (Berlin and Boston: De Gruyter, 2014), 137.
182 Terence Parsons, "A Prolegomenon to Meinongian Semantics", *Journal of Philosophy* 71 (1974) No. 16, 562.
183 *Über Gegenstandstheorie* (1904): Alexius Meinong, "The Theory of Objects", in *Realism and the Background of Phenomenology*, ed. Roderick M. Chisholm (Atascadero, CA: Ridgeview, 1981 [reprint]), 76–117. Cf. Janet Farrell Smith, "The Russell-Meinong Debate", *Philosophy and Phenomenological Research* 45, No. 3 (March 1985) 305–50; Richard Routley and Valerie Routley, "Rehabilitating Meinong's Theory of Objects", *Revue Internationale de Philosophie* 27 (1973), No. 104/105, 224–54.
184 On the problem of existence in Meinong, cf. Routley, op. cit., especially pp. 227 and 247 (in context of subsistence). The problems of the "subsistence theory" are explained further in: *Exploring Meinong's Jungle and Beyond: An Investigation of Noneism and the Theory of Items* (Canberra: Australian National University, 1980), 442–4; following Meinong, Parsons distinguishes nuclear and extranuclear properties, existence belonging to the latter. Terence Parsons, "Fictional Characters and Indeterminate Identity", in *Truth in Fiction*, ed. Franck Lihoreau (Frankfurt: Ontos Verlag. 2011), 29.

185 Cf. Terence Parsons, "A Meinongian Analysis of Fictional Objects", *Grazer Philosophische Studien* 1 (1975), 73–86; Terence Parsons: "A Prolegomenon to Meinongian Semantics", *Journal of Philosophy* 71 (1974) No. 16, 561–80.

186 Lewis, "Fiction", 37; Gottfried Gabriel has offered an alternative: Gabriel, "Fictional objects", loc. cit.

187 Liheoreau's summary of Graham Priest in: Frank Lihoreau, *Truth in Fiction* (Frankfurt: Ontos Verlag. 2011), 17.

188 Werner, "Fiktion", 134.

189 Frank Lihoreau, *Truth in Fiction*, 14; For Saul Kripke's position, see G.W. Fitch, *Saul Kripke* (London and New York: Routledge, 2014 [2004]).

190 G.W. Fitch provides a good introduction to Saul Kripke's treatment of truth respective possible world theory: in: Fitch, *Saul Kripke*, 1–26. Please also note his criticism of Kripke's theory, e.g. on p. 12.

191 Gabriel, "Semantic Approach", 252.

192 Goodman, "Five Fingers", 163.

193 Umberto Eco, *The Role of the Reader: Explorations in the Semiotics of Texts* (Bloomington: Indiana UP, 1984).

194 Lubomír Doležel, *Heterocosmica. Fiction and Possible Worlds* (Baltimore and London: Johns Hopkins UP, 1998); id. *Possible Worlds of Fiction and History. The Postmodern Stage* (Baltimore and London: Johns Hopkins UP, 2010): possible world theory now applied to history.

195 Thomas Pavel, op. cit.

196 Marie-Laure Ryan, "The Modal Structure of Narrative Universes." *Poetics Today* 6, No. 4, 717–56; id., "From Parallel Universes to Possible Worlds: Ontological Pluralism in Physics, Narratology and Narrative", *Poetics Today* 24, No. 7, 633–74; id., "The Text as World versus the Text as Game: Possible Worlds Semantics and Narrative Theory," *Journal of Literary Semantics* 27, No. 3, 137–63.

197 Goodman, "Five Fingers", 163: "While all Fiction is literally false, some is metaphorically true". Gabriel seems to aim at a similar notion of a "truth of literature": Gabriel, "Semantic Approach", 253–5; Gabriel, "Fiction and Truth, Reconsidered", 547–50.

198 Alf Ross assumes a similar viewpoint: "It is as if the novelist were to write: 'Suppose that (…)', with the brackets surrounding the novel", Alf Ross, *Directives and Norms*, 29. Though assuming a speech act approach, Ross, however, also assumes that what is said in a novel "will most often be false", ibid.

199 Lewis's account of fiction was preceded by a theory of counterfactuals by Stalnaker (Robert Stalnaker, "A Theory of Conditionals", in *Studies in Logical Theory*, ed. Nicholas Rescher (Oxford: Blackwell, 1968), 98–112, and Lewis's book *Counterfactuals* (Cambridge: Harvard UP, 1973). Also Saul Kripke is noteworthy in this context, cf. Saul Kripke, "Semantical Considerations on Modal Logic", *Acta Philosophica Fennica* 16 (1963), 83–94. Kripke, however, considerably revised his position in a 1970 lecture (which later appeared in print):" The quoted assertion gives the erroneous impression that a fictional name such as [Sherlock] 'Holmes' names a particular possible-but-not-actual individual", Saul Kripke, *Naming and Necessity* (London: Harvard UP, 1980), 158.

200 Lewis, "Truth in Fiction", *American Philosophical Quarterly* 15, No. 1 (1978), 41.

201 Lewis, "Truth", 42.

202 Lewis, "Truth", 45.

203 Lewis, "Truth", 45.

204 Gabriel, "Fictional Objects", 375; Gabriel, however, also uses Lewis's method of paraphrasing and prefixing.

205 Toutoulon writes: "All our institutes have an original fictive character. If one would like to rid the law of fiction past and present, not much would be left", Tourtoulon, 452 (my translation); Lecocq states: "[A]ll the law is nothing but fiction. The relations it determines between people and things have no real 'consistence', they don't exist beyond the human esprit, their creator, and are not of the realm of fact, don't exist in the nature"): Lecocq, *De la Fiction*, 23 (my translation); he later repeats: "le droit entire est une succession de fictions", 265. Lecocq extends this idea to language in general: "Tout le language est forme de fiction [...] le langue humain, dans son ensemble, n'est que métaphors: les substantifs don't nous servon n'exprimait autrefois qu'une qualite qu'ils désignent aujourd'-hui", 264. Kelsen and Fuller also comment on the issue: Fuller, *Legal Fictions*, 130; Kelsen, "Theorie", 634, 637; Kelsen, *Hauptprobleme*, 181. Lecocq also comments on the relation of abstraction and fiction, e.g. on p. 265. Pfersmann also comments on the matter, especially in paragraphs 5 and 31 (Otto Pfersmann, "Les modes de la fiction: droit et literature", in: *Usages et theories de la fiction*, ed. Francoise Lavocat (Rennes: Presses Universitaires, 2004), 39–61).

206 Cf. Marie-Laure Ryan, "Postmodernism and the Doctrine of Panfictionality", *Narrative* 5, No. 2 (May 1997), 165–87; Emily Caddick Bourne, "Fictionalism", *Analyses Reviews* 73 (2013), 147–62; Rorty, op. cit.; Vaihinger also comments on the issue of fictionalism in his English foreword to Ogden's translation: Vaihinger, *The Philosophy*, viii.

207 Fuller, *Legal Fictions*, 123.

208 Fuller, *Legal Fictions*, 130.

209 Baker, op. cit.

210 Maclean, "Legal Fictions", 9.

211 Douglas Lind, "Pragmatic Value", 93.

212 "Whether a corporation is a real or only a fictitious entity is a question which I shall not undertake to solve. [...] According to an old saying, everybody is born either a nominalist or a realist" (Gray, *Sources*, 51).

213 Cf. H.L.A. Hart, *Essays in Jurisprudence and Philosophy* (Oxford: Clarendon, 1983), 265–77 (Chapter 12: "Jhering's Heaven of Concepts and Modern Analytical Jurisprudence"); it must be noted, however, that Jhering issued repeated attacks against this idea (and its propagators, the scholars of a "conceptual jurisprudence" ("Begriffsjurisprudenz")).

214 Kelsen, "Fiktionen", 633; Kelsen, however, rejects the idea: "A natural reality is stipulated with the concept of the 'legal person' that never and nowhere exists in reality. The same applies to the 'physical' and the 'corporate person'", p. 637 (my translation).

215 Kuntze, *Obligation*, 89–90.

216 Paul Krückmann, "Fiktionen und Bilder in der Rechtswissenschaft", *Annalen der Philosophie* 3 (1923), 426 (my translation); cf. id., "Verschuldensaufrechnung, Gefährdungsaufrechnung und Deliktsfähigkeit", *Jherings Jahrbücher für die Dogmatik des bürgerlichen Rechts* 55 (109), 1–208, Krückmann claims here, that, in legal causality, a *post hoc* is rendered a *propter hoc*, and that the supposed control of an external movement might be a fiction (Krückmann, "Fiktionen", 1).

217 Such as Samek, who suggested that legal fictions "have their own reality" (Samek, "Fictions", 290) and Biet, who refers to the "virtual reality" created by the legislator (Christian Biet, "Judicial Fiction and Literary Fiction. The Example of the Factum", *Law and Literature* 20, No. 3 (2008), 415).

218 "Unwesentliche Modifikation"(insignificant modification), Kelsen, "Theorie", 632.

219 Kelsen, *Hauptprobleme*, 180-1 (my translation, emphasis added).

220 „erweiterter Fiktionsbegriff", Kelsen, „Fiktionen", 632

221 Kelsen, "Fiktionen", 631–4, 637, 641, 644, 647–8. The "legal reality" ("Rechtswirklichkeit", 634), or "Legal order, as the 'reality', which is the object of legal cognition" (648) is opposed here to the "'real' reality" which Kelsen also denotes by the terms "natural reality" ("Naturwirklichkeit" 647, "natürliche Wirklichkeit", 637) or "Sense-Reality" ("Sinneswirklichkeit", 632). While fictions is understood in the latter world to relate to "real, natural facts" ("reale Naturtatsachen", 643), legal fictionality for Kelsen can only exist pertaining to legal facts as elements of the "legal reality" or "legal world" ("Wirklichkeit des Rechts", Rechtswelt", 639), which is synonymous with "legal order" ("Rechtsordnung, 633, 644, 647, 648) and is a "human creation" ("Menschenwerk", 636); my translations.

222 To be distinguished from the factual pertaining to "Naturtatsachen" (natural facts), Kelsen, "Fiktionen", 643.

223 "Wirklichkeit" is used with this restricted connotation on pp. 631, 637, while e.g. on p. 639 it is used in a wider sense: "[...] reality, be it the natural one, or the reality of law." It is also noteworthy that Kelsen uses "Realität" and "Wirklichkeit" interchangeably, which are in fact synonyms that, however, only have one English translation ("reality"), since "wirklich" is the German translation of the Latin loanword "real".

224 It is unclear here, however, if Kelsen also rejects certain fictions for lacking expediency. He seems to do so in the case of jurisprudential fictions, but the passages are ambivalent regarding the question of whether Kelsen himself considered expediency a necessary criterion, or if he only demonstrates that Vaihinger incorrectly understands these "fictions", since they do not fulfill the criteria Vaihinger has established (including expediency), cf. infra note 224.

225 Kelsen, "Fiktionen", 647–8.

226 Kelsen, "Fiktionen", 650.

227 Kelsen, "Fiktionen", 650; Kelsen raises similar claims on pp. 638–9, 641, 643. Kelsen follows Somlò here, who claimed that fictionality was not possible in law since law's clauses were directives, and not assertives. Somlò states: "Since legal clauses are not assertive, but directive clauses, and [...] the realm of fiction are assertive clauses, directives cannot contain fictions in this general, non-legal sense" (Somlò, 424–5). That the prerequisite of an assertive proposition is not Vaihinger's criterion alone also becomes manifest in Kelsen's habilitation, where he insists that law is not "explanatory", but "normative": Kelsen, *Hauptprobleme*, 180. Correspondingly, Kelsen assesses the legitimacy of legal fictionality dependent on which propositional content is asserted ("insofern sie ein Seiendes zu beinhalten ausgiebt"), loc. cit.

228 Repeatedly, Kelsen explicitly clarifies that the legal fictions he investigates cannot be fictions in the sense of Vaihinger, e.g. 638: "Regarding statutory fictions [...] no fictions in Vaihinger's sense are existent".

229 Kelsen, "Fiktionen", 634.

230 Kelsen, "Fiktionen", 647–8; Kelsen understands the judicial fiction as a special kind of assertion: as a legal assertion ("Rechtsbehauptung"), which needs to be distinguished from an assertion of (natural) facts ("Tatsachenbehauptung"), Kelsen, "Fiktionen", 647.

231 Cf. Peter Cane, *Responsibility in Law and Morality* (Oxford: Hart, 2002), Chapter 4 (p. 113–40); Guido Calabresi, "Concerning Cause and the Law of Torts", *University of Chicago Law Review*, 43 (1975): 69–108; H.L.A. Hart and Tony Honoré, *Causation in the Law* (Oxford: Clarendon, 1985). William Lucy, *Philosophy of Private Law* (Oxford: Clarendon, 2007), especially Chapter 5, p. 144–205; Jane Stapleton, "Law, Causation and Common Sense", *Oxford Journal of Legal Studies*, 8 (1988): 111–31.

232 George P. Fletcher, *Rethinking Criminal Law* (Oxford and New York: Oxford UP, 2001), 589.
233 Cf. on the topic of expectation damages, lost profit, and hypothetical bargain awards: Adam Kramer, *The Law of Contract Damages* (Oxford and Portland: Hart, 2017) esp. 144, 150, 186; Graham Virgo, "Hypothetical Bargains: Compensation or Restitution?" *The Cambridge Law Journal* 65, No. 2 (July 2006), 272–5.
234 Cf. e.g. Bruce R. Hopkins and Jody Blazek, *The Tax Law of Private Foundations* (Hoboken, NJ: Wiley, 2018), 329.
235 "The doctrine of judicial estoppel, in its most generic form, prevents a party from asserting a position in one legal proceeding that directly contradicts a position taken by that same party in an earlier proceeding." Kira A. Davis, "Judicial Estoppel and Inconsistent Positions of Law Applied to Fact and Inconsistent Positions of Law Applied to Fact and Pure Law", *Cornell Law Review* 89, No. 1 (2003), 192.
236 Liebs, *Rechtsregeln*, 43: "A thing adjudicated is accepted as the truth"; cf. Peter Barnett, *Res Judicata, Estoppel, and Foreign Judgments: The Preclusive Effects of Foreign Judgments in Private International Law* (Oxford: Oxford UP, 2001), 8.
237 Cf. Gregory Currie, "Fictional truth", *Philosophical Studies* 50 (1986) 195–212; Marc Currie, ed., *Metafiction* (New York: Longman/Routledge 1995); Lewis, op. cit.; Monika Fludernik, "Metanarrative and Metafictional Commentary: From Metadiscursivity to Metanarration and Metafiction", *Poetica* 35, 1–39; Nünning, Ansgar "Towards a Definition, a Typology and an Outline of the Functions of Metanarrative Commentary", in *The Dynamics of Narrative Form: Studies in Anglo-American Narratology*, ed. J. Pier (Berlin: de Gruyter, 2004), 11–57.
238 Cf. David Novitz, *Knowledge, Fiction & Imagination* (Philadelphia: Temple UP, 1987).
239 E.g. with respect to love and sexuality: Niklas Luhmann, *Love as Passion: The Codification of Intimacy*, transl. William Whobrey (Cambridge: Cambridge UP, 1998).
240 Currie, *Fictional Truth*, 200.
241 Gregory Currie, "On Being Fictional", *The Journal of Aesthetics and Art Criticism* 55 (1997), 425–7.
242 Searle, "Fictional Discourse", 322.
243 Op. cit., 324.
244 Gabriel, "Fiction", 248.
245 Beardsley, "Aesthetic Intentions", 169–70.
246 Monroe Beardsley, "Fiction as Representation", *Synthese* 46 (1981) 295.
247 Op. cit., 297.
248 Beardsley, "Aesthetic Intentions", 169–70.
249 Nicholas Wolterstorff, "Response to Beardsley on 'Fiction as Representation'", *Synthese* 46, No. 3 (1981), p. 322.
250 Maria Reicher, "Knowledge from Fiction", in *Understanding Fiction. Knowledge and Meaning Jürgen*, ed. Jürgen Daiber, Eva-Maria Konrad, Thomas Petraschka and Hans Rott (Paderborn: Wilhelm Fink: 2012), 114–34 (cited by Werner, "Fiktion", 145).
251 Gregory Currie, "What is fiction?" *Journal of Aesthetics and Art Criticism* 43, No. 4 (1985), 386, 390.
252 Currie, "What is fiction?", 385
253 Currie, "What is fiction?", 387
254 Loc. cit.
255 From "What is Fiction?" (1985) over "The Nature of Fiction" (1990) to "On Being Fictional" (1997), where he admits some errors of his previous conception.

In "Standing in the Last Ditch: On the Communicative Intentions of Fictions Makers" (*The Journal of Aesthetics and Art Criticism* 72, No. 4, 351–63) he further explains his claim of an "identification of fiction with the to-be-imagined" in form of a "supervenicnce thesis".

256 Walton actually reserves the term "fictional" for the function of a prop within a make-belief game. Kendall L. Walton, *Mimesis as Make-Believe* (Cambridge, MA: Harvard UP, 1990), 11.

257 Within analytical philosophy, Derek Matravers is one of the critics both of Currie's and of Walton's approaches, though Matravers also focuses on the question of "doing" – he, however, understands imagination as an inadequate criterion for fictionality: Derek Matravers, *Fiction and Narrative* (Oxford: Oxford UP 2014).

258 Cf. Ryan, Marie-Laure. "Fiction, Cognition and Non-Verbal Media", in *Intermediality and Storytelling*, ed. Marie-Laure Ryan and Marina Grishakova (Berlin and New York: De Gruyter, 2010).

259 Gerard Genette, *Fiction and Diction*, transl. Catherine Porter (Ithaca, NY: Cornell UP, 1993).

260 Dorrit Cohn, *The Distinction of Fiction* (Baltimore and London: Johns Hopkins UP, 1999); id., "Signposts of Fictionality. A Narratological Perspective." *Poetics Today* 11, No. 4 (Winter 1990), 775–804.

261 Wolfgang Kayser, "Wer erzählt den Roman?" in: *Die Vortragsreise. Studien zur Literatur*, ed. Wolfgang Kayser (Bern: Francke: 1958) 82–101.

262 Käte Hamburger, *Die Logik der Dichtung* (Stuttgart: Klett, 1957). The second edition was translated into English: *The Logic of Literature*, transl. Marilynn J. Rose, Bloomington: Indiana UP, 1973.

263 Searle, "Logical Status", 325 ("pretending to recount us a series of events").

264 Searle, "Logical Status", 328.

265 Third-person speech.

266 Cohn, *The Distinction of Fiction*, 23. Hamburger's approach has instead been characterized as a syntactic theory of fiction.

267 Op. cit., 6.

268 Frank Zipfel, *Fiktion, Fiktivität, Fiktionalität: Analysen zur Fiktion in der Literatur* (Berlin: Erich Schmidt Verlag, 2001), 68–113 and 115–70; especially: 115–22 and 165–71.

269 E.g. Lutz Rühling, "Fiktionalität und Poetizität", in *Grundzüge der Literaturwissenschaft*, ed. H. L. Arnold and H. Detering (Munich: dtv, 1996), 29–30, and Ulrich Keller, *Fiktionalität als Literaturwissenschaftliche Kategorie* (Heidelberg: Carl Winter, 1980), 10–12 (both cited by Zipfel, *Fiktion*, 166–7). Following Margaret Macdonald ("The Language of Fiction"), Zipfel instead propagates an interrelation between both levels: "the fictitiousness of the story implies the fictionality of the discourse", rendering the fictitiousness of discourse a necessary condition for fictionality (Zipfel, *Fiktion*, 165–7). Zipfel explicitly opposes Wolterstorff's claim that "the essence of fiction consists not in the nature of the states of affaires indicated, nor in the truth or falsity of those states of affairs" (Zipfel, *Fiktion*, 166, note 193, quoting from Nicholas Wolterstorff's *Works and the Worlds of Art* (Oxford: Clarendon, 1980), 234).

270 Sir Philipp Sidney, "The Defense of Poesy", in *Englische Literaturtheoretische Essays*, ed. Ruediger Ahrens (Heidelberg: Quelle & Meyer, 1975), 1:45; cited by Zipfel, *Fiktion*, 21.

271 Cited by Ogden, *Bentham's Theory of Fiction*, xciii.

272 Monroe Beardsley, Aesthetics. *Problems in the Philosophy of Criticism*, 2nd edition (Indianapolis and Cambridge: Hackett, 1981), 420–1, found at Lamarque/Olsen.

273 Currie, "What is Fiction?", 388; Currie, *The Nature of Fiction*, 48.

274 Currie, *The Nature of Fiction*, 48.
275 Currie, "What is fiction?", 391.
276 Lewis, "Fiction", 40.
277 Gabriel, "Fiction", 253. On p. 252 Gabriel, however, argues for a parsimonious approach that avoids the idea of fictive reference, since fictive reference would entail that fictional entities do exist – and, according to Gabriel, "we receive no benefits for accepting the ontological commitments of the fictive world theory".
278 Currie, "On Being Fictional", 425.
279 Currie, *The Nature of Fiction*, 73–5.
280 Currie, "On Being Fictional", 425.
281 The above is an assessment of Gale's theory by Lamarque and Olsen (Lamarque, *Truth Fiction and Literature*, 60).
282 Cf. Ross, "Legal Fictions", 224–31. Cf. Ross, *Directives and Norms*, 57, note 1. In the latter work, Ross also comments on the question of fiction on pp. 30–33.
283 Ross, *Directives and Norms*, 32.
284 Cf. Andrei Marmor's chapter (Chapter 5.4 of this volume); and Soifer, "Reviewing Legal Fictions", 882–3.
285 Cf. the position of H.L.A. Hart and this collaboration with J.L. Austin: Neil MacCormick and Zenon Bankowski, "Speech Acts, Legal Institutions, and Real Laws" in *The Legal Mind: Essays for Tony Honore*, ed. Neil MacCormick and Peter Birks (Oxford: Clarendon, 1986), 121–33; Sanford Schane," Contract Formation as a Speech Act", in *The Oxford Handbook of Language and Law*, ed. Peter M. Tiersma and Lawrence M. Solan (Oxford: Oxford UP, 2012), 100–13; Jan Woleński, "'Doing Things with Words' and the Law," in *Selected Papers in Legal Philosophy*, ed. Jan Woleński and Kazimierz Opałek (Dordrecht: Springer, 1999), 311–21.
286 Most notably John Austin, "every positive law, or every law strictly so called, is a direct or circuitious command" (Austin, *Lectures on Jurisprudence*, 183). Bülow presumes the same in his 1879 account of fictionality: Oskar Bülow, "Civilprozessualische Fiktionen und Wahrheiten", *Archiv für die civilistische Praxis* 62 (1879), 3.
287 "[W]hen the legislator desires to accomplish his object, he need not feign, he commands": John Bouvier, *A Law Dictionary. Adapted to the Constitution and Laws of the United States and the Several States of the American Union; with References to the Civil and other Systems of Foreign Law* (Philadelphia, PA: T. & J.W. Johnson, 1856), 1: 520.
288 Infra Chapter 5.2.
289 Bülow in his 1879 essay formulates (my translation): "The Legislator [...] directs the judge to assume something that never happened as happened, he commands to treat something non-existing as existing", Bülow, "Fiktionen", 3; Krückmann in his 1923 essay also understands legal fictionality as an "order" ("Befehl"): the order to act as if ("befehlsmäßiges Handeln Als Ob"). Krückmann, "Fiktionen und Bilder", 426. Already Kelsen (Kelsen, "Fiktionen") mentions the idea of legal fictionality as a "demand" ("Aufforderung"), e.g. on p. 655; however, he rejects the idea of an "as-if". Instead, the command is construed to treat "as-well" (Ebenso Wie"), p. 639.
290 For Assmann, it was Aristoteles who successfully elaborated the first draft of a fictional contract: Assmann, *Legitimität der Fiktion*, 153. See also: Martin Price, "The Fictional Contract", in: *Literary Theory and Structure: Essays in Honor of William K. Wimsatt*, ed. Frank Brady, John Palmer, and Martin Price (New Haven, Yale UP, 1973), 151–78.
291 Christian Metz and Alfred Guzzetti, "The Fiction Film and Its Spectator: A Metapsychological Study". *New Literary History* 8, No. 1 (Autumn, 1976),

75–105. Metz's text is related to Jean Louis Bauydry's apparatus theory established in his essays "Cinéma: effets idéologiques produits par l'appareil de base" (first published in *Cinéthique* 7–8, Paris 1970, available in translation as: Jean-Louis Baudry and Alan Williams, "Ideological Effects of the Basic Cinematographic Apparatus", *Film Quarterly* 28, No. 2, (Winter 1974–1975), 39–47) and "Le dispositif: approches métapsychologiques de l'impression de réalité" (first published in *Communications* 23, Psychanalyse et cinéma, Seuil, Paris, 1975, available in translation: Jean Louis Baudry, "The apparatus: Metapsychological approaches to the impression of reality in cinema", in *Narrative, Apparatus, Ideology: A Film Theory Reader*, ed. Philip Rosen (New York: Columbia UP, 1986), 299–318.

292 Cf. Derek Matravers, *Fiction and Narrative* (Oxford: Oxford UP, 2014), Chapter 7, though he strongly criticizes both Currie's and Walton's approaches. Walton also replaces the usual criterion of a suspension of disbelief by a pretense of belief: Kendall L. Walton, "Appreciating Fiction: Suspending Disbelief or Pretending Belief?" *Dispositio* 5, No. 13/14 (1980), 1–18.

293 Richard Gerrig, *Experiencing Narrative Worlds: On the Psychological Activities of Reading* (New Haven: Yale UP, 1993).

294 Gerrig, *Narrative Worlds*, 230.

295 The term "Rezeptionsvorgabe" had been introduced by Naumann: Manfred Naumann, "Einführung in die theoretischen und methodischen Hauptprobleme", in *Gesellschaft – Literatur – Lesen. Literaturrezeption in theoretischer Sicht*, ed. Manfred Naumann et al. (Berlin and Weimar: Aufbau-Verlag: 1975 [1973]), 17–97.

296 "Rezeptionsanweisungen".

297 "Apellstrukturen", a related term Iser uses in his 1970 monograph: Wolfgang Iser, *Die Appellstruktur der Texte. Unbestimmheit als Wirkungsbedingung literarischer Prosa* (Konstanz: Universitätsverlag, 1970).

298 Wolfgang Iser, *The Act of Reading: A Theory of Aesthetic Response* (Baltimore: Johns Hopkins UP, 1978 [1976]); the term has been translated as "structured prefigurement" (p. 36, 107) but the latter deviates considerably from the original meaning. "Vorgabe" literally means "prescription", "requirement" or "demand", and in contrast to its opposing pole in Iser's Theory (the "Rezeptionsangebot" receptional offer, invitation), it has a clear authoritative connotation. Cf. Wolfgang Iser, "The Reading Process: a Phenomenological Approach," *New Literary History* 3, No. 2, On Interpretation: I (Winter, 1972), 279–299; id., *The Implied Reader: Patterns of Communication in Prose Fiction from Bunyan to Beckett* (Baltimore: Johns Hopkins UP, 1974). Hans Robert Jauß has developed a similar theory, cf. Hans Robert Jauss, Aesthetic Experience and Literary Hermeneutics, transl. Michael Shaw (Minneapolis: University of Minnesota Press, 1982); Hans Robert Jauss, *Toward an Aesthetic of Reception*, transl. Timothy Bahti (Minneapolis: University of Minnesota Press, 1982).

299 "Rezeptionsangebote" bzw. "Angebote": e.g. Wolfgang Iser, *Der Implizite Leser* (München: Wilhelm Fink, 1972), 355; id., *Der Akt des Lesens: Theorie ästhetischer Wirkung* (München: Wilhelm Fink, 1976), 60.

300 Scholars have stressed that a substantial part of what nowadays is considered "fiction" has initially been read as factual. Jonathan Culler raises the question (Jonathan Culler, *Literary Theory* (New York: Sterling: 2009), Chapter 2). The issue has also been debated pertaining to the recipients of ancient myth (e.g. Paul Veyne, *Glaubten die Griechen an ihre Mythen? Ein Versuch über die konstitutive Einbildungskraft* (Frankfurt a.M.: Suhrkamp: 1987)). Also fictional theory has controversially debated the question whether a text that is intentionally produced as factual but is instead read as factual becomes fictional, and vice versa. The problem is related to the question whether clear textual markers (or "signposts") for

fictionality exist, or whether fictional discourse is a merely pragmatic feature, making it impossible to discern the question of fictionality from the syntactical form or propositional content of an utterance alone (cf. Cohn, *Signposts*). While Searle (Searle, "Fictional Discourse", 320) is of the opinion that it "is for the author to decide", "whether or not" a speech act is fictional, for Walsh (Walsh, op. cit.) and Anderegg, fiction is a mere question of reception (Zipfel, *Fiktion*, 231). Consequently, the above "mandate" is one that rather follows from fiction as an "institution". A similar position is taken by Kendall Walton: "The institution of fiction centers not on the activity of fiction makers, but on the objects [...] and their role in the appreciators' activity", Walton, *Mimesis as Make Belief*, 88. Curry treats the problem under the header "secondary fiction", Currie, "What is fiction?", 387.

301 It is well known, however, that performance artists, such as Marina Abramovic, have played with these cultural rules of reception. In "Rhythym 5", Abramovic's life in fact depended on the audience to interrupt the performance and save her life. Also in the dramatic arts, breaking the fourth wall and engaging the audience has long become common.

302 Searle, "Illocutionary Acts", 11.

303 Walton, *Mimesis as Make Belief*, 88.

304 Walton's approach is, however, not considered to be strictly recipient-oriented, but rather "functional": Zipfel, *Fiktion*, 231.

305 Lamarque, *Truth, Fiction and Literature*, 256

306 Ibid.

307 Marie-Laure Ryan, "Fiction, non-factuals, and the principle of minimal departure", *Poetics* 9, No. 4 (August 1980), 333–422; id., "Possible Worlds and Accessibility Relations: A Semantic Typology of Fiction." *Poetics Today* 12, No. 3, 553–76.

308 Cf. Fuller, *Legal Fictions*, 10–11; Lind, "Pragmatic Value", 94; Baker, *Bodies*, 54. See also supra note 300, infra Chapter 3.2 note 51 and infra Chapter 5.2 notes 158 and 163 (and accompanying text).

309 Harmon, "Falling", 2.

310 Ludwig Wittgenstein, *Philosophical Investigations*, transl. G.E.M. Anscombe (New York: Macmillan: 1953), § 66.

311 Ibid. § 65.

312 Taylor, lemma "Prototype Semantics", 239; also: John R Taylor, *Linguistic Categorization: Prototypes in Linguistic Theory* (Oxford: Oxford UP, 2003 [1989]), Chapter 4.

313 Eleanor Rosch and Carolyn Mervis, "Family Resemblances: Studies in the Internal Structure of Categories", *Cognitive Psychology* 7 (1975), 575.

314 Rosch, "Family Resemblances", 574.

315 Taylor, loc. cit.

316 Leonard Lipka, "Prototype semantics or feature semantics: an alternative?" in *Perspectives on Language in Performance: Studies in Linguistics, Literary Criticism, and Language Teaching and Learning*, ed. W. Lörscher (Tübingen: Narr, 1987), 2:283.

317 Taylor, loc. cit.; Piotr Winkielman, Jane Halberstadt, Tedra Fazendeiro and Steve Catty, "Prototypes are attractive because they are easy on the mind", *Psychological Science*, 17 (2006), 799–806.

318 Rosch, "Family Resemblances", 575.

319 In the context of Wittgenstein, Mandelbaum discusses the problem: Maurice Mandelbaum, "Family Resemblances and Generalization concerning the Arts", *American Philosophical Quarterly* 2, No. 3 (July 1965), 219–28 (220–2). Cf. Michael A. Simon, "When is a Resemblance a Family Resemblance?", *Mind, New Series*, 78, No. 311 (July 1969), 408–16; Colin McGinn, *Truth by Analysis: Games,*

*Names, and Philosophy* (Oxford, Oxford UP: 2012), especially Chapter 2: Definition and Family Resemblance. In Prototype Semantics the question is raised whether prototypicality is identified "perceptually" (Rosch), thus as "image". Especially one passage in Rosch is unclear here: the definition of prototypes as "the objects which most strongly reflect the attribute structure of the category as a whole" (Lipka, "Prototype Semantics", 282) can be read in both ways, depending whether "reflect" is understood literally or metaphorically.

320 Rosch, "Family Resemblances", 583.

321 Rosch, "Family Resemblances", 584.

322 Cf. Kathryn Pyne Parsons, "Three Concepts of Clusters", *Philosophy and Phenomenological Research* 33, No. 4 (June 1973), 514–23.

323 Morris Weitz, "The Role of Theory in Aesthetics", *The Journal of Aesthetics and Art Criticism* 15, No. 1 (September 1956), 27–35; cf. Noël Carroll, *Philosophy of Art: A Contemporary Introduction* (London and New York: Routledge: 1999), 225.

324 Genette, *Fiction and Diction*, 1.

325 Charles L. Stevenson, "On 'What is a Poem?'", *The Philosophical Review* 66, No. 3 (July 1957), 329–62.

326 John Searle, "Literary Theory and its Discontents", in *Theory's Empire: An Anthology of Dissent*, ed. Daphne Patai and Wilfrido H. Corral (New York: Columbia UP, 2005), 147.

327 Hempfer has suggested a prototype-theory-based approach to fictionality: Klaus W. Hempfer, *Literaturwissenschaft. Grundlagen einer systematischen Theorie* (Stuttgart: J.B. Metzler, 2018), 99–100.

328 Rosch, "Family Resemblances", 575.

329 Cf. Klaus Hempfer, "Some Problems Concerning a Theory of Fiction(ality)", *Style* 38, No. 3 (Fall 2004), 304, 308–9; Zipfel, *Fiktion*, 65–7; A more extensive critique of family resemblance as applied to the concept of "art" in general provides Mandelbaum: Maurice Mandelbaum, "Family Resemblances and Generalization concerning the Arts", *American Philosophical Quarterly*, Vol. 2, No. 3 (July 1965), 219–28.

330 Cf. infra Chapter 5.2 notes 18–38 and accompanying text (pp. 202–3)

## Bibliography

Anker, Elisabeth and Bernadette Meyler. *New Directions in Law and Literature.* Oxford UP, 2017.

Assmann, Aleida. "Fiktion als Differenz", *Poetica* 21 (1989), 239–60.

Assmann, Aleida. *Die Legitimität der Fiktion: Ein Beitrag zur Geschichte der literarischen Kommunikation.* München: Wilhelm Fink Verlag, 1980.

Austin, John L. *How to do Things with Words: The William James Lectures Delivered at Harvard University in 1955.* Oxford: Oxford UP, 1962.

Austin, John. *Lectures on Jurisprudence or the Philosophy of Positive Law. Abridged from the Larger Work for the Use of Students by Robert Campbell.* London: John Murray, 1880.

Baker, John. *The Law's Two Bodies: Some Evidential Problems in English Legal History.* Oxford: Oxford UP: 2001.

Balkin, Jack. "Deconstructive Practice and Legal Theory". *Yale Law Journal* 96 (1987), 743–86.

Balkin, Jack. "The Construction of Original Public Meaning", *Constitutional Commentary* 31 (2016), 71–98.

Ballentine, James. *A Law Dictionary*. Rochester, NY: Lawyers Co-operative Pub. Co, 1969.

Barnett, Peter. *Res Judicata, Estoppel, and Foreign Judgments: The Preclusive Effects of Foreign Judgments in Private International Law*. Oxford: Oxford UP, 2001.

Baudry, Jean Louis. "The apparatus: Metapsychological approaches to the impression of reality in cinema". In *Narrative, Apparatus, Ideology: A Film Theory Reader*. Edited by Philip Rosen, 299–318. New York: Columbia UP, 1986.

Baudry, Jean-Louis and Alan Williams. "Ideological Effects of the Basic Cinematographic Apparatus", *Film Quarterly* 28, No. 2 (Winter, 1974–1975), 39–47.

Baumgarten, Alexander Gottlieb. *Reflections on Poetry*. Translated by Karl Aschenbrenner and William B. Holther. Berkeley: University of California Press, 1954.

Beardsley, Monroe. "Aesthetic Intentions and Fictive Illocutions". In: *What is Literature?* Edited by Paul Hernadi, 161–77. Bloomington: Indiana UP, 1978.

Beardsley, Monroe. "Fiction as Representation", *Synthese* 46 (1981), 291–313.

Beardsley, Monroe. *Aesthetics. Problems in the Philosophy of Criticism*. Indianapolis and Cambridge: Hackett, 1981.

Bentham, Jeremy. *A Fragment on Government*. Edited by J.H. Burns and H.L.A. Hart. Cambridge: Cambridge UP, 1988.

Bentham, Jeremy. *The Works of Jeremy Bentham, published under the Superintendence of his Executor, John Bowring*. 11 Volumes. Edinburgh: William Tait, 1838–1843.

Biet, Christian. "Judicianal Fiction and Literary Fiction. The Example of the Factum", *Law and Literature* 20, No. 3, 403–22.

Binder, Gyora and Robert Weisberg. *Literary Criticism of Law*. Princeton: Princeton UP, 2000.

Birks, Peter. "Fictions ancient and modern". In: *The Legal Mind: Essays for Tony Honoré*. Edited by Neil MacCormick and Peter Birks, 83–101. Oxford: Clarendon, 1986.

Black, Henry. *A Law Dictionary*. 6th edition. St. Paul, MN: West Group, 1990, 516.

Blackstone, William. *The Oxford Edition of Blackstone's Commentaries on the Laws of England*. Vol. 3. Ed. T. Gallanis. Oxford: Oxford UP, 2016.

Bouvier, John, *A Law Dictionary*. Philadelphia, PA: T. & J.W. Johnson, 1856.

Bradley, Francis. *Essays on Truth and Reality*. Oxford: Clarendon, 1914.

Brooks, Peter and Paul Gewirtz (eds). *Law's Stories: Narrative and Rhetoric in the Law*. New Haven: Yale UP, 1998.

Bruck, Jan. "Zum Begriff literarischer Fiktion". *Zeitschrift für gemanistische Linguistik* 6 (1978), 283.

Bülow, Oskar. "Civilprozessualische Fiktionen und Wahrheiten". *Archiv für die civilistische Praxis* 62 (1879), 1–96.

Caddick Bourne, Emily. "Fictionalism". *Analysis* 73 (2013), No. 1, 147–62.

Calabresi, Guido. "Concerning Cause and the Law of Torts". *University of Chicago Law Review* 43 (1975), 69–108.

Campbell, Kenneth. "Fuller on Legal Fictions". *Law & Philosophy* 2 (1983), 339–70.

Cane, Peter. *Responsibility in Law and Morality*. Oxford: Hart, 2002.

Carroll, Noël. *Philosophy of Art: A Contemporary Introduction*. London and New York: Routledge, 1999.

Champs, Emmanuelle de. "The Place of Jeremy Bentham's Theory of Fictions in Eighteenth-Century Linguistic Thought", *Journal of Bentham Studies* 2 (1999). Available from: www.uclpress.co.uk/pages/journal-of-bentham-studies [Accessed 13 Jan 2020].

Charles L. Stevenson. "On 'What is a Poem?'" *The Philosophical Review* 66, No. 3 (July 1957), 329–62.
Clark, Frank. *A Treatise on the Law of Surveying and Boundaries.* Indianapolis: The Bobbs-Merrill Company, 1922.
Cohen, Felix. "Review of Bentham's Theory of Fictions by C.K. Ogden and The Theory of Legislation by Jeremy Bentham", *Yale Law Review* 42, No. 7 (1933), 1149–52.
Cohn, Dorrit. "Signposts of Fictionality. A Narratological Perspective", *Poetics Today* 11, No. 4 (Winter 1990), 775–804.
Cohn, Dorrit. The *Distinction of Fiction.* Baltimore and London: Johns Hopkins UP, 1999.
Cornell, Drucilla. *The Philosophy of the Limit.* New York: Routledge, Chapman & Hall, 1992.
Currie, Gregory. "Fictional truth", *Philosophical Studies* 50 (1986), 195–212.
Currie, Gregory. "On Being Fictional", *The Journal of Aesthetics and Art Criticism* 55 (1997), 425–7.
Currie, Gregory. "Standing in the Last Ditch: On the Communicative Intentions of Fictions Makers". *The Journal of Aesthetics and Art Criticism* 72, No. 4, 351–63.
Currie, Gregory. "What is fiction?" *The Journal of Aesthetics and Art Criticism* 43, No. 4 (1985), 385–92.
Currie, Gregory. *The Nature of Fiction.* Cambridge: Cambridge UP, 1990.
Currie, Marc (ed.). *Metafiction.* New York: Longman/Routledge, 1995.
Davidson, Donald. "The Structure and Content of Truth", *The Journal of Philosophy* 87, No. 6 (June 1990), 279–328.
Davis, Kira. "Judicial Estoppel and Inconsistent Positions of Law Applied to Fact and Inconsistent Positions of Law Applied to Fact and Pure Law", *Cornell Law Review* 89, No. 1 (2003), 191–230.
Dekkers, René. *La fiction juridique: étude de droit romain et de droit comparé.* Paris: Sirey, 1935.
Del Mar, Maksymilian and William Twining (eds). *Legal Fictions in Theory and Practice.* Cham: Springer, 2015.
Demelius, Gustav. *Die Rechtsfiktion in ihrer geschichtlichen und dogmatischen Bedeutung.* Weimar: Hermann Boehlau, 1858.
Dewey, John. "The Historic Background of Corporate Legal Personality", *Yale Law Journal* 35 (April 1926), 655–73.
Dewey, John. *Logic: The Theory of Inquiry.* New York: Holt, 1938.
Doležel, Lubomír. *Heterocosmica. Fiction and Possible Worlds.* Baltimore and London: Johns Hopkins UP, 1998.
Doležel, Lubomír. *Possible Worlds of Fiction and History. The Postmodern Stage.* Baltimore and London: Johns Hopkins UP, 2010.
Eco, Umberto. *The Role of the Reader: Explorations in the Semiotics of Texts.* Bloomington: Indiana UP, 1984.
Eggert, Kurt. "Deference and Fiction: Reforming Chevron's Legal Fictions after King v. Burwell", *Nebraska Law Review* 95 (2016), 702–86.
Einstein, Albert and Leopold Infeld. *The Evolution of Physics: The Growth of Ideas from Early Concepts to Relativity and Quanta.* Cambridge: Cambridge UP, 1938.
Farrell Smith, Janet. "The Russell-Meinong Debate", *Philosophy and Phenomenological Research* 45, No. 3 (March 1985), 305–50.
Finch, Henry. *Law, Or, a Discourse Thereof.* London: Henry Lintot & J. Shuckburg, 1759.

Fludernik, Monika. "Metanarrative and Metafictional Commentary: From Metadiscursivity to Metanarration and Metafiction", *Poetica* 35 (2003), 1–39.

Foucault, Michel. *Power/Knowledge: Selected Interviews and Other Writings, 1972–1977.* Edited by C. Gordon. Brighton, Sussex: Harvester Press, 1980.

Foucault, Michel. "Truth and Power". In: *Contemporary Sociological Theory.* Edited by Craig J. Calhoun. Hoboken: Blackwell, 2007.

Foucault, Michel. "Truth and Juridical Forms". In: *Power. The Essential Works of Michel Foucault 1954-1984.* Edited by James Faubion. New York: New Press, 2000, 31–45.

Fuller, Lon. "Legal Fictions", *Illinois Law Review* 1931, 877–910.

Fuller, Lon. *Legal Fictions.* Stanford: Stanford UP, 1967.

Gabriel, Gottfried. "Fiction – A Semantic Approach", *Poetics* 8 (1979), 245–55.

Gabriel, Gottfried. "Fiction and truth reconsidered", *Poetics* 11 (1982), 541–51.

Gabriel, Gottfried. "Fictional Objects? A 'Fregean' Response to Terence Parsons", *Modern Logic* 3, No. 4 (October 1993), 367–75.

Gabriel, Gottfried. *Fiktion und Wahrheit.* Stuttgart: Frommann und Holzboog, 1975.

Genette, Gerard. *Fiction and Diction.* Translated by Catherine Porter. Ithaca, NY: Cornell UP, 1993.

George P. Fletcher. *Rethinking Criminal Law.* Oxford and New York: Oxford UP, 2001.

Gerrig, Richard. *Experiencing Narrative Worlds: On the Psychological Activities of Reading.* New Haven: Yale UP, 1993.

Glasersfeld, Ernst von and Paul Cobb. "Knowledge as Environmental Fit", *Man-Environment* 13 (1983), 216–24.

Glasersfeld, Ernst von. "An Interpretation of Piaget's Constructivism", *Revue Internationale de Philosophie* 36, No. 142/143, 612–35.

Glasersfeld, Ernst von. *Radical Constructivism.* A Way of Knowing and Learning. London: Falmer, 1995.

Goodman, Nelson. "Fiction for Five Fingers", *Philosophy and Literature* 6 (1982), 162–4.

Goodman, Nelson. *Of Mind and Other Matters.* Cambridge, MA: Harvard UP, 1984.

Gray, John. *The Nature and Sources of the Law.* New York: Columbia UP, 1909.

Habermas, Jürgen. "Wahrheitstheorien". In: *Wirklichkeit und Reflexion: Walter Schulz zum 60. Geburtstag.* Edited by Helmut Fahrenbach, 211–65. Pfullingen: Neske, 1973.

Habermas, Jürgen. *On the Pragmatics of Social Interaction.* Translated by Barbara Fultner. Cambridge: Polity Press, 2003.

Habermas, Jürgen. *Truth and Justification.* Translated by B. Fultner. Cambridge, MA: MIT Press, 2003.

Hamburger, Käte. *The Logic of Literature.* Translated by Marilynn J. Rose. Bloomington: Indiana UP, 1973.

Harmon, Louise. "Falling Off the Vine: Legal Fictions and the Doctrine of Substituted Judgment", *Yale Law Journal* 100 (1990), 1–71.

Hart, H.L.A. *Essays in Jurisprudence and Philosophy.* Oxford: Clarendon, 1983.

Hart, H.L.A. and Tony Honoré. *Causation in the Law.* Oxford: Clarendon, 1985.

Hartshorne, Charles and Paul Weiss (eds). *The Collected Papers of Charles Sanders Peirce,* Volumes 5–6: Pragmatism and Pragmatism/Scientific Metaphysics. Cambridge, MA: Harvard UP, 1974.

Hempfer, Klaus W.. *Literaturwissenschaft. Grundlagen einer systematischen Theorie.* Stuttgart: J.B. Metzler, 2018.

Hempfer, Klaus. "Some Problems Concerning a Theory of Fiction(ality)", *Style* 38, No. 3 (Fall 2004), 302–23.
Hernadi, Paul (ed.). *What is Literature?* Bloomington: Indiana UP, 1978.
Hopkins, Bruce R. and Jody Blazek. *The Tax Law of Private Foundations.* Hoboken, NJ: Wiley, 2018.
Iser, Wolfgang. "The Reading Process: a Phenomenological Approach", *New Literary History* 3, No. 2 (Winter, 1972), 279–99.
Iser, Wolfgang. *Der Akt des Lesens: Theorie ästhetischer Wirkung.* München: Wilhelm Fink, 1976.
Iser, Wolfgang. *Der Implizite Leser.* München: Wilhelm Fink, 1972.
Iser, Wolfgang. *Die Appellstruktur der Texte.* Konstanz: Universitätsverlag, 1970.
Iser, Wolfgang. *The Act of Reading: A Theory of Aesthetic Response.* Baltimore: Johns Hopkins UP, 1978 [1976].
Iser, Wolfgang. *The Implied Reader: Patterns of Communication in Prose Fiction from Bunyan to Beckett.* Baltimore: Johns Hopkins UP, 1974.
James, William. "Pragmatism's Conception of Truth", *The Journal of Philosophy, Psychology and Scientific Methods* 4, No. 6 (March 14, 1907), 141–55.
James, William. *Pragmatism.* Cambridge, MA: Harvard UP, 1975 [1907].
James, William. *The Meaning of Truth.* Cambridge, MA: Harvard UP, 1975 [1909].
Jauss, Hans Robert. *Aesthetic Experience and Literary Hermeneutics.* Translated by Michael Shaw. Minneapolis: University of Minnesota Press, 1982.
Jauss, Hans Robert. *Toward an Aesthetic of Reception.* Translated by Timothy Bahti. Minneapolis: University of Minnesota Press, 1982.
Jhering Rudolf. *Geist des römischen Rechts auf den verschiedenen Stufen seiner Entwicklung.* Leipzig: Breitkopf und Härtel, 1853–1869.
Kamlah, Wilhelm and Paul Lorenzen (eds). *Logische Propädeutik: Vorschule des vernünftigen Redens.* Stuttgart: Metzler, 2016.
Keller, Ulrich. *Fiktionalität als Literaturwissenschaftliche Kategorie.* Heidelberg: Carl Winter, 1980.
Kelsen, Hans. "Zur Theorie der juristischen Fiktionen. Mit besonderer Berücksichtigung von Hans Vaihingers Philosophie des Als Ob", *Annalen der Philosophie und philosophischen Kritik* 1 (1919), 630–58.
Kelsen, Hans. *Hauptprobleme der Staatsrechtslehre, entwickelt aus der Lehre vom Rechtssatze.* Tübingen: Mohr, 1911.
Knauer, Nancy. "Legal Fictions and Juristic Truth". *St. Thomas Law Review* 23, 1–49.
Kramer, Adam. *The Law of Contract Damages.* Oxford and Portland: Hart, 2017.
Kripke, Saul. "Semantical Considerations on Modal Logic", *Acta Philosophica Fennica* 16 (1963), 83–94.
Kripke, Saul. *Naming and Necessity.* London: Harvard UP, 1980.
Krückmann, Paul. "Fiktionen und Bilder in der Rechtswissenschaft", *Annalen der Philosophie* 3, No. 3 (1923), 418–26.
Krückmann, Paul. "Verschuldensaufrechnung, Gefährdungsaufrechnung und Deliktsfähigkeit", *Jherings Jahrbücher für die Dogmatik des bürgerlichen Rechts* 55 (109), 1–208.
Kunz, Lena. "Posessio civilissima in Spanish and German Law". In: Poss*ession between Fact and Fiction: Consequences of Possession*, edited by Elspeth Reid and Eric Descheemaeker, 141–0. Edinburgh: Edinburgh UP, 2014.

Lamarque, Peter and Stein Olsen. *Truth, Fiction and Literature: A Philosophical Perspective*. London: Oxford UP, 1996.

La Rue, Lewis. *Constitutional Law as Fiction. Narrative in the Rhetoric of Authority*. University Park, PA: Pennsylvania State UP, 1995.

Lecocq, Lucien. *De la Fiction comme procede juridique*. Paris: Arthur Rousseau, 1914.

Lewis, David. "Truth in Fiction", *American Philosophical Quarterly* 15, No. 1 (1978), 37–46.

Lewis, David. *Counterfactuals*. Cambridge, MA: Harvard UP, 1973.

Liebs, Detlev. *Lateinische Rechtsregeln*. München: C.H. Beck, 2007.

Lind, Douglas. "The Pragmatic Value of Legal Fictions". In: *Legal Fictions in Theory and Practice*. Edited by William Twining and Maksymilian Del Mar, 83–107. Cham: Springer, 2015.

Lind, Hans Jochen. "Fictio Legis". In: *Formen der Fiktion*. Edited by Remigius Bunia. Munich: Wilhelm Fink, forthcoming.

Lind, Hans Jochen, Christina Mulligan, Michael J. Douma and Brian P. Quinn. "Translation Approaches in Constitutional Hermeneutics". *The International Journal for the Semiotics of Law*. Special Issue: *Situating Jurilinguistics across Cultures using Translation and Discourse Approaches* (forthcoming, Springer: 2020).

Lockwood, Thornton. "Aristotle on the (alleged) inferiority of history to poetry". In *Reading Aristotle: Argument and Exposition*. Edited by William Wians and Ron Polansky, 315–33. Leiden and Boston: Brill, 2017.

Lucy, William. *Philosophy of Private Law*. Oxford: Clarendon, 2007.

Luhmann, Niklas. *Love as Passion: The Codification of Intimacy*. Translated by William Whobrey. Cambridge: Cambridge UP, 1998.

MacCormick, Neil and Zenon Bankowski. "Speech Acts, Legal Institutions, and Real Laws". In *The Legal Mind: Essays for Tony Honore*. Edited by Neil MacCormick and Peter Birks, 121–33. Oxford: Clarendon Press, 1986.

MacDonald, Margaret and M. Scriven. "Symposium: The Language of Fiction", *Aristotelian Society Supplementary Volume* 28, No. 1 (July 1954), 165–96.

Maclean, Ian. "Legal Fictions and Fictional Entities in Renaissance Jurisprudence", *The Journal of Legal History* 20 (1999), 1–24.

Maine, Henry. *Ancient Law: Its Connection with the Early History of Society, and Its Relation to Modern Ideas*. London: John Murray, 1861.

Mandelbaum, Maurice. "Family Resemblances and Generalization Concerning the Arts", *American Philosophical Quarterly* 2, No. 3 (July 1965) 219–28.

Matravers, Derek. *Fiction and Narrative*. Oxford: Oxford UP, 2014.

McGinn, Colin. *Truth by Analysis: Games, Names, and Philosophy*. Oxford: Oxford UP, 2012.

Meinong, Alexius. "The Theory of Objects". In *Realism and the Background of Phenomenology*. Edited by Roderick M. Chisholm, 76–117. Atascadero, CA: Ridgeview, 1981 [reprint].

Metz, Christian and Alfred Guzzetti. "The Fiction Film and Its Spectator: A Metapsychological Study", *New Literary History* 8, No. 1 (Autumn 1976), 75–105.

Miller, Sidney. "The reasons for some legal fictions", *Michigan Law Review* 8 (1910): 623–36.

Mulligan, Christina, Michael J. Douma, Hans J. Lind and Brian Patrick Quinn. "Founding-Era Translations of the United States Constitution", *Constitutional Commentary* 31, No. 1 (2016), 1–53.

Naumann, Manfred. "Einführung in die theoretischen und methodischen Hauptprobleme". In *Gesellschaft – Literatur – Lesen. Literaturrezeption in theoretischer Sicht.* Edited by Manfred Naumann et. al., 17–97. Berlin and Weimar: Aufbau-Verlag, 1975.

Neurath, Otto. "Soziologie im Physikalismus". *Erkenntnis* 2 (1931), 393–431.

Ng Boyte, Alina. "The Conceits of Our Legal Imagination: Legal Fictions and the Concept of Deemed Authorship." *N.Y.U. Journal of Legislation & Public Policy* 17 (2014), 707–62.

Ngaire, Naffine. "Legal Persons as Abstractions: The Extrapolation of Persons from the Male Case." In: *Legal Personhood: Animals, Artificial Intelligence and the Unborn.* Edited by Visa A.J. Kurki and Tomasz Pietrzykowski, 15–28. New York: Springer, 2017.

Norris, Christopher. "Truth in Derrida". In: *Companion to Derrida* . Edited by Zeynep Direk and Leonard Lawlor. Hoboken, NJ: Wiley Blackwell, 2015.

Novitz, David. *Knowledge, Fiction & Imagination.* Philadelphia: Temple UP, 1987.

Nünning, Ansgar. "Towards a Definition, a Typology and an Outline of the Functions of Metanarrative Commentary." In: *The Dynamics of Narrative Form: Studies in Anglo-American Narratology.* Edited by J. Pier, 11–57. Berlin: de Gruyter, 2004.

Ogden, Charles. *Bentham's Theory of Fictions.* New York: Harcourt, Brace & Co., 1932.

Olivier, Pierre. *Legal Fictions in Practice and Legal Science.* Rotterdam: Rotterdam UP, 1975.

Oort, Richard van. "Three Models of Fiction: The Logical, the Phenomenological, and the Anthropological (Searle, Ingarden, Gans)", *New Literary History 29* (1998), 439–65.

Parsons, Terence. "A Meinongian Analysis of Fictional Objects", *Grazer Philosophische Studien* 1 (1975), 73–86.

Parsons, Terence. "A Prolegomenon to Meinongian Semantics", *Journal of Philosophy* 71 (1974) No. 16, 561–80.

Parsons, Terence. "Fictional Charaters and Indeterminate Identity". In *Truth in Fiction.* Edited by Franck Lihoreau, 27–42. Frankfurt: Ontos Verlag, 2011.

Paul Feyerabend. "Realism and Instrumentalism: Comments on the Logic of Factual Support". In: *The Critical Approach to Science and Philosophy.* Edited by M.A. Bunge. London: The Free Press, 1964.

Pavel, Thomas. *Fictional Worlds.* Cambridge, MA: Harvard UP, 1986.

Payne, Michael. "The survival of truth after Derrida" *Cultural Values* 4 (2000), No. 1, 127–43.

Petroski, Karen. "Legal Fictions and the Limits of Legal Language". In: *Legal Fictions in Theory and Practice.* Edited by William Twining and Maksymilian Del Mar, 131–56. Cham: Springer, 2015.

Petroski, Karen. *Fiction and the Languages of Law: Understanding Contemporary Legal Discourse.* New York: Routledge, 2018.

Pettit, Philip. "Habermas on Truth and Justice", *Royal Institute of Philosophy Lectures* 14 (1982), 207–28.

Pfersmann, Otto. "Les modes de la fiction: droit et literature". In: *Usages et theories de la fiction.* Edited by Francoise Lavocat, 39–61. Rennes: Presses universitaires, 2004.

Phelps, Charles. *Juridical Equity. Abridged, for the Use of Students.* Baltimore: M. Curlander, 1894.

Pound, Roscoe. *Jurisprudence.* Vol. 3. St. Paul, MN: West, 1959.

Pyne Parsons, Kathryn. "Three Concepts of Clusters", *Philosophy and Phenomenological Research* 33, No. 4 (June 1973), 514–23.

Quinn, Michael. "Fuller on Legal Fictions. A Benthamian Perspective". In: *Legal Fictions in Theory and Practice.* Edited by Maksymilian Del Mar and William Twining, 55–82. Cham: Springer, 2015.

Reicher, Maria. "Knowledge from Fiction". In *Understanding Fiction. Knowledge and Meaning.* Edited by Jürgen Daiber, Eva-Maria Konrad, Thomas Petraschka, and Hans Rott, 114–34. Paderborn: Wilhelm Fink, 2012.

Reichmann, Rant. "Law's affective thickets?" In: *New Directions in Law and Literature.* Edited by Elisabeth Anker and Bernadette Meyler, 109–22. Oxford UP, 2017.

Reid, Elspeth and Eric Descheemaeker (eds). *Consequences of Possession.* Edinburgh: Edinburgh UP, 2014.

Reiffenstuel, Anaclet. *Ius Canonicum universum, clara method iuxta titulus quinque librorum. Tomus Primus.* Monachij (=Munich): Joannis Hermmanni, 1702.

Rescher, Nicholas. *The Coherence Theory of Truth.* Oxford: Clarendon, 1973.

Ricoeur, Paul. *Temps et Récit.* Paris: Seuil, 1985.

Rorty, Richard. *Consequences of Pragmatism: Essays, 1972–1980.* Minneapolis: University of Minnesota Press, 1982.

Rorty, Richard. *Contingency, Irony, and Solidarity.* Cambridge: Cambridge UP, 1989.

Rosch, Eleanor and Carolyn Mervis. "Family Resemblances: Studies in the Internal Structure of Categories", *Cognitive Psychology* 7 (1975), 573–605.

Ross, Alf. "Legal Fictions". In: *Law, Reason and Justice: Essays in Legal Philosophy.* Edited by Graham Hughes, 217–34. New York: New York UP, 1969.

Ross, Alf. *Directives and Norms.* Routledge & Kegan Paul, 1968.

Routley, Richard and Valerie Routley. "Rehabilitating Meinong's Theory of Objects". *Revue Internationale de Philosophie* 27 (1973), No. 104/105, 224–54.

Routley, Richard. "The Semantical Structure of Fictional Discourse", *Poetics* 8 (1979), 3–30.

Routley, Richard. *Exploring Meinong's Jungle and Beyond: An Investigation of Noneism and the Theory of Items.* Interim Edition. Canberrra: Australian National University, 1980.

Rühling, Lutz. "Fiktionalität und Poetizität". In *Grundzüge der Literaturwissenschaft.* Edited by H. L. Arnold and H. Detering, 25–51. Munich: dtv, 1996.

Russel, Bertrand. *An Inquiry into Meaning and Truth.* London: Pelican Books, 1962.

Ryan, Marie-Laure. "From Parallel Universes to Possible Worlds: Ontological Pluralism in Physics, Narratology and Narrative". *Poetics Today* 24, No. 7, 633–74.

Ryan, Marie-Laure. "Possible Worlds and Accessibility Relations: A Semantic Typology of Fiction." *Poetics Today* 12, No. 3, 553–76.

Ryan, Marie-Laure. "The Text as World Versus the Text as Game: Possible Worlds Semantics and Narrative Theory", *Journal of Literary Semantics* 27, No. 3, 137–63.

Ryan, Marie-Laure. "Fiction, Cognition and Non-Verbal Media". In *Intermediality and Storytelling.* Edited by Marie-Laure Ryan and Marina Grishakova. Berlin and New York: De Gruyter, 2010.

Ryan, Marie-Laure. "Fiction, non-factuals, and the principle of minimal departure", *Poetics* 9, No. 4, (August 1980), 333–422.

Ryan, Marie-Laure. "Postmodernism and the Doctrine of Panfictionality", *Narrative* 5, No. 2 (May 1997), 165–87.

Ryan, Marie-Laure. "The Modal Structure of Narrative Universes." *Poetics Today* 6, No. 4, 717–56.

Samek, Robert. "Fictions and the Law". *University of Toronto Law Journal* 31 (1982), 290–317.

Savigny, Friedrich Carl von. *Vom Beruf unsrer Zeit für Gesetzgebung und Rechtswissenschaft.* Heidelberg: Mohr und Zimmer, 1814.

Schane, Sanford. "The Corporation is a Person: The Language of a Legal Fiction", *Tulane Law Review* 61, No. 3 (1987).

Schane, Sanford. "Contract Formation as a Speech Act". In *The Oxford Handbook of Language and Law.* Edited by Peter M. Tiersma and Lawrence M. Solan, 100–13. Oxford: Oxford UP, 2012.

Schlick, Moritz. "Das Wesen der Wahrheit nach der modernen Logik". *Vierteljahrsschrift für wissenschaftliche Philosophie und Soziologie 34* (1910), 386–477.

Schlick, Moritz. "Die Grenze der naturwissenschaftlichen und philosophischen Begriffsbildung". *Vierteljahrsschrift für wissenschaftliche Philosophie und Soziologie* 34 (1910), 121–42.

Schofield, Philip. *Utility and Democracy: The Political Thought of Jeremy Bentham.* Oxford: Oxford UP, 2006.

Searle, John. "A Classification of Illocutionary Acts", *Language in Society* 5, No. 1 (April 1976), 1–23.

Searle, John. "Literary Theory and its Discontents". In: *Theory's Empire: An Anthology of Dissent.* Edited by Daphne Patai and Wilfrido H. Corral, 637–67. New York: Columbia UP, 2005.

Searle, John. "The Logical Status of Fictional Discourse", *New Literary History* 6, No. 2 (1975), 319–32.

Searle, John. *Speech Acts: An Essay in the Philosophy of Language.* Cambridge: Cambridge UP, 1969.

Shain, Ralph. "Derrida on Truth". *Philosophical Forum* 49, No. 2, 193–213.

Sidney, Philipp. "The Defense of Poesy". In *Englische Literaturtheoretische Essays.* Edited by Ruediger Ahrens, 31–66. Heidelberg: Quelle & Meyer, 1975.

Simon, Michael. "When is a Resemblance a Family Resemblance?" *Mind, New Series,* 78, No. 311 (July 1969), 408–16.

Smith, Peter. "New Legal Fictions". *Georgetown Law Journal* 95 (2007), 1435–95.

Soifer, Aviam. "Reviewing Legal Fictions", *Georgia Law Review* 20 (1986), 871–915.

Stalnaker, Robert. "A Theory of Conditional". In *Studies in Logical Theory.* Edited by Nicholas Rescher, 98–112. Oxford: Blackwell, 1968.

Stapleton, Jane. "Law, Causation and Common Sense", *Oxford Journal of Legal Studies,* 8 (1988), 111–31.

Stern, Simon. "Legal and Literary Fictions". In: *New Directions in Law and Literature.* Edited by Elizabeth S. Anker and Bernadette Mayler, 313–26. Oxford: Oxford UP, 2017.

Stern, Simon. "Legal Fictions and Exclusionary Rules", in: *Legal Fictions in Theory and Practice.* Edited by Maksymilian Del Mar and William Twining, 157–73. Cham: Springer, 2015.

Stolzenberg, Nomi. "Bentham's Theory of Fictions – A Curious Double Language", *Cardozo Studies in Law and Literature* 11, No. 2 (1999), 223–62.

Stone, Marjorie. "Dickens, Bentham, and the Fictions of the Law: A Victorian Controversy and Its Consequences", *Victorian Studies 29,* No. 1 (Autumn 1985), 125–54.

Taylor, John. *Linguistic categorization: Prototypes in Linguistic Theory.* Oxford: Oxford UP, 2003 [1989].

Tourtoulon, Pierre de. *Les Principes philosophiques de L'histoire du Droit.* Lausanne/Paris: Librairie Payot, 1908–1919.

Vaz Barbosa, Simon. *Prinzipia et Loci Communies seu Regulae tam decisionum, quam Argumentorum U.J. cum plenissima Doctorum allegatione collecta.* Trajecti ad Rhenum [=Utrecht]: 1651.

Veyne, Paul. *Glaubten die Griechen an ihre Mythen? Ein Versuch über die konstitutive Einbildungskraft.* Frankfurt a.M.: Suhrkamp, 1987.

Virgo, Graham. "Hypothetical Bargains: Compensation or Restitution?" *The Cambridge Law Journal* 65, No. 2 (July 2006), 272–5.

Walsh, Richard. *The Rhetoric of Fictionality.* Columbus, OH: Ohio State UP, 2007.

Walton, Kendall. "Aesthetics – What?, Why?, and Wherefore?" *Journal of Aesthetics and Art Criticism* 65, No. 2 (2007), 147–62.

Walton, Kendall. "Appreciating Fiction: Suspending Disbelief or Pretending Belief?" *Dispositio* 5, No. 13/14 (1980), 1–18.

Walton, Kendall. *Mimesis as Make-Believe.* Cambridge, MA: Harvard UP, 1990.

Ward, Ian. *Law and Literature. Possibilities and Perspectives.* Cambridge and New York: Cambridge UP, 1995.

Weitz, Morris. "The Role of Theory in Aesthetics", *The Journal of Aesthetics and Art Criticism* 15, No. 1 (September 1956), 27–35.

White, Hayden. "Historical Pluralism", *Critical Inquiry* 12, No. 3 (Spring 1986), 480–93.

White, Hayden. "The History–Fiction Divide". *Holocaust Studies* 20 (2014), Nos 1–2, 17–34.

White, Hayden. "The Value of Narrativity in the Representation of Reality", *Critical Inquiry* 7, No. 1, On Narrative (Autumn, 1980), 5–27.

White, Hayden. *Methahistory: The Historical Imagination in Nineteenth-Century Europe.* Baltimore: Johns Hopkins UP, 1973.

Winkielman, Piotr, Jane Halberstadt, Tedra Fazendeiro and Steve Catty. "Prototypes are attractive because they are easy on the mind". *Psychological Science*, 17 (2006), 799–806.

Wittgenstein, Ludwig. *Philosophical Investigations.* Translated by G.E.M. Anscombe. New York: Macmillan, 1953.

Woleński, Jan. "'Doing Things with Words' and the Law". In: *Selected Papers in Legal Philosophy.* Edited by Woleński Jan and Kazimierz Opałek, 311–21. Dordrecht: Springer, 1999.

Wolfgang Kayser. *Die Vortragsreise. Studien zur Literatur.* Bern: Francke, 1958.

Wolterstorff, Nicholas. "Characters and their names", *Poetics* 8 (1979), 101–27.

Wolterstorff, Nicholas. "Response to Beardsley on 'Fiction as Representation'". *Synthese* 46, No. 3 (1981), 315–32.

Wolterstorff, Nicholas. *Works and Worlds of Art.* Oxford: Clarendon, 1980.

Zetterberg Gjerlevsen, Simona. "A Novel History of Fictionality." *Narrative* 24, No. 2 (2016), 174–89.

Zipfel, Frank. *Fiktion, Fiktivität, Fiktionalität: Analysen zur Fiktion in der Literatur.* Berlin: Erich Schmidt Verlag, 2001.

# Part 2

# The ubiquity of fictional discourse in legal theory and practice

Chapter 2.1

# Fictions of constitutional privacy

## Toward a linguistic subject

*Cynthia A. Merrill*

In *Griswold v. Connecticut*, the 1965 Supreme Court case that struck down a Connecticut prohibition on contraceptive use and inaugurated a constitutional right to privacy, Justice Douglas famously queried: "Would we allow the police to search the sacred precincts of marital bedrooms for telltale signs of the use of contraceptives?"[1] In so doing, Douglas inscribed constitutional privacy as crucial to the protection of sacred domestic space. In fact, the *Griswold* defendants suffered no domestic invasion; they had been convicted as accessories in contraceptive use due to their participation in *public* family planning clinics.[2] Nor was there any reasonable apprehension that police raids of private homes were in the offing. Four years earlier in *Poe v. Ullman*, dismissing a challenge to the same statute for lack of justiciability, the Supreme Court had observed that in the 86 years since the law's enactment, enforcement had been attempted only once.[3] That prosecution, like *Griswold*, had targeted medical personnel for allegedly counseling and assisting contraceptive use.[4] Justice Douglas nevertheless warned darkly in his *Poe* dissent that "[i]f we imagine a regime of full enforcement of the law ... we would reach the point where search warrants issued and officers appeared in bedrooms to find out what went on."[5]

Douglas was not alone in his imagining. He echoed a 1955 Planned Parenthood advertisement urging repeal of the Connecticut statute with cartoons of police lurking under beds, pads and pencils at the ready to document illicit activity.[6] "A policeman in every home is the only way to enforce this law," the ad exhorted.[7] In 1964, a year before *Griswold* was decided, Vance Packard repeated the threat in *The Naked Society*, his wide-ranging critique of assaults on privacy throughout American society.[8] The sanctified marital home so featured in the *Griswold* decision thus sprang from cultural and judicial imagination, not the facts of the case. Constitutional privacy not only emerged as an *unwritten* right (as its detractors have long complained), but was founded, from its very beginnings, on a fiction.

Justice Douglas's discursive invention legitimized the privacy right by rendering it homologous with Fourth Amendment protections against unwarranted searches and seizures. At the same time, *Griswold*'s evocation of a sacred domestic enclosure occluded more controversial social histories and diffuse cultural anxieties underwriting the opinion. But privacy's spatialization—which persisted even as privacy doctrine increasingly centered on notions of autonomous decision-making—has obscured the extent to which privacy requires not only the right to be free from governmental proscription of certain acts, but also the freedom to author for oneself the *meaning* of such acts. Although courts and scholars have noted a kinship between substantive due process privacy and First Amendment expressive and associational freedoms, they have rarely conceived of the subject protected by the privacy right as linguistically constituted.

The lack of such a conception has left a significant void in protection of the rights—notably reproductive rights—that the privacy doctrine initially secured. My aim in the larger project from which this chapter is drawn is to reconceive of the constitutional right once dubbed "privacy" as a right to meaningful agency in intimate self-constitution, requiring attention to the linguistic mechanisms by which the state and the individual interact in the process of identity formation. Such a reconceptualization is necessary, even urgent, as rights protected by substantive due process privacy are not only assailed broadside, but eroded through discursive interventions that reformulate the meanings of those rights. Examining the myriad fictions of privacy need not move us to jettison privacy as a constitutional liberty altogether, as some have urged, but can prompt us to recognize the subject of privacy as crucially—though not exclusively—linguistic.

## I *Griswold*'s fictions

Seeking to legitimate privacy as a constitutional right in *Griswold*, Justice Douglas turned to *Boyd v. United States,* which held a compulsory production of papers unconstitutional, citing"'the sanctity of a man's home and the privacies of life.'"[9] Quoting *Boyd*, Douglas deftly aligned the privacy right not only with the Fourth and Fifth Amendments, but with an idealized, almost divinely ordained domesticity.[10] Even as this domestic trope secured reproductive freedoms, however, it also undermined women's efforts to defy gender orthodoxies and deflected attention from the more fraught issues of female sexuality and speech in the case's pre-history.[11]

The law at issue in *Griswold* was a lingering example of the "Comstock laws," so-named after Anthony Comstock, an evangelical Christian reformer and prime mover behind the 1873 federal Act for the Suppression of Trade in, and Circulation of, Obscene Literature and Articles of Immoral Use.[12] Part of a larger movement to wrest reproductive control from women, the federal Comstock Act banned the interstate mailing of contraceptive devices and information, as well as obscene and sexually explicit publications. By targeting through a single prohibition such disparate items as advertisements for birth control devices, tracts urging women to avoid unwanted sex, pamphlets describing "natural" birth control methods, "free love" prints, and descriptions of the reproductive cycle, the statute conflated female reproductive control and frank female speech as that which could not be expressed within the bounds of the law.

Prosecutions under Comstock laws had threatened to silence early twentieth-century reformers such as Margaret Sanger, who "visualized the birth control movement as part of the fight for freedom of speech."[13] Sanger proposed "a new conception of sex ... as a psychic and spiritual avenue of expression"[14] and argued that "[n]o woman can call herself free who does not own and control her body."[15] The Comstock laws thus struck at an important nexus of rights in women's efforts to achieve self-governance. Some of Comstock's most ardent opponents formed the Free Speech League to fight for freedom of expression and supported, among other causes, Sanger's efforts at providing birth control.[16]

By 1965, when *Griswold* was decided, controversy over contraception had abated, but women still struggled for the full public participation that contraception enabled. The American Civil Liberties Union's *amicus* brief in *Griswold* argued that the Connecticut contraceptive ban violated equal protection—a doctrine that did not yet protect gender equality—by limiting women's professional opportunities. "[E]ffective means of contraception rank equally with the Nineteenth Amendment in enhancing the opportunities of women who wish to work in industry, business, the arts, and the professions," the ACLU contended.[17]

*Griswold*'s reliance on the domestic trope repressed this history, in which contraception was intertwined with transgressive speech and resistance to normative gender ideologies. Doctrinally, Justice Douglas located a constitutional right to privacy in "emanations" from explicit guarantees in the Bill of Rights.[18] Substantively, however, he located the privacy right in "the sacred precincts of marital bedrooms" and in a marriage bond "intimate to the degree of being sacred": "an association that promotes a way of life, not causes; a harmony in living, not political faiths; a bilateral loyalty, not commercial or social projects."[19] Distinguishing marriage from economic and political associations, Douglas pointedly distanced the decision from discredited Lochnerism, which had employed substantive due process to shield economic contracts from government regulation.[20] But the invocation of a timeless bond also muted the transformative potential of the ruling for women's roles in and outside of marriage.

More broadly, *Griswold*'s denunciation of the fictional police invasion affirmed the Court's ability to check state power in an era of post-New Deal regulation and diffuse governmental intrusion. As Deborah Nelson has compellingly argued, *Griswold*'s invocations of domesticity drew on Cold War rhetoric that fashioned the idealized home as a fortress against totalitarian invasions of the private realm, a symbol of democratic liberty.[21] Indeed, in his *Poe* dissent, Justice Douglas had endorsed a privacy right as precisely that which distinguishes a democracy from a totalitarian state.[22] At the same time, however, denunciations of communism as an infiltrating virus, the "enemy within," prompted unprecedented governmental intrusions into private spaces—through personality testing, electronic surveillance, and FBI interviews with federal employees about their marriages.[23] The tactics of Comstockery resurfaced as the Post Office tracked recipients of "physique" magazines purportedly favored by homosexuals.[24] Even as boundaries between the public and the private thus grew increasingly unstable, the Court installed a fiction of inviolate space as the central trope for conceptualizing relations between individuals and the state in intimate matters of reproduction and sexuality.

That fiction persisted even as the Court increasingly equated constitutional privacy with decisional autonomy and self-determination. In the abortion cases, for example, the Court self-consciously abandoned a rhetoric of enclosure—"The pregnant woman cannot be isolated in her privacy"[25]—but rhetorically reinscribed spatialized privacy by declaring that "[i]t is a promise of the Constitution that there is a realm of personal liberty that the government may not enter."[26] And in striking down a law criminalizing same-sex sodomy in *Lawrence v. Texas,* the Court adverted to spatial privacy as well as "autonomy of self."[27]

Although *Lawrence* characterized autonomy and spatial privacy as distinct concerns, in many ways these discourses converge. The concept of personal autonomy derives from Enlightenment individualism, with its notion of the self-contained, rational, unified subject.[28] In law, as Joel Feinberg has pointed out, "personal autonomy" is at root a political metaphor, implicitly modeling the autonomous self on the independent, self-governing state, "sovereign over its own territory."[29] Susan Williams likewise notes that "the underlying dimension in the liberal model of autonomy is space (because the self is understood in terms of boundaries)."[30] Thus the privacy decisions wrestle over "domains" and "zones" and even discursively construct the protected legal right as a territorial body: "Only where state regulation imposes an undue burden on a woman's ability to make this [abortion] decision does the power of the State reach in the heart of the liberty protected by the Due Process Clause."[31] Here, the state has hands to "reach" and liberty has a "heart";[32] decisional autonomy, imagined as territorial sovereignty, is mapped over the corporeal.

The spatialization of autonomy stems in part from the bare fact of our embodiment and the way in which self-conception may be founded, in the first instance, on visual recognition of a corporeal outline. Psychoanalyst Jacques Lacan locates the genesis of identity formation in what he terms the "mirror phase."[33] As Lacan explains, the very young child, still physically uncoordinated and helpless, nevertheless recognizes its unified form in a mirror. This vision becomes a totalizing ideal, by means of which the child can conceive of itself *as* a self, a unique and coherent being. Thus the capacity for what legal theorists call autonomy or personhood initially derives from "the lure of spatial identification."[34]

In an analogous sense, spatial fictions rendered unwritten privacy and autonomy rights legally cognizable. The American tendency to figure rights contests as boundary disputes dates back to the Federalists' preoccupation with protecting private property against the feared tyranny of a democratic populous.[35] Mary Ann Glendon points out that the early American fixation on property had its roots in the "myth-making" of "story-teller" John Locke who characterized property rights, beginning with ownership of one's body, as natural, prepolitical, and absolute—virtually sacred.[36] A Lockean mythology of property defined limits on state encroachment, and a rhetoric of boundaries, enclosures, and inviolable spaces permeated American rights discourses. "Individual autonomy was conceived of as protected by a bounded sphere—defined primarily by property—into which the state could not enter," Jennifer Nedelsky explains.[37] By the 1960s, the New Deal and economic regulation had dislodged the property paradigm (and its concomitant right to contract), as evidenced by *Griswold*'s anxious distinguishing of *Lochner*. Thus the challenge for the *Griswold* Court was to reconceive the fundamental constitutional liberty that could check government power. Privacy furnished the abstract concept, while the physical boundaries of the marital bedroom and invocations of a right "older than the Bill of Rights"[38] subtly recollected the Lockean model of rights antecedent to government.

However, insofar as discourses of autonomy imply a boundary between public and private, metaphorically spatializing privacy rights, they foster a fiction as fully as did *Griswold*'s sacred enclosure. They figure subjectivity as isolate, ignoring the subject's relationality. As Nedelsky and others have argued, a dichotomy between autonomy and collectivity ignores how one creates oneself through relations with others, through the social matrix in which one is embedded.[39] Cultural institutions are deeply constitutive of subjectivity, not merely forces arrayed against it. Even Lacan's mirror stage figures the way experience of the bounded self is necessarily mediated—initially by the external and stable image, ultimately by what Lacan calls the social-symbolic order, primarily language.[40]

A spatialized model of bounded autonomy also overlooks the diffuse and invisible operations of power. As Foucault has famously argued, networks of power "produce" subjects in the most fundamental sense; they do not exert force from without, but through their constitutive effects.[41] They operate through state control of everyday practices, through the generation and circulation of signs, through structures imposed on interpersonal relations—and through discourse.[42] Such power normalizes subjects, not through fear of encroachment on a private domain, but through its production of knowledge, desire, truth, and identity.

## II A linguistic subject of privacy

The fictions of constitutional privacy—figuring sacred enclosures and autonomous selves—have obscured how privacy doctrine implicates a subject embedded in language. Although the Supreme Court's privacy jurisprudence acknowledges self-definition as a liberty interest, it fails to recognize the constitutive role of language in identity formation or how a subject is defined not only by its acts but by the *meaning* that attaches to those acts. Privacy doctrine lacks what Susan Williams has called a "narrative model of autonomy," which construes autonomy "not as an act of volition, but as an act of interpretation and narration."[43]

Although commentators have noted privacy doctrine's conceptual relation to the rights of free expression and association, such observations focus on the significance of association to self-definition and the expressive power of life-defining acts—not the linguistic constitution of privacy's subject.[44] Jed Rubenfeld, who interprets privacy doctrine as embodying an anti-totalitarian principle, has intimated such an understanding. He argues that privacy confers a right to "author" one's own life, not to be instrumentalized by the state.[45] "By the right to be let alone ... we should understand just this: a right not to have the law script or conscript our lives."[46]

I would take more literally than does Rubenfeld the self-authoring that constitutional privacy enables. Subjectivity, as consciousness of self, takes shape in the discourse in which the "I" is enunciated, addressing a "you" that is other.[47] The subject continually constructs and reconstructs itself through language, at the intersection of multiple discursive practices. Any account of oneself, even *to* oneself, is already overdetermined by publicly circulated conceptual frameworks, narratives, and images—the available structures of meaning. At the same time, authorship is agency. While an act of self-authorship is inevitably constrained, inherited paradigms are revisable, open to contestation, and vulnerable to subversion. Autonomy as discursive self-authorship thus coexists with social construction. Attention to self-authoring, rather than the prerogatives of an inviolate subject, shifts attention to autonomy as dialogic process, to the ways law first produces, then regulates the subject.[48]

The *Griswold* opinion broached privacy's linguistic dimension, but failed to confront it directly.[49] Justice Douglas initially addressed the constitutional foundation of a privacy right by citing *Meyer v. Nebraska*,[50] which held unconstitutional a statute forbidding foreign language instruction before the ninth grade, and *Pierce v. Society of Sisters*,[51] which struck down an Oregon law requiring children to attend public (rather than private) schools through the eighth grade. Commentators often cite these cases as establishing a private realm of family life and child-rearing, off limits to state regulation,[52] but Justice Douglas offered them as exemplars of First Amendment rights "to educate one's children as one chooses," "to study the German language in a private school," to inquire, to think, and to teach.[53] In fact, *Meyer* and *Pierce* were not decided under the First Amendment, but on substantive due process grounds;[54] the First Amendment had not been applied to the states at the time they were decided[55] and nowhere in the opinions is it mentioned. If Douglas sought to confirm a privacy right legitimately embraced by the Constitution, why resurrect these two *Lochner*-era cases at all?

What apparently interested Douglas about *Meyer* and *Pierce* was that the cases protect a subject's right to choice and agency in critical linguistic encounters that shape identity. In *Meyer,* the state had required children to study English "'until it had become a part of them'"[56] and the Court thus interrogated the extent to which the state might "foster a homogeneous people" by limiting children's linguistic capacities.[57] Similarly, in *Pierce* the Court rejected "any general power of the State to standardize its children by forcing them to accept instruction from public teachers only."[58] *Griswold* thus recognized, as established doctrine, a right to participate in crucial processes of idea and identity formation free from coercive socialization—especially linguistic colonization. The Court nevertheless failed to address the informational aspect of the Connecticut statutes—that is, the bar on counseling erected by the accessory statute. But in characterizing the privacy right as emanating from the First Amendment, the Court sketched a framework for conceiving of the subject of privacy as linguistic.

In subsequent cases, however, such a conception has not emerged. In the abortion cases, in particular, judicial analysis of the linguistic dimension of the privacy right is strikingly inadequate. Although *Eisenstadt v. Baird* dislodged the marital home and couple from the center of privacy doctrine by extending contraceptive rights to unmarried individuals,[59] a conception of privacy as sheltering a privileged site and relation still exerted a powerful, if repressed, force in *Roe v. Wade,* decided a year later.[60] The opinion stoutly declared that "this right of privacy ... is broad enough to encompass a woman's decision whether or not to terminate her pregnancy,"[61] characterizing the right at issue as a woman's decisional autonomy. Later in the opinion, however, the Court seemingly conferred decisional authority on a woman's *doctor*, not the woman herself. Prior to the points when the state's interests in maternal health and fetal life become "compelling," the Court held, "the attending physician, in consultation with his patient, *is free to determine*, without regulation by the State, that, in his medical judgment, the patient's pregnancy should be terminated."[62] Until then, "basic responsibility for [the abortion decision] must rest with the physician."[63] This incongruity at the very core of the decision marks a return of *Griswold*'s spatialized privacy paradigm. The doctor's office replaces the marital bedroom as the inviolable space; masculinized medical authority stands in for patriarchal domestic rule. As in *Griswold,* a culturally sanctioned narrative of spatialized and entity privacy rhetorically mutes the transformative potential of the decision for women's self-determination.

Even as it fashioned the abortion decision as a doctor–patient consultation, however, the Court failed to analyze the dynamics of that dialogue. A deep irony of the *Roe* decision, Nelson points out, is that the privacy right it announced could only be effected by the pregnant woman's rhetorical *disclosure* to a powerful other—a "forced confession."[64] To achieve a favorable medical judgment, a woman must author herself in a manner cognizable by and acceptable to the physician. So understood, the *Roe* doctrine disabled the very autonomy it purported to protect. As Foucault has elaborated, in confession one "authenticates" oneself by the "discourse of truth" one is able or obliged to produce about oneself.[65] The subject revealed through such revelatory discourse is simultaneously *produced* by the other—the interlocutor or institutional structure—within a dynamic of power and subjection.

The Court's failure to interrogate the doctor–patient exchange that it mandated has contributed in no small measure to contemporary abortion controversies as states have sought to regulate the field by "informed consent" provisions—statutes mandating specific information physicians or clinics must provide to a woman before terminating a pregnancy. In the first decades after *Roe*, the Supreme Court struck down provisions it regarded as attempting to persuade women to abandon the procedure. In *City of Akron v. Akron Center for Reproductive Health, Inc.*, for instance, the Court held that requiring physicians to inform their patients that "'the unborn child is a human life from the moment of conception'" was "inconsistent with the Court's holding in *Roe v. Wade* that a State may not adopt one theory of when life begins to justify its regulation of abortions."[66] In effect, *Akron* held, the state could not regulate the meaning of a woman's decision.

In *Planned Parenthood of Southeastern Pennsylvania v. Casey*,[67] the Court famously reversed course. At the outset, the plurality opinion offered a full-throated endorsement of self-authoring as a constitutionally protected liberty:

> At the heart of liberty is the right to define one's own concept of existence, of meaning, of the universe, and of the mystery of human life. Beliefs about these matters could not define the attributes of personhood were they formed under compulsion of the State.[68]

The decision acknowledged that a woman could not legally be bound to a "dominant" vision of her proper role; her "destiny" must be shaped by "her own conception of her spiritual imperatives and her place in society."[69] In such passages, *Casey* appears to echo and magnify *Griswold*'s hints that privacy embraces the self-authoring of identity and meaning.

But the decision failed to fulfill this promise. The plurality did reject a fictive bounded autonomy: "What is at stake is the women's right to make the ultimate decision, not a right to be insulated from all others in doing so."[70] Yet it neglected the woman's own status as a linguistic subject and instead asserted the *state*'s expressive interests: "Regulations which do no more than create a structural mechanism by which the State … may express profound respect for the life of the unborn are permitted, if they are not a substantial obstacle to the woman's exercise of the right to choose."[71] To assess whether regulations infringe a right to abortion, the plurality developed an "undue burden" test that, in the context of informed consent provisions, requires primarily that the information given be "truthful and not misleading."[72] On its face, this holding supports the autonomy interests served by common law requirements for medical informed consent, which seek to ensure that patients make fully informed decisions.[73] Yet under *Casey*, even measures expressly designed to "persuade" a woman to elect childbirth over abortion may pass constitutional muster.[74] Restricting the woman's right to "the ultimate decision," while authorizing the full might of the state's normalizing power, the Court adopted a narrow model of autonomy as a singular volitional act, failing to consider whether, in the context of a physician's office, the distinction between linguistic persuasion and coercion might be blurred.

The *Casey* Court's cramped focus on "the ultimate decision" contrasts with "a narrative model of autonomy," which locates autonomy not in the volitional act—the decision itself—but in the public and private narrativization of that act.[75] In a narrative model, "the meaning of autonomy is that one's identity and life are not 'the object or medium of someone else's speech, [but rather] the subject of one's own.'"[76] Autonomy arises from using a symbolic system—usually language—to create meaning. Such a model acknowledges not only the constitutive role of discourse in shaping meaning and identity, but also the need for *self*-authorship. From this perspective, self-governance requires protection of deliberative processes, which in turn requires keen attention to the linguistic—just as deliberative democracy depends on the protections of the First Amendment.[77] A narrative model recognizes that autonomy takes shape in the reasoning and narration that produce a decision, not merely in the decision reached. To protect autonomy, constitutional liberty must protect the preconditions that enable its exercise—self-authoring, narration, and deliberation.

A narrative model of autonomy reveals that certain contemporary "informed consent" abortion regulations violate the concept of liberty putatively endorsed by *Casey* because they foist on women the state's narration of the *meaning* of the procedure, wresting from them the power of self-authoring. For example, four states require that women seeking abortions be informed that the procedure "will terminate the life of a whole, separate, unique, living human being."[78] In South Dakota, a woman must also be advised that she "has an existing relationship with that unborn human being and that the relationship enjoys protection under the United States Constitution and under the laws of South Dakota," and "[t]hat by having an abortion, her existing relationship and her existing constitutional rights with regard to that relationship will be terminated."[79]

The impact of such provisions on women's autonomy has largely been eclipsed by claims that the requirements compel ideological speech by physicians, violating the physicians' First Amendment rights. For example, the Eighth Circuit upheld the South Dakota advisory that abortion terminates the life of a "human being," rejecting claims that it would unduly burden women's abortion rights.[80] But in doing so, the court relied upon an earlier en banc decision (vacating a preliminary injunction against the statute) that addressed only physicians' First Amendment rights, not the rights of the pregnant woman.[81] The en banc decision concluded that, in light of the statutory definition of "human being" as a "member of the species of Homo sapiens" from fertilization onward,[82] a physician could readily grasp the biological sense of the advisory.[83] But even if a physician were to include the species-based definition of "human being" when advising patients, as the court suggested, that would not erase the connotations provoked by describing the human being as "whole, separate, unique," suggesting that it is "a member of the community of human persons whose life possesses dignity and warrants respect."[84] This second meaning of "human being" gains force through the advisory that the woman "has an existing relationship with that unborn human being."[85] Although *Casey* permits regulatory mechanisms that express the state's "respect for the life of the unborn,"[86] South Dakota presents its position as objective fact, alongside such verifiable information as "statistically significant medical risks" of abortion and childbirth.[87] The advisories perform what Jerome Bruner calls "the narrative construction of reality,"[88] an imposition of design, intention, and, most importantly, meaning on raw data. Directing the pregnant woman's decision-making, the advisories deny the deliberative independence necessary for autonomy.

Moreover, women must acknowledge, even tacitly accept, the state's proffered meaning as a precondition to the procedure. As Judge Murphy pointed out, in dissenting from the Eighth Circuit's en banc opinion, requirements that the physician certify in writing that she or he believes that the woman "understands the information imparted" and that a woman's questions and comments be entered into a permanent medical record "are mechanisms likely to compel a woman to conform her speech to the state's chosen message."[89] A statutory mandate that the woman herself confirm in writing that she "understands" the advisories[90] likewise requires her to inscribe herself into the state's stigmatizing narrative.

Efforts to deny women's own scripting of their abortion choices can also be seen in ultrasound regulations. Seven states currently mandate ultrasound imaging for women seeking abortions,[91] and four more require that women both view the image and receive a verbal description of it.[92] Although the Fifth Circuit described fetal sonograms as "the purest conceivable expression of 'factual information,'"[93] the potency of the images results less from the visual information they convey than from the multiple narratives in which they are embedded. To the untrained eye, fetal sonograms (particularly in pregnancy's earliest stages) typically present as a greyish blur.[94] More than the image itself, the sonographer's interpretation may transform the woman's understanding of the potential life within her. Rather than supply a woman with "truthful" information, mandatory ultrasound procedures compel a woman's body to confess a purported "truth," read *to* her from an authoritative site both within and outside her. Contrast this with the common law regime that governed abortion in the nineteenth century, which permitted the procedure prior to quickening, when a pregnant woman first feels fetal movement.[95] The common law's implicit definition of fetal life worthy of protection relied on a woman's subjective relation to the fetus developing within her. A sonogram operates as a "technological quickening," as Carol Sanger has put it,[96] supplanting a woman's experience of pregnancy with a scientific, purportedly objective narrative of fetal development. The image magnifies and frames the fetus as a "free-floating independent entity,"[97] providing visual (but biologically fictive) confirmation that, as the South Dakota and other advisories proclaim, the fetus is a "separate" and "whole" human being.

At the same time, a mandatory ultrasound attempts to capture women within what has become a cultural rite of desired pregnancy: the first picture of the life within, to be shared with family and friends.[98] Whether she confronts or refuses to look at the image, the woman choosing abortion must pointedly reject a celebrated life script. But the sonogram offers only a partial narrative—a single frame divorced from the events leading up to the pregnancy (which may include rape, incest, an abusive marriage) and those that may ensue if the pregnancy is carried to full term, including the social and material conditions of motherhood. Again, privileging the sonogram abstracts the reality of a pregnancy away from a woman-authored narrative.

While any decision to terminate a pregnancy will necessarily occur in the context of multiple, competing discourses—religious, medical, personal, and ethical—regulations compelling a woman to submit to an ultrasound show-and -tell or to attest that she understands a fetus to be a "separate" human capture the woman within master narratives as a precondition for the exercise of her constitutional right. Such coercive narrativization of intimate acts betrays *Casey*'s promise of liberty as "the right to define one's own concept of existence, of meaning."[99] The self-defining power of intimate acts flows no less from their cultural and personal narration than from the consequences of the acts themselves.

However, the *Casey* Court's own "undue burden" analysis of Pennsylvania abortion regulations was primarily consequentialist. A spousal notification requirement might literally prevent a woman from terminating her pregnancy, the Court reasoned, while the state's persuasive efforts purportedly leave her free to make the "ultimate decision."[100] Such reasoning assumes a subject whose autonomy results only from volitional acts—a model as fictional as *Griswold*'s bedroom invasion. And, like the *Griswold* fiction, it ignores how reproductive rights require and produce women's re-writing of gendered cultural narratives extending far beyond motherhood itself. As Margaret Sanger recognized, the struggle for reproductive rights is inextricably intertwined with a struggle for expressive freedom. The Court's successive fictions of privacy have obscured that dual struggle, undermining women's narrative autonomy at critical junctures of self-definition.

Meaningful substantive due process liberty requires not only acknowledgement of a linguistically-constituted subject that exercises self-governance through discursive self-authoring, but recognition of law's own imposition of meaning and identity through regulatory discourses. A full examination of the doctrinal tools that might frame such acknowledgements is beyond the scope of this chapter, but certain doctrines do hold promise. The

Supreme Court has recognized an individual interest in being free from coerced listening, although as yet it has addressed the interest only as a legitimate check on other individuals' exercise of free speech.[101] However, as Robert Goldstein has pointed out, the Court *has* regulated the interrogation of persons in custody, limiting communication that "overwhelms" autonomous choice and dissolves distinctions between the individual and the state.[102] Because reproductive rights have been deemed "fundamental," discursive tactics in this context should likewise be recognized as infringing protected rights. Liberty requires not only the right to make self-defining choices, but the opportunity to script the meaning of such choices through dialogic interaction with, not subordination to, the state's narratives. Liberty interests compel the recognition of a linguistic subject.

## Acknowledgment

I am grateful to the UCLA Center for the Study of Women for its ongoing support of this project. And I am profoundly indebted to Claudia Ingram for her incisive reading of earlier drafts and thought-provoking comments.

## Notes

1 *Griswold v. Connecticut*, 381 U.S. 479, 485 (1965).
2 Id. at 480. The statutes at issue included the General Statutes of Connecticut sections 53-32 and 54-196 (1958). Section 53-32 provided: "Any person who uses any drug, medicinal article or instrument for the purpose of preventing conception shall be fined not less than fifty dollars or imprisoned not less than sixty days nor more than one year or be both fined and imprisoned." Section 54-196, the accessory statute, provided: "Any person who assists, abets, counsels, causes, hires or commands another to commit any offense may be prosecuted and punished as if he were the principal offender."
3 *Poe v. Ullman*, 367 U.S. 497, 501 (1961).
4 See *State v. Nelson*, 11 A.2d 865, 857–8 (Conn. 1940).
5 *Poe*, 367 U.S. at 519–20 (Douglas, J., dissenting).
6 See Leigh Ann Wheeler, *How Sex Became a Civil Liberty* (New York: Oxford University Press, 2013), 97–8.
7 Wheeler, *How Sex Became a Civil Liberty*, 98.
8 Vance Packard, *The Naked Society* (New York: David McKay Co., 1964), 162–3; see also Deborah Nelson, *Pursuing Privacy in Cold War America* (New York: Columbia University Press, 2002), 14–15, 79. Nelson examines the construction, dissolution, and reimagining of privacy in constitutional law and confessional poetry in the twentieth century, and her rich work has influenced my own. While Nelson is keenly alert to the discursive construction of privacy, she does not argue for a linguistic legal subject.
9 *Griswold*, 381 U.S. at 484 (quoting *Boyd v. United States*, 116 U.S. 616, 630 (1886)).
10 See Kathryn Abrams, "Disenchanting the Public/Private Distinction," in *Imagining New Legalities*, ed. Austin Sarat, Lawrence Douglas, and Martha Merrill Umphrey (Stanford, CA: Stanford University Press, 2012), 26–8.

11 The trope also shielded domestic violence from state interference. See Reva B. Siegel, "The Rule of Love: Wife Beating as Prerogative," *Yale Law Journal* 105 (June 1996), 2150–74. For this and other reasons, feminists have regarded privacy as a problematic vehicle for protecting reproductive rights. See, e.g., Catharine A. MacKinnon, "Reflections on Sex Equality Under the Law," *Yale Law Journal* 100 (March 1991), 1311; Abrams, "Disenchanting the Public/Private Distinction," 34–6.

12 Act for the Suppression of Trade in, and Circulation of, Obscene Literature and Articles of Immoral Use, ch. 258, 17 Stat. 598 (1873); see *Poe*, 367 U.S. at 520 n.10 (Douglas, J., dissenting); *Poe*, 367 U.S. at 546 n.12 (Harlan, J., dissenting); Sandra F. VanBurkleo, *"Belonging to the World": Women's Rights and American Constitutional Culture* (New York: Oxford University Press, 2001), 167–8. Connecticut's anti-contraceptive statute was enacted in 1879 as an amendment to an obscene literature law; only later was the prohibition on contraceptive use enacted as an independent statute. See Carol Flora Brooks, "The Early History of the Anti-Contraceptive Laws in Massachusetts and Connecticut," *American Quarterly* 18, No. 1 (Spring 1966), 9–12 and n. 23.

13 Margaret Sanger, *Margaret Sanger: An Autobiography* (New York: W.W. Norton, 1938), 113.

14 Margaret Sanger, *The Pivot of Civilization* (New York: Brentano's Publishers, 1922), 140.

15 Margaret Sanger, *Woman and the New Race* (New York: Brentano's Publishers, 1920), 94.

16 David M. Rabban, "The Free Speech League, the ACLU, and Changing Conceptions of Free Speech in American History," *Stanford Law Review* 45 (November 1992), 91–3.

17 Brief for the American Civil Liberties Union and the Connecticut Civil Liberties Union as Amicus Curiae at 16, *Griswold v. Connecticut*, 381 U.S. 479 (1965) (No. 496). See also Melissa Murray, "Overlooking Equality on the Road to *Griswold*," *Yale Law Journal Forum* 124 (March 2, 2015), 324–31, www.yalelawjournal.org/forum/overlooking-equality-on-the-road-to-griswold; Neil S. Siegel and Reva B. Siegel, "Contraception as a Sex Equality Right," *Yale Law Journal Forum* 124 (March 2, 2015), 349–58, www.yalelawjournal.org/forum/contraception-as-a-sex-equality-right.

18 *Griswold*, 381 U.S. at 484–5.

19 Id. at 486.

20 See id. at 481–2; *Lochner v. New York*, 198 U.S. 45 (1905).

21 See Nelson, *Pursuing Privacy*, 76–80, 93–5; see also Elaine Tyler May, *Homeward Bound: American Families in the Cold War Era*, rev. ed. (New York: Basic Books, 2008), 1–38.

22 *Poe*, 367 U.S. at 521–2 (Douglas, J., dissenting).

23 See David K. Johnson, *The Lavender Scare: The Cold War Persecution of Gays and Lesbians in the Federal Government* (Chicago: University of Chicago Press, 2004), 30–8, 119–30; Nelson, *Pursuing Privacy*, 9–14; Packard, *The Naked Society*, 68–72, 148–68.

24 See Wheeler, *How Sex Became a Civil Liberty*, 112–13, 154–5; Richard M. Fried, *Nightmare in Red: The McCarthy Era in Perspective* (New York: Oxford University Press, 1990), 167.

25 *Roe v. Wade*, 410 U.S. 113, 159 (1973).

26 *Planned Parenthood of Southeastern Pennsylvania v. Casey*, 505 U.S. 833, 847 (1992).

27 *Lawrence v. Texas*, 539 U.S. 558, 562–3 (2003). Ironically, the *Griswold* bedroom invasion was literalized in *Lawrence*. Id. The Court has also invoked the privacy

right in cases involving interracial marriage, *Loving v. Virginia*, 388 U.S. 1, 12 (1967), possession of pornography in the home, *Stanley v. Georgia*, 394 U.S. 557, 564 (1969), and family life, *Moore v. City of East Cleveland*, 431 U.S. 494 (1977).

28 See, e.g., Susan H. Williams, *Truth, Autonomy and Speech: Feminist Theory and the First Amendment* (New York: New York University Press, 2004), 41–4.

29 Joel Feinberg, "Autonomy, Sovereignty, and Privacy: Moral Ideas in the Constitution," *Notre Dame Law Review* 58 (1983), 446, 452.

30 Williams, *Truth, Autonomy and Speech*, 149.

31 *Casey*, 505 U.S. at 874.

32 Alan Hyde's work alerted me to the metaphorics of this passage. See Alan Hyde, *Bodies of Law* (Princeton, NJ: Princeton University Press, 1997), 83.

33 Jacques Lacan, "The mirror stage as formative of the function of the 'I,'" in *Écrits: A Selection*, trans. Alan Sheridan (New York: W.W. Norton, 1977), 1–7.

34 Lacan, "Mirror stage," 4.

35 See Jennifer Nedelsky, *Law's Relations: A Relational Theory of Self, Autonomy and Law* (Oxford: Oxford University Press, 2011), 127–9; Mary Ann Glendon, *Rights Talk: The Impoverishment of Political Discourse* (New York: Simon & Schuster, 1991), 18–46, 48–61.

36 Glendon, *Rights Talk*, 21–2, 31; John Locke, "On Property," in *Two Treatises of Government*, ed. Thomas I. Cook (New York: MacMillan Publishing Co., 1947), 133–46.

37 Nedelsky, *Law's Relations*, 128; see also Jean L. Cohen, *Regulating Intimacy: A New Legal Paradigm* (Princeton, NJ: Princeton University Press, 2002), 64–7.

38 *Griswold*, 381 U.S. at 486.

39 See, e.g., Nedelsky, *Law's Relations*, 130–3; Williams, *Truth, Autonomy and Speech*, 58–68.

40 See Michel Rosenfeld, "Law and the Postmodern Mind: The Identity of the Constitutional Subject," *Cardozo Law Review* 16 (1995), 1058–9.

41 See, e.g., Michel Foucault, "Áfterward: The Subject and Power," in Herbert L. Dreyfus and Paul Rabinow, *Michel Foucault: Beyond Structuralism and Hermeneutics*, 2nd ed. (Chicago: University of Chicago Press, 1983), 208–26.

42 Michel Foucault, "Interview—Truth and Power," in *Power/Knowledge: Selected Interviews and Other Writings 1972–1977*, ed. Colin Gordon (Brighton, UK: Harvester Press, 1980), 119.

43 Williams, *Truth, Autonomy and Speech*, 149.

44 See, e.g., Laurence H. Tribe, "*Lawrence v. Texas*: The 'Fundamental Right' That Dare Not Speak Its Name," *Harvard Law Review* 117 (April 2004), 1939–40; Charles Fried, *Saying What the Law Is: The Constitution in the Supreme Court* (Cambridge, MA: Harvard University Press, 2004), 200.

45 Jed Rubenfeld, *Freedom and Time: A Theory of Constitutional Self-Government* (New Haven, CT: Yale University Press, 2001), 221–55. For Rubenfeld, the legitimacy of privacy as an unwritten constitutional right flows from his model of democratic government as collective self-authorization; totalitarian practices deprive citizens of the foundational right to participate as co-authors in the democratic process.

46 Rubenfeld, *Freedom and Time*, 253.

47 Émile Benveniste, "Subjectivity in Language," in *Problems in General Linguistics*, trans. Mary Elizabeth Meek (Coral Gables, FL: University of Miami Press, 1971), 223–30.

48 See Judith Butler, *Gender Trouble: Feminism and the Subversion of Identity* (New York: Routledge, 1990), 2.

49 Although the *Griswold* co-defendants challenged the accessory statute as a First Amendment violation, arguing that it prohibited even private and clinical

discussions of contraception, they addressed the First Amendment rights of only the medical personnel. See Brief for Appellants at 90–2, *Griswold v. Connecticut*, 381 U.S. 479 (1965) (No. 496). The majority opinion did not address these arguments.

50 *Meyer v. Nebraska*, 262 U.S. 390 (1923).
51 *Pierce v. Soc'y of Sisters*, 268 U.S. 510 (1925).
52 See, e.g., *Moore*, 431 U.S. at 499.
53 *Griswold*, 381 U.S. at 482. Justice Harlan had earlier discussed *Meyer* and *Pierce* as exemplifying First Amendment values. See *Poe*, 367 U.S. at 544 (Harlan, J., dissenting).
54 *Meyer*, 262 U.S. at 399–403; *Pierce*, 268 U.S. at 533–5.
55 See Erwin Chemerinsky, "The Rhetoric of Constitutional Law," *Michigan Law Review* 100 (August 2002), 2015–16 and n. 44.
56 *Meyer*, 262 U.S. at 398 (quoting the state opinion, 187 N.W. 100, 102 (Neb. 1922)).
57 *Meyer*, 262 U.S. at 402–3.
58 *Pierce*, 268 U.S. at 535.
59 *Eisenstadt v. Baird*, 405 U.S. 438 (1972).
60 *Roe*, 410 U.S. 113.
61 *Roe*, 410 U.S. at 153.
62 Id. at 163 (emphasis added).
63 Id. at 166.
64 Nelson, *Pursuing Privacy*, 112–16, 128–30.
65 Michel Foucault, *The History of Sexuality, Vol. 1: An Introduction*, trans. Robert Hurley, Vintage Books ed. (New York: Random House, 1990), 61–2.
66 *City of Akron v. Akron Ctr. for Reprod. Health, Inc.*, 462 U.S. 416, 444 (1983) (quoting Akron, Ohio Codified Ordinances ch. 1870, No. 160-1978, § 1870.06 (B) (1978); citing *Roe*, 410 U.S. at 159–62) (overruled in part by *Casey*, 505 U.S. at 882); see also *Thornburgh v. Am. Coll. of Obstetricians & Gynecologists*, 476 U.S. 747, 759–64 (1986) (overruled in part by *Casey*, 505 U.S. at 882).
67 *Casey*, 505 U.S. 833.
68 Id. at 851.
69 Id. at 852.
70 Id. at 877.
71 Id.
72 Id. at 881–3.
73 See *Stuart v. Camnitz*, 774 F.3d 238, 251 (4th Cir. 2014); see also Ian Vandewalker, "Abortion and Informed Consent: How Biased Counseling Laws Mandate Violations of Medical Ethics," *Michigan Journal of Gender and Law* 19, No. 1 (2012), 5.
74 *Casey*, 505 U.S. at 877–8.
75 Williams, *Truth, Autonomy and Speech*, 148–56.
76 Williams, *Truth, Autonomy and Speech*, 149 (quoting Susan J. Brison, "The Uses of Narrative in the Aftermath of Violence," in *On Feminist Ethics and Politics*, ed. Claudia Card (Lawrence, KS: University of Kansas Press, 1999), 214).
77 See James E. Fleming, "Securing Deliberative Autonomy," *Stanford Law Review* 48 (November 1995), 19–23, 64–71.
78 Kan. Stat. Ann. § 65-6709(b)(5) (2019); N.D. Cent. Code § 14-02.1-02(11)(a)(2) (2019); S.D. Codified Laws § 34-23A-10.1(1)(b) (2019). Missouri requires that women receive materials stating: "The life of each human being begins at conception. Abortion will terminate the life of a separate, unique, living human being." Mo. Rev. Stat. § 188.027(2) (2019).

79 S.D. Codified Laws § 34-23A-10.1(1)(c)–(d) (2019).
80 See *Planned Parenthood Minn., N.D., S.D. v. Rounds*, 653 F.3d 662, 667–8 (8th Cir. 2011).
81 Id. at 667 (citing *Planned Parenthood Minn., N.D., S.D. v. Rounds*, 530 F.3d 724, 737 (8th Cir. 2008)).
82 See S.D. Codified Laws § 34-23A-1(4).
83 *Rounds*, 530 F.3d at 734–6 (2019).
84 Robert Post, "Informed Consent to Abortion: A First Amendment Analysis of Compelled Physician Speech," *University of Illinois Law Review* 2007, No. 3 (2007), 954–5.
85 S.D. Codified Laws § 34-23A-10.1(1)(c) (2019).
86 *Casey*, 505 U.S. at 877.
87 S.D. Codified Laws § 34-23A-10.1(1)(g) (2019).
88 Jerome Bruner, "The Narrative Construction of Reality," *Critical Inquiry* 18, No. 1 (1991), 1–21.
89 *Rounds*, 530 F.3d at 747 (Murphy, J., dissenting); see generally S.D. Codified Laws § 34-23A-10.1 (2019) and subsection 34-23A-10.1(1).
90 S.D. Codified Laws § 34-23A-10.1(1) (2019).
91 Ala. Code § 26-23A-4(b)(4) (2019); Ariz. Rev. Stat. § 36-2156(A)(1)(a) (2019); Fla. Stat. § 390.0111(3)(a)(1)(b) (2019); Ind. Code Ann. § 16-34-2-1.1(a)(5) (2019); Iowa Code § 146A.1(1) (2019); Miss. Code Ann. § 41-41-34(1) (2019); Va. Code Ann. § 18.2-76(B) (2019).
92 Ky. Rev. Stat. Ann. § 311.727(2) (2019); La. Stat. Ann. § 40:1061.10(D) (2019); Tex. Health & Safety Code Ann. § 171.012(a)(4)-(5) (2019); Wis. Stat. § 253.10 (3gm) (2019). Similar laws in North Carolina and Oklahoma have been enjoined. See *Stuart*, 774 F.3d 238 (N.C. Gen. Stat. § 90-21.85); *Nova Health Sys. v. Pruitt*, 2012 OK 103, 292 P.3d 28 (Okla. 2012) (Okla. Stat. tit. 63, § 1-738.3d (2010)). The Supreme Court recently declined to review a decision by the Sixth Circuit upholding Kentucky's ultrasound requirement against a challenge that it violated doctors' First Amendment speech rights. See *EMW Women's Surgical Ctr., P.S.C. v. Meier*, 920 F.3d 421 (6th Cir. 2019), *cert. denied*, 2015 L. Ed. 2d 387 (2019). In some states, a woman may refuse to hear the sonogram explanation if she certifies that she comes within a statutory exception, such as for rape victims.
93 *Tex. Med. Providers Performing Abortion Servs. v. Lakey*, 667 F.3d 570, 577 n.4 (5th Cir. 2012) (rejecting challenge to Texas statute).
94 Carol Sanger, "Seeing and Believing: Mandatory Ultrasound and the Path to a Protected Choice," *UCLA Law Review* 56 (December 2008), 367–72. My argument has been significantly informed by Sanger's powerful examination of mandatory ultrasounds. While Sanger focuses on ultrasounds' visual power, I examine the narrativization that ultrasounds enable, even compel. See also Jessica Silbey, "Picturing Moral Arguments in a Fraught Legal Arena: Fetuses, Photographic Phantoms and Ultrasounds," *Georgetown Journal of Gender and Law* 593 (Summer 2015), 593–631; Vicki Toscano and Elizabeth Reiter, "Úpholding a 40-Year-Old Promise: Why the Texas Sonogram Act Is Unlawful According to *Planned Parenthood v. Casey*," *Pace Law Review* 34 (Winter 2014), 128–83.
95 See Reva Siegel, "Reasoning from the Body: A Historical Perspective on Abortion Regulation and Questions of Equal Protection," *Stanford Law Review* 44 (January 1992), 281–2.
96 Sanger, "Seeing and Believing," 382.
97 MacKinnon, "Reflections on Sex Equality," 1310.
98 Sanger, "Seeing and Believing," 382–3.

99 *Casey*, 505 U.S. at 851.
100 Id. at 881–98.
101 See *Hill v. Colorado*, 530 U.S. 703, 716–8 (2000); *Erznoznik v. Jacksonville*, 422 U.S. 205, 208–10 (1975). See also Caroline Mala Corbin, "The First Amendment Right Against Compelled Listening," *Boston University Law Review* 89 (June 2009), 939–1016.
102 Robert D. Goldstein, "Reading *Casey*: Structuring the Woman's Decisionmaking Process," *William and Mary Bill of Rights Journal* 4 (Summer 1996), 848–9.

Chapter 2.2

# Adultery, criminality and the fiction of the king's body

*Erin Sheley*

On June 5, 1820 Lord Liverpool delivered a message to the House of Lords concerning the impending trial of Caroline of Brunswick, wife of the recently ascended King George IV, for divorce on the grounds of adultery. "The King," the Lord Chancellor read aloud, "has felt the most anxious desire to avert the necessity of disclosures and discussions, which must be as painful to his people as they can be to himself," but Caroline's decision to return from self-imposed exile in Italy to claim her place as Queen of England "leaves him no alternative."[1] From both a social and a political standpoint Caroline's trial was one of the most notorious and divisive episodes in the history of the modern British monarchy; many witnesses testified to her romantic relationship with her Italian steward Bartolomeo Pergami and a bill of divorce passed the House of Lords.[2] Nonetheless, due to Caroline's immense popularity as a figure of reform and George's reputation as a cruel husband and dissolute monarch, the bill was not submitted to the House of Commons.[3] Beyond its much-discussed political significance, Queen Caroline's trial was also an important moment of cultural ferment surrounding the nature of adultery as a legal wrong.

The king's message for Parliament on that first day of the divorce proceedings, alluding to the harm to "the people" arising from disclosure of Caroline's alleged indiscretions, is clearly a case of political grandstanding. Yet he made the statement in the context of a trial that was, due to the parties involved, at once a private divorce and a proposed public bill. It should therefore also be understood as a particular sort of legal claim, with relevance to the basic classification of a wrong as a tort or a crime. When Blackstone distinguishes between "public" and "private" wrongs at the start of Book Four of his *Commentaries*, he states that English criminal law is known as "the doctrine of the pleas of the crown" because "the king, in whom centers the majesty of the whole community, is supposed by the law to be the person injured by every infraction of the public right belonging to that community, and is therefore in all cases the proper prosecutor for every public offence."[4] In many cases the public/private wrong model is a useful, if oversimplified, means of distinguishing between a crime and a civil injury such as a tort or a breach of contract, and in democracies it does not depend upon the physical body of a monarch. Individuals may recoup losses for civil injuries, while the government prosecutes a crime to vindicate the harms it imposes on the polity as a whole. When one commits an intentional assault on another person, for example, he has wronged that person and may owe him compensation under civil law, but he has also done violence to the whole community by violating the collective moral prohibition on assault; he therefore may also be prosecuted by the sovereign.

Yet Blackstone's turn of phrase suggests something in the English common law imagination that sees a potentially interdependent relationship between tort and crime, centered on the body of the sovereign. John Goldberg and Benjamin Zipursky suggest that one way to distinguish between a tort and a crime is the "relational" component of the tort. As they put it, where "a criminal prohibition states 'For all x, x shall not A,' a tort occurs when someone violates the directive 'For all x and for all y, x shall not do A to y.'"[5] Blackstone's famous dichotomy is striking in that—counter to this modern understanding—it relies upon the language of relationality to describe criminal liability as well as tort: x shall not do A to *the king*. In most cases this legal fiction will not matter much in the common law's disposition of wrongs both public and private. But King George's invocation of the "people's" wellbeing in his own divorce proceeding brings to light a very specific legal wrong that has been fluid in nature at common law precisely *because* of the body of the king: adultery. I argue that in Britain over the course of the eighteenth and nineteenth centuries, the understanding of adultery as a tort is complicated by an accompanying discourse of what I will call "quasi-criminality." Specifically—while formally trivialized—adultery remains discursively linked to a threat to British kingship. The tension between the weight of relevant monarchical history and the absence of criminal enforcement creates a new cultural discourse of adultery which attempts, itself, to serve an explicitly penal function.

The image of adultery occupied a curious position in English political discourse throughout the Revolution and Restoration and the accompanying ideological struggles as to the sources of royal authority. Stuart apologist Sir Robert Filmer famously analogized the relationship between a subject and his sovereign to the subjection of Eve to Adam, and James I declared to Parliament "What God has conjoined let no man separate. I am the husband and the whole island is my lawful wife."[6] The discourses of marital relations and kingship have been intertwined throughout the development of Anglo-American laws related to adultery.[7] And even after the liberalizing shifts after the Revolution, it remained the case that a woman's murder of her husband constituted petty treason, punishable by burning; thus, adultery-related murders of husbands by wives were inescapably reiterations, in the public sphere, of the husband-as-sovereign legal trope.[8]

Indeed, it was precisely this potential relationship between adultery and violence that reinforced the cultural narrative of adultery as a public concern. It is therefore perhaps unsurprising that the famous eighteenth-century cause of action in tort for adultery was known as "criminal conversation." A form of trespass, the cause of action was first recognized in the latter part of the century, and exploded in popularity immediately. The very name of the action compresses the criminal into the commonplace; "conversation" suggests the highly regulated social interactions of the eighteenth century that so frequently formed the backdrop for instances of adultery. The cause of action recognized both the quasi-criminality and basic *impoliteness* of seducing someone's spouse. Indeed, in the courtroom, lawyers for plaintiffs in these cases expended a lot of effort to play up harm to the *public* morality occasioned by an act of adultery, even though such public concerns are traditionally the territory of the criminal prosecution which, as Blackstone would have it, is concerned with the rights of the king, not the plaintiff.[9]

The increasing popularity of the criminal conversation lawsuit resulted in a new form of popular literature: the publication of the proceedings of trials for both criminal conversation and divorce. In these cases observers attended the trials and took short-hand notes on the attorneys' arguments and the testimony of each witness. These were then collected into volumes containing the proceedings of multiple trials which were often illustrated like novels, with detailed drawings of the various pairs of lovers at their moment of discovery.

While meant for entertainment, these compendiums also assumed a self-consciously punitive purpose. In the preface to *Trials for Adultery: or, The History of Divorces* (1799), the editor laments the de-criminalization of adultery and suggests that his text, itself, might rectify it: "[t]his publication may effect what the law cannot: the transactions of the adulterer and the adulteress will, by being thus *publickly circulated*, preserve others from the like crimes, from the fear of shame."[10] Another volume, *A New and Complete Collection of the Most Remarkable Trials for Adultery &c* (1780), makes its public function even more explicit. While including several of the same famous eighteenth-century society adulteries chronicled in *The History of Divorces*, this "Complete" collection begins with the 1542 trial and execution of Henry VIII's fifth queen, Catherine Howard. While *The History of Divorces* is concerned with presenting the criminal relationship between aristocratic sexual behavior and public morals, this collection takes it a step further. In using an English queen's trial for treason as the starting point for a project on eighteenth-century tort cases, the text's editors reify the relationship between adultery, criminality, and sovereignty.

Consequently, the chapter on Catherine Howard explains:

> This trial is put at the head of this Work, not only on account of its being the earliest in point of time, but on account of the dignity of the party tried. It is a trial of a most curious and interesting nature; the principal facts proved were committed before marriage; the punishment of the Queen's relations, who were no way accessory to her lewd practices, was contrary to every rule of law and justice; and the act of Parliament that

> passed, in order to oblige any lady the King intended to marry, to reveal any former incontinence she had been guilty of, was considered a most extraordinary effort of tyranny.[11]

From this introduction, it is clear that Catherine's trial is significant in part because she is the archetypical adulteress: as she is the queen and therefore "first" in "dignity," Catherine's adultery has the most important general effects on the kingdom, its legal order, and its security vis-à-vis the rest of the world. The editors of the compendium emphasize this by including a long extract from a letter sent by the king's privy council to William Paget, the English Ambassador in France, which states that the King had desired in the first place to marry Catherine so that "his Majesty might have some more store of fruit and succession, to the comfort of his realm."[12] The inclusion of his fifth queen's adultery trial at the start of this compendium demonstrates how the criminality of adultery had come to function as a form of English legal origins story. In addition, at least with respect to Catherine Howard's affairs prior to her marriage to the king, the text notes that investigations "shewed that the Queen had thrown aside all sense of modesty, as well as all fear of discovery."[13] The concept of "discovery" as the touchstone for legal liability remained deeply important to the eighteenth-century discourse on adultery. When closely considered under the logic of those who would criminalize adultery, it is in fact the discovery of the private sin that brings it into the public sphere and thereby causes the harms complained of.

These same anxieties can be seen in the following century in Tennyson's epic Arthurian poem *Idylls of the King*. At the time of its publication Tennyson drew criticism for his emasculation of Malory's highly masculine Arthur, in part due to his role as a cuckold. Swinburne complained that Tennyson had "lowered the note and deformed the outline of the Arthurian story, by reducing Arthur to the level of a wittol, Guinevere to the level of a woman of intrigue, and Launcelot to the level of a 'co-respondent,'" an allusion to the trivial culture of cuckoldry associated with tort and divorce law.[14] Nonetheless, in dedicating the epic to the late Prince Consort Albert, Tennyson designates the poem as a tribute to marital fidelity, idealized as a component of sovereignty. He compares Albert to Arthur, reimagined as both loyal husband and obedient subject to his conscience. While Arthur (and Albert) "loved one only and … clave to her," he also "reverenced his conscience as his king."[15] The dissolution, through death, of the marriage of Victoria and Albert becomes a threat to the cohesion of the former's empire, over which "commingled with the gloom of imminent war,/The shadow of His loss drew like eclipse,/Darkening the world."[16] Victoria's sovereignty appears destabilized by the loss of a partner who cleaved to her, as if marital completeness were a necessary condition for hegemonic political authority.

It is clear that both political order and humanity depend upon the purity of the union between Arthur and Guinevere. Tennyson suggests that unification of husband and wife into one legal entity is a precondition for the consolidation of warring factions into one political entity. In contemplating Guinevere as a potential queen in the first book of the poem, Arthur recalls that her father King Leodegrance had said of his warring lands that "there between the man and beast they die," and wonders, "Shall I not lift her from this land of beasts/Up to my throne,/and side by side with me?'"[17] In the language of physical motion he describes Guinevere's transition from the realm of beast to that of man to that of queen. Her personal elevation to the literal and figurative throne next to him turns out to be critical to Arthur's project of unification and humanization described at the outset:

> [F]or saving I be joined
> To her that is the fairest under heaven,
> I seem as nothing in the mighty world,
> And cannot will my will, nor work my work
> Wholly, nor make myself in mine own realm
> Victor and lord. But were I joined with her
> Then might we live together as one life,
> And reigning with one will in everything
> Have power on this dark land to lighten it,
> And power on this dead world to make it live.[18]

Arthur here establishes the central problem of the poem: much like Victoria's empire, which is "eclipsed" by the darkness of her consort's death, the unification of England as a political state depends upon a conjugal "joining" of its king with his wife. His "will"—both as an individual man and as a source of political legitimacy—is impotent without collapse into the will of another, to form "one," either as a unified legal entity under his direction or as an example of companionate leadership, with both parties working together. The priest who marries the royal couple reiterates this charge: "Reign ye,/and live and love, and make the world/Other, and may thy queen be one with thee,/And all of this Order of thy Table Round/Fulfill the boundless purpose of their King!"[19] Again, Tennyson conflates Arthur's "purpose" of "making the world other" into being "one" with Guinevere.

In the chapter "The Marriage of Geraint," Tennyson foregrounds a lesser-known Arthurian figure whose story reinforces the conflict between sovereignty and adultery. In this episode, Guinevere's betrayal with Lancelot sparks a chain of causation through which the "flyers from Justice" escape punishment and unmake the kingdom, which in turn begins to unmake the union between Geraint and Enid. Unlike most of the other characters in the *Idylls*, Geraint does not figure in the primary French and English Arthurian texts but is known mostly from the collection of medieval Welsh manuscripts known as the *Mabinogion*. Tennyson's Geraint marries the beautiful Enid, a favorite of Guinevere's who in turn "with true heart,/Adored her, as the stateliest and the best/And the loveliest of all women upon earth."[20] The text's first direct reference to Guinevere's affair with Lancelot comes indirectly through Geraint's observations of his wife's relationship with the queen:

> Long in their common love rejoiced Geraint
> But when a rumour rose about the Queen,
> Touching her guilty love for Lancelot,
> Though yet there lived no proof, nor yet was heard
> The world's loud whisper breaking into storm,
> Not less Geraint believed it, and there fell
> A horror on him, lest his gentle wife,
> Through that great tenderness for Guinevere,
> Had suffered or should suffer any taint
> In nature ...[21]

Geraint's views on the potential effects of the queen's rumored affair on his own wife's chastity reflect the same concern, expressed in the eighteenth-century adultery trial compendiums, of the particular dangers of upper-class adulteresses corrupting through example. Furthermore, the moment the hint of adultery enters the text, the action immediately shifts to the peripheries of the legal order established by Arthur. Geraint makes the excuse that he needs to leave Camelot because his princedom is "Close on the borders of a territory,/Wherein were bandit earls, and caitiff knights,/Assassins, and all flyers from the hand/Of Justice and whatever loathes a law."[22] Geraint thereby establishes himself as an iteration of Arthur, intending to impose a system of justice on another pre-legal state of nature. Upon arriving in his own lands, however, Geraint instead spends his time on romantic pleasures with Enid, who laments that he is "forgetful of his promise to the King." Though she describes their situation as an act of infidelity to Arthur, her husband overhears her accusing herself—as the cause of her husband's lapse—of being "no true wife," from which he concludes that she, like Guinevere, has committed adultery.[23]

As punishment for her perceived betrayal, Geraint makes Enid put on her shabbiest gown and ride out with him on an adventure. Numerous altercations with lawless knights ensue and they eventually take shelter at an inn. Lord Limours, a former suitor of Enid's whom Geraint had defeated many years before, happens to arrive at the inn and, seeing the couple at odds, takes the opportunity to declare to her that losing her had "turned him wild." His existence at the periphery of Arthur's realm, participating in the lawless conduct of the local knights was the direct consequence of failing to achieve matrimony.

Just as the first rumors of adultery lead to the unraveling of the Arthurian legal order, however, the reinforcement of fidelity begins to restore it, at least for a time. After Geraint is wounded in a fight with Limours' men, he is taken—assumed dead—to the hall of the "brute Earl" Doorm, who attempts to force Enid to eat and drink with him. After her many refusals out of loyalty to Geraint, he shouts, "I compel all creatures to my will,"[24] and "unknightley with his flat hand" slapped her.[25] It is only upon hearing Enid's many professions of loyalty to her fallen husband that Geraint is able to rise, take his sword, and "shore through the swarthy neck" of Earl Doorm, whose "russet-bearded head rolled on the floor."[26] The "brute" lord who rules over "creatures" rather than men has been removed as head of authority by the restoration of a monogamous marriage.

Indeed, after the pair escape Doorm's castle, they immediately reunite with Arthur, who had taken it upon himself to visit the lawless lands Geraint had mentioned and "cleanse this common sewer" of the realm. As Geraint's wounds healed physically, Arthur "rooted out the slothful officer/Or guilty, which for bribe had winked at wrong,/And in their chairs set up a stronger race"[27] and "cleared the dark places and let in the law,/And broke the bandit holds and cleansed the land."[28] With the threat of adultery cleared away, the legal order in this part of the kingdom can evolve out of the state of nature, away from the "darkness" that seems to recur throughout the text whenever a marriage is disrupted. Yet the chapter closes on an ambiguous note: Geraint's reunion with Arthur occasions Enid's reunion with Guinevere, and Geraint "could never take again/That comfort from their converse which he took/ Before the Queen's fair name was breathed upon."[29] Geraint's discomfort, of course, presaged the inevitable end to the Arthurian saga in future books.

Tennyson's selection of source material so deeply linked to the English originary story suggests that this preoccupation with sovereignty traces a particular historical vector. Arthur's cuckolded identity was—as George IV had suggested of his own—a wrong to the people, as whose head and conscience he was supposed to serve. With the faithful matrimonial bodies of Tennyson's own sovereign and her late spouse so vividly invoked at the start of the poem, the temporal remove to the Arthurian period necessarily implicates the various historical queens whose alleged adulteries complicated and reconstituted English sovereignty in the centuries between Guinevere and Victoria. Furthermore, the proliferation of adultery throughout the text, with non-royal couples moving in a kind of network with Guinevere and Arthur, suggests the same anxiety over contagion seen in the eighteenth-century compendiums. *Idylls of the King* may, therefore, be considered to function as a uniquely English adultery text. Far from avoiding the subject, Tennyson narrates it as inextricably interwoven with—while destructive of—the English legal order.

## Notes

1 *The Important and Eventful Trial of Queen Caroline, Consort of George IV, for "Adulterous Intercourse" with Bartolomo Bergami*, ed. George Smeeton (1820), 11.

2 Robins Jane, *Rebel Queen: How the Trial of Caroline Brought England to the Brink of Revolution* (New York: Simon & Schuster, 2006), 192–3.

3 Ibid., 200–10.

4 William Blackstone, *Commentaries on the Laws of England*, 4 vols. [1765–1769], ed. William Cyrus Sprague (Chicago: Callaghan & Co., 1915), 4:7.
5 John C.P. Goldberg & Benjamin Zipursky, "Torts as Wrongs," *Texas Law Review* 88 (2010), 949.
6 C.H. McIlwain, *The Political Works of King James I.* (Cambridge: Cambridge UP, 1918), 272.
7 Mary Beth Norton, *Founding Mothers and Fathers: Gendered Power and the Forming of American Society* (New York: Vintage, 1996), 6.
8 Blackstone, *Commentaries*, 4, 88–9.
9 Ibid., 179.
10 *Trials for Adultery: or, the History of Divorces* (7 vols. London: S. Blandon, 1799), iii.
11 *A New and Complete Collection of the Most Remarkable Trials for Adultery &c* (London: J. Fleeming. 1780), 14.
12 Ibid.
13 Ibid., 15.
14 Algernon Charles Swinburne, "On the Idylls", in *Tennyson: The Critical Heritage*, ed. John D. Jump (London: Routledge and Kegan Paul, 1967), 319.
15 Alfred, Lord Tennyson, "Idylls of the King," in *The Complete Works of Lord Tennyson*, ed. Charles Howard Johnson (1859; repr., New York: Frederick A. Stokes, 1891), ll. 8–10.
16 Ibid., ll. 12–14.
17 Ibid., ll. 78–80.
18 Ibid., ll. 84–93.
19 Ibid., ll. 471–4.
20 Ibid., ll. 19–21.
21 Ibid., ll. 22–3.
22 Ibid., ll. 34–7.
23 Ibid., l. 108.
24 Ibid., l. 628.
25 Ibid., l. 717.
26 Ibid., l. 728.
27 Ibid., l. 939.
28 Ibid., l. 943.
29 Ibid., ll. 949–50.

Chapter 2.3

# Memory, history, and forgetting

## *Shelby County, Alabama v. Holder*

*Laura Cisneros*

> One does not remember alone.
>
> Paul Ricoeur, *Memory, History, Forgetting*[1]

## I Introduction

Collective memory and the law share a paradoxical relationship. They exist independently of each other, yet they are interdependent in their construction; collective memory influences the representation of the law, but law influences the representation of collective memory. Collective memory has been investigated as the impetus for political change[2] and as a narrative of civil society.[3] This essay engages the relationship between collective memory and the law. It has been said that "Law in the modern era is ... one of the most important of our society's technologies for preserving memory."[4] The judicial opinion, for example, stands as a piece of historical datum that archives and materializes memory. Indeed, the act of interpretation in which judges engage is performed in part as a carrier of social memory. Judicial decisions, therefore, "help to constitute and reaffirm the nation's understanding of its past and how that past shapes our present and future. But not every decision engages memory in the same way or engages the same type of memory."[5] This essay explores that differential memory engagement. It looks at the relationship between law and collective memory descriptively by reading the U.S. Supreme Court's decision in *Shelby County, Alabama v. Holder* through the lens of Paul Ricoeur's *Memory, History, Forgetting* to investigate how and where the law helps us to remember and to forget.

In the short term, it is fair to say that the Roberts Court represents another chapter in the reaction against the socially progressive Warren Court era. Since its inception in 2005, the Roberts Court has handed down decisions that signify that the debate over what direction the Court is taking on issues of race, federal power, and state sovereignty has not abated. In the long term, the shift in the Court's composition gives rise to questions about how the Court's decisions may fundamentally alter the experience of the Constitution for the next generation of Americans. The Court's last few terms have turned out to be especially significant. The Court has weighed in on some of the most hotly contested cultural and legal issues of our time. Given this, it is easy to see the power that Supreme Court opinions have as an agent of one of the most important social institutions affecting our lives—the law. The Roberts Court is poised to reexamine the Warren Court's landmark decisions from the 1950s and 1960s and, in its current composition, that re-examination will be performed by a majority block of justices who interpret the Court's role to be less socially progressive and more oriented to state's rights/small government than their predecessors. The narratives the Court adopts, rejects, and constructs in their opinions—which already affect how issues in subsequent cases can be framed and litigated in court —will take on a larger significance if they also fundamentally restructure the basis for or objects of constitutional protection.

In this chapter, I use Paul Ricoeur's analysis in *Memory, History, Forgetting*[6] and extend it to an examination of the majority and dissenting opinions in the Court's 2013 Voting Rights Act decision: *Shelby County, Alabama v. Holder.*[7] I chose to focus on the *Shelby* decision because its holding directly negates the Warren Court's foundational Voting Rights Act decision, *South Carolina v. Katzenbach.*[8] Analyzing the two *Shelby* opinions through a Ricoeurian lens provides a means for examining and critiquing the sacrifices and implied legal consequences that judicial opinions produce through their construction of narrative forgetting.

Part II of this chapter sets forth some of Ricoeur's ideas on memory, history, and forgetting. Part III provides a few relevant aspects of the judicial context of the *Shelby* decision. Part IV examines the *Shelby* decision. After a brief summary of the case outcome, I analyze Chief Justice Roberts's majority opinion and Justice Ginsburg's dissenting opinion and demonstrate how they rhetorically grapple with the representation of equality and the meaning of the Voting Rights Act through the judicial production of memory and forgetting.

## II Ricoeurian concepts of memory, history, forgetting

Ricoeur investigates why some historical events occupy the forefront of the collective consciousness, while other events, just as profound, recede into the background. He reveals how the reciprocal relationship between remembering and forgetting influences both the perception of historical experience and the production of historical narrative. Ricoeur's description of the phenomenology of memory begins with a focus on the object of the memory (*souvenir*) that one has in mind, then proceeds to the search for that given object, a stage that Ricoeur calls recollection (*anamnesis*).[9] This process of memory-capture through recollection and reflection requires an active remembering that creates the bridge to history making and, ironically, to active forgetting. He explains that individuals recall memories and construct narrative histories to make those individual memories intelligible to others.[10] Once intelligible or recognizable, those constructed narratives can then be transformed into collective memories that function as history.[11]

Ricoeur then explains how the construction of these narratives emerges from the historian's assemblage and evaluation of evidence made available from competing sources. The historiographical operation proceeds from the documentary phase (collecting evidence) to the explanatory phase (making sense and understanding of the evidence) to the representation phase (articulating that understanding into a representation of the past).[12] The explanatory phase also actively engages with history. Here, the historian tests his/her collection of documentary proof against variously posited explanatory modalities.[13] This critical interrogation provides a means to verify the plausibility, probability, or likelihood of a particular historical account.

Accepting the view that human action proceeds through a series of repeatable events produced by singular, unrepeatable human action such that these events are not susceptible to generalization, Ricoeur maintains that the historian's representation of the explanatory phase requires a narrative form so that it can be made comprehensible.[14] He submits that the literary narrative form is an effective means to rhetorically stage the events of history into an intelligible narrative.[15] Ricoeur cites Hayden White's work on emplotment as "[t]he major contribution to the exploring of the properly rhetorical resources of historical representation."[16] In *Metahistory*, White discusses emplotment and its contribution to the historiographical operation of moving from chronicle to story to history.[17] Ricoeur emphasizes that emplotment operates as a powerful rhetorical device. Through emplotment, the organization of the narrative controls the meanings of the individual events contained within it.[18] Thus, the narrative form itself tends to legitimize the evidence selected for inclusion in the narrative.

Finally, Ricoeur suggests that this narrative process involves two types of "forgetting"—one positive, in that one needs to forget some things to create a path to forgive and transcend trauma, and one negative, in the sense that forgetting may create space for repeating past mistakes or silencing minority voices.[19] A Ricoeurian reading of *Shelby* reveals how Chief Justice Roberts's majority opinion works as a misappropriation of the positive aspect of forgetting, while the narrative of Justice Ginsburg's dissent cautions against the negative aspect of forgetting.

## III Juridical context of the *Shelby* decision

One can better appreciate the interpretive possibilities that *Shelby*'s rhetoric provides by understanding the decision's context. *Shelby* can be contextualized from two main sources: statutory law—here, the Voting Rights Act—and case law. In this instance, the 1966 decision *South Carolina v. Katzenbach* serves as the Court's foundational interpretation of the purpose and reach of the Voting Rights Act. Additionally, the Roberts Court's 2009 decision in *Northwest*

*Austin Municipal Utility Dist., No. 1 v. Holder*[20] provides the initial interpretive turn from *Katzenbach* that foreshadows the eventual interpretive departure the Court makes in *Shelby*.

The Fifteenth Amendment to the United States Constitution prohibits the federal and state governments from denying a citizen the right to vote based on that citizen's "race, color, or previous condition of servitude."[21] The impetus for enacting this post-Civil War Reconstruction Amendment was to prohibit the practice of states, especially Southern states, from enacting laws that had the intent and effect of restricting the freedom of and discriminating against African Americans. One of the crowning achievements of the Civil Rights movement was the Voting Rights Act of 1965, which prohibits racial discrimination in voting.[22] Its purpose was "to foster our transformation to a society that is no longer fixated on race."[23] In 1965 that meant that the VRA needed to employ extraordinary measures to address the extraordinary problem of entrenched racial discrimination in voting in the Jim Crow South. One of the most controversial provisions of the VRA, Section 5, required certain states and local governments to obtain federal permission (called preclearance) before enacting any law related to election standards or voting requirements. The purpose of Section 5's preclearance requirements was to "freeze" election practices and procedures in covered jurisdictions until new procedures, compliant with the VRA, could be established—either after the Attorney General's administrative review or litigation in the federal court. Section 4(b) of the Act contains the coverage formula that determines which jurisdictions are subjected to preclearance based on their histories of discrimination in voting. The coverage formula targeted those jurisdictions with a history of Jim Crow racism and discrimination in voting. Since its enactment, Congress has amended the VRA five times to expand its protections.

South Carolina was the first to challenge the constitutionality of the VRA,[24] arguing that the VRA unconstitutionally encroached on states' rights and violated the doctrine of equality among the states.[25]

Chief Justice Warren's majority opinion recounted the deplorable history of disenfranchisement and minority voter intimidation in the South. "The VRA was designed by Congress to banish the blight of racial discrimination in voting, which has infected the electoral process in parts of our country for nearly a century."[26] Because of that century-long record, he continued, "The constitutional propriety of the VRA must be judged with reference to the historical experience which it reflects."[27] The opinion cited the failed congressional attempts at remedying racial discrimination in voting on a case-by-case basis, and noted, "the damage to our national conscience is too great not to adopt more effective measures than exist."[28]

These passages frame the Court's narrative of the VRA. The first frame is the metaphor of disease ("the *blight* of racial discrimination in voting, which has *infected* the electoral process"). The second is the VRA's narrative on the historical experience of racial discrimination and our national conscience. The opinion's relation of racial discrimination in voting to the threat and destruction of disease supports the Court's decision to uphold the VRA as constitutional. However, as Ricoeur notes in *The Rule of Metaphor*, use of metaphor can extend language beyond its very limits by establishing a form of meaning making that can "forever discover new resonances within itself."[29] Thus, while the Court's use of the metaphor of disease successfully conveys the experience of the severity of racial discrimination in voting, it also opens up two distinct ways of interpreting disease: as chronic or curable. Understood as chronic, congressional attempts to eradicate the disease of racial discrimination in voting are presumed to be perpetual and thus perpetually justified; understood as curable frames congressional attempts within the problem–solution modality, which imagines a determinate endpoint to congressional remedial efforts. The majority opinion recognized that the VRA upset basic federalism principles, but acknowledged that, based on this history of abuse, "exceptional conditions can justify legislative means not otherwise appropriate."[30] The *Katzenbach* opinion privileges the narrative of race-memory[31] over a narrative of robust federalism to support its decision that not only had Congress exercised its power under the Fifteenth Amendment in an appropriate manner, but that in all likelihood this memory of racial subjugation was so strong as to leave Congress with no other choice but to invent this particular regulatory scheme. The opinion concludes:

> Whatever legislation is appropriate, that is, adapted to carry out the objects the Civil War Amendments have in view, whatever tends to enforce submission to the prohibitions they contain, and to secure to all persons the enjoyment of perfect equality of civil rights and equal protection of the laws against State denial or invasion, if not prohibited, is brought within the domain of congressional power.[32]

*Katzenbach* illustrates the Court's implicit acknowledgment that it has an institutional duty to use the Constitution to protect race-memory. What then does it mean to judicially protect race-memory? It may simply mean that the Court must remedy past abuses.[33] More radically, it might also mean that the Court must normatively consider slavery and racism on a conceptual level. Under this second interpretation, the motivation to protect is not limited to a focus on correcting specific instances of past abuse. Rather, protecting race-memory includes protection methods geared toward apologizing for the existence of slavery and racism in the first place. *Katzenbach* showed a Court willing to deploy the Constitution to protect the memory of slavery and racism as a hedge against their repetition.

*Northwest Austin* involved a small municipal utility district with an elected board in Texas, a covered jurisdiction under the VRA. Thus, the utility district had to seek federal preclearance before it could change any of its election standards. The Roberts Court applied the principle of constitutional avoidance and decided the case on statutory interpretation grounds.[34] Notwithstanding its statutory grounding, the unanimous opinion written by Chief Justice Roberts signaled a shift from *Katzenbach* in how the Court framed the memory and history of race and in the Court's response as to whether the time had come to impose institutional forgetting.

*Northwest* acknowledges the atrocities of the past described in *Katzenbach* and thus elides criticism that *Northwest* is a blatant disregard of *stare decisis.*[35] His homage continues and captures the Warren Court's *Katzenbach* opinion:

> We upheld the temporary [VRA] as an appropriate exercise of congressional power in *Katzenbach*, explaining that "[t]he constitutional propriety of the VRA [had] to be judged with reference to the historical experience it reflects."
>
> We concluded [in *Katzenbach*] that the problems Congress faced when it passed the Act were so dire that "exceptional conditions [could] justify legislative measures not otherwise appropriate."[36]

By historicizing the conceptions of race-memory in the *Katzenbach* precedent, Roberts lays the foundation for a construction of race-memory and the history of racial discrimination in voting that will ultimately support the judicial forgetting in the Court's majority opinion in *Shelby.* He acknowledges that "the historic accomplishments of the VRA are undeniable," pointing to the fact that the registration gap between white and black voters in the covered jurisdictions shrunk from "roughly 50 percentage points to single digits," but then Roberts shifts the Court's focus from the object of the VRA's protection (minority voters) to the object of its regulation (the covered jurisdictions): "the federalism intrusion into sensitive areas of state and local policymaking, impose substantial 'federalism costs.'"[37] The narrative thread is seamless: Once Upon a Time the South had a problem of racial discrimination in voting, which led Congress to enact a law with some constitutionally dubious *but at the time* necessary requirements. We all went along with it because things were so bad … back then. In a line that will embed itself in Roberts's legacy on the Court, he writes: "Things have changed in the South."[38] He continues, "Blatantly discriminatory evasions of federal decrees are rare."[39] And as a result, he concludes that "the current burdens [of the preclearance requirement of the VRA] must be justified by current needs."[40] By rhetorically relegating the story of the South's racial discrimination in voting to the past, the Chief Justice can place the history of racial abuse and the Warren Court's interpretation of the purposes of the VRA in that defined historical moment in time. This clear break from the protection of race-memory by constructing a history of Southern transcendence of racial discrimination creates the space for the narrative of a redeemed South. This narrative operates a juridical forgetting by replacing judicial discourse about the protection of race-memory with judicial discourse about the protection of the equality and dignity of the states.

## IV The *Shelby County, Alabama v. Holder* opinion

In *Shelby County, Alabama v. Holder*, the United States Supreme Court declared Section 4(b) VRA, which effectively nullified Section 5. In noting that "things have changed in the South," the decision reasoned that reliance on the memory and history of Jim Crow racism in the South was no longer warranted for purposes of protecting the substantive right to vote guaranteed by the Fifteenth Amendment; it was time to forget the past.

### *Chief Justice Roberts's majority opinion*

Chief Justice Roberts's majority opinion constructs a teleological slavery-to-freedom narrative that creates the conditions for the juridical forgetting of the history of racial discrimination in voting.[41] His narrative follows a progressive linear conception of history. Roberts's opinion focuses on what it perceives as the most important story: not slavery, but the end of slavery; not Jim Crow, but the end of Jim Crow. Ultimately, Roberts's opinion relegates the memory of slavery and racism to the status of a historical artifact.

The opening sentence of Roberts's majority opinion frames the memory of the VRA: "The Voting Rights Act of 1965 employed extraordinary measures to address an extraordinary problem."[42] Although the word "extraordinary" can be understood as both special and strange, as his first paragraph develops, it becomes clear that the construction of the majority's historical narrative will depict the VRA as strange and abnormal. Roberts calls the VRA "a drastic departure from basic principles of federalism," a "dramatic departure from the principle that all States enjoy equal sovereignty," and "strong medicine [that] Congress determined [...] was needed to address entrenched racial discrimination in voting."[43] He constructs this framing of irregularity and variance to describe the VRA's measures not as innovative but as "unprecedented"[44] and, in so doing, transforms the memory of the VRA from a vital piece of civil rights legislation and bulwark of racial justice to a historical anomaly.

The majority next articulates the amendment history of the VRA. After briefly acknowledging the initial failures of Congress to adequately enforce the voting rights protections of the Fifteenth Amendment, noting that the case-by-case litigation remedies "were slow and expensive" and states were creative in coming up "with new ways to discriminate as soon as existing ones were struck down,"[45] Roberts describes the multiple subsequent extensions Congress passed to continue the VRA's measures (1970, 1975, 1982, and 2006).[46] Each time, Roberts describes the actions of Congress without mention of context, congressional deliberation, or even what type of testamentary or statistical evidence was made available to Congress for review.[47] He presents a narrative of the VRA's amendment that depicts Congress as lazy and willing to reauthorize the "extraordinary" measures of the VRA absent deliberation, resulting in federal overreaching into and encroachment of the sovereignty of the states.

The next move the majority makes is the crux of Roberts's reconfigured narrative. Proceeding from the basic premise that the need to secure equality among voters necessitated the VRA's measures, the opinion captures this essence of equality and repositions it to cover not minority voters but *states*. Invoking the memory of his 2009 *Northwest Austin* opinion, Roberts writes:

> [In *Northwest*] we explained that §5 "imposes substantial federalism costs" and "differentiates between the States, despite our historic tradition that all the States enjoy equal sovereignty."[48] And we concluded that "a departure from the fundamental principle of equal sovereignty requires a showing that a statute's disparate geographic coverage is sufficiently related to the problem that it targets. These basic principles guide our review of the question before us.[49]

Here, Roberts shifts the focus from minority voters to the states themselves while maintaining the narrative of equality. He recasts what was a civil rights violation issue into an issue about equal sovereignty among the states. Through this rhetorical shift, Roberts is able to hold out the VRA as unnecessary under current conditions given that "[t]hings have changed in the South [because v]oter turnout and registration rates now approach parity. Blatantly discriminatory evasions of federal decrees are rare. And minority candidates hold office at unprecedented levels."[50] More importantly, he suggests that the VRA is anathema to the American principle of freedom and dignity: "Over a hundred years ago, this Court explained that our Nation 'was and is a union of States, equal in power, dignity and authority … The Voting Rights Act sharply departs from these basic principles.'"[51]

Roberts writes that the conditions of racial discrimination in voting in the South have changed dramatically since the VRA was enacted nearly 50 years ago.[52] In 1966, Roberts notes:

> [This Court] concluded that "[u]nder the compulsion of these unique circumstances, Congress responded in a permissibly decisive manner." … At the time, the coverage formula—the means of linking the exercise of the unprecedented authority with the problem that warranted it—made sense.[53]

However, Roberts continues, the formula that Congress uses to determine which states are covered by the preclearance requirements is no longer applicable, and the law itself is not in keeping with the times. Here, the majority draws on distinct lessons from the history of the Civil Rights Movement for support, such as Philadelphia, Mississippi, where three civil rights workers were murdered during the 1964 Freedom Summer and Selma, Alabama: "Today both of these towns are governed by African-American mayors. Problems remain in these States and others, but there is no denying that, due to the Voting Rights Act, our nation has made great strides."[54] In stating that "[O]ur nation has made great strides," the opinion implies we no longer need federal enforcement over voting procedure.[55]

By attaching the VRA entirely to the memories of slavery and Jim Crow, Roberts constructs a linear slavery-to-freedom narrative that he can then rhetorically transpose from minority voters to Southern states. Under the frame of equal sovereignty and dignity, the Southern states are "forgiven" for their sins of slavery and Jim Crow, and the VRA becomes obsolete. Roberts's opinion replaces minority voters with the Southern states as the subject of the equality narrative but maintains the narrative's form, thereby preserving the connection to equality's virtue. Through this narrative reconfiguration Roberts capitalizes on the power of the equality trope and uses it to the states' advantage.

Roberts's narrative invokes two powerful generic norms that a majority of the bench found more persuasive than the empirical evidence on which Justice Ginsburg's dissent relies. First, as mentioned above, Roberts's construction invokes the norm of equality, which has tremendous purchase on the American legal imagination. Second, his recitation of the myriad ways in which the Southern states have risen above their ignoble history with respect to racial discrimination in voting speaks to the post-racial identity that America wishes to claim.

### *Justice Ginsburg's dissent*

Justice Ginsburg's dissent attempts to construct a "remember Jim Crow" story as a counterpoint to Roberts's "slavery-to-freedom" narrative. Ginsburg's narrative considers slavery, the Black Codes, Jim Crow, and the Civil Rights Movement not simply in terms of their occurrence or their vestiges, but as objects that create a modern-day affect. In her construction of this history of slavery and racism, she insists on acknowledging slavery and racism's continuing influence on racial justice issues.

In her dissent, Justice Ginsburg, joined by Justices Breyer, Sotomayor, and Kagan, begins by articulating the twofold congressional purpose behind the legislative body's most recent reauthorization of the controversial measures of the VRA: "First, continuance would facilitate completion of the impressive gains thus far made; and second, continuance would guard against backsliding."[56] In contrast to Roberts's conception of the VRA as a backward-looking, compensatory, remedial statute geared toward specific and particularized past abuses, Ginsburg frames the VRA as a backward- *and* forward-looking statute. It is remedial *and* preventative in its ability to enforce the substantive protection of the voting rights granted in the Fifteenth Amendment. Understood in this light, the purpose of the VRA becomes (1) to stamp out the vestiges of slavery and Jim Crow racism, *and* (2) to address racism as a present problem in American politics.

Like Roberts's majority opinion, Ginsburg also draws lessons from the history of the Civil Rights Movement for support, calling on the legacy of Martin Luther King, Jr., the need for a longstanding commitment to civil rights progress:

> Alabama is home to Selma, site of "Bloody Sunday" beatings of civil rights demonstrators that served as the catalyst for the VRA's enactment.

> Following those events, Martin Luther King, Jr., led a march from Selma to Montgomery, Alabama's capital, where he called for passage of the VRA. If the Act passed, he foresaw, progress could be made even in Alabama, but there had to be a steadfast national commitment to see the task through to completion.[57]

However, Ginsburg's use of the Civil Rights Movement is markedly different from the majority's use of similar incidents. Whereas the majority imports the Civil Rights Movement to showcase a problem–solution model, the dissent's use of it emphasizes that the individual, isolated instances of the movement created an enduring commitment—a struggle. Ginsburg uses the Civil Rights Movement to argue that these instances of resistance should be understood not as discrete moments of reaction to specific occasions of oppression, but as indicators of a culture collectively committing to racial justice and equality.

Next, unlike the majority, Ginsburg's dissent tackles head-on what Ricoeur calls the first phase of active engagement with history, the documentary phase:

> Congress approached the 2006 reauthorization of the VRA with great care and seriousness. The same cannot be said of the Court's opinion today. The Court makes no genuine attempt to engage with the massive legislative record that Congress assembled. Instead, it relies on increases in voter registration and turnout as if that were the whole story.[58]

Her dissent recounts the "21 hearings" Congress held, in which it heard testimony from "scores of witnesses, received a number of investigative reports, and other written documentation of continuing discrimination in covered jurisdictions," culminating in a legislative record of "more than 15,000 pages."[59] Using details from this documentary evidence, Ginsburg constructs a historical narrative that, while acknowledging the impressive strides and improvements made in the South, including in Alabama specifically, denotes the still deeply entrenched problem of voter discrimination in the covered jurisdictions.

Part of her ability to weave a historical narrative about the South's history of voter discrimination is that unlike the majority, which looks at whether current conditions resolved past problems, such as voter registration and turnout, Ginsburg evolves the definition of voter discrimination to include first-generation barriers and second-generation barriers. The former include the kind of blatant voter discrimination laws that the majority opinion uses as its metric. The latter include more subtle attempts to block minority access to the ballot, such as racial gerrymandering or the "adoption of a system of at-large voting in lieu of district-by-district voting in a city with a sizable black minority."[60] This substantive understanding of voter discrimination allows Ginsburg to construct a narrative that is open-ended in the sense that it avoids the teleology accomplished by Roberts's redemption narrative.

When Ricoeur discusses forgetting and manipulated memory, he acknowledges the inherent weakness in the work of narrative configuration. He writes, "[Because] the narrative necessarily contains a selective dimension … one can always recount differently, by eliminating, by shifting the emphasis, by recasting the protagonists of the action in a different light along with the outlines of the action."[61] Ginsburg admonishes the majority for just such a narrative reconfiguration, noting:

> The sad irony of today's decision lies in its utter failure to grasp why the VRA has proven effective. The Court appears to believe that the VRA's success in eliminating the specific devices extant in 1965 means that preclearance is no longer needed. … With that belief, and the argument derived from it, history repeats itself.[62]

While Ricoeur notes that there is a positive aspect of forgetting that can lead to forgiveness and transcendence, compelled or manipulated forgetting may not afford the same transcendent benefit. The treatments of memory, history, and forgetting expose the core disagreements between Roberts's and Ginsburg's opinions: whether the fight for racial justice is limited to alleviating the vestiges of slavery and Jim Crow *or* includes investigations into present structures and systems, as well as the role that the federal government should play in supporting or administering that fight.

The awareness of memory as malleable and as a source of political contestation has serious implications for the practice of constructing memory and historical narrative in judicial discourse. A Ricoeurian reading of *Shelby* demonstrates the narrative power of language to affect patterns of judicial discourse and precedent that shape the production of memory and forgetting on an institutional level.

## Notes

1 Ricoeur, Paul, *Memory, History, Forgetting*, trans. Kathleen Blamey and David Pellauer (Chicago: University of Chicago Press, 2004), 121.
2 Assman, Aleida, and Linda Short, eds., *Memory and Political Change* (New York: Palgrave MacMillan, 2012).
3 Halbwachs, Maurice, *Les cadres sociaux de la mémoire* (Paris: F. Alcan, 1925).
4 Sarat, Austin and Thomas R. Kearns, eds., *History, Memory, and the Law* (Ann Arbor: University of Michigan Press, 2002), 12.
5 Sarat and Kearns, *History, Memory, and the Law*, 17–18.
6 Ricoeur, Paul, *Memory, History, Forgetting*, trans. Kathleen Blamey and David Pellauer (Chicago: University of Chicago Press, 2004).
7 570 U.S. 529 (2013).
8 383 U.S. 301 (1966).
9 Ricoeur, *Memory*, xvi.
10 Ibid., 120.
11 Ibid.
12 Ibid., 136. Ricoeur attributes his adoption of the phrase "historiographical operation" for his epistemological analysis of history as well as his triadic structural framework of the operation to the work of Michel de Certeau. See Michel de

Certeau, "L'opération historique," in *Faire de l'histoire* (Jacques Le Goff and Pierre Nora, eds., 3 vols. Paris: Gallimard, 1974), partially translated as *Constructing the Past: Essays in Historical Methodology* (New York: Cambridge University Press, 1984). In this essay, Certeau proposes the expression "historic operation." See also, Michel de Certeau, *The Writing of History* (trans. Tom Conley, New York: Columbia University Press, 1988). In this longer work, Certeau adopts the phrase "historiographical operation."

13 Ricoeur, *Memory*, 182–233.

14 Ibid., 238–48.

15 Ibid., 238.

16 Ibid.

17 White, Hayden, *Metahistory: The Historical Imagination in Nineteenth-Century Europe* (Baltimore: Johns Hopkins University Press, 1973), 5–10.

18 Ricoeur, *Memory*, 252.

19 Ricoeur, *Memory*, xvi. "[B]uried under the footprints of memory and history then opens the empire of forgetting, an empire divided against itself, torn between the threat of the definitive effacement of traces and the assurance that the resources of anamnesis are placed in reserve."

20 *Northwest Austin Municipal Utility District No. 1 v. Holder*, 557 U.S. 193 (2009).

21 U.S. Const. amend. XV.

22 The Voting Rights Act, Voting Rights Act of 1965, Pub. L. No. 89-110, 79 Stat. 437 (1965) (codified as amended at 42 U.S.C. §§ 1971, 1973 to 1973bb-l (2006)); 52 U.S.C. § 10101, et seq.; 52 U.S.C. § 10301 et seq.; 52 U.S. C. § 10501 et seq. (formerly cited as §§ 42 U.S.C. 1973).

23 Georgia v. Ashcroft, 539 U.S. 461, 490 (2003).

24 *South Carolina v. Katzenbach*, 383 U.S. 301 (1966).

25 *Katzenbach*, at 323.

26 *Katzenbach*, at 308.

27 Id.

28 Id., at 315.

29 Ricoeur, Paul, *The Rule of Metaphor: Multi-disciplinary Studies of the Creation of Meaning in Language*, trans. Robert Czerny (University of Toronto Press, 1981).

30 Id., at 334.

31 Here, let me acknowledge that I am using the term "race-memory" to refer to the memory of slavery and the memory of racism in the United States, specifically in the American South. Moreover, my use of the term "racism" is meant in terms of the black/white binary, focusing on the understanding pertinent to the post-Civil War Black Codes, Jim Crow laws, and the Civil Rights Movement.

32 *Katzenbach*, at 327.

33 *See Wygant v. Jackson Bd. of Educ.*, 476 U.S. 267, 279-80 (1986); *Fullilove v. Klutznick*, 448 U.S. 448, 480 (1980); *University of California Regents v. Bakke*, 438 U.S. 265, 301 (1978); and *Swann v. Charlotte-Mecklenburg Bd. of Educ.*, 402 U.S. 1, 26 (1971).

34 The canon of constitutional avoidance is a tool for choosing between competing plausible interpretations of a statutory provision and holds that "Where an alternative interpretation of a statute is fairly possible, courts construe legislation in a manner that avoids serious constitutional problems raised by an otherwise acceptable construction," *Artis v. Dist. of Columbia*, 138 S. Ct. 594, 606 (2018).

35 *Stare decisis* is Latin for "to stand by things decided" and articulates the legal principle of determining questions of law according to previous rulings. Cf. *Kimble v. Marvel Entertainment*, LLC, 135 S. Ct. 2401, 2409 (2015).

36 *Northwest*, at 199.

37 Id., at 224.
38 Id., at 202.
39 Id.
40 Id., at 203.
41 For a discussion on the teleological narrative of slavery to freedom, see e.g. Ariela Gross and Chantal Thomas, "The New Abolitionism, International Law, and the Memory of Slavery," 35 *Law and History Review* 99 (2017) (arguing that the slavery to freedom narrative "undergirds an argument that the debt to slavery has been paid"); and Ariela Gross, "When is the Time of Slavery? The History of Slavery in Contemporary Legal and Political Argument," 96 *California Law Review* 283, 286–94 (2008) (discussing the slavery-to-freedom narrative as presenting slavery as "a prelude to the inevitable unfolding of freedom").
42 *Shelby*, at 534.
43 Id.
44 Id.
45 Id., at 536.
46 Id., at 537–8.
47 Id.
48 Id., at 540.
49 Id., at 542.
50 Id.
51 Id., at 544.
52 Id., at 547.
53 Id.
54 Id.
55 Id.
56 Id., at 559–60 (Ginsburg, J., dissenting).
57 Id., at 581.
58 Id., at 580.
59 Id., at 565.
60 Id., at 563.
61 Ricoeur, *Memory*, 448.
62 *Shelby*, at 592 (Ginsburg, J., dissenting).

Chapter 2.4

# Boilerplate

## Deconstructing the fiction of contract

*Tal Kastner*

Contract, the legal obligation resulting from the parties' agreement,[1] has long been imagined in the United States as an exercise in agency and a manifestation of free will.[2] With the turn toward emancipation in the nineteenth century, contract figured in contrast to slavery. It offered a worldview that idealized self-ownership and voluntary exchange, and it served as a manifestation of freedom.[3] Notwithstanding courts' so-called "objective" approach to contract since the nineteenth century, they continue to invoke the rhetoric of a "meeting of minds" between parties.[4] Judges routinely examine contract terms to ascertain parties' intent,[5] and they summon a master narrative involving parties freely transacting, negotiating terms, and meaningfully agreeing. This traditional paradigm of contract involves "dickered for" or meaningfully considered terms reflecting agency and choice.[6]

The traditional story of contract implicates a number of fictions. These include a validating original moment of agreement involving knowledge and unconstrained choice as well as a delineated context, which enables such agreement. The framework of contract eschews a counter-model—that of "boilerplate," or the non-negotiated fine-print contract language recognized as an attenuated expression of will. A notionally distinct form of contract language, boilerplate also functions as the very medium of contract. Boilerplate thereby demonstrates the tensions inherent in contract as a vehicle of freedom. In addition, although the idea of boilerplate implicitly marks its distinction from the traditional notion of contract terms, boilerplate arguably serves as a paradigm of contractual expression. As such, a view of contract as boilerplate could serve to facilitate experiences of autonomy and choice—the ideals contract imagines.[7]

A brief parable featured in contract case law makes salient the imagined terrain of contract. In a case involving the timing and implications of contractual notice, Judge Pierre Leval presented a story of contractual relations by analogy. This anecdote can also be read as a story about the fictional elements that inform contract in the law.[8]

In *Register.com v. Verio* (2004),[9] the Second Circuit Court of Appeals rejected a firm's claim that it was not bound by terms it received following a similar transaction. Judge Leval's opinion in the case illustrates the dynamic of obligations accruing to a party as a result of notice—or presumed knowledge—and an act of free choice. Telling a tale of contract, the opinion conjures plaintiff, "P," who "maintains a roadside fruit stand displaying bins of apples." It also tells of "defendant D," "a visitor" who "takes an apple and bites into it." The moral of Judge Leval's story is explicit; the opinion explains that D, after seeing a sign that "says 'Apples—50 cents apiece,'" "cannot continue on a daily basis to take apples for free, *knowing full well* that P is offering them only in exchange for 50 cents in compensation."[10] Instead, "such circumstances" involve a choice, specifically, "to take the apple on the known terms of the offer or not to take the apple."[11] Knowledge and agency thereby serve as the lynchpins to the resulting obligation in the tale. At the same time, the fictional backdrop and elements of the parable (including the roadside stand, the apple, the clear terms, two individuals transacting,[12] and the possibility of leaving the apple at the stand) reflect a circumscribed context in which power, constraint, and attenuated communication fail to figure. The roadside stand suggests a level field as a backdrop for an intuitive story of obligation and agency. Indeed, the bite of an apple itself conjures knowledge and free choice in our imagination.

The actual case in *Register.com* involved sophisticated actors, business entities in conflict about, among other things, the binding nature. Yet the fictional parties at the fruit stand figure implicitly as individuals, which in turn suggests the primacy of individual will and the model of unmediated meeting of minds in contract's master narrative. The fruit-stand vignette also recurs in subsequent case law in a way that highlights the limits of this imagined landscape. A district court invoked this same parable to enforce a forum-selection clause in Facebook's terms of service against an individual user (who was thus prevented from suing Facebook in his home state).[13] In contrast to the fruit-stand story, the parties to the case occupied starkly different bargaining positions confronting terms more opaque than "Apples, 50 cents apiece." In fact, terms indicating product and price have been identified as particularly accessible articulations of the parties' desires in a - transaction.[14] As such, these essential terms[15] arguably constitute contract's *special* case or the exception to contract expression, while the Facebook scenario hews closer to the (non-fictional) experience of contract. Given the reality of the fine print, in attempting to invoke the framework suggested in *Register .com*, the district court insisted, "For purposes of this case, suppose that above the bins of apples are signs that say, 'By picking up this apple, you consent to the terms of sales by this fruit stand. For those terms, turn over this sign.'"[16] As the court's instruction suggests, the obscure, non-negotiated standard terms —the so-called "boilerplate" ubiquitous in contract documents—either fail to figure in the fictional story of contract or, when they do, threaten to undermine the coherence of the parable.

Jacques Derrida's work in deconstructive theory illuminates various fictions of contract, including the marginalization of boilerplate. Most fundamentally, perhaps, deconstruction "consist[s] ... in reversing and displacing a conceptual order."[17] This approach of upending a hierarchy invites us to reconsider the place in our thinking of boilerplate, contract's presumptively parasitic form. Doing so also prompts an examination of the presumed context in which contract purportedly operates.

Derrida counters an understanding of expression as representative of a pre-existing originary signified; he suggests instead a process of meaning-making in which "every sign ... presupposes a certain absence."[18] He identifies the possibility of an absent sender—an elusive origin—and/or indeterminate destination as a necessary condition of writing, which for Derrida encompasses all meaning-making. Challenging the presumptive primacy of intentional expression, Derrida points instead to citation, whereby any sign can "break with every given context," as the conceptual standard.[19]

Boilerplate—language designated as standard or reiterated—is thus necessarily unmoored from an identifiable intentioned origin or context of production. As such it epitomizes this possibility of repetition, which Derrida suggests is implicit in all human experience.[20] In addition, he asserts, not only must the mark signify out of context, but context itself (rather than existing as a "determining center") must be understood as contingent and constituted by the expression in question.[21] Boilerplate instantiates this process as well, at times manifesting disparities in power. It thereby calls into question the circumscribed and presumed-level terrain suggested in the fruit-stand scenario.

The etymological origins of the term "boilerplate" further reveal a figure of portability and standardization. Coined in connection with the steam engines of the Industrial Revolution, "boilerplate" referred by the end of the nineteenth century to the syndicated newsprint casts, conveyed from one newspaper to another.[22] Boilerplate's etymological antecedents invoke physically transportable and recontextualized writing,[23] suggesting the disseminative process of meaning-making.[24] By the twentieth century, boilerplate referred figuratively to generic expression, especially the formalized standard language of contract.[25] As suggested by its signification in legal discourse, as well, the concept of boilerplate highlights and challenges the dominant contract narrative.

A Supreme Court opinion that is the first to use the term "boilerplate" in connection with contract illustrates the way boilerplate figures in relation to both the imagined and experienced contract framework. In *National Equipment Rental, Ltd. v. Szukhent* (1964),[26] Justice Hugo Black's dissenting opinion invokes a narrative of contract as an expression of intention and unconstrained agency through fixed, legible signs. Yet the opinion also suggests the way boilerplate complicates this model and challenges the fiction of contract as unequivocal agreement. Addressing whether two farmers in Michigan could be sued in New York for payment on their leased equipment because they agreed to submit to the jurisdiction of courts in New York,[27] the case engages, among other things, the issue of meaningful choice at the heart of contract. While the majority of the Court found jurisdiction to have been established, the decision rested on the ultimate delivery to the farmers of service of process by a New York resident designated in the terms of the contract as their agent.[28] The majority opinion implicitly treated contract as a vehicle for the realization of actual intentions and it this view that Justice Black's dissenting opinion pointedly explores.[29]

Justice Black's dissenting opinion marshals a stark distinction between "genuine agreement" and its ostensible "weak" counterpart—a bright line that boilerplate ultimately blurs. His dissenting opinion rejects the validity of the contractual appointment of an agent for service of process to establish jurisdiction of a distant court over the parties. In doing so, Justice Black's dissent tells a story of inequity at odds with contract. It highlights deviations from the notional paradigm of contract in the company's "standard printed form obviously prepared by [its] New York lawyers."[30] Among other things,[31] Justice Black's dissenting opinion asserts that it "def[ies] common sense" to treat this case, involving one party which "at its leisure and drawing upon expert legal advice, drafts a form contract" as "an agreement coolly negotiated and hammered out by equals."[32] Indeed, he doubts the likelihood "that these Michigan farmers ... were in any position to dicker over what terms went into the contract they signed."[33] As such, Justice Black views the "printed form provision buried in a multitude of words" as "too weak an imitation of a genuine agreement" to serve as an effective waiver of the right to be tried in one's home state.[34] Instead, he argues, such a waiver "must be deliberately and understandingly made and can be established only by clear, unequivocal, and unambiguous language."[35] Dismissing the claim that the farmers read or could understand the implications of the provision, he asserts, "The idea that there was a knowing consent of [these individuals] to be sued in the courts of New York is no more than a fiction—not even an amiable one at that."[36]

One might be inclined toward Justice Black's reading of the inequities in this case and his characterization of a fiction of consent. At the same time, deconstruction complicates his account of the actualization of "genuine agreement" and the paradigm of the "clear, unequivocal, unambiguous language" of contractual waivers. As Derrida suggests, the production of meaning through signs inherently involves a rupture that is "inscribed in the structure of the mark."[37] Thus, as a condition of possibility of meaning, "intention ... will strive or tend in vain to actualize or fulfill itself, for it cannot, by virtue of its very structure, ever achieve this goal."[38] Thus, even a speech act communicating "genuine agreement" necessarily manifests a "re-move,"[39] or attenuation enabling re-contextualization and standardization.

Indeed, Justice Black offers a warning that disturbs the distinction he invokes between a fiction of consent and genuine agreement undergirding his story of contract. He asserts that, as a result of the Court's holding, clauses such as the one being considered "will soon find their way into the 'boilerplate' of everything."[40] Thus, "boilerplate" complicates the categories on which Justice Black attempts to rely. Boilerplate figures as both the very medium of contract as well as a parasitic imitation of a paradigm of agreement—and this very paradigm of contract, Justice Black's opinion suggests, might already itself be a fiction. Justice Black acknowledges the pervasiveness of form language as well as the potential for regularized terms—"the 'boilerplate' of everything"—to proliferate and echo previous iterations in a new context.

Legal scholars have noted this proliferation, arguably heightened in the electronic age.[41] Non-negotiable fine-print terms are all but inescapable in American life if one uses a credit card or surfs the Internet, to name just a couple of hard-to-avoid acts. Rather than manifesting the understanding of both parties, these transaction documents—overwhelmingly consisting of non-negotiable form language—reflect the asymmetrical relation of power between an individual and a repeat-player drafting firm. Even beyond consumer contracts, in transactions in which both parties are represented by lawyers,[42] agency and subjectivity are necessarily attenuated. Documented terms typically originate in a pre-existing template, parts of which may or may not be specifically negotiated.[43] As such, the dominant paradigm of salient or "dickered" terms reflecting "genuine agreement" serves as an imagined paradigm rather than an actuality of the practice of contract.

A collective view of language considered boilerplate reveals the expressive range of "form language":[44]

As I note elsewhere,[45]

> among other things, boilerplate has been characterized as standardized and customizable;[46] clear and obscure, depending on the reader;[47] opaque to all, but valuable as familiar;[48] context-specific,[49] and portable, thus context-independent.[50] So called "standard" terms signal and perform meaning in various ways, beyond, and at times in contrast with the words' "plain meaning,"[51] screening meaning, manifesting fairness or instantiating a deal.[52]

Notwithstanding the expressive range of so-called boilerplate terms and the fact that courts treat form language as presumptively enforceable,[53] "dickered for" or negotiated language functions as privileged evidence of intent.[54] A bankruptcy case following the 2008 financial crisis demonstrates the way the category of "negotiated language" is itself subject to contextual reframing. By telling two stories about contract terms as negotiated or standard, the case illustrates how contract expression constitutes its context and vice versa. As such, it reveals the fiction of a particularly bounded contract landscape.

The case involved an account established by Lehman Brothers at the Bank of America (BOA) only weeks before Lehman Brothers' 2008 market-shaking collapse. When Lehman Brothers failed, BOA seized the account, claiming a right to set off debt as per the agreement between the parties. Seeking "to determine the intention of the parties as derived from the language employed,"[55] the court considered whether the right to set off debt under New York law[56] had been established by the agreement. Specifically, it examined a common provision preserving "all rights ... given to the Bank by virtue of any ... law."[57] Challenging the conventional view of this provision as a "catch all," BOA presented the provision as a negotiated term. In this way the bank sought to underscore the provision's role as a reflection of the parties' considered intent to preserve the right to offset debt. Moreover, BOA offered evidence of the term's negotiation, pointing to an evolution of exchanged drafts containing, and later removing, and thereafter reinserting this provision. Ultimately, the court rejected BOA's framing of the deal and the provision, drawing a different contextual boundary as informed by (and informing) its view of the term. The court noted that this term was part of BOA's—and likely other banks'—standard forms.[58] Thus, the court characterized the provision as "boilerplate" and found it did not express intent to establish an account subject to such rights.[59]

The court's acknowledgement of a stressful negotiating context and the lack of a record of explicit discussion of the issue at hand[60] underscores the attenuation of intent inherent in a contractual process. In no transaction can every possibility be anticipated and articulated. Similarly, the question of characterizing terms as negotiated or boilerplate—and the possibility the case suggests of terms operating as both standard and negotiated terms—illustrate the contingency and dynamism of contractual relations, and of the language that manifests them. As this case suggests, the designation of certain terms as standard form implicates a particular contestable contractual context. In this way, boilerplate makes salient the imagined contractual landscape.

In reality, contract serves as a necessary fiction of agreement to facilitate transaction and exchange. Courts routinely enforce so-called standard terms, both in sophisticated party transactions and in situations in which a distinctly more powerful party offers a "take-it-or-leave-it" deal to a less powerful one. Courts invoke the rhetoric of traditional contracts, and cite notice[61] and formal signs of assent. In doing so, they enforce terms that implicate significant rights, such as access to a court or recourse from harm, even as these terms remain nearly impossible for only one party to assess.[62] As a result, the process of ceding fundamental rights has become normalized as a function of agreement, perhaps as Justice Black feared.

A deconstructive lens not only highlights the fictions inherent in the prevailing notion of contract, but it also implicitly recognizes the cultural significance, the dominance, of this influential fiction. Specifically, the rhetoric of case law gestures toward meaningful agency—knowledge and choice in a level landscape with salient equitable terms. A recognition of boilerplate as the framework of contract calls attention to the imagined landscape in which contract happens. In doing so it points to the limits in reality that can compromise the goal of meaningful choice. In some contexts, courts implicitly recognize the limits of the posited landscape with an eye to fairness, as demonstrated by the bankruptcy court's rejection of an idiosyncratic meaning of a negotiated term that impacted other creditors beyond the deal.[63] Yet, with respect to consumer contracts, in which transactions parties inhabit markedly asymmetrical relations of power, courts tend to point to contract as an indication of free choice and intent, situated in an imagined landscape of salient signs.

A view of contract as a weak form of boilerplate—rather than boilerplate as contract's weak imitation—suggests a way to further, if never absolutely achieve, the goals of contract. An acknowledgement of the limits of contract, and also of the significance of the fiction as aspiration, paradoxically creates the possibility to address unjust structural challenges to meaningful agency or agreement. It opens the possibility of reframing a limitation of waivers of rights or other oppressive terms as a means of furthering (rather than hindering) the aspiration to autonomy and choice.

In reality, the absolute realization of the goals of freedom, agency, and agreement may be elusive or impossible. A view of contract through the framework of boilerplate might enable the possibility of mitigating the injustice of contract as unamiable fiction.

## Notes

1 The Uniform Commercial Code (UCC), for example, defines contract as "the total legal obligation that results from the parties' agreement as determined by the Uniform Commercial Code as supplemented by any other applicable laws." *Uniform Commercial Code* (2013), § 1-201(12).
2 See Amy Dru Stanley, *From Bondage to Contract* (Cambridge: Cambridge University Press, 1998).
3 Ibid., x. Cf. Tal Kastner, "The Persisting Ideal of Agreement in an Age of Boilerplate," *Law and Social Inquiry* 35 (2010), 793–823.
4 See *May v. Wilcox*, 182 A.D.2d 939, 939-40 (N.Y. App. Div. 3d Dep't 1992)
5 See e.g. *In re Lehman Bros. Holdings Inc.*, 439 B.R. 811, 825 (Bankr. S.D.N.Y. 2010).
6 Whereas the court in *ConocoPhillips Alaska, Inc. v. Williams Alaska Petroleum, Inc.*, 322 P.3d 114, 129 (Alaska 2014) ultimately equated "dickered-for terms" with those deemed "sufficiently important," in *Bowen v. Young*, 507 S.W.2d 600, 605 (Tex. Civ. App 1974), the court granted "'dickered' aspects of the individual bargain," which go "so clearly to the essence of the bargain," the power to override words of disclaimer in a purchase agreement.
7 Aspects of this chapter have been developed in Tal Kastner, "Form Contract," in Simon Stern, Maksymillian Del Mar, and Bernadette Meyler, eds, *Oxford Handbook of Law and Humanities* (Oxford, 2020).
8 Discussion of this case draws in part on Tal Kastner, "How 'Bout Them Apples?: The Power of Stories of Agreement in Consumer Contracts," *Drexel Law Review* 7 (2014), 67.
9 *Register.com, Inc. v. Verio, Inc.*, 356 F.3d 393 (2d Cir. 2004).
10 Ibid., 401 (emphasis added).
11 Ibid., 404.

12 As "D" "bites into" an apple, the analogy suggests at least one human actor, who by implication conjures a parallel individual seller in "P."
13 See *Fteja v. Facebook, Inc.*, 841 F. Supp. 2d 829 (S.D.N.Y. 2012).
14 See Steven J. Burton and Eric G. Andersen, "The World of a Contract," *Iowa Law Review* 75 (1990), 873.
15 See *Bowen v. Young*, 605.
16 *Fteja*, 839.
17 Jacques Derrida. *Limited Inc*, Gerald Graff ed. (Evanston: Northwestern University Press, 1988), 21.
18 Ibid., 7.
19 Ibid., 12.
20 Ibid., 9–10, 12.
21 See ibid., 18.
22 Carol Bast, "A Short History of Boilerplate," *Scribes Journal of Legal Writing* 5 (1994–1995), 155; Tina I. Stark, *Negotiating and Drafting Contract Boilerplate* (New York: ALM Publishing, 2003), 9.
23 As Derrida explains, "writing can and must be able to function in the radical absence of the sender, the receiver and the context of production." Derrida, *Limited Inc*, 8.
24 See J. Hillis Miller, *Speech Acts in Literature* (Stanford: Stanford University Press, 2001), 67–68, 83 (discussing Derrida's *Limited Inc*).
25 Bast, "Short History," 155.
26 *National Equipment Rental, Ltd. v. Szukhent*, 375 U.S. 311 (1964).
27 Ibid., 313.
28 Ibid., 314.
29 The majority opinion penned by Justice Potter Stewart quotes the relevant paragraph of the lease to discuss its purpose and the parties' intent, thereby engaging the language of the document as a reflection of the original will of the parties. Ibid., 316. He underscores the significance of the parties' notification, and thus the document's role as an indication of will and reflection of agency by noting the proximity of the farmers' signatures to the relevant provision. Ibid., 313. Justice William J. Brennan's dissenting opinion similarly taps into this vision of contract as a reflection of meaningful consent, seeking evidence of "knowin[g] and intelligen[t] consent." Ibid., 334.
30 Ibid., 319.
31 Justice Black argued that the Court ought to defer to New York State law on the question of agency, and if not, the standard it formulates should reject a "sham" appointment, as he views the one in this case. Ibid., 323.
32 Ibid., 326.
33 Ibid.
34 Ibid., 332.
35 Ibid.
36 Ibid., 333. For Justice Black, this "strains" and "exhausts credulity." Ibid., 332–3.
37 Derrida, *Limited Inc*, 8, 48.
38 Ibid., 56.
39 Ibid.
40 *National Equipment Rental*, 328.
41 See Omri Ben-Shahar, "Preface: Or: A Boilerplate Introduction," in *Boilerplate: The Foundation of Market Contracts*, ed. O. Ben-Shahar (Cambridge: Cambridge University Press), ix–xiv; Margaret Jane Radin, *Boilerplate: The Fine Print, Vanishing Rights, and the Rule of Law* (Princeton: Princeton University Press, 2012); Cheryl B. Preston and Eli W. McCann, "Unwrapping Shrinkwraps, Clickwraps, and

Browsewraps: How the Law Went Wrong from Horse Traders to the Law of the Horse," *Brigham Young University Journal of Public Law* 26, No. 1 (2012), 1–35; Nancy S. Kim, "Situational Duress and the Aberrance of Electronic Contracts," *Chicago-Kent Law Review* 89, No. 1 (2014), 265, 274–5.

42 The presence of lawyers and the nature of a corporate entity underscore the attenuation of subjectivity.

43 Russell A. Hakes, "Focusing on the Realities of the Contracting Process—An Essential Step to Achieve Justice in Contract Enforcement," *Delaware Law Review* 12 (2011), 103.

44 I discuss the range of significations of boilerplate in Tal Kastner, "Form Contract," in *Oxford Handbook of Law and Humanities* (forthcoming); Tal Kastner, "The Persisting Ideal of Agreement in an Age of Boilerplate," *Law and Social Inquiry* 35 (2010), 804–6 from which these findings and citations derive.

45 See Tal Kastner, "The Persisting Ideal of Agreement in an Age of Boilerplate," *Law and Social Inquiry* 35 (2010), 804–6.

46 See Margaret Jane Radin, "Boilerplate Today: The Rise of Modularity and the Waning of Consent," in *Boilerplate: The Foundation of Market Contracts*, 190.

47 See Michelle E. Boardman, "Contra Proferentem: The Allure of Ambiguous Boilerplate," in *Boilerplate: The Foundation of Market Contracts*, 176.

48 See Stephen J. Choi and G. Mitu Gulati, "*Contract as Statute*," *Michigan Law Review* 104, No. 5 (2006), 1152 n.83, 1160; Marcel Kahan and Michael Klausner, "Standardization and Innovation in Corporate Contracting (or 'The Economics of Boilerplate')," *Virginia Law Review* 83 (1997), 721 n.16.

49 Todd D. Rakoff, "The Law and Sociology of Boilerplate," in *Boilerplate: The Foundation of Market Contracts*, 200–10.

50 See Henry E. Smith, "Modularity in Contracts: Boilerplate and Information Flow," in *Boilerplate: The Foundation of Market Contracts*, 164.

51 See e.g. Mark C. Suchman, "The Contract as Social Artifact," *Law and Society Review* 37, No. 1 (2003), 111–2; Robert B. Ahdieh, "The Strategy of Boilerplate," *Michigan Law Review* 104, No. 5 (2006), 1033–73; David Gilo and Ariel Porat, "The Unconventional Uses of Transaction Costs," *Michigan Law Review* 104, No. 5 (2006), 983–1030; Anna Gelpern and Mitu Gulati, "Public Symbol in Private Contract: A Case Study," *Washington University Law Quarterly* 84 (2006), 1627–715.

52 Gilo and Porat, "Unconventional Uses," 983–1030.

53 *Graham v. Scissor-Tail*, 623 P.2d 165 (Cal. 1981).

54 In *In re Bremen v. Zapata*, 407 U.S. 1, 14 (1972), for example, the Supreme Court enforced a forum-selection provision in a transaction between sophisticated actors precisely because it was "unrealistic" to imagine that the term did not "figure[] prominently in [the parties'] calculations" in their negotiations. Moreover, the opinion contrasts the negotiated term with "boilerplate," stating "this was not simply a form contract with boilerplate language that [the party] had no power to alter." Ibid., 14 n.14.

55 *In re Lehman Bros. Holdings Inc.*, 825.

56 By claiming its right to set off, BOA sought to establish a claim to these funds superior to those of other Lehman creditors.

57 Ibid., 818.

58 Ibid., 827 n.18.

59 Ibid., 827–8.

60 Ibid., 815–6.

61 Such notice may be "constructive," an acknowledgement that it need not be experienced. See e.g. *Major v. McCallister*, 302 S.W.3d 227, 229 (Mo. Ct. App. 2009).

62 Tess Wilkinson-Ryan aptly characterizes fine-print disclosures as "functionally unreadable (or at least indigestible) for consumers with bounded cognitive capacity —i.e., everyone." Tess Wilkinson-Ryan, "A Psychological Account of Consent to Fine Print," *Iowa Law Review* 99, No. 4 (2014), 1749.

63 *In re Lehman Bros. Holdings Inc.*

# Part 3

# A matter of evidence?

## Fact and fiction in the courtroom

# Chapter 3.1

# Dying declarations

*Peter Brooks*

The grim case of *Chavez v. Martinez* turns on a late-night shooting in Oxnard, California, in which Oliverio Martinez was badly wounded by gunshot from police officer Peña; he would be left blind and quadriplegic.[1] Taken to the ER, he was interrogated relentlessly by Officer Chavez as he slipped in and out of consciousness and medics attempted to minister to his wounds. Later, he sued Chavez, but did not win. A deeply divided Supreme Court rejected his Fifth and Fourteenth Amendment claims that his interrogation was coercive on the grounds that his admissions in the ER were never used against him in a court of law. He was never tried. This set off a debate between Justices Thomas and Scalia on the one hand, and Stevens and Kennedy on the other, as to whether *Miranda v. Arizona* bans only coerced confessions used against a defendant in court—or reaches further, to ban brutal police behavior. Stevens in particular cites passages from the audio recording of the interrogation to make his point; just a short excerpt:

*O. M.* : I don't want to say anything anymore.
*Chavez:* No?
*O. M.* : I want them to treat me, it hurts a lot, please.
*Chavez:* You don't want to tell [sic] what happened with you over there?
*O. M.* : I don't want to die, I don't want to die.
*Chavez:* Well if you are going to die tell me what happened, and right now you think you are going to die?
*O. M.* : No.
*Chavez:* No, do you think you are going to die?
*O. M.* : Aren't you going to treat me or what?
*Chavez:* Look, think you are going to die, [sic] that's all I want to know, if you think you are going to die? Right now, do you think you are going to die?
*O. M.* : My belly hurts, please treat me.
*Chavez:* Sir?
*O. M.* : If you treat me I tell you everything, if not, no.

*Chavez:* Sir, I want to know if you think you are going to die right now?
*O. M.* : I think so.

(at 786)

And this macabre exchange goes on and on. But in his insistence that Martinez tell his story if he is about to die—indeed, *because* he is going to die—Officer Chavez represents a venerable legal doctrine as well as a long literary tradition. Justice Kennedy calls Chavez's continued interrogation of Martinez in his agony "torture," but he concedes that the pain of the dying witness may not necessarily preclude his wanting to speak. His fear of death may indeed constitute a motive to speak. Kennedy continues:

> The words of a declarant who believes his death is imminent have a special status in the law of evidence. See, *e. g., Mattox* v. *United States,* 146 U. S. 140, 152 (1892) ("The admission of the testimony is justified upon the ground of necessity, and in view of the consideration that the certain expectation of almost immediate death will remove all temptation to falsehood, and enforce as strict adherence to the truth as the obligation of an oath could impose"); see also Fed. Rule Evid. 804(b)(2) (providing an exception from the hearsay rule for certain statements uttered under belief of impending death). A declarant in Martinez's circumstances may want to tell his story even if it increases his pain and agony to do so. The Constitution does not forbid the police from offering a person an opportunity to volunteer evidence he wishes to reveal.
>
> (at 797)

Kennedy may remind us of the dying Hamlet, and his urgent request to Horatio:

> Absent thee from felicity awhile,
> And in this harsh world draw thy breath in pain
> To tell my story.
>
> (V, ii, 347–9)

But such does not appear to be Oliverio Martinez's concern at this moment.

In law, then, the blanket rule against hearsay evidence—the acceptance in court of sworn testimony only, subject to confrontation of one's witness—finds an exception in the ancient doctrine of dying declarations, which according to *McCormick on Evidence* existed long before the rule against hearsay took root in the early 18th century. *Mattox v. U. S.*, the 1892 case cited by Kennedy, itself cites an English case from 1840, *Regina v. Perkins*:

> [T]he deceased received a severe wound from a gun loaded with shot, of which wound he died at five o'clock the next morning. On the evening of

> the day on which he was wounded, he was told by a surgeon that he could not recover, made no reply, but appeared dejected. It was held by all the judges of England that a declaration made by him at that time was receivable in evidence on the trial of a person for killing him as being a declaration *in articulo mortis*. There, the declaration was against the accused, and obviously no more rigorous rule should be applied when it is in his favor. The point is to ascertain the state of the mind at the time the declarations were made. The admission of the testimony is justified upon the ground of necessity, and in view of the consideration that the certain expectation of almost immediate death will remove all temptation to falsehood and enforce as strict adherence to the truth as the obligation of an oath could impose.[2]

In other words, the certainty of impending death will remove any temptation to lie—because, as the Perkins court will further note, of the imminence of eternal damnation if one does. The "dying declarations" doctrine was given a characteristically aphoristic form by Justice Cardozo in 1933: "The patient must have spoken with the consciousness of a swift and certain doom."[3] Cardozo also states, citing an 1860 English case, *Regina v. Peel*: "There must be 'a settled hopeless expectation' ... that death is near at hand, and what is said must have been spoken in the hush of its impending presence" (at 291).

The dying declarations doctrine has fallen into some disrepute, yet as the Federal Rule of Evidence 804(b)(2) cited by Justice Kennedy demonstrates, it still stands as good law. Like the oath, it responds to some sense of a *mysterium tremendum*—to use the evocative term of Rudolph Otto in his book, *The Idea of the Holy*—that prevents falsehood.[4] Faced with imminent death (and all the cases contend it must be imminent, not simply likely or probable), one does not lie. I have long been dubious about what *tremendum* may be left in the oath in a secular age—but at least the lie under oath provides grounds for prosecution for perjury. The dying declaration seems to have a more absolute sort of status—"mystical," Charles McCormick calls it—since the declarant is gone by the time it becomes evidence in a court of law.[5]

The religious dimension of the dying declarations doctrine may be even more evident when we juxtapose it to the "Newgate Biography"—those confessional narratives collected by the Ordinary (the chaplain) of Newgate Prison at the foot of the Tyburn gallows, and published by him in chapbooks costing sixpence that tended to sell quite well, and to bring in a handsome supplement—as much as £200—to his ecclesiastical stipend. The genre continued for about a century, from 1676 to 1772, and offered accounts of some 2,500 hangings. They are pathetic stuff, tales both sensationalistic and moralistic, recounting how ordinary lives could slip gradually, though moral negligence, into crime. Many an idle apprentice, for instance, will end up robbing his master or setting his house afire. They are presented often as first-person accounts. But, of course, they are "as told to"—to this professional biographer who is also a representative of the Church of England.[6] While the

Newgate biographies are considered an exceptionally rich source of information on ordinary lives in seventeenth- and eighteenth-century England, those of us who worry about narrative forms and veracity must harbor some doubts. They may resemble the confessions produced in present-day custodial interrogations, where the words of the suspect-perpetrator are lent to him or her by the police. Though narrated in the first person, they might be characterized as hearsay.

The classical novel generally prefers to have its dying declarations take place at center stage. I have not done a typology of novelistic death scenes, but I have the impression that they range from the sacrificial/Christologic through the Gothic to the Socratic, as in J.-L. David's tableau of the Death of Socrates, where he sits abed exhorting his disciples as he prepares to drink the hemlock. The sacrificial, of course, stands early in the tradition in Clarissa Harlowe's death with the words "Oh death! Where is thy sting!" on her lips. And is worthily continued with Sydney Carton's "It is a far, far better thing that I do, than I have ever done" in Charles Dickens's *Tale of Two Cities.* The best example of the Socratic in the novel (though it is also Gothic) might be the death of Old Goriot in Balzac's *Père Goriot*, a long personal confession and diatribe, a scathing lesson addressed to the entire nineteenth century in which all familial relations have become denatured, so that he declares there shall be "No more marriages!" Marriage is a financial transaction by which fathers are replaced by rapacious sons-in-law, and daughters become whores. Society will perish if fathers are trodden underfoot, Goriot declares; and the repudiation of paternity echoes throughout the *Human Comedy*, where the "law of disorganization" that characterizes contemporary French society can be traced directly to the parricide of 1793, the killing of the father-king Louis XVI on the guillotine. Goriot's death rant is all about a failure in the transmission of wisdom through traditional routes, most often figured as father to child.[7]

One could accumulate versions of the death scene as the passing-on of wisdom from one generation to another in many different registers, from the sentimental to the ironic or even the blasphemous. Dickens in particular wrings illumination from the death bed and its legacies in nearly all his novels. Barkis's "going out with the tide," in *David Copperfield*, is the least talkative but possibly the most effective of his death scenes: Barkis has only to repeat the famous single line that characterizes him, "Barkis is willing," to achieve the effect of transmission on Davy and the Peggottys. Other death scenes are far more elaborate: Magwitch, Little Nell. At times, unbearably maudlin. Though also important, as in Stephen Blackpool's death in *Hard Times:* "I ha' fell into th' pit, my dear, as have cost w'in the knowledge o' old fok now livin', hundreds and hundreds o' men's lives"—an indictment of industrial England somewhat compromised by his hope that the star he has seen from deep in the abandoned mine will lead to an understanding of masters and workers. Then there is the extraordinary twist given to the resolution of death in Wilkie Collins's *The Woman in White* in the chapter called "The Narrative of the Tombstone," which reads: "Sacred to the Memory of Laura, Lady Glyde"—who does not in fact lie under the tombstone, but rather her unfortunate half-sister, Anne Catherick. A couple of hundred more pages will be needed to sort out the true meaning of the deceptive tombstone, and to get the legacies in the novel correctly aligned.

Flaubert, I note, offers us parodies of the Christologic dying declaration in Emma Bovary's suicide, and her encounter at the final moment of her agony with the blind beggar, singer of obscene ballads:

> "The blind man!" she cried out.
>
> And Emma burst into laughter, horrible, frantic, despairing laughter, thinking she saw the hideous face of the poor wretch looming like terror itself in the darkness of eternity.[8]

Flaubert will also parody the Socratic dying declaration in *Sentimental Education*, with the demise of the rapacious capitalist and fixer Dambreuse, who cherished "Power with such love that he would have paid to be able to sell himself." Here, as in so many nineteenth- and early twentieth-century novels, what seems to be at stake in moments of ultimate truth and transmission is a legacy larger than a single person. Will the ilk of Dambreuse inherit France? What is the legacy of this historical moment to the future? E. M. Forster in a famous chapter of *Howards End* pursues a mediation, looking down from the Purbeck Hills, on the question: To whom does England belong? Across the Channel, you see a variant in the question thrown up by a revolutionary century: Who shall inherit France? This is the crucial question posed by Julien Sorel's life and death in Stendhal's *The Red and the Black*. The usurpatory career of Julien Sorel—modeled, of course, on Napoleon's—puts into question all the traditional lines of inheritance.

One could go on accumulating examples, in George Eliot, Thomas Hardy, Virginia Woolf, Emile Zola, Marcel Proust (whose entire novel may be a dying declaration)—in all those novelists who, however experimental, feel an attachment to the central moral and political questions of the traditional novel, and who see the novel as engaged in the transmission of wisdom, to reprise the term used by Walter Benjamin in talking about the oral tale. It is because, as Benjamin suggests, the reader of novels is solitary, uncounseled, that the wisdom passed on in the death he or she reads about matters so much. "Death is the flame at which we warm our shivering lives," he writes.[9] We confer on the death scene and the dying declaration an authority because we can never know it in our own lives, since the "meaning of life" can become apparent only retrospectively.

Joseph Conrad dramatizes this very problem over and over, most succinctly and dramatically in *Heart of Darkness*, where Marlow the narrator comes to fix his attention on Kurtz's dying declaration: "The horror! The horror!" Kurtz has appeared to Marlow especially as "a voice" discoursing eloquently of life's meanings. Following Kurtz's death, Marlow comes close to death himself, and discovers: "I was within a hair's breadth of the last opportunity for pronouncement, and I found with humiliation that probably I would have nothing to say." Kurtz had stepped over the edge, "while I had been permitted to draw back my hesitating foot." Marlow goes on to address what seems to me the crucial issue, in literature as in law:

> And perhaps in this is the whole difference; perhaps all the wisdom, and all truth, and all sincerity, are just compressed into that inappreciable moment of time in which we step over the threshold of the invisible. Perhaps! I like to think that my summing-up would not have been a word of careless contempt. Better his cry—much better. It was an affirmation, a moral victory paid for by innumerable defeats, by abominable terrors, by abominable satisfactions.[10]

The passage is a crucible of all our problems with Marlow as narrator: a "word of careless contempt" would seem to be just what "the horror! the horror!" is—yet Marlow insists on seeing it as a moral victory following a life of abomination. Yet Kurtz's affirmation is such that when Marlow later meets Kurtz's Intended and she asks him for her hero's last words, he can only offer her a lie. "I was on the point of crying at her: 'Don't you hear them?'" But instead of repeating the words of horror he hears "like the first whisper of a rising wind," he pulls himself together to offer the conventional dying declaration: "'The last word he pronounced was—your name'" (p. 161) I knew it, she replies, assuring transmission of a lie.

Conrad gives us the theory of the last utterance in the novel he was composing contemporaneously with *Heart of Darkness*, *Lord Jim*, where Marlow meditates:

> And besides, the last word is not said,—probably shall never be said. Are not our lives too short for that full utterance which through all our stammerings is of course our only and abiding intention? I have given up expecting those last words, whose ring, if they could only be pronounced, would shake both heaven and earth. There is never time to say our last word ...[11]

Here I think Conrad offers his justification of the modernist novel with its incomplete, restless endings—as in Henry James, for instance—and gives us a profound critique of the law, which wants to believe in last words to the extent that it still today recognizes an exception to the hearsay rule in "dying declarations."

That seems to me important beyond the one example of dying declarations doctrine: the law is invested in believing in all sorts of words whose ring is supposed to shake heaven and earth. Law speaks from a place of mystified authority from which it can pronounce, in the words that so often conclude Supreme Court opinions: "It is so ordered." Legal adjudication requires finality, of course. But that finality, as Justice Jackson long ago noted, offers an illusion of the authoritative and indeed the infallible that is deceptive.[12] Legal actors become used to assuming that the performative function of their words confers on them the *mysterium* of the dying declaration, the testimony from beyond the grave that cannot, by its very nature, be questioned. How often do we feel that legal speech needs to be more Conradian, to understand that the finality of the judicial word needs to be met with the skepticism of Marlow if not the cynicism of Kurtz.

## Notes

1 *Chavez v. Martinez*, 538 U.S. 760 (2000). This chapter was originally delivered to the annual conference of the Association of Law, Culture, and the Humanities at Georgetown Law Center in March 2018. My thanks to Sarah Raff for organizing the panel in which it figured.
2 *Mattox v. United States*, 146 U.S. 140 (1892), at 152.
3 *Shepard v. US*, 290 U.S. 96 (1933), at 290.
4 See Rudolph Otto, *The Idea of the Holy*, trans. J. W. Harvey (Oxford: Oxford University Press, 1958).
5 Charles T. McCormick, *Law of Evidence* (St. Paul: West Publishing, 1954), §258.
6 See my discussion of these accounts in *Troubline Confessions: Speaking Guilt in Law and Literature* (Chicago: University of Chicago Press, 2000), 159–60.
7 See my Introduction to *Père Goriot*, trans. Henry Reed (New York: Signet Classics, 2004), ix–xvii.
8 Gustave Flaubert, *Madame Bovary*, trans, Lydia Davis (New York: Penguin, 2010), 290.
9 Walter Benjamin, "The Storyteller," in *Illuminations*, trans. Harry Zohn (New York: Schocken 1978), 101.
10 Joseph Conrad, *Heart of Darkness* in *Youth and Two Other Stories* (Garden City: Doubleday Page and Co., 1924), 151.
11 Joseph Conrad, *Lord Jim* (Garden City: Double Page and Co., 1924), 225.
12 See Justice Robert Jackson's famous comment on the Supreme Court: "We are not final because we are infallible, we are infallible because we are final."

Chapter 3.2

# Rap as courtroom reality

*Hans J. Lind*

In *Greene v. Commonwealth*,[1] the Kentucky State Supreme Court considered whether portions of a home-made hip-hop video in which the defendant rapped about murdering his wife were admissible as evidence. Although parts of the video were clearly fictitious (Greene rapped about being in a jail cell, which was obviously not (yet) the case), the video nevertheless matched the killer's *modus operandi*, cutting "her throat from ear to spine so deeply that it scraped the spine".[2] The lyrics provided:

> B— made me mad, and I had to take her life. My name is Dennis Greene and I ain't got no f— wife./I knew I was gonna be givin' it to her when I got home./I cut her mother—in' neck with a sword.

In a similar case, after allegedly killing a man at an Olive Garden restaurant parking lot, Gonzalez Wardlow a.k.a. Snoop wrote: "[H]it 'em in his chest [...] caught 'em dead at da Olive Garden".

This list can easily be continued. In 2009, California resident Alex Medina was charged, based, in part, on rap lyrics composed before and after his arrest ("Never did it for the fame/'cuz that ain't right,/Did it cause I had love for my homies and the life"), and Colorado's Jonair Tyreece Moore was indicted with "conspiracy to distribute crack cocaine and cocaine", using a video recording of Moore rapping as evidence.[3] Both defendants were convicted. In the case of Dennis Greene, the State Supreme Court upheld the conviction, finding that the video referred to Greene's "actions and emotions regarding the crime" and thereby established "premeditation and motive in appellant's own words".[4]

Presumably hundreds of cases have been tried since, using defendant-authored rap lyrics as evidence of character, knowledge, motive or intent, often pertaining to serious matters such as aggravated assault, rape or murder. In a number of cases, the rap lyrics even constituted criminal acts: Olutosin Oduwole was charged with attempted terrorist threats based on a handwritten draft containing rap lyrics, and Blake Jones, who regularly exchanged rap lyrics with his high school friend, was convicted of terroristic threatening in the first degree for a manuscript containing the following lines:

> I'm a motherf— murderer, I slit my mom's throat and killed my sister. You gonna keep being a bitch, and I'm gonna cliche [click], [...]. I'll murder you before you can think twice, cut you up and use you for decoration to look nice.[5]

For prosecutors in particular, rap lyrics seem to be an especially fruitful source of evidence, and unsurprisingly, law enforcement officials are carefully instructed not to overlook this opportunity. The statement "[p]erhaps the most crucial element of a successful prosecution is introducing the jury to the real defendant" is found in a 2004 brochure of the American Prosecutors Research Institute titled *Prosecuting Gang Cases: What Local Prosecutors Need to Know*.[6] The manual continues:

> Through [...] notes, and even music lyrics, prosecutors can invade and exploit the defendant's true personality. Gang investigators should focus on these items of evidence during search warrants and arrests.[7]

Donald Lyddane's "Understanding Gangs and Gang Mentality: Acquiring Evidence of Gang Conspiracy" includes a similar passage:

> In today's society many gang members compose and put their true-life experiences into lyrical form [...] Law enforcement officials must remain mindful of [...] the opportunities to obtain inculpatory evidence in gang-related investigations and cases.[8]

Although convictions were not disputed in the case of Dennis Greene and Gonzales Wardlaw, a number of recent cases have especially aroused discussion, leading to a number of federal or State Supreme Court decisions on the matter. In *Commonwealth v. Steward*, prosecutors decided not to introduce into evidence defendant-authored rap lyrics that the local police had understood as confessions of a murder committed,[9] and in the case of Vonte Skinner, charged with "attempted murder and related charges", a conviction based on defendant-authored rap lyrics was later overturned by the State Supreme Court.[10]

Both defendants and scholars have long argued that, within the courtroom, rap lyrics need to be treated with extreme caution due to their artificial nature and fictional status. In *United States v. Moore*, the defendant stated that rapping was his "art"and that "his provocative lyrics were not literally true, but were meant to draw a response from the crowd".[11] Blake Jones claimed he was "modeling his writing after [rap artist] Eminem"and further stated: "It was a rap and pretty gruesome."[12] Similarly, Antwain Steward had maintained that he was "in the lane of hardcore rap", and that he just wanted to build up his "brand". In *United States v. SB 12 13*, defendant Melvin Colon argued that the rap lyrics used as evidence to show an ongoing gang feud and his gang affiliation were merely "fictional artistic expressions" and "puffery" that should not have been admitted against him, and in *Elonis v. United States*, the Marion B. Brechner First Amendment Project submitted an amicus brief on behalf of Rapper Anthony Douglas Elonis,[13] arguing that his rap lyrics need to be understood as "a recognized form of artistic expression"[14] that uses "invented stories and characters".[15] Along the same lines, scholar Erik Nielson emphasized that rappers were "creating characters, not diaries" and highlights that, in the case of rap lyrics, prosecutors constantly missed the distinction between author and narrator while they "seem to able to grasp that concept with every other art form that uses first person narrative".[16] Such warnings are not without reason. If Henry Louis Gates Jr. is correct in his assessment that rap lyrics are "the new vanguard of American poetry"[17] and consequently should not be excluded from the literary canon, literary theory needs to enter the courts when rap is on trial. What would be required then, as an initial distinction, is not whether the material presented in the lyrics is true, but whether the discourse is factual, taking into account not only that the material used in gangsta rap lyrics often is fictitious, but also that the songs might in fact need to be qualified as fictional discourse.

It is my position that a speech act approach is particularly fruitful when assessing rap lyrics in court, both because it allows the perlocutionary function of rap music (as the utterances ultimate goal) to be taken into account, and, as I will later argue, because it also raises the bar, forcing legal interpreters to further justify their claims of an alleged factuality of the particular lyrics in question.

As explained in Chapter 1 of this volume,[18] the basic assumption of speech act theory is that speaking is "doing", that it consists in performing illocutionary acts, and that its perlocutionary function might differ considerably from the locution's propositional content. From a theoretical perspective, the issue of fictionality is treated in two very distinct ways within speech act theory: either an illocutionary act is said to be only pretended, or an illocutionary act *sui generis* is said to be actively and seriously performed. In the case of rap lyrics used in trials, however, the practical consequences are nevertheless the same: taking rap lyrics at face value as an assertion, or even as a confession, confuses two distinct and incomparable types of discourse – and thus means to commit a categorical error.[19] The latter is particularly problematic for a version of speech act theory that considers fictional discourse as non-assertive, and thus understands fictional illocutions as devoid of truth values.[20]

Furthermore, a performative approach is adequate with regard to rap lyrics, since within rap culture the issue of performance stretches much further than the sole notion of rap lyrics as illocutionary pretense: the complete set of communicative behavior that rap artists employ is of performative nature, from the creation of a stage name to a legend that is also supposed to govern their private lives. Correspondingly, the amicus brief submitted in *Elonis v. United States* compares rap artists to wrestlers that stay in character even after they have left the stage, evoking what Tricia Rose coined "[r]ap's pretense of no pretense": rap artists "act as if they live the life they rap about".[21] Having understood that "gangsta-rap is the most profitable genre", record companies in fact soon began encouraging artists to focus on gangsta-style lyrics.[22] Artists are also well aware that rap is not only a form of art, but a commercial product requiring a certain kind of pretense. After having been acquitted, Antwain Steward commented in an interview on the divergent perlocutionary function of his music as follows: "I just found something that I'm talented at and found a way to make money of it [and] like it or not, gangsta rap is what sells."[23]

While sometimes the question of factuality is not difficult to negate (Rick Ross, for example, contrary to his persona's legend, had a college education and even served as corrections officer),[24] lines can also easily become blurred. Particularly in the case of gangsta rap's creation of a criminal persona, usually accompanied by graphic accounts of violence, audiences can easily overlook that these are genre conventions and begin to "conflate artist with character and fiction with fact".[25] The problem furthermore gains complexity if it is understood that also in rap lyrics, fictionality and literariness are distinct[26] though interdependent factors, inhibiting simplistic factual readings. Additionally, with literariness a recognized feature of rap, intertextual questions will inevitably enter the discussion. The text in rap lyrics is also often servant to form (thus understood only as basic material that needs to be subjected to rhythm and meter, leading to a particular "style" and "flow"). As in literature generally, the propositional content of a work might often be a result of a certain genre chosen and other preceding texts in this tradition, rather than the result of real events in the author's life – an insight the history of literature will inevitably teach any scholar invested in the field.

Rap lyrics prove to be rather typical in this latter aspect. Using the stock characters and stock narratives its genre provides, explicitly quoting, referring to or even contesting other rap lyrics, makes it challenging for an outsider to participate in this literary game as a reader or listener, and this particularity is likely to inhibit understanding or even foster misunderstanding. Umberto Eco once maintained that the reception of any art form requires an intertextual encyclopedia that is consciously or unconsciously activated at every instance of reception, and rap music seems to be a particularly strong example here. That rap draws on the "use of collective consciousness"[27] is not a new insight, and it is not surprising that this insight has already found its way in the amicus brief submitted in *Elonis v. United States.*[28] Being "highly focused on form", the brief explicitly positions rap in a "long tradition of African American storytelling [...] which privileges exaggeration, metaphor, [...] wordplay", "parody", and "pastiche".[29] Characterized by "dense slang" and "coded references", it is not only characterized as requiring "knowledge"of the "complicated conventions" of rap music to be properly understood,[30] but is even said to "defy interpretation at every turn", "with rap's 'rhetorical flexibility' being an essential challenge for interpretation".[31] In a similar fashion, the amicus brief submitted by the American Civil Liberties Union of New Jersey in *State v. Skinner* quotes scholar Andrea Dennis:

> Rap lyrics have their own artistic conventions [...] Rappers tell long, evolved, sometimes abstract stories with catchy and memorable phrases and beats that lend themselves to black sound bite packaging, storing critical fragments in fast paced [...] rhythms [....] For rap's language wizards, all images, sounds, ideas and icons are ripe for recontextualization, pun, mockery and celebration.[32]

Drawing on the notion of playfulness of rap lyrics, rap has long been qualified as part of Postmodernism's literary movements.[33] The notion of rap's literariness, including intertextuality and genre-dependent narratives, is supported by a considerable number of investigations on rap's form and narrative content,[34] with the *African American Review* even devoting a special issue to the topic titled *Hip Hop and the Literary.*[35] For some, rap constitutes "a contemporary stage for the theatre of the powerless", and as "enacted ideological insubordination" it poses a critical voice in form of "jokes and stories",[36] also allowing "young men and women of color to create a poetic universe in which they are masters of their environments".[37] For others, gangsta rap, as a newer sub-form of the genre, is not only a form of expression, but politically and socially performative, constituting "an act of resistance and defiance in a society that seeks to demean a group based on an inalterable trait".[38] At the same time, gangsta rap has proven to be particularly prone to misinterpretation. Having a reduced set of stereotypical characters, topics, and narratives, rap music in general already presents a "unique blend of metaphors, boasts, and narratives deriving from oral and literary traditions of the black community"[39] that might unsettle unacquainted recipients:

> The intention of the narrator of the [rap music] yarn is to tell outrageous stories that stretch and shatter credibility, overblown accounts about characters expressed in superlatives [...] by definition the traditional yarn is always [...] one outrageous lie after another.[40]

Gangsta rap is characterized by an even narrower scope of narratives and characters, actually embracing the stereotype of the "bad black man",[41] and as a typically first-person narrative, performances on- and off-stage are closely interlinked. With the performer's self-portrayal off- and on-stage also following a set of given rules and codes,[42] it readily invites a confusion of fact and fiction, artist and criminal persona. Consequently, it is not surprising that the amicus brief in *State v. Skinner* positioned the defendant's rap lyrics precisely in the latter context:

> Mr. Skinner's lyrics [...] depict a world where violence is so intense and so all-pervasive that it makes the reader hold his or her breath. True to the "boast", the lyrics contain "exaggerated and invented boasts of criminal acts [...] where the narrator is ringmaster of violence [...] The narrator is portrayed as a virtual Angel of Death [...] who will 'have you in front of heaven prayin' to God, body parts displaying the scars". [...] [T]the language Mr. Skinner uses is offensive, outrageous and inappropriate [...] Mr. Skinner's rap lyrics, with their anger, profanity, their misogyny, and their brutal and unremitting violence paint a portrait of a city and of a people seemingly beyond help and without hope. Whether these lyrics represent an assertion of power, an embrace of stigma, or something else, they convey messages of profound public concern.[43]

That said, it is understandable that the lines between fact and fiction can easily become blurred, especially in the case of gangster rap – and here not only by material of factual origin entering fictional discourse, but also by fictional discourse overshadowing the factual world. It has already been stated in secondary literature that in the history of hip-hop, it was not uncommon for both former and present gang members to engage in music; in the case of break-dance and rap's oral competitions even substituting actual violence with represented and thus enacted violence, relocating the fights from the street into the realm of art – which might have served in preventing violence instead of causing it.[44] Examples for the contrary topical movement have also been noted. In the case of Anthony Johnson, accused of murder and allegedly bragging about it in songs, the defendant's attorney declared:

> We're talking about a bunch of guys who think they are hip-hop stars in San Antonio. They're not living the dream – they're living in a dream. They started to believe in their own image [...] when in fact it wasn't (real).[45]

Unfortunately, for a judicial interpretation of rap, such blurring is understood as the rule rather than the exception, with the prosecutors and judges readily assuming that rap lyrics have at least some factual background – either in the life or in the character of the lyrics' author – and therefore can be taken at face value, disregarding the particular illocutionary status of rap as discourse.

For speech act theory, the amalgamation of factual and fictional material often present in rap lyrics is not, in and of itself, a problem, since fictionality is, from the onset, understood as a question of mere form. A speech act is either factual or fictional, depending on its markers[46] or the context it is framed by, and speech acts that are partly fictional and partly factual simply do not exist. At the same time, speech act theory accounts for content of factual origin in fictional speech acts. According to Searle, most fictional utterances actually "contain nonfictional elements".[47] For Searle's understanding of fictional discourse, this is, however, only relevant as a genealogical question: as the question where the "material" is taken from or what "propositional content" the pretended speech act contains. Once part of a pretended illocutionary act, any former non-fictional assertions or references have inevitably lost hitherto existing truth values.

This does not mean that fictional speech acts cannot be used as evidence. That the question of the fictional nature of a speech act is not a quantitative question (depending on the amount of "referentiality" or "factuality" present) but a merely formal one, however, considerably changes the proceeding to be used during a trial. Once qualified as potentially fictional (e.g. by the use of stage names or by other pragmatic framing of the utterance as fictional), a literary critic's process needs to be applied in order to discern whether the propositional content nevertheless represents true events. One could even claim that the illocutionary status in fact heightens the requirements of proof, and that the propositional content of such speech acts is to be treated *prima facie* as non-factual, with the consequence that the alleged factuality of the material has to be meticulously established if courts wish to use such fictional utterances as evidence.

What speech act theory demands depends on how courts permit rap lyrics to be used in trial. As said above, two distinct types of cases usually occur: either rap lyrics are used as evidence in order to establish knowledge, motive or intent, or they are understood as criminal acts themselves (usually qualified as criminal threats). Under speech act theory, whether a rap song constitutes a criminal threat is solely a question of the status of the speech act: if the speech act in itself was serious[48] or only pretended. The question of whether rap lyrics can be used as evidence in order to establish motive and knowledge, or can even be treated as a confession, is more complicated, however, since it involves two subsequent questions: first, whether the song as speech act is a factual or fictional one, and, second, if classified as fictional, whether it nevertheless contains material of factual origin. Speech act theory does not facilitate the task of discerning whether material integrated in a possible artefact (rap songs) has a factual origin. Actually, the contrary is the case; since fictionality is to be regarded as the rule in rap lyrics, the evidentiary requirements are considerably altered, now demanding that factual ties are convincingly established first before such texts can even be taken into account as criminal evidence.

Instructive is the United States Court of Appeals decision in *Elonis v. United States.* The defendant had posted on Facebook:

> Did you know that it is illegal for me to say I want to kill my wife.[...] It's indirect criminal contempt [...] Now it was okay to say for me to say it right then because I was just telling you that it's illegal for me to

> say I want to kill my wife. I'm just letting you know that it is illegal for me to say that. [...] Um, what's interesting is that it's very illegal to say I really, really think someone out there should kill my wife. [...] But not illegal to say with a mortar launcher. Because that's its own sentence. It's an incomplete sentence but it may have nothing to do with the sentence before that. So that's perfectly fine. Perfectly legal. I also found out that it's incredibly illegal, extremely illegal, to go on Facebook and say something like the best place to fire a mortar launcher at her house would be from the cornfield behind it because of easy access to a getaway road and you'd have a clear line of sight through the sun room.[49]

Since the defendant had gone to great lengths to hide the illocutionary status of his utterances, obfuscating a threat as a *prima facie* assertory speech act, the appellate court had to decide whether a "criminal threat" was uttered. In compliance with speech act theory, the court did not bother with phrasal semantics,[50] but instead solely relied on the performative status of the utterance when asking whether a "true"[51] threat was actually made. In order to decide the latter, the court furthermore raised a question which is also manifest both in speech act theory and in fictional theory:[52] whether the performative status of the utterance has to be judged from the recipient's perspective, requiring solely that the victim understood it as an intentional threat, or whether the actual intent of the speaker to perform a threat was necessary.

While in the case of such "true threats" the judicial decisions generally show an adequate consciousness of the linguistic issues at hand, critical scrutiny is often absent in those cases where a potentially or evidently fictional speech act has a propositional content that might contain elements of factual origin: the paradigm case of rap lyrics to be used as evidence of a crime committed, establishing knowledge, intent or motive. As shown, here, courts regularly do not discern at all whether a real or a fictional (assertive) speech act, which might even amount to a confession, was uttered. Due to this common omission, a Supreme Court decision had been tensely awaited, and was celebrated among civil rights activists once it was pronounced: the NJ State Supreme Court opinion in *State v. Skinner*. In its decision, the court seems to exhibit a clear understanding of the issue when deeming defendant-authored rap lyrics inadmissible by stating:

> Fictional forms of inflammatory self-expression such as poems, musical compositions, and other writings about bad acts, wrongful acts, or crimes, are not properly evidential.[53]

The defendant Vonte Skinner was initially convicted of attempted murder, using defendant-authored rap lyrics. Skinner's lyrical persona, called "Threat", shared a number of similarities with the author of these lyrics (notably a tattoo of the word "Threat"), and the lyrics depicted "in graphic detail, using violent metaphors, racial epithets, and profanity, acts of violence that the narrator has committed or anticipates to commit".[54]

Skinner's appeal was backed up by an amicus brief of the American Civil Liberties Union of New Jersey, claiming that Skinner's rap songs constitute "a form of expression, however distasteful, which the constitution tolerates and protects" as laid out in *Street v. New York*.[55] As "expressive conduct" which includes artistic expression such as painting, music, poetry and literature, the lyrics were entitled to protection under the First Amendment to the US Constitution and Art. I, paragraph 6 of the New Jersey constitution, and, by providing "social and political commentary on impoverished black neighborhoods", qualified as "speech on matters of public concern" as defined in *Snyder v. Phelps* – and thus were entitled to an even higher protection than other artistic expressions.[56] In this case, the State Supreme Court declared:

> [W]e detect little probative value to the lyrics whatsoever. The difficulty in identifying probative value in fictional or other forms of artistic self-expressive endeavors is that one cannot presume that, simply because an author has chosen to write about certain topics, he or she has acted in accordance with those views. One would not presume that Bob Marley, who wrote the well-known song "I Shot the Sheriff," actually shot a sheriff, or that Edgar Allan Poe buried a man beneath his floorboards, as depicted in his short story "The Tell-Tale Heart," simply because of their respective artistic endeavors on those subjects. The defendant's lyrics should receive no different treatment. In sum, we reject the proposition that probative evidence about a charged offense can be found in an individual's artistic endeavors absent a strong nexus between specific details of the artistic composition and the circumstances of the offense for which the evidence is being adduced.[57]

Already in *State v. Hanson*, "the proposition that an author's character can be determined by the type of book that he writes" had been strongly contested – in clear contrast to the well-known use of literary evidence already in the paradigm trial against writer Oscar Wilde, where excerpts taken from *The Picture of Dorian Gray* had been used to prove the accused's deviant behavior. The long-awaited, now articulated criterion for admissibility of fictional evidence in *State v. Skinner* – the criterion of a "strong nexus" – at first glance could well fulfill expectations, since it can be read as the requirement to establish a genealogical relationship between facts in the real world and their representation in a fictional speech act, as literary criticism commonly prescribed (and in recent times even more often refutes). However, both the court's argumentation in section III A of the decision and the examples provided in section III B (including a reference to *Greene v. Commonwealth* and *Bryant v. State*) show that a "substantial similarity with the alleged crime" is understood to be sufficient to fulfill the requirement of establishing a "strong nexus" – and would thus allow rap lyrics to be used as evidence even in dubious cases. The latter should, however, not come as a surprise. In *Skinner*, the requirements enumerated above were part of the so-called Cofield test, which is not concerned with questions of fictionality, but, as the court is explicitly aware, was developed to "avoid the over-use of extrinsic evidence of other crimes or wrongs". The Cofield requirement's aim thus is not to discern whether a fictional speech act has a factual background, but to address the fact that "the jury may convict the defendant because he is a 'bad person in general'", which is understood to be "the underlying danger of admitting other-crime [or bad-act]". Since the Cofield test is only designed to exclude factual evidence if such facts have no immediate relation to the crime (but instead need to be considered as unrelated crimes or "bad acts"), the test is neither aimed at nor capable of accounting for the categorical differences between fictional and non-fictional speech acts. Accordingly, in *State v. Skinner*, the rap lyrics in question were not excluded because of their fictional nature. It was in fact considered irrelevant in Skinner's case whether the lyrics were factual or fictional. The only relevant criterion was whether the lyrics had "the capacity" to "poison the jury against a defendant" and therefore needed to be treated equally with "other crimes [or bad acts]" under N.J.R.E. 404(b).

Comparably, in *United States v. Moore*, although the Court of Appeals ruled in favor of the appellant, defendant-authored lyrics were taken at face value as a factual account of events. As in *State v. Skinner*, no particular effort has been made to name or establish criteria for how fictional accounts can be distinguished from factual ones, which, however, should be a prerequisite of determining the probative value of the lyrics in the case tried. That the hermeneutical circle is a vicious one, and especially when the court's fictionality test is solely based on the criterion of a "substantial similarity with the alleged crime" – and thus on the same *adequatio ad rem* relation that the lyrics as evidence are supposed to establish in the first place – should, however, have already provided sufficient grounds for the court to be doubtful in both above cases.

The introductory passage to section III C in the decision in *State v. Skinner*, which comments on the "difficulty of pronouncing a hard and fast rule to govern the admission of rap lyrics", demonstrates that courts are in fact quite aware of some of the issues at stake. That courts often do not sufficiently determine the nature of the respective speech acts might not be due to a naïve understanding of fictionality (only). Practical considerations also play a part – such as the fact that a speech act approach, instead of facilitating the process, rather complicates the matter by raising the evidentiary bar. The problem is furthered by a fact that has recently been addressed by scholars.[58] It has been monitored that not only legal practice engages in problematic readings of rap songs, but that also outside the field of law, a "complicity with legal interpretative violence" existed. Especially regarding rap and R&B songs that participate in what scholars have termed "rape" or "rapey culture", a tendency of the general public to engage in what Eve Kosofsky Sedgwick has called "paranoid readings"[59] has been described. It is in fact argued that "the project of weeding out [rape culture] in cultural products has certain affective elements and epistemic learnings. One of its learnings is a commitment to [...] 'a hermeneutic of suspicion'".[60] From "the weak evidence that connects certain songs to sexual coercion", it has also been concluded that "the terms 'rapey' and 'rape culture' operate as negative fetish concepts", and that a "racialized fetishization" underlies the "disproportionate and more vehement targeting of black performers".[61] Scholars have furthermore directed their attention to the performative nature not only of the songs but also of the discourse criticizing and persecuting such utterances.[62]

Evidently, legal discourse might not be completely immune to such general tendencies, and, as already mentioned above, reasons for a non-critical use of rap lyrics in trials might thus subsist on two very different levels of consciousness. The latter may especially explain legal practice's harsh neglect of insights from other fields such as linguistics,[63] literary theory, media studies, performance studies and sociology. That in *United States v. Wilson* the court simply rejected a scholar's expert witness testimony on the premise that rap lyric interpretation was not a subject "worthy of expert witness testimony"[64] seems to be indexical for a general trend of courts to consciously or unconsciously adjourn the problematic task of determining the specific hermeneutical challenges of rap lyrics interpretation.

## Notes

1 *Greene v. Commonwealth of Kentucky*, No. 2004-SC-000046-MR, Decided: May 18, 2006.
2 Medical testimony, cited ibid.
3 The case led to an appeal (*United States v. Jonair Tyreece Moore*, No. 10-2001, Decided April 06, 2011)
4 *Greene v. Commonwealth*, ibid.
5 *Jones v. State of Arkansas*, No. 01-695, Decided: January 17, 2002.
6 Alan Jackson, *Prosecuting Gang Cases: What Local Prosecutors Need to Know* (Alexandria, VA: American Prosecutors Research Institute, 2004), www.nationalpublicsafetypartnership.org/clearinghouse/Resource/467 (last accessed: 01/08/20).
7 Op. cit., 19.
8 Donald Lyddane, "Understanding Gangs and Gang Mentality: Acquiring Evidence of Gang Conspiracy", *United States Attorney's Bulletin* 2006, 1 (the passage is quoted by: Andrea Dennis, "Poetic (In)Justice? Rap Music Lyrics as Art, Life, and Criminal Evidence", *Columbia Journal of Law and the Arts* 31 (2007), 1).
9 *Commonwealth of Virginia v. Antwain Donte Steward*, No. JA092055-03.
10 *State of New Jersey v. Vonte L. Skinner*, Decided: August 04, 2014.
11 *United States v. Moore*, No. 10-2001, Decided: April 06, 2011.
12 *Jones v. State of Arkansas*, No. 01-695, Decided: January 17, 2002.
13 *Anthony D. Elonis v. United States for America*, *AMICI CURIAE* BRIEF OF THE THOMAS JEFFERSON CENTER FOR THE PROTECTION OF FREE

EXPRESSION, THE MARION B. BRECHNER FIRST AMENDMENT PROJECT, AND THE PENNSYLVANIA CENTER FOR THE FIRST AMENDMENT IN SUPPORT OF THE PETITION FOR A WRIT OF CERTIORARI (No. 13-983), available at: http://firstamendment.jou.ufl.edu/pubs/ElonisAmicusBrief.pdf (last accessed: 05/27/2019).

14 Op. cit., 4.
15 Op. cit., 12.
16 Nielson in an interview on NPR.
17 *Elonis, AMICI CURIAE* BRIEF, 8; see also Brent Wood, "Understanding Rap as Rhetorical Folk-Poetry", *Mosaic* 32, No. 4 (December 1999), 129–46.
18 See supra Chapter 1, Section V.
19 Ibid.
20 On the question of assertion vs. non-assertion: cf. Chapter 1, Section V.
21 Tricia Rose, *The Hip Hop Wars: What We Talk About When We Talk About Hip Hop—and Why It Matters* (New York: Basic Civitas, 2004), cited in the amicus brief on p. 14.
22 Charis Kubrin and Erik Nielson, "Rap on Trial", *Race and Justice* 4 (2014), 190.
23 PBS Newshour, June 29, 2014, transcript available at: www.pbs.org/newshour/show/rap-lyrics-used-evidence-court (last accessed: 02/05/2019).
24 *Elonis, AMICI CURIAE* BRIEF, 15.
25 *Elonis, AMICI CURIAE* BRIEF, 15; Kubrin, "Rap on Trial", 197.
26 Searle is one of the strongest proponents of a clear distinction between fictionality and literariness (John Searle, "The Logical Status of Fictional Discourse", *New Literary History* 6, No. 2 (1975), 320). Although Searle's criterion for fictionality is disputed, the necessity to distinguish fictionality and literariness seems to be majorly accepted – e.g. by Tzvetan Todorov, who claims fictionality is neither a necessary nor a sufficient condition of literature (cf. Beardsley, "Aesthetic Intentions and Fictive Illocutions", 172; see supra Chapter 1 note 3 and 4 and accompanying text).
27 Dennis, "Poetic (In-)Justice", 20.
28 Rap "requires some level of expertise to be fully understood", p. 10 of the brief.
29 *Elonis, AMICI CURIAE* BRIEF, 3.
30 Op. cit., 5, 10.
31 Op. cit., 9.
32 BRIEF OF *AMICUS CURIAE* AMERICAN CIVIL LIBERTIES UNION OF NEW JERSEY IN SUPPORT OF DEFENDANT RESPONDENT, *State of New Jersey v. Vonte L. Skinner*, A-57/58-12 (071764), 8–9.
33 Russell A. Potter. *Spectacular Vernaculars: Hip-Hop and the Politics of Postmodernism* (Albany: State University of New York Press, 1995), 2.
34 Just to name a few: Eithne Quinn, *Nuthin' but a "G" Thang: The Culture and Commerce of Gangsta Rap* (New York: Columbia UP, 2004); Id., "Who's the Mack?: The Performativity and Politics of the Pimp Figure in Gangsta Rap", *Journal of American Studies* 34, No. 1, 115–36; id., *Representing and Affronting: The Politics and Poetics of Gangsta Rap Music* (Keele University [Diss.] 1999); Candice M. Jenkins, "Introduction: 'Reading' Hip-Hop Discourse in the Twenty-First Century", *African American Review* 46, No. 1 (Special issue: *Hip Hop and the Literary*, Spring 2013), 1–8; Denise Herd, "Changing Images of Violence in Rap Music Lyrics: 1979–1997", *Journal of Public Health Policy* 30, No. 4 (December 2009), 395–406; Ralph M. Rosen and Donald R. Marks, "Comedies of Transgression in Gangsta Rap and Ancient Classical Poetry", *New Literary History* 30, No. 4 (Autumn, 1999), 897–928; James Peterson, "'Dead Prezence': Money and Mortal Themes in Hip Hop Culture", *Callaloo* 29, No. 3 (*Hip-Hop Music and Culture*, Summer, 2006), 895–909; Gwen Hunnicutt and Kristy Humble Andrews,

"Tragic Narratives in Popular Culture: Depictions of Homicide in Rap Music", *Sociological Forum* 24, No. 3 (September 2009), 611–30; Mtume ya Salaam, "The Aesthetics of Rap", *African American Review* 29, No. 2, *Special Issue on The Music* (Summer, 1995), 303–15; Greg Dimitriadis, "Hip Hop: From Live Performance to Mediated Narrative", *Popular Music* 15, No. 2 (May 1996), 179–94.

35 *African American Review* 46, No. 1, *Special Issue: Hip Hop and the Literary* (Spring 2013)

36 Rose, loc. cit.

37 Imany Perry, "Prophets of the Hood: Politics and Poetics in Hip-Hop", cited in *Elonis, AMICI CURIAE* BRIEF, 13.

38 Alexander, cited in *Skinner, AMICUS CURIAE* BRIEF, 8

39 *Skinner, AMICUS CURIAE* BRIEF, 8 (now citing Dennis)

40 *Skinner, AMICUS CURIAE* BRIEF, 9.

41 Cf. Begonya Enguix, "Male Bodies and the Black Male Gaze: Is There a Cultural Interpretation of Masculinities?", in: *African Realities: Body, Culture and Social Tensions*, ed. Josep Martí (Newcastle upon Tyne: Cambridge Scholars, 2014), 114.

42 Charis Kubrin, "Gangstas, Thugs, and Hustlas: Identity and the Code of the Street in Rap Music," *Social Problems* 53, No. 3, 360–78.

43 *Skinner, AMICUS CURIAE* BRIEF, 11–15.

44 Rose, op. cit.

45 Kubrin, "Rap on Trial", 193.

46 It is, however, highly disputed whether clear textual markers (or "signposts") for fictionality exist, or whether fictional discourse is a merely pragmatic feature, making it impossible to discern the question of fictionality from the syntactical form or propositional content of an utterance alone. Cf. Dorrit Cohn, "Signposts of Fictionality. A Narratological Perspective." *Poetics Today* 11, No. 4 (Winter 1990), 775–804, as well as supra Chapter 1, note 300.

47 Searle, "Fictional Discourse", 330.

48 For speech act theorists as Searle the label is "serious", not "true" (since only assertions can be true). Courts however treated the matter under the question of truth ("true threat", etc.)

49 *US v. Elonis*, No. 12-3798, Decided: October 28, 2016, at I.

50 On p. 16, the court, however, clearly saw the issues at stake when stating "we read 'statements where the speaker means to communicate a serious expression of an intent to commit an act of unlawful violence' to mean that the speaker must intend to make the communication".

51 As already said (supra note 48), courts usually use the inadequate term "true" in this context, instead of the label "serious" (which would be the correct terminology according to speech act theory). What they, however, correctly investigate, is the issue, whether the utterance in question was meant or had to be understood by the recipient as being "serious" – thus they correctly investigate the illocutionary status of the speech act in question.

52 Cf. supra Chapter 1 note 300 and infra Chapter 5.2 note 163 (and accompanying text).

53 A-5365-14T2 (decided August 04, 2014).

54 *Skinner, AMICUS CURIAE* BRIEF, 5.

55 *Skinner, AMICUS CURIAE* BRIEF, 4.

56 *Skinner, AMICUS CURIAE* BRIEF, 8–9, 11

57 *State v. Skinner*, V.A. at para 9.

58 Cf. Ummni Khan, "An Incitement to Rapey Discourse. Blurred Lines and the Erotics of Protest", in *Synesthetic Legalities: Sensory Dimensions of Law and Jurisprudence*, ed. Sarah Marusek (London/NY: Routledge, 2016), 200–13; id., "Fetishizing Music as

Rape Culture", *Studies in Gender and Sexuality* 18, No. 1, 19–30; Eve Kosofsky Sedgwick and Adam Frank, "Paranoid Reading and Reparative Reading, Or, You're So Paranoid, You Probably Think This Essay Is About You," in *Touching Feeling: Affect, Pedagogy, Performativity* (Durham: Duke UP, 2002).

59 Eve Kosofsky Sedgwick, cited in Khan, "Incitement", 201.

60 Khan, "Incitement", 201–2.

61 Khan, "Fetishizing Music", 19.

62 Khan, "Incitement", 202, 210.

63 Which is inconsistent, since legal theory addressed the field of linguistics early, including speech act theory. Cf. Chapter 1, notes 227, 285–6 and Chapter 5.2 notes 37 and 39 (and accompanying text).

64 Dennis, "Poetic (In-) Justice", 13.

Chapter 3.3

# Fiction as courtroom fact?

## Exploration accounts as evidence in aboriginal rights and title litigation

*Luis Campos*

### I Introduction

In a reversal of Canada's historically problematic treatment of aboriginal peoples, Canadian courts have demonstrated a willingness to consider traditional aboriginal perspectives as meaningful to legal proceedings. The cases concern aboriginal rights and title, a highly contested legal terrain. Inclusion of aboriginal perspectives represents judicial concession to the value of oral histories as evidence in legal proceedings. This chapter will problematize evidentiary narratives in aboriginal rights and title litigation. Rather than addressing traditional aboriginal narratives, which have received significant scholarly attention, this work focuses on the body of texts against which they are measured: the written observations, journals, diaries, and papers of European explorers and traders. This *explorer record* has been both fashioned and then tapped as an authoritative archive, factually demonstrative of the historical relationship of aboriginal peoples to the land and its resources. Canadian courts and litigants have been complicit, willingly acceding to the European narratives as powerful testimony—indeed, as "eyewitness accounts."[1] The law's commitment sharply contrasts with the skepticism for this literature commonly held by scholars working outside of the law.[2]

### II The Canadian jurisprudence

Canada continues to be the home to more than 600 First Nations. And First Nations have vigorously filed numerous legal claims to assert, retain, or recover aboriginal rights and title to land. Aboriginal rights are comprised of traditional cultural activities related to sustenance such as fishing, hunting, and harvesting timber. These should be distinguished from aboriginal title, which concerns ownership of the land itself. The Supreme Court of Canada (SCC) has delineated the substantive tests for proving aboriginal rights and title, and has imposed an onerous evidentiary burden on aboriginal litigants to describe the historical relationship of their ancestors to the land or its resources or both. To prove aboriginal title to land, the seminal *Delgamuukw*[3] case emphasized the necessity of demonstrating the sufficient, continuous, and exclusive occupation by a First Nation claimant prior to the assertion of European sovereignty. By contrast, in aboriginal rights cases the aboriginal activity asserted must have been—at the time of contact—an element of a practice, custom, or tradition integral to the distinctive culture of the aboriginal group asserting the right.[4] The respective legal tests share a common retroactive orientation. Evidence must speak to events from hundreds of years ago and therefore must be *historical* in some sense. They also impose an additional problem for aboriginal litigants: how to satisfy an evidentiary burden by recourse to their oral histories—and without the aid of a written record. Fundamentally, the challenge is to make an ancient form fit a modern, Western legal regime.

The SCC in the *Delgamuukw* and *Van der Peet* cases addressed this evidentiary challenge. The Court mandated the accommodation and more flexible and equitable treatment of aboriginal perspectives in rights and title litigation.[5] The response, however, has proven difficult. The British Columbia Supreme Court (BCSC) reflected on the need for change:

> Courts that have favoured written modes of transmission over oral accounts have been criticized for taking an ethnocentric view of the evidence. ... In order to truly hear the oral history and oral tradition evidence presented in these cases, courts must undergo their own process of decolonization.[6]

The BCSC acknowledged its assumptions about the historical record, saying, "There is always a Eurocentric tendency to look for and rely on the written word. Try as one might, it is difficult to read these words and not see in them events as they really were."[7] Despite the cautionary language, the provincial court considered the extensive explorer record with clear deference, perhaps even reverence:

> Western Canada is a repository of the most complete records of first contact between Europeans and aboriginal peoples anywhere in the world. This record is contained in the detailed journals kept by the Officers and Gentlemen of the HBC. Copies of the relevant journals, where available, form a valuable part of the record of this trial.[8]

The implementation of the SCC's imperative has remained uncertain in the lower courts. Treating the spoken history with the same level of credibility as the written history continues to confound. The SCC did little to clarify the confusion in its 2014 *Tsilhqot'in* decision. The Court held that aboriginal "ancestral practices" should not be forced "into the square boxes of common law concepts."[9] However, and despite the complex relationship between indigenous communities and the land, the SCC resorted to familiar common law narratives: *sufficiency*, *continuity*, and *exclusivity* of occupation are "useful lenses through which to view the question of aboriginal title."[10] As the writings of European explorers tend to conform to these European depictions of land ownership, aboriginal plaintiffs find themselves disadvantaged and forced into the "square boxes" of an acceptable narrative form—at least to the extent that they desire to adduce persuasive evidence. The explorer record beckons to aboriginal plaintiffs.

## III Constructing narratives: Law's alternate universe

The law is incorrigibly possessed of a discourse that idealizes truth. From the fact-finder's (that is, judge or jury) perspective, "getting at the truth is her job,"[11] while witnesses providing testimonial evidence, for example, are obligated to tell "nothing but the truth." In practice, however, the law does not contemplate arriving at absolute truth for successful fact-finding. The law's standard of proof in Canadian civil proceedings, for example, is a more modest *preponderance of the evidence* or *balance of probabilities*, which expresses the notion that legal fact-finding can and should proceed on something less than full factual knowledge. The inference is that partial truth may occasionally suffice as adequate truth.

Law maintains a system of rules to ascertain facts. At trial, fact-finders evaluate (1) the admissibility of evidence and (2) the weight or appreciation of evidence. Determining *admissibility* acts as initial review/acceptance of the evidence for inclusion in the judicial record. Here admitted evidence is understood as *reliably* representing reality, *or* having the potential to do so—to an extent that satisfies minimum legal requirements. If, during the maturation of proceedings, the fact-finder ultimately assigns sufficient weight to the evidence, it may be regarded as compelling enough to influence belief in the factual proposition that it represents.[12] Although one may generally know what evidence has been heard and considered—the record of the proceedings will reveal the evidence (and associated narrative) that was admitted—the weight assigned to specific evidence (or the reasoning for its appreciation) may not always be articulated in the record. Indeed, the factors that influence the weight attributed may also be imperceptible to the fact-finder herself. It is not often that we ask *why* we believe.

Consideration of the explorer record directs us to the concept of *reliability*, a central question of admissibility. Significantly, the question of "reliability is one which bridges the issue of admissibility and weight."[13] Reliability is clearly one of the most important considerations in the assessment of evidence. The term *reliability* escapes easy definition or description, except by reference to the often-quoted *freedom from suspicion*, and, by extension, its connection to the idea of *plausibility*.[14]

The *rule against hearsay* is fundamental to considerations of reliability. This is the best known of the common law's evidentiary exclusionary rules.[15] Frederick Koch refers to hearsay evidence as "any oral or written statement made by a person who did not testify at trial when such a statement is used to prove the truth of any facts asserted in that statements."[16] As an example, the explorer record is hearsay because its authors are unavailable to testify in court[17] *and* their asserted truth, as tendered by litigants, is relevant to a fact at issue. At trial, out-of-court hearsay statements function like formal in-house testimony,[18] except that the declarant is unavailable to the tribunal. The main problem with hearsay and the general need for its prohibition relates to the inability to test the reliability of the statement. If the declarant is unavailable, how can one determine sincerity, memory, perception, as well as narration problems?[19]

Modern evidentiary practice has introduced the concept of a *principled* approach to address hearsay problems. Fact-finders have utilized it extensively in aboriginal rights and title cases to clear a path, at least in theory, for the admission of the ancient aboriginal stories. The principled strategy functions on the notion that "the rules of evidence are not cast in stone nor are they enacted in a vacuum."[20] It eschews formality and favours flexibility, permitting hearsay to be more freely admitted, provided threshold reliability and necessity can be established.[21] It is a common principle in law that reliability can be established if the fact-finder can infer that the statement is free from suspicion. Expert witnesses, like historians, may be called to help establish such trustworthiness. The principled approach has a different starting point: rather than being focused on exclusion, it generally favours inclusion. Precisely within this inclusive space have imperial and colonial writings proliferated, allowing them to flourish in the legal record.

## IV Ahousaht Indian Band and Nation v. Canada

Although the use of the explorer writings as evidence is not uncommon in the proceedings, *Ahousaht Indian Band and Nation v. Canada*[22] is particularly notable for its robust discussion surrounding the explorer record. The litigants introduced a wide range of historical documents, offering readers a veritable archive of early explorer writings from Canada's west coast. We find various journal narratives representing: texts at various stages of completion; conflicting texts or versions of the same account; and distinct classes of authorship, from questing-conquering authors and fur traders, to captive-victim writers and even non-observing editorial interveners. Moreover, the case also illustrated the attraction of explorer records for both the aboriginal plaintiff, who relied on explorer and trader journals to frame and sustain a viable claim, and defendants, who turned to many of the same explorers to refute the plaintiff's claims.

The plaintiffs were five aboriginal bands whose territories are on the west coast of Vancouver Island. Among their claims, the plaintiffs asserted an aboriginal right to fish on a commercial basis, a position refuted by governmental authorities. Aboriginal parties claimed that Canada Fisheries' statutory and policy regimes unjustifiably infringed their right to catch and sell fish, severely limiting their harvesting opportunities, particularly on a commercial level. As a rights claim, Plaintiffs understood the need to prove that at 1774, the date of their first contact with Europeans, they already fished and traded in fish. The plaintiffs maintained that since before contact with Europeans, continuing to the present, they (and their ancestral predecessors) owned, used, and occupied territories within the claim areas. They also alleged that prior to and at contact they were a fishing people, whose way of life was characterized by trade, including the trade in fish. As required by the relevant legal test, the plaintiffs argued that these pre-contact practices translated into a modern aboriginal right to continue to harvest all species of fisheries resources within the claim areas and to do so for any purpose—from food and ceremonial reasons to trade on a commercial scale.

The complexity of fact-finding emerged at an early stage of the trial, during the May 26, 2008, Mid-Trial Hearings on the Admissibility of Ancient Explorer Records. The parties disagreed over the admissibility of the documents referred to by the Court as the *Explorer Records.*[23] Dating from 1774 to 1874, the collection was comprised of "primarily the journals of the maritime explorers, traders, and missionaries who came into contact with the plaintiffs' ancestors."[24] The defendant government requested that "Explorer Records be admitted into evidence for the truth of their contents,"[25] despite their status as hearsay. The defendant relied on an obscure doctrinal "ancient document" exception to the hearsay rule or, alternatively, under the principled exception to the hearsay rule as described in *R v Kahn*, [1990] 2 SCR 531 and *R v Smith*, [1992] 2 SCR 915. The defendants went further, contending that the whole collection should be admitted (for the Court's consideration) without the necessity of providing independent evidence of their reliability, such as the testimony of an expert.[26] The aboriginal plaintiffs countered that the Explorer Records were not ancient documents entitled to an exception to the hearsay rule, were not free from suspicion, and were not admissible as evidence in their own right, for the truth of their content. The historical record, the plaintiffs submitted, was suspect because of "ghost written manuscripts, omission or embellishments in the reproduced text, unreliable translations, errors in observation and many other issues."[27]

Despite their concerns, the plaintiffs nonetheless understood the value of these writings, asserting that Explorer Records were "necessary, useful evidence for determining historical facts necessary to this case."[28] However, they insisted on a more measured assessment, which would require the special interpretive skills of expert witnesses, such as "anthropologists and ethnographers."[29] They maintained that experts could place records in context. The plaintiffs also advanced a narrower position that only those passages specifically referred to by the experts should form part of the evidentiary record. Critically, the disagreement demonstrated that the ultimate evidentiary question for the Court was one of *how* to admit, and not *whether* to admit the Explorer Records into the evidentiary record.

Having to determine historical events, the Court chose admission of the hearsay evidence, as permitted by a principled method.[30] The Court's Mid-Trial ruling also seemed to split the difference between the parties: Madam Justice Garson would not limit the narratives' admission to specific passages, but instead would admit entire documents. However, the Court would have to determine reliability, which could require the use of expert witnesses.[31] The Court paved a way for early explorers to be "present" in the contemporary proceedings:

> These Explorer Records were used *testimonially*, mostly as eyewitness accounts of post-contact indigenous activities. And with the aid of expert witness testimony to construct a framework for inference, the Explorer Records were submitted, in particular, to support the first element of the claim: the existence of pre-contact trade by the plaintiff's ancestors ...[32]

The Court thus "received testimony" from Captain James Cook; the Spanish explorers Juan Perez, Bruno de Hezeta, and Don Estevan Josef Martinez; the Spanish naturalist Jose Mariano Mozino; the American fur trader (captive of the *Nuu-chah-nulth* and Chief Maquinna) John R. Jewitt; Alexander Walker of a British fur trade expedition commanded by James Strange; British fur trader John Mears; and several other "explorers" and early "ethnographers" of the west coast and island of Vancouver.

Ultimately, the Court was swayed by the plaintiff's rights-based claims. As far as the weight of evidence is concerned, the Cook and Jewitt journals,[33] in particular, seemed to persuade the Court. John R Jewitt was a captive of the Nootka from 1803 to 1805, who published his journal in 1807. The plaintiffs (and plaintiff's expert) relied principally on this version. Subsequently, Richard Alsop interviewed Jewitt and published *The Adventures and Sufferings of John R. Jewitt* (1815). The defendant's experts relied on this version of Jewitt's account. The judge, as the appellate court noted, also placed "some reliance" on the narratives of Gilbert Sproat, *Scenes and Studies of Savage Life*,[34] a settler and colonial bureaucrat whose ethno-graphic report was published in 1868.[35] The factual findings were also tempered by a court coming to terms with its own limitations. The Court stated:

> The task facing courts in aboriginal rights and title cases is one usually reserved for historians, anthropologists, archaeologists, and ethnographers. Courts have sufficient difficulty determining what happened a few months or years ago, never mind a few centuries ago.[36]

These concerns were not new. Indeed, Madam Justice Garson adopted Justice Binnie's analysis in an earlier aboriginal rights case before the SCC (*R v Marshall*): "The Courts have attracted a certain amount of criticism from professional historians for what these historians see as an occasional tendency on the part of judges to assemble a 'cut and paste' version of history" (Binnie's citations omitted).

Madam Justice Garson continued, referring to Justice Binnie's view that:

> While the tone of some of this criticism strikes the non-historian as intemperate, the basic objection as I understand it, is that the judicial selection of facts and quotations is not always up to the standard demanded of the professional historian, which is said to be more nuanced. ... *The law sees a finality of interpretation of historical events* where finality, according to the professional historian, is not possible. The reality of course is that the courts are handed disputes that require for their resolution the finding of certain historical facts. The litigating parties cannot await the possibility of a stable academic consensus. The judicial process must do as best it can.[37]

The Court's ambivalence manifested an acute self-awareness of its discipline's limitations, while implicitly exposing an attachment to the law's narrative: (1) that history is knowable and determinate and (2) that there exists a specific site that contains the necessary knowledge for the determination of facts. It must be so. Without the existence of historical quarry from which to mine facts, disputes over aboriginal rights and title could never be resolved and adjudicated. The Explorer Record, the *archive*, exists to service the legal tests for aboriginal rights and title.

## V Competing stories: Fictions and factions

During the *Ahousaht* Mid-Trial Proceedings, the parties understood that the *original* journals and manuscripts resided in archives or perhaps rare book rooms around the world. The court record, rather, was mainly comprised of transcriptions, reprints, facsimiles, translations, and various other *secondary* texts.[38] Indeed, Madam Justice Garson expressed her reluctance to engage the handwritten originals, saying she had no intention of "booking my ferry passage over to the archives. Don't worry. I can tell you without any doubt."[39]

Without original manuscripts, the parties quarreled over the superior edition of the Journals of Captain James Cook. Plaintiff's counsel referred to the problem as trying to make sense of "competing versions of the same event."[40] The two were: (1) The 1967 J.C. Beaglehole (editor) version (*The Journals of Captain James Cook on His Voyages of Discovery, the Voyage of the Resolution and Discovery, 1776-1780*) and (2) the James Douglas's *A Voyage to the Pacific Ocean Performed under the Direction of Captains Cook, Clerke, and Gore in His Majesty's Ships Resolution and Discovery in the Years 1776, 1777, 1778, 1779, and 1780*, in Three Volumes written by James Cook, A.W. Strahan, 1784. The defendants' expert relied on the Douglas version, while the plaintiff's expert used Beaglehole.

The Court questioned the editorial liberties taken by Mssrs Beaglehole and Douglas and their published texts possible absence of Cook's original entries. Who were Beaglehole and Douglas? The Hakluyt Society (on account of the Cook Bicentennial celebrations in 1978 and 1979) favoured the scholar John Cawte Beaglehole (1901–1971), and his texts of the Cook journals were deemed as *the* authoritative accounts.[41] Dr. John Douglas, Canon of Windsor and St. Paul's, published his "Cook Journals" in 1777 and 1784.[42] Notably, what remains beyond the Court's scrutiny is Captain James Cook himself—that is, his objectivity and qualifications as an observer and transcriber of aboriginal practices. The wrangling between the parties neglected to consider the faculties, biases, and agenda of the adventurer-author, but rather seemed to question which subsequent publication had fewer embellishments or distortions.

The main disagreement between the experts related to Cook's statement in the Beaglehole version: "[F]ish seemed to be in greater plenty, though we got none but by truck from the natives, who after the first week supplied us pretty plentifully with a small fish like sardines, if they were not of them, and a small fish like bream, now and then cod."[43] The statement is not contained in the Douglas version. The plaintiffs argued that the statement was an "important piece of evidence because it tends to support the contention that the natives traded fish with the early explorers."[44] They also discredited the Douglas edition: "Douglas took literary license and added his own content."[45] Plaintiff's expert also noted that Douglas may have had commercial literary interests and may have been "catering to his intended audience." Indeed, the "1784 edition was a best seller that sold out in three days."[46] Ultimately, the Court concluded: "[F]rom the evidence ... that the weight of scholarly opinion on this topic is that the Beaglehole version is *more authoritative and reliable* than the Douglas version."[47]

The Court emphasized that the expert testimony was used to better understand the documents' provenance,[48] a process that Eva-Marie Kroller characterizes as "the tortured textual history that arises out of the corporate authorship involved in producing Captain James Cook's travels".[49]

The Court summarized how journals were constructed:

> There are four distinct processes involved in the preparation of Explorer Records, although not every explorer record went through the same four stages of publication. The first stage is the log or field book, which is a record of daily activities and is usually written close to the time of the activities described. The second stage is a journal, which is a retrospective account written after a voyage, or part of a voyage, has been completed. The journal is next re-worked into a draft manuscript, which is the third stage of production. The journal manuscript is then re-worked into an edited and published text.[50]

The Court recognized how this would impact her evidential assessment:

> [T]he distinction between these various stages becomes relevant when I consider the reliability and weight of the various Explorer Records.[51]

Issues of construction, as perceived and addressed by the Court, seemed to be reserved for the last stage. The first three stages of journal construction were largely left unaddressed by all the parties.

The willingness by the parties and the Court to embrace the journal narratives as eyewitness testimony should be assessed against the available and substantial scholarly treatment of the subject. Non-legal scholars commonly question the authority of Explorer Records as "eyewitness narrative."[52] Elizabeth Vibert, who has written about early traders in British Columbia, argues that the notion that such documents could be "treated as objective eyewitness accounts is an illusion."[53] Felix Driver reminds us that historians increasingly view the purported accuracy of scientific accounts, as recorded by explorers, for its aesthetic and literary dimensions.[54] Eva-Marie Kroller notes: "Because of its proximity to sensationalism makes it popular, revision for profit, performed by an editor *or the author himself*, can be extensive, and the borderline between truth and fiction becomes blurred."[55] I.S. McLaren states that "the reliability of the eyewitness traveler thus became and should remain for the contemporary scholars a complex matter of some considerable doubt."[56] McLaren, who writes extensively on contact zones in British Columbia, adds: "Explorer and travelers were usually chiefly people of action. Books about their movements were demanded of them, but demand alone could not transform them into authors."[57] For him:

> [H]astily drawing a straight line between travel and narrative, that is, between eye witness observer, on the one hand, and recorder, on the other, is precarious. Not only is the caught zone fraught with "enormous" problems of communication, but also the records of what happened at contact are deeply conflicted.[58]

Courts have failed to take into account that explorer record may in fact harbor fictions in the sense that its authors "set out to encounter real knowledge along imaginary roads."[59] Or perhaps they may have constructed imaginary knowledge on real roads. By using fictional as a descriptive term in my title, I do not mean to insinuate that the explorer writings are entirely fictitious or that they are compilations of mistruths. Rather, literature generally, and fiction specifically, are highly imaginative and expressive genres of writing and use various narrative devices and artifices. The comparison may be apt. In the eighteenth and nineteenth centuries parallels between fiction and history were discussed and debated among novelists and critics. Both genres could be concerned with describing and moralizing about human behaviour and social institutions. In making the comparison, "it is important to consider the use each genre makes of the other," as well as verisimilitude, probability, and the requirement that readers "suspend their disbelief."[60] At the very least, the explorers' writings are never purely descriptive: they comment, opine, and interpret and define patterns of behaviour (in groups) and social organization.

## VI Why are courts enticed by explorer records (and why should they not be)?

Embracing problematic narratives to determine contemporary rights is puzzling and provocative for the questions it engenders. The charitable explanation may be that courts simply wish to accommodate the aboriginal plaintiffs' difficulty in admitting evidence. The use of flexible principles, however, may in fact be the only prudent strategy. Without it, there would be no familiar evidentiary form to prove the critical element of the case.[61] Reliance on the observational and authorial skill of early explorers to North America seems indispensable.

A softened or diminished evidential threshold requires more considered attention in its application to the explorer record. It privileges an imperial narrative, one which prioritizes the perspectives of agents of dispossession, subverting Canada's reconciliatory efforts vis-à-vis First Nations.[62] The liberal admission also has the effect of reinforcing culturally entrenched assumptions about what constitutes good legal evidence and foreclosing a meaningful interrogation of these assumptions. In *Narrative Fallacy*,[63] Doron Menashe and Hamutal Esther Shamash address the potentially harmful impact of hegemonic stories in legal fact-finding.[64] These accounts "provide familiar and comprehensible narrative frameworks within which to process information."[65] Easier admission of already conventional histories—those that are easiest to process cognitively—allows "fact-finders or parties to rely on generally accepted narratives to fill out stories about specific events."[66] Menashe and Shamash note that "fact-finders will assess relative plausibility of those ostensibly specific stories on the basis of their coherence with the general socially constructed narratives."[67] The imperial story becomes entrenched as an epistemic paradigm, which cannot help but subordinate aboriginal perspectives in contradiction to the SCC's efforts at their accommodation.

## VII Archival practices

Explorer records are alluring to all parties in litigation. But how does one begin to assess judicial practices as a product of seduction rather than prudence? *Ahousaht* demonstrates not only juridical attachment to the authority of explorers, but also suggests a necessary proclivity for archival associations. Why? Simply, the *archive* provides cover for what are otherwise problematic documents. It allays potential reliability concerns. The affinity is particularly evident in the Court's chosen lexicon. Use of the terms *primary*, *records*, *repository*, and *collection* to describe the writings may have been convenient, but they also had the effect of being tropes for authority and credibility.

The plaintiff's counsel was adamant that the Explorer Records were secondary sources. During the May 26, 2008 Mid-Trial Hearing, the plaintiff's attorney stated:

> It's our submission that these records are secondary sources in the way that they have been compiled both in ancient times or at least in the 1700s and 1800s and they have been reproduced now. In both circumstances, the way they've been prepared makes them secondary sources, and these are sources that the experts have relied upon, have turned to.[68]

Despite the plaintiff's contentions, the Court chose to call the documents *primary*. The Court stated:

> The experts relied on a combination of what I will call primary evidence and secondary evidence. Characterized loosely, primary evidence is original evidence in the sense of being a first-hand description of an observation of an event. Primary evidence may also be a study of original artifacts … Secondary evidence is what I would call commentary. For convenience, I will characterize the Explorer Records as primary evidence, though I acknowledge that they are not necessarily so in the truly historical sense.[69]

Despite the disclaimer, the approach is hazardous. By choosing to couch the documents in *primary* terms, the Court also enhanced their promise and status. Readers will perceive primary documents to occupy a privileged place from which authority and authenticity flows and from which factual inferences are more easily justified. The judicial choice of phrasing bolsters the archival association (as the root *arch* also denotes chief, principal, earliest in time). The danger resides in the exercise of rhetorical license to help construct an artificial, perhaps non-existent reality.[70]

The Court's fact-finding process relied on accessing *primary* records and collections and then ordering, classifying, and generally disciplining such data in order to reach some factual finality—that is, a legal truth. It is difficult to resist the obvious comparisons: court as archive, judge as archivist, and judicial fact-finding as a process of *archivization*. Although parsing, ordering, and classifying are not unusual for courts, their relation to the concept of *archive* in *Ahousaht* is inescapable.

Underlying the Court's method is a powerful mimetic force for archival action: legitimizing the explorer literature and justifying its own interpretation of this literature. Tom Nesmith's comments on archival process are compelling for understanding the Court's strategies:

> Archivists not only attempt to acquire *primary* (or original) sources, or records, which are thus thought to have special (even unique) integrity as means of access to the past; *they believe that providing information about the record "origin" and respecting the original order of their creation are essential to ensure that archiving is a neutral means of communication of the recorded past.*[71]

The Court defined certain historical events as relevant, and proceeded to measure and catalogue them into historical periods.[72] The Court adopted an active role in constructing a "neutral" chronicle, while ensuring protection of the conventional historical narrative, at least as told by the European sources. *Judicial Archivization* cannot be entirely innocent or objective. The chosen facts have not merely been found, nor have past events simply retrieved or transmitted dispassionately. Instead, they have been disciplined to reflect cultural choices:

> This mediation of reality occurs as archivists interact with broader process of archivization. Their personal backgrounds and social affiliations, and their professional norms, self-understanding, and public standing, shape and are shaped by their participation in the process. As they selectively interpret their experiences of it, archivists help fashion formative contexts of their work, which influences their understanding of recorded communication and position particular archives to do particular things.[73]

## Notes

1 *Ahousaht Indian Band and Nation v. Canada (Attorney General)*, 2009 BCSC 1494 at para 55.
2 See footnotes 53–58, discussion and comments of scholars critical of these texts as truth-bearing documents.
3 *Delgamuukw v. British Columbia*, [1997] 3 SCR 1010, at para 153.
4 *R v. Van der Peet*, [1996] 2 SCR 507, at para. 85.
5 *Delgamuukw*, *supra* n 3, at paras 80–1.
6 *Tsilhqot'in v. British Columbia*, 2007 BCSC 1700 [2008] at para 132.
7 *Tsilhqot'in (BCSC)* at para 203.
8 Ibid. at para 198.
9 *Tsilhqot'in Nation v. British Columbia*, [2014] 2 SCR 257, at p. 279, at para 32.
10 Ibid.
11 H.L. Ho, *A Philosophy of Evidence Law, Justice in the Search for Truth* (Oxford: Oxford University Press, 2008), at 68.
12 The fact-finder must have adequate epistemic justification for her factual findings. In other words, the trier-of-fact, in finding a fact, must *believe* in its propositional content. Ho, *supra* note 11 at 71.
13 *Ahousaht* Mid-Trial (see fn 24) at para 18.
14 *See* generally Vern R Walker, "Preponderance, Probability and Warranted Factfinding" (1996) 62 *Brook Law Review* 1075 at 1081.
15 David M Tanovich, "Starr Gazing: Looking into the Future of Hearsay in Canada" (2003) *Queen's Law Journal* 372.

16 Frederick W.J. Koch, "The Hearsay Rule's True *Raison de Etre*: Its Implications for the New Principled Approach to Admitting Hearsay Evidence" (2006) 37 *Ottawa Law Review* 251 at 251.
17 Lenora Ledwon, "Diaries and Hearsay: Gender, Selfhood, and the Trustworthiness of Narrative Structure" (2000) 73 *Temple Law Review* 1185 at 1214. Aboriginal histories passed down inter-generationally also constitute hearsay.
18 Michael Pardo, "Testimony," [2007] 82 *Tulane Law Review* 119, 150; see also Paul S. Milich, "Hearsay Antinomies: The Case for Abolishing the Rule and Starting Over" 71 *Oregon Law Review* 723 at 725–6.
19 Pardo, "Testimony," 151.
20 *R v Levagiannis* [1993] 4 SCR 475, 487.
21 *See R v Khan* (criminal context) [1992] 2 SCR 915 and *Ares v Venner* (civil context) [1970] SCR 608. *See also R v Smith* [1992] 2 SCR 915 and *R v Hawkins* [1996] 3 SCR 1043. The bench is careful to emphasize that ultimate reliability (and weight) cannot be determined until experts, for example, have provided context and insight for documentary interpretation. *Ahousaht*, Pre-Trial Admissibility Ruling (cited below at fn 24) at para 18.
22 *Ahousaht Indian Band and Nation v Canada (Attorney General)*, 2009 BCSC 1494.
23 Apparently, plaintiff's counsel first coined the term in *Ahousaht* Mid-Trial Ruling. Transcript of May 26, 2008, Hearing (No. SO33335, Vancouver Registry, Proceedings at Trial), at 16, lines 7–12 ["Ahousaht Mid-Trial Transcript"].
24 *Ahousaht v. Canada (Attorney General)*, 2008 BCSC 768 at para 9 [*Ahousaht* Mid-Trial Ruling]. In its judgment, the Court referred to these documents as the "only written evidence regarding the earliest interactions between Europeans (and some Americans) and aboriginal groups on the WCVI" (ibid. at para 66).
25 Ibid. at para 1. It should be emphasized that this hearing did not address questions of how evidence should be weighed (ibid. at para 18). Moreover, the parties did not disagree about the authenticity of the documents (ibid. at para 40).
26 Ibid. at para 40.
27 Ibid.
28 Ibid. at para 1
29 Ibid. Interestingly, the plaintiffs failed to mention historians here.
30 Ibid. at para 21.
31 Adopting Justice Vickers' reasoning in *Tsilhqot'in*, Justice Garson stated: he found that the meaning of historical documents may not be clear without expert assistance (ibid. at para 32).
32 *Ahousaht*, Mid-Trial Ruling, *supra* note 24 at para 55.
33 Notably, the Alsop account is just one example of a genre known as *captivity narratives.* In Canada, these include There Gowanlock's *Two Months in the Camp of Big Bear* (1885) and Samuel Goodrich's *The Captive of the Nootka* (1835).
34 London: Smith, Elder, and Co., 1868.
35 See ibid. at 279.
36 *Ahousalt* Mid-Trial Ruling, *supra* note 24 at para 55.
37 *Ahousaht* Mid-Trial Ruling, *supra* note 24 at para 82; italics added for emphasis.
38 Plaintiff's counsel Kirchner emphasized that although he would use Explorer Records, they were in fact secondary sources.
39 *Ahousaht*, Mid-Trial Hearing Transcript, *supra* note 23 at 81, lines 13–43.
40 *Ahousaht*, Mid-Trial Hearing Transcript *supra* note 23 at 65, line 27.
41 "Founded in 1846, the Hakluyt Society seeks to advance knowledge and education by the publication of scholarly editions of primary records of voyages, travels and other geographical material." See online: www.hakluyt.com.

42 See Captain Cook Society, online: www.captaincooksociety.com/home/collectables/books/eighteenth-century-books.
43 *Ahousaht*, Mid-Trial Ruling, *supra* note 24 at para 115.
44 Ibid. at para 115.
45 Ibid. at para 118.
46 Ibid. at para 116, 118.
47 *Ahousaht*, Mid-Trial Ruling, *supra* note 24 at para 119.
48 Ibid. at para 76
49 Eva-Maria Kroller, "Exploration and Travel," in Eva-Maria Kroller, ed, *The Cambridge Companion to Canadian Literature* (Cambridge: Cambridge UP, 2004 at 75.
50 *Ahousaht*, Mid Trial Ruling, *supra* note 24 at para 74.
51 Ibid. at para 75.
52 See e.g. Felix Driver, "Distance and Disturbance: Travel, Exploration and Knowledge in the Nineteenth Century" (Paper presented at the Transactions of the RHS, 14 2004), 73–92.
53 Elizabeth Vibert, *Traders Tales, Narratives of the Encounters in the Columbia Plateau 1807–1846* (Norman: U of Oklahoma Press, 1997), 5.
54 Driver, "Distance and Disturbance", 76.
55 Kroller, "Exploration and Travel", 76.
56 I.S. McLaren, "Herbert Spencer, Paul Kane, and the Making of the Chinook," in John Sutton Lutz, ed., *Myth and Memory: Stories of Indigenous European Contact* (Vancouver: UBC Press, 2007), 91.
57 Ibid.
58 Ibid.
59 Michael Wood, *Literature and the Taste of Knowledge* (Cambridge: Cambridge UP, 2005) at 190.
60 Morroe Berger, *Real and Imagined Words: The Novel and Social Science* (Cambridge: Harvard UP, 1977) at 162.
61 Here I call attention to her statement in the Mid-Trial Ruling: "can an expert give an opinion based on the contents of an un-provable document?" (*Ahousaht* Mid-Trial Ruling, *supra* note 24 at para 37). She seems to allude to a problem of evidential causality: no document, no expert; no expert, no evidence.
62 *See Delgamuukw* and *Van der Peet* for SCC discussions surrounding the need for reconciliation.
63 Doron Menashe and Hamutal Esther Shamash, "Pass the Sirens By: Further Thoughts on Narrative and Admissibility Rules" (2007) 5 (1) *International Commentary on Evidence*, Article 3 (on file with the author); also available online at SSRN: https://ssrn.com/abstract=1137429.
64 Ibid. at 2; including marginalizing non-hegemonic groups.
65 Ibid.
66 Ibid.
67 Ibid.
68 *Ahousaht*, Mid-Trial Hearing Transcript, *supra* note 23, lines 21–31.
69 *Ahousaht*, Mid-Trial Ruling, *supra* note 24 at paras 73, 74.
70 Grace Li Xiu Woo, *Ghost Dancing with Colonialism: Decolonization and Indigenous Rights at the Supreme Court of Canada* (Vancouver: UBC Press, 2011), at 150.
71 Tom Nesmith, "Seeing Archives: Postmodernism and the Changing Intellectual Places of Archives", *The American Archivist* 65 (2002), 27
72 *Ahousaht*, Mid-Trial Ruling, *supra* note 24 at para 89; italics added for emphasis.
73 Nesmith, "Seeing Archives", 30–31.

# Part 4

# Fictional discourse as law's mirror and cradle

## Metafictional qualities of law in literature

Chapter 4.1

# "A fearful and wonderful institution"

## Representing law in sensation novels

*Sara Murphy*

"It is curious to note how much of modern fiction has a legal tone about it. Some its very best efforts it owes to the law." Thus observed an essayist writing in the popular British magazine *Belgravia* in 1869. But after that promising beginning, the author goes on to take novelists to task; for "while the law from the novelist's point of view, in truth, is often a fearful and wonderful institution," it seems as though many of the novelists who use legal themes and procedures to fuel their plots are rather ignorant about that institution.[1] Exempting from this reproach Dickens, Collins, and Bulwer Lytton—as well as a certain "lady novelist," most certainly *Belgravia* editor Mary Elizabeth Braddon—the author offers several examples drawn from recent popular novels of mistakes about law or legal procedure. As it happens, these examples constitute a catalogue of nearly every plot device most commonly associated with sensation fiction, from bigamy to lost or stolen wills to murder. But as the author ticks off examples of legal ignorance, the essay's force shifts. While, at first, it seems to be taking writers to task for failing to adhere with sufficient rigor to the conventions of realist representation, it turns out that this is not entirely the case. What began as a demand for adherence to realist conventions ultimately collapses its critique on itself, admitting that only a legal expert would notice these mistakes, and for that reader, the errors about law would offer an extra boost to the novel's entertainment value. According to this author, the accuracy of the depiction of law and its procedures both matters a good deal—and it doesn't at all. Law has become a resource for literary effect, which at once links the world of the novel to the world outside it, and operates as an autonomous set of devices for the production of ever more intricate and suspenseful plots.

What this article refers to as "novelists' law" forms an intriguing site upon which to signal some of the broader tensions coursing through an apparently "unserious" popular genre. In this apparent critique of novelists' deployment of law, we see not only a delineation of sensation as a Victorian sub-genre, but a suggestive way of rethinking the relations between law and popular narratives. Taking the *Belgravia* article as an instigation, this chapter proposes that the intersection of a Victorian popular genre and law helps us think both about the place of sensation in the literary landscape and of the place of law in relation to its subjects. Exploring the significance of that "novelists' law," including these mistakes or errors in representing legal procedures and discourse, clarifies the stakes of the representation of the "fearful and wonderful institution" in popular mid-century fiction. But, to the extent that sensation fiction also marks a key moment in the development of mass print culture, this exploration also permits us to engage some issues that ramify beyond the Victorians. What does the tension between a certain kind of commitment to realism, on the one hand, and, on the other hand, legal quirk and procedure deployed as plot infrastructure, indifferent to accuracy, tell us about the intersections of popular fiction and law? About the relations between fiction and the emergence of a modern form of legal consciousness?

The "sensation"—or, sometimes, "newspaper" or "railway"—novel is said to emerge in the early 1860s, with the publication of Wilkie Collins's *The Woman in White* (1859–1860) often pointed to as the first of the genre—although Charles Dickens's *Bleak House* (1853) is clearly a major predecessor. It is not insignificant to note here that the very existence of genre itself owes no small debt to law; the repeal of the "taxes on knowledge" had made for a much more prolific, if more commercial, press. Anxieties about the ramifications of this commerciality animate critics of sensation; as one lacerating review put it, "a commercial atmosphere floats around works of this class, redolent of the manufactory or the shop."[2] Founded in 1866, the journal *Belgravia* was a decidedly middle-brow publication known for its serialization of sensation novels, which appeared interleaved with articles about aristocratic life, current events, celebrities of the day, and popular trials.[3] For many years, *Belgravia* was edited by the "queen of sensation," Mary Elizabeth Braddon, known for her bestselling *Lady Audley's Secret.*

Rewriting many of the conventions of earlier Gothic novels, sensation fiction expressly displaces the maze-like architecture of the Gothic castle to the level of plot. Twists, turns, surprises, suspense are all characteristic of plots featuring battles over wills, bigamy, imposture, murder and attempted murder. Most often, these crimes take place in the upper-class or bourgeois private sphere: whereas criminality in English fiction had most often been represented as a dimension of life among the dangerous classes, here it moves to the drawing room and the salon. In fact, while violent crimes against the person are far from unheard of in sensation novels, where they arise, they do so in the context of non-violent crimes or civil disputes. While readers of sensation fiction have long remarked that the genre thematizes the instability of identity, less noted is the fact that this instability is articulated in terms of the disparities between civil identity and subjectivity. Assuming a number of different identities, Braddon's Lady Audley commits arson and attempted murder—but only to conceal fraud and bigamy. In Braddon's later *John Marchmont's Legacy*, a will produces many complications, including, as is the case in Collins's *Woman in White*, the villain falsely imprisoning the legal heiress. Charles Reade's *Griffith Gaunt* features a heroine on trial for the murder of her estranged husband—who, as it turns out, is not dead after all, though he experiences a kind of civil death and resurrection. And in Collins's *Man and Wife*, the heroine's quandary is uncertainty about whether she has unwittingly entered into a Scottish irregular marriage with her best friend's fiancé. Apparently fulminating at the way some contemporary novelists treat the ever-popular bigamy plot, our Belgravia essayist points out that all too often novelists seem to think that marriage certificates or entries in parish registers are sufficient evidence of a marriage, but, in fact, "nothing is more difficult of absolute proof [than] a secret marriage."[4] Principally at stake in much sensation fiction are not criminal biographies or criminal acts; it is the ways in which law mediates characters' identities and circumscribes their relations to each other that forms the central focus.

Scholarship on nineteenth-century literature and law has often represented the relationship as rivalrous; in the work of Kieran Dolin, Jan-Melissa Schramm, Lisa Rodensky, and Alexander Welsh, literary realism emerges as a competitor to the claims of law to represent a normative reality. It is, from one standpoint, unsurprising that scholarship has highlighted rivalry, for this is frequently how the relation between law and literature is constructed in the period itself. As Thackeray cheerily admits in "The War Between the Press and the Bar" (1845), novelists have contributed to the public representation of lawyers as a "dangerous, slippery, wicked set of practitioners."[5] Dickens famously satirizes not only the practitioners, but the institutions of law and government themselves. If law and lawyers often come off poorly in nineteenth-century fiction, legal professionals are not only avid to point out novelists' mistakes, but to refute their claims about the ethical status of legal practice and the clarity of legal language. In one of his several essays on law and the novel, Fitzjames Stephen, the leading criminal law jurist of the period, laments "the almost universal inability of novelists to write about law without making mistakes."[6] Dickens is one of his favorite, if not his only, targets. In "The License of Modern Novelists," for instance, Stephen remarks that Dickens's "notions of law, which occupy so large a space in his books, are precisely those of an attorney's clerk,"[7] while Charles Reade is a "petulant littérateur who has arraigned [the authorities] at *his* Bar."[8]

At stake in this rivalry are a number of factors, central among them the increasing dominance of the novel as the major form of cultural production; as Stephen himself repeatedly notes in his essays of the 1850s, the novel's influence is great, particularly on younger readers. Equally consequential is the growing professionalization of the legal field. Julie Stone Peters's remarks on the disaggregation of disciplines, a particularly nineteenth-century project, are apposite here; she suggests that the emergence of law and literature as distinct arenas of knowledge production owe as much to "attempts to rationalize the legal sphere by ridding it of the customary and natural law traditions" as it does to the emergence of modern aesthetics as a sphere free of the instrumentalist claims of utilitarian calculus.[9] At a moment when it seemed that law had more and more of a presence in people's everyday lives, its language and procedures appeared more and more incomprehensible to the layperson. Discussing legal professionals' mid-century "attempt to define the marks of exclusive expertise," Nicola Lacey sees "a double bind":

> [T]he most obviously legally exclusive techniques were precisely those whose complexity opened them up to the Benthamite critique of law as deliberately fostering archaic and obfuscatory fictions. Modernizing the law … implied making it more transparent. But this seemed to cut across the need for cognitive exclusiveness.[10]

We might speculate, then, that the novel as a genre took advantage of this double bind: if, at moments, novelists appear to concur with Bentham's distaste for opaque language, they also exploit its literary possibilities.

This would suggest that the relations between law and the literary in the Victorian era are more complex than a "model of rivalry" might permit us to see. Even, or especially, if this rivalry argument can be supported with regard to high literary realism, sensation fiction seems to offer an alternative scenario. As Clare Pettit remarks, "much Victorian fiction seeks to resituate the law in a wider cultural debate."[11] The anonymous *Belgravia* essayist hints at such an alternative view, describing a form of fiction that, with regard to its treatment of law, is mediated by certain standards and expectations of literary production associated with realism, but only to the extent that it falls short of them. That falling short has, as one of its effects, the confirmation of the specialized professional knowledge of the novel-reading lawyer, who will enjoy spotting novelists' errors. On this view, the relationship between law and literature is far from rivalrous; through its misrepresentations, popular fiction affirms the distinction between itself and the discourse of the lawyer. In so far as the novelist makes mistakes, law as a specialized field of knowledge, discrete from other symbolic fields, becomes visible—as does this particular genre of fiction. With their appeal both to the general reader and the professional, sensation novels underscore, and perhaps even play a role in, the disaggregation of the discourses of law and literature. Law is rhetorically constituted as a "fearful and wonderful institution," in so far as it is represented as requiring a kind of occult knowledge, at which novel-writers, avowedly excluded from it, can only gesture in the manufacture of plots. If novelists refer to this arena in their work, it is literally as a fiction: legal procedures and institutions acquire a kind of shadow-life as literary devices.

On the face of it, then, it could seem that these "legal fictions" function to buttress the power of law and the authority of its practitioners as its privileged interpreters. We might also see operating here something like what Jacques Rancière describes as the "partition of the sensible": "the implicit law that parcels out places and forms of participation in a common world by first establishing the modes of perception within which these are inscribed."[12] With regard to sensation fiction, we can track in the contemporary critical reception an attempt to constitute such a mode of perception, specifically a mode of reading. In his 1869 *Quarterly Review* takedown of sensation fiction, for instance, Henry Mansell polices the boundaries of appropriate literature for a rising middle-class readership, delineating these novels, "written to meet an ephemeral demand, aspiring only to an ephemeral existence," from those works which exhibit a "deep knowledge of human nature, graphic delineations of individual character, and representations of the aspects of Nature or the workings of the soul."[13] Sensation novels present a social danger, because one reads them with the body: they "preach to the nerves," inciting visceral responses rather than reflective, or appropriately aesthetic, ones. For all of Mansell's worries, more recent analysts of the politics of sensation fiction have seen a more or less conservative trend in these novels. Critics such as Jonathan Loesberg and Patrick Brantlinger have pointed to the genre's emergence in an era of parliamentary reform, arguing that sensation novels themselves register anxieties over shifting power structures and an expanding public sphere; writing particularly of *Belgravia* as an example of Victorian popular print culture, Alberto Gabriele has made the case that the magazine simultaneously instigated and contained critical affect toward the upper classes. In short, the precise class politics of sensation are legible in a number of different ways, but in so far as these novels thematize law and legal proceedings, negotiating a distribution of the sensible between law and fiction and between sensation and realism, they appear to expose a particular relation between modern law and its subject.

It is a private sphere permeated by the expanding grasp of law, rather than any determinate political alignment, that sensation fiction registers in particular ways. In the course of the British nineteenth century, law's reach extended in many directions; reforms bearing on finance, the law of contract, trusts and estates, women's civil status, as well as multiple attempts at criminal law reform, mark the mid and late century especially. We can add, of course, the two major parliamentary reforms in 1832 and 1867. In addition to a print public sphere increasingly saturated by law and law's stories, there was a perception of law's expanding presence in the private lives of middle- and upper-class individuals. Many sensation novels, whether their authors get the procedural details correct or not, seek to represent the effects of this intervention. Perhaps more to the point, the effects that these novels tend to represent are indifferent to the particularities of procedure or rule; they are frequently, *pace* Mansell, psychic or corporeal effects. For this is neither the *ancien régime* body, at the mercy of the sovereign, nor even at stake necessarily is the institutionalized body in the grip of the state, "only … touching the body in order to reach something other than the body itself," as Foucault memorably remarked.[14] At stake is not, in other words, the body that the logic of Victorian culture marked as criminal, but rather that of the putatively law-abiding citizen, the autonomous liberal subject in all its supposed abstraction.

One example is provided by Wilkie Collins's 1870 *Man and Wife*. Collins's avowed aim with this novel was to do what he could to hasten the reform of "the present scandalous condition of the Marriage Laws of the United Kingdom."[15] Indeed, the disparities of marriage laws across the United Kingdom had recently been the subject of a Royal Commission and there had been at least one highly publicized and, in fact, sensational legal case bearing on this issue.[16] But the novel itself is less a reformist screed than a suspense-filled, highly entertaining examination of how law constitutes and effects its subjects. Attempting to salvage her compromised honor, the heroine of this novel plans to meet her seducer at a secluded inn on the border of the Highlands to enact an irregular marriage. That seducer sends his friend instead, and complications, including the possibility of bigamy, ensue. More than simply finding themselves before an institution or a collocation of rules, prohibitions, and obligations expressed in language that they do not understand, the characters in this novel find their lives shaped by forces of law that they cannot perceive until they are already deeply embroiled in them—and which even then remain occult. The power of law is manifested by jurisdictional differences; one only discovers oneself as a subject of law when confronted by the disparities between English and Scottish laws. And this discovery is frequently traumatic; English characters not only find civil status and social position compromised, but identity itself threatened through a chance encounter with disparities in territorial jurisdiction.

The novel underscores that there is no place outside of law. The domestic sphere is defined and striated by legal frameworks, though in the course of their everyday life individuals may not recognize this fact. Rather than cognitively assessing their interpellation by law, characters experience it as a physical impact; early in the novel, the heroine's mother is told that her husband has determined that their long marriage is invalid, due to a loophole in English marriage law. The impact is immediately physical: "she dropped … senseless at his feet."[17] When, much later, the heroine is told that she is likely married to her best friend's fiancé, she too faints dead away at the words, underscoring the repetition of the mother's fate in the daughter's life. That legal status is inherited is not surprising, but here it operates less like title or property and more similarly to inherited physiological conditions as they circulate in nineteenth-century medicine; a woman's legal status is not simply a formal attribution, but forms a deeply inscribed component of subjectivity, a component that might well remain latent, or unconscious, until circumstances awaken it. Completing the repetition of her mother's story, the heroine Anne flees and assumes another name, but it is clear that, rather than exiting a crushing legal order, she has only been repositioned within it.

Seeking a professional opinion avails nothing. The novel's main lawyer character, the benevolent Sir Patrick, is quick to point out that legal authorities are "everywhere at variance" on the question of Scottish irregular marriages. And, crucially, it isn't simply that nobody knows the law, but that the law is impossible to know: "No individual opinion in a matter of this kind is to be relied on," Patrick explains. Everyone is left equally confused before the mysteries of

Scottish marriage law, with its curious capacity to alter the civil status of individuals without their knowledge. Where even the specialized knowledge of professionals fails, law is represented as a curiously mystical disembodied institution, wielding inexorable authority over the private fates of citizens.

We could say this particular late sensation novel indexes the emergence of a modern state, marking a centralization of power that entails soliciting its citizens to see themselves as unmarked subjects of law, a process engaged by rendering uniform laws regarding the registration of marriages, births, and deaths, among other technologies. It is not insignificant, in this light, that the unmarked subject is represented as middle or upper class. To the extent that the fast-paced, suspense-filled plot depicts a fairly unlikely scenario—real-world difficulties around jurisdictional disparity with respect to marriage laws notwithstanding—this is also an instance of what *Belgravia* ruefully refers to as "novelists' law," the real legal world's fictional shadow, providing entertainment value in a burgeoning mass culture. But law here is not simply a scaffolding for a page-turner; its ability to shape the domestic sphere and alter the psychic landscape of its subjects forms the infrastructure of the plot, an infrastructure that Collins might not have been able to explore had he adhered rigorously to the facts of procedure and rule. And so while the animating problem of the novel is legible as historically linked to the consolidation of the modern state, its deeper concern is the constitution of the modern legal subject of that state. The nature of that concern, however, is readily represented neither by mid-century realism nor case law, nor even the endless Royal Commission reports that Victoria's reign produced.

Collins is a particular case; while, like more than one nineteenth-century novelist, he had studied law as a young man, he retained a fascination for legal peculiarities and loopholes—of which Scottish irregular marriage is one. The peculiarity, the residual customary practice, the "weird case," seem particularly appropriate for the exposure of a broader dynamic specific to the relations constituted between its citizens by modern law. In *Man and Wife*—but, I would contend, in other sensation novels as well—the embodied psyche emerges as a kind of excess to the legal subject supposed by formal legal discourse: desiring, gripped by unreason, fragile, violent, and autonomous only in fantasy. John Kucich has described Collins's apprehension of legal systems as "tragic" in so far as the novelist conceptualizes law as both unreliable and indispensable.[18]

Collins is very much of his sensational generation in this regard, for what the sensation novel renders sensible is that the modern legal subject's excess cannot be understood simply as a series of independent affects and embodiments that law can control or regulate; these affects, emotions, and embodiments are in fact law's constitutive other. In this relation, the effects of law are best articulated through a particular kind of fictionality. At the moment when Benthamite jurists are driving for greater transparency of language and for codification to displace legal fictions, popular novelists are transforming law into a "fearful and wonderful institution."

## Notes

1 Anon, "Novelists' Law," *Belgravia: A London Magazine* 7 (February 1869), 124.
2 Henry Mansel, "Sensation Novels," *The Quarterly Review* 113 (1862), 485.
3 For more on *Belgravia*, see Alberto Gabriele, *Reading Popular Culture in Victorian Print* (New York: Palgrave Macmillan, 2009).
4 Anon, "Novelists' Law," 126.
5 William Thackeray, "The War Between the Press and the Bar," *Punch* 9 (August 1845), 64.
6 James Fitzjames Stephen, "The Relations of Novels to Life," in *Cambridge Essays* (London: Saville and Edwards, 1855), 167–8.
7 James Fitzjames Stephen, "The License of Modern Novelists," *The Edinburgh Review* 106, No. 215 (July 1, 1857), 128.
8 Ibid., 151.
9 Julie Stone Peters, "Law, Literature and the Vanishing Real," *PMLA* 120, No. 2 (March 2005), 449.
10 Nicola Lacey, "The Way We Lived Then: The Legal Profession and the Nineteenth-Century Novel," *Sydney Law Review* 33, No. 4 (December 2011), 616.
11 Claire Pettitt, "Legal Subjects, Legal Objects: The Law in Victorian Fiction," in *A Concise Companion to the Victorian Novel*, 71–90, ed. Francis O'Gorman (Malden, MA, and Oxford, UK: Blackwell, 2005), 87.
12 Jacques Rancière, *The Politics of Aesthetics*, trans. Gabriel Rockhill (New York: Continuum, 2005), 85.
13 Mansell, "Sensation Novels," 486.
14 Michel Foucault, *Discipline and Punish: The Birth of the Prison*, trans. Alan Sheridan (New York: Vintage, 1979), 11.
15 Wilkie Collins, *Man and Wife* (Oxford and New York: Oxford UP, 1995), 5.
16 The Royal Commission on the Laws of Marriage was convened in 1865 and published its findings in 1868. The case in question is *Thelwall v. Yelverton*, which is echoed in Collins's novel.
17 Wilkie Collins, *Man and Wife*, 38.
18 John Kucich, *The Power of Lies: Transgression in Victorian Fiction* (Ithaca: Cornell UP, 1994), 85.

Chapter 4.2

# Fictions of corporate intention

## The epistemological problem of the good corporation

*Lisa Siraganian*

In one of the more polished chapters of F. Scott Fitzgerald's final novel, *The Love the Last Tycoon* (1940), left incomplete at his sudden death, an executive film producer stands on the verge of making an apparently disastrous financial decision for a major Hollywood studio. "Money man" Monroe Stahr, modeled on the legendary producer Irving Thalberg at Metro Goldwyn Mayer (MGM), announces that he plans to green-light a new "South America picture."[1] Although the film is budgeted at $1.75 million, Stahr expects that it will yield revenue of not "more than a million and a half" (*LLT* 47). This admission shocks his colleagues, "poised breathlessly on whether Stahr had slipped on his figures" and thus might be vulnerable to a leadership challenge (*LLT* 47). But Stahr swiftly divulges his reasoning, dashing their seditious plans:

> 'For two years we've played safe,' said Stahr. 'It's time we made a picture that'll lose some money. Write it off as good will—this'll bring in new customers ... [W]e have a certain duty to the public, as Pat Brady says at Academy dinners. It's a good thing for the production schedule to slip in a picture that'll lose money.' (*LLT* 48)

The other executives, "all blinking quickly," are too stunned to respond: hoping to catch their boss in a costly error, they instead witness new depths of financial strategizing (*LLT* 48). According to Stahr's logic, a single unprofitable picture is a "good thing" not only because it will "bring in new customers," but because it will advertise the corporation's willingness to place cultural value over economic profit. Stahr calculates the cost (and potential earnings) of the corporation's "duty to the public," working to maximize its returns. Corporate "good will" turns out to have a lucrative value they had not accurately estimated or even envisioned. His command of the studio remains secure.

In essence, Stahr intuits that "a certain duty to the public" should be incorporated into corporate decision-making. Although the idea of such responsibility was not new in 1940, it was less pervasive and more contested than it is today. The idea that for-profit businesses also have public obligations—a concept later labeled "corporate social responsibility" (or CSR)—began to be seriously debated among legal scholars, business ethicists, corporate managers, politicians, and the public at large beginning in the 1950s and escalating thereafter.[2] Founded on the premise that a corporation's responsibilities extend "beyond the traditional Anglo-American objective of providing financial returns to its shareholders," CSR often included "broader objectives [such] as sustainable growth, equitable employment practices, and long-term social and environmental well-being."[3] Although critics perched in economics departments or business schools contended that "welfare and society are not the corporation's business," the CSR philosophy became mainstream by the end of the twentieth century.[4] But, to this day, neither CSR's detractors nor its promoters delve too deeply into the movement's fundamental conceptual difficulty—one might even call it a conceptual incoherence or incapacity—explored in the pages that follow. I term this the epistemological problem of the good business corporation. Specifically, how can we know the ethical basis of any corporate action, or discern why a corporation is making what appears to be a socially responsible business decision? And without that assurance, why should we assume that CSR is necessarily a social good?

This epistemological problem develops out of a set of assumptions about the fictional status of corporate entities (cf. p. 208, p. 228 note 77, p. 38 note 42 and p. 48 note 214) along with subsequent implications about corporate intentionality. Often in these discussions, corporate duties and intentions are constructed analogously to a natural person's. We understand that, like a human being, the corporation has a legal identity—that is, legal personhood. Yet a corporation's personhood, unlike that of natural persons, stands distinct and apart from the human person's functioning as agent for the corporation. For that reason, the legal fiction of the corporate entity requires conceptualizing corporate "artificial" persons slightly differently from how we think about "natural" human beings. However, jurisprudence and legal theorizing have not always risen to this task. Moreover, the question of whether or not a corporate person has moral or social duties is a specific problem of corporate fictionality, directly related to the question of whether or not "corporate intentions" are necessarily identical to a natural person's (or persons') intentions. To assume from a legal metaphor, used for expediency and ease, that a corporation's extra-legal moral or social duties can simply map on to natural persons' obscures the problems at hand.

A version of this general dilemma structures the episode in Fitzgerald's novel. Initially, the studio executives are convinced that Stahr's authorization of the South America film indicates fuzzy sentimentality and idealism: they suspect that he is operating not with the corporation's bottom line but with some conception of society's bottom line. But Stahr's tactics evince a longer time horizon and subtle maneuvering for the company's benefit. Not only is he focusing on burnishing the studio's brand reputation, but he is also planning what is now known as a "loss-leader": selling a commodity or service at a price below market cost to attract new customers and stimulate future, more profitable sales.[5] Like Black Friday doorbusters at Target or BestBuy, his scheme to "slip in" an unprofitable social commentary film about South America promises to "bring in new customers" (presumably of a different socioeconomic class) to pay for a broader range of films (*LLT* 48). Potential justifications for producing an unprofitable film (corporate good will, brand reputation, or loss-leader) are aligned, and thus the corporation makes a socially responsible decision because Stahr can financially justify it. But that his colleagues could not anticipate his reasons—and, indeed, have no way of knowing which of many possible reasons he relies on to make that decision—highlights the problem I analyze in the pages to follow.

CSR introduces a different type of corporate strategizing that may, or may not, have a moral basis even while most observers assume it must. Quite simply, they mistake a metaphor, a legal fiction, for the real thing, a conceptual error with real consequences. Although both CSR's admirers and its critics have discussed various issues with the movement, when they acknowledge the basic conceptual and epistemological problem emerging from this fundamental metaphorical gesture, they tend to view it as a hurdle to be overcome rather than a constitutive attribute of corporate decision-making that undermines CSR doctrine. After briefly investigating how and why legal scholars and business ethicists struggle to conceptualize the epistemological problem of CSR, I then turn to a contemporary literary examples by way of contrast. Following on Fitzgerald's intuition, Dave Eggers's *The Circle* (2013) explores why the good corporation's reasoning remains both inscrutable and dubiously moral. Hollywood executives, writes Fitzgerald, "gave well but … [i]t was not charity" (*LLT* 57). Eggers's novel feels out and illustrates the fundamental ethical challenges of the corporate creature and its agents. Simply developing better versions of CSR cannot eliminate the dilemma of knowing whether, when the corporation gives "well," it is well for the many or for a very select few.

## I

On the one hand, CSR can be understood as principally a question of and for management: how should executives and a board of directors manage a company best? In this regard, CSR primarily looks like a question of the obligations of management to identify and avoid possible conflicts between management's moral duties and their fiscal responsibilities (such as profit maximization). Socially responsible corporate actions are thereby justified by claiming that CSR is not opposed to profit maximization, but serves precisely that aim albeit on a different time horizon. As Stahr recognized with his cinematic loss-leader, even the appearance of corporate morality can have a positive marketing effect long-term.

But, on the other hand, the more vital and intriguing problem CSR poses works a little differently. In this formulation, rather than framing CSR as a management decision, we can think of it instead as a larger conceptual and moral philosophical problem of corporate intentionality. The fictional nature of corporate personhood suggests that how corporations intend, and the subsequent moral and legal rules that should apply to corporations, might differ substantially from expectations demanded of a natural person (for example, that a corporate aim to maximize shareholder value might differ from a natural person's desire to act ethically). Utilitarian or moral decisions might only be duties for natural persons, not corporate ones, since corporate persons are only legal constructs. When Immanuel Kant observes that external duties cannot be duties of virtue but only duties of right—"no external lawgiving can bring about someone's setting an end for himself (because this is an internal act of the mind)"—he is anticipating precisely the problem I explore here.[6] Namely, can corporations possess CSR-type duties of virtue, following the legal fiction of corporate personhood, if they do not have anything like a human natural mind that acts and sets obligations for itself?

This legal and moral quandary of CSR, and the story of corporate charity more generally, arose with the prominent Michigan Supreme Court decision *Dodge v. Ford Motor Company* (1919). In 1916, the Ford Motor Company's Board of Trustees decided to withhold special dividends to shareholders and instead invest that money into the corporation. John and Horace Dodge, previously Henry Ford's major business partners, owned a substantial percentage of Ford stock and had been counting on a dividend that never arrived. They sued. Having just formed a competing car company—you can guess which one—the Dodge brothers suspected that Henry Ford was trying to starve them of capital needed to build their business.[7] Ford disputed this charge, claiming that the purpose of investing in his company, rather than paying dividends to the brothers Dodge, was "to employ still more men; to spread the benefits of this industrial system to the greatest possible number, [and] to help [Ford employees] build up their lives and their homes."[8] Under cross-examination, he further asserted that the Ford Motor Company was "organized to do as much good as we can, everywhere, for everybody concerned. And incidentally to make money."[9] The Michigan Supreme Court was not convinced by this line of argument. Rejecting Ford's claim of "incidental" capitalism, they held that a corporation cannot take actions that harm its shareholders and which are motivated solely by humanitarian, as opposed to business, concerns.[10] Ford was required to pay the dividend the Dodge shareholders demanded.

*Dodge* is now "routinely cited as recognizing the norm of shareholder supremacy within corporate law," as Kent Greenfield notes.[11] Less noticed is that this early case highlighted the challenge of determining exactly why a corporation was making a socially beneficial decision in the first place. Consider the competing arguments in play. First, Henry Ford argued that withholding dividends simply permitted the corporation "to do as much good" as possible, a claim that might have been justifiable on utilitarian grounds were Ford workers benefiting more than Ford shareholders. Second (and rather differently), his point was that in doing this "good," he was adding to the company's bottom line. Specifically, Ford explained in court, by adopting a "policy to force the price of the car down as fast as production would permit, and give the benefits to users and laborers," the Ford Corporation ended up accruing "surprisingly enormous benefits to ourselves."[12] Doing good to workers was a roundabout way of doing good to the corporate self. Third, although Ford never stated it, he was surely attempting to thwart the Dodge brothers, expanding his own dominance in car manufacturing—while, again, helping his company's bottom line. Faced with these competing rationales, the Court had to decide which version of Ford's reasoning truly motivated the corporation's business decision. But the Michigan judges had no calculus that would help them select from the corporation's charitable explanations versus its profitable ones. They simply took Ford at all of his (contradictory) words.

Following *Dodge*, mid-century CSR advocates strategized ways to circumvent the shareholder primacy principle that the decision seemed to shore up but never quite did. As Einer Elhauge, David Millon, Lynn Stout, and others have explored, shareholder primacy was not an established legal doctrine, despite assumptions to the contrary.[13] By the 1980s, the American Law Institute adopted essential CSR ideas in their influential advisory treatise, *Principles of Corporate Governance: Analysis and Recommendations.*[14] Federal rules authorized corporate philanthropy and many states (including Delaware, the corporate law behemoth) passed legislation adopting CSR principles.[15] As an editor of *The Economist* griped in 2005, corporate social responsibility "commands the attention of executives everywhere."[16] During this time, companies developed the idea of the "triple bottom line," in which economic, social, and environmental performance would be considered in addition to financial accounting.[17] New twenty-first-century business entities such as Benefit ("B") Corporations or Social Purpose Corporations downgraded shareholders to one of several stakeholders. Yet once shareholder primacy was relaxed, a new problem emerged: so-called "skin-deep CSR" or "greenwashing" scenarios. CSR was becoming a necessary business expense or commodity subjected to cost–benefit analysis, inextricable from advertising and brand management.[18]

Legal analysts have examined this skin-deep CSR problem from various angles. In addition to legislating alternative business entities for socially conscious enterprises, scholars have recommended more governmental regulation. For example, Miriam Cherry and Judd Sneirson acknowledge "that there currently are no ready solutions for policing CSR claims," and advocate "additional policing of CSR" to redress that absence.[19] But even if regulating CSR curtailed the worst greenwashing or faux CSR abuses, more policing would not touch the difficulty of knowing when a Hollywood producer like Monroe Stahr or an automobile executive like Henry Ford was acting to demonstrate charity, on the one hand, or to angle for corporate hegemony, on the other. As Elhauge asserts, "managerial discretion to sacrifice corporate profits … is inevitable because it cannot be disentangled from the discretion managers need to make profit-enhancing corporate decisions."[20] The establishment of the business judgment rule (holding that courts shall not second-guess the actions of corporate directors), obviated the legal requirement that courts disentangle motives.

More recently, some scholars have argued that such disentangling is unnecessary in a more basic sense, asserting that the specific intent behind corporate philanthropy is inessential: “Asking why firms produce altruism is like asking why Toyota produces the Camry,” write M. Todd Henderson and Anup Malani; “The answer is that they do so because there is consumer demand for it and the company is able to produce it at competitive cost.”[21] Henderson and Malani portray altruism as a market good, while acknowledging that the altruism market differs from other kinds of markets.[22] Because corporate philanthropy invariably “reflects a blend of motives,” as do nearly all business decisions, the choice either to act charitably or not “is a quintessential business decision” which courts now refrain from investigating.[23]

But, as we have already seen, the difficulty remains when making a determination about what counts as charitable intent or not. Moreover, it is not clear that a corporation’s motives for engaging in philanthropy could be as truly irrelevant as Henderson and Malani imply. They assume that as long as the altruistic results are consistent, and the business judgment rule holds, then the corporation’s motives in acting “generously” could not be pertinent. According to this view, a corporation limiting its greenhouse gas emissions to combat climate change would be doing the same thing as one limiting those emissions to gild its brand image. But to see those actions as identical is in some real sense not to see them fully or accurately. Intentional actions, writes the celebrated philosopher of action Elizabeth Anscombe, “are the ones to which the question ‘Why?’ is given application.”[24] In these two instances the answers to the “why” question would diverge sharply: to save the planet or to save BP’s image are not the same answers to “why” BP claims that the “goal of achieving no damage to the environment guides our actions.”[25]

To think that the decisions of a corporate being matter only in their effects, and not in their “why’s,” is to understand these decisions as the external effects caused, rather than intended, by an insensate creature. Yet in all sorts of ways, laws and the people who abide by them assume that corporations can have intentions and act on those intentions, even if we are rarely sure what those precise aims are and how to discover them. In these moments, we assume the legal fiction of corporate personhood is a reality that maps cleanly on to our own sense of how and why humans intend and act. Moreover, while more CSR in the world is largely understood to be a legitimate, evident good, it might not be. As John M. Conley and Cynthia A. Williams note, “[r]ather than redressing the power imbalance between corporations and civil society, [CSR] processes may be reinforcing it in subtle but effective ways.”[26] CSR builds up corporations as more powerful players in society, even while their basic intentions remain unknown or unknowable.

## II

Corporate theorists want to rectify the problem of skin-deep CSR with better policy. I am suggesting that a broader, more intractable problem is how to determine potential charitable intent by a corporate entity that is a legal fiction. Despite the business judgment rule, determining such intent is necessary in order to know whether or not CSR is skin-deep or sincerely meant. As we observed with *Dodge*, this epistemological puzzle looks unsolvable, which in part explains why the business judgment rule is a better strategy for courts. If judges cannot make reasonable judgments about managerial decisions, then it might be better for them not to make any judgments about corporate intent at all—assuming they can abide by that stricture. But it is not clear that the business judgment rule, as necessary as it might be for the legal system, is a sufficient reason for ordinary persons to support CSR.

Dave Eggers's *The Circle: A Novel* (adapted as a mediocre film starring Tom Hanks and Emma Watson) begins to focus on the problems with this compromise by envisioning a corporation that has CSR baked into its very mission statement.[27] To be sure, the novel is not explicitly focused on corporate philanthropy and its various dilemmas. Instead, it depicts a dystopian nightmare about an ostensibly progressive social media behemoth "that subsumed Facebook, Twitter, Google" and their Silicon Valley progeny (*C* 23). Unifying all of a person's various identities and information across the internet, the Circle Corporation advocates radical transparency and transforms the web into a more collegial, courteous, and socially guarded space. But in becoming a profitable, conscientious corporation, the Circle also becomes a diabolical entity and dangerous social force that cannot be checked by law—even while its supposedly upstanding motives are presumed by almost everyone. The Circle's CSR is not skin-deep, but in being deeply meant it is all the more deeply damaging.

The ostensibly beneficial qualities of the corporation complement the Circle's more typical portfolio of CSR acts: sustainable housing, support for the arts (specifically, the painters, artists, musicians, comedians, and writers struggling in the hostile media environment the Circle helped create), and general support for "the passions of the community" or Circle workers (*C* 17–18). On her first day, impressionable protagonist Mae Holland, a recent college graduate disheartened by her first job working nine-to-five tech support for a local utility company, eagerly absorbs the Circle pitch delivered by the HR department: "*Community First* ... making sure this is a place where our humanity is respected, where our opinions are dignified, where our voices are heard—this is as important as any revenue, any stock price, any endeavor undertaken here" (*C* 47). They voice the triple-bottom-line CSR philosophy in a nutshell, in which "community" and "humanity" are "as important as revenue" or shareholders' desires for a rising stock price. "We want this to be a workplace, sure," Mae's HR handlers explain patiently, but "it should also be a *human*place" (*C* 47).

Predictably, the Circle "had been voted the world's most admired company four years running" (*C* 2).

So far, so good. Mae finds ample evidence to experience the Circle campus as "heaven," as she does in the book's opening line (*C* 1). But very quickly the novel exposes how thoroughly and seamlessly CSR and exploitative profitability have become intertwined, as Eggers relishes illustrating what a toxic blend of for-profit social ethics might look and sound like. Sometimes the mix is subtle. A "do-gooder" employee is "trying to get tablets into schools that right now can't afford them" (*C* 57). That phrase, "right now," is key: charity in the present will always come due as a bill (and revenue) in the future, when those schools *can* afford tablets. Circle's HR department is more explicit about the need for profitability: "If we don't give the customers a satisfying, human, and *humane* experience, then we have no customers" (*C* 47–8). In other words, the Circle product *is* "humane experience": the experience customers have of a company that can act with humanity while reaping profits. In this sense, CSR has become the chief commodity that they are peddling, along the lines that Henderson and Malani envision (where altruism is a market good). Moreover, this "*human*place" is one where an hour-long lunch break is officially provided but never observed, where after-hour "parties" turn out to be mandatory, where visits home to ill parents are frowned upon, and where the company encourages employees to move into its "campus dorms." Along the way, the Circle attempts to monetize all aspects of human existence in order to eventually erase the distinction between working and living.

The corporation will also do anything—legal or not—to defend its dominance. When a U.S. Senator launches an antitrust crusade against the Circle, pushing the Justice Department "to break it up, just as they did with Standard Oil, AT&T and every other demonstrated monopoly in our history," that Senator is almost immediately disgraced and neutralized: "a hundred weird searches, downloads—some very creepy stuff" are discovered on her laptop (*C* 173, 206). By the novel's end, we learn that for years Circle management had been planting fake evidence on its critics' computers to silence them (*C* 483). The novel's point is not that you cannot know what a corporation intends because its motives are complicated, but that too often you know all too well because its motives are straightforwardly brutish. The Circle is functioning just like one of the blind carnivorous sharks its corporate executives keep in the company aquarium. The corporation cannot fully see the effects of its actions. It simply uses CSR if that doctrine helps the organism eat and grow, just as it will use any other technique that enhances its supremacy (such as framing someone for a crime she did not commit). The appearance, versus the reality, of corporate ethics happens to be entirely profitable. In this regard, the novel takes a cynical, even hysterical view of what corporate philanthropy or goodwill offers: it will become dangerous and abused to support "the world's first tyrannical monopoly," a "totalitarian nightmare" (*C* 401, 481).

The novel's warning is blatantly clear. Even a "good" corporation's actions will become predatory and must be checked.

*The Circle* also suggests that the real danger of the socially conscious corporation is its knowability and legibility. We can know all of the Circle and it can know all of us if we offer the corporation our private realm of experiences. As Mae releases more of her life, beliefs, and experiences to the Circle, she rises precipitously in the Circle ranks, yet also struggles to sleep and begins drinking more, supplied with endless free alcohol in her corporate dorm refrigerator. She simultaneously has powerful feelings of elation and astronomical popularity combined with an encroaching sense of self-annihilation. She feels that "a tear was growing within her, opening quickly, a fathomless blackness spreading under her" (*C* 333). The tearing accelerates as she disavows private experiences such as kayaking on the San Francisco bay in the dark by herself (and with a swimming seal or two), and not sharing the moment on social media. Eggers thus portrays the vastness of nature, enabled by privacy and solitude, as a soothing reservoir of selfhood. As in classic Romantic poetry, what William Wordsworth depicted as the "bliss of solitude" (in "I Wandered Lonely as a Cloud") once rejuvenated the depleted Mae; without that regular wandering and dreaming she feels herself unmoored, hollowed out from the inside. From the novel's perspective, the danger here is that Mae is opening herself to a corporate entity lacking a conception of the private realm. That entity acts "ethically" not out of conviction but for the particular ends of maintaining and increasing customers. She is destructively shaping herself in the corporation's image of a public entity composed of contracts rather than a private, human being.

That self-fashioning is all the more destructive because the Circle's business model requires openness and transparency and can assign no fiscal (or other) value to privacy. Until the corporation finds a way to monetize secrecy, solitude becomes an inhibitor to the corporation's success and growth. As the novel draws out the calamity that ensues, the corporation's agents describe privacy and discretion as unethical: "secrets are the enablers of antisocial, immoral and destructive behavior," one Circle executive pontificates (*C* 289). Revealed secrets are knowledge in the sense of public exposure rather than reserved revelation. But having recognized this intriguing truth about corporate ontology, the novel retreats. That is, rather than conceiving of the problem of corporate morality and responsibility as one of an entity constitutively unable to experience a private realm of solitude—and thus a space of reflection, moral or otherwise—the novel tends to see the problem of corporate ethics as the influx of *too much* knowledge (the familiar moniker of "the information age"). Progressively entranced by the corporation's vision of humanity, Mae is represented as in a crisis of information overload. Her estranged friend Mercer tries to make her aware of this: "We are not meant to know everything, Mae. Did you ever think that perhaps our minds are delicately calibrated between the known and the unknown?" (*C* 430). What we need instead, Eggers suggests with idealistic characters like Mercer, is to recalibrate ourselves with more mysticism and profound opacity because "[t]he ceaseless pursuit of data to quantify the value of any endeavor is catastrophic to true understanding" (*C* 485).

The novel turns to the spiritual and ethereal as the solution to the entanglements of CSR in our lives. That is, *The Circle* implies that not knowing how the corporation functions—or how we function—might be the better, safer course of action for humanity in the early twenty-first century. In that sense, the novel's final position ends up surprisingly indistinguishable from—and ultimately as unsatisfying as—law's business judgment rule. Just as the courts would rather not make judgments questioning or challenging the rationale of management, so would *The Circle* prefer not to judge the rationale of management. Eggers takes the epistemological problem of CSR and implies that it might be better not to know how the sausage is made if it means that the corporation, in turn, will not know how your soul is made. Deliberate ignorance—what law more derisively terms "willful blindness"—becomes a potential protection from a corporation like the Circle's ravenous desires.[28]

## III

Contemporary novels like Eggers's offer a powerful critique of corporate do-gooding as a problem of knowing. They imply in different ways that corporations aiming to do well for themselves and others both know too much about us and expose what is often the paucity of law's own account of "fictionality." At least in CSR discussions, that term functions more often as a synonym for "convention" or "formality" applied for ease of analysis and expediency, rather than as a robust topic with a set of conventions, expectations, and speculations of its own.

However, the question remains whether the problems of CSR (that is, the problem of assessing the "why" of corporate social actions) spring from a lack of understanding of the fictional nature of corporate personhood and corporate intentions, or from a determination to ignore the legal fictionality of corporate personhood. As this essay has explored, when CSR is debated, the consciousness that corporate personhood is a legal fiction, and that corporations are not actually natural persons but are treated instead "as if" they are persons, is mostly elided. Such omissions are hard to justify. The crucial questions in these debates are closely related to the status of corporate personhood as a legal fiction: namely, can corporations have moral duties, intentions, and social responsibilities?[29] Once discussions of CSR more clearly examine the ontological and metaphysical nature of these issues, we will be able to advance in our debates—in whatever way legal scholars or society ultimately answers these questions.

## Notes

1 F. Scott Fitzgerald, *The Love of the Last Tycoon*, ed. Matthew J. Bruccoli (New York: Scribner, 1993), 46. Hereafter cited parenthetically in the text as *LLT*.
2 Kevin T. Jackson, "Global Corporate Governance: Soft Law and Reputational Accountability," *Brooklyn Journal of International Law* 35 (2010), 48–9.
3 John M. Conley and Cynthia A. Williams, "Engage, Embed, and Embellish: Theory Versus Practice in the Corporate Social Responsibility Movement," *Journal of Corporate Law* 31 (2005), 1–2.
4 Theodore Levitt, "The Dangers of Social Responsibility," *Harvard Business Review* 41 (1958), 47.
5 "A loss leader is a product or service that is offered at a price that is not profitable, but is sold or offered in order to attract new customers or to sell additional products and services to those customers … in the hope of building a customer base and securing future recurring revenue." www.investopedia.com/terms/l/lossleader.asp.
6 Immanuel Kant, *The Metaphysics of Morals*, trans. and ed. Mary Gregor (Cambridge: Cambridge University Press, 1996), 31. On Kant and corporate morality, see Matthew C. Altman, "The Decomposition of the Corporate Body: What Kant Cannot Contribute to Business Ethics," *Journal of Business Ethics* 74, No. 3 (September 2007), 253–66; Wim Dubbink and Luc van Liedekerke, "A Neo-Kantian Foundation of Corporate Social Responsibility," *Ethical Theory and Moral Practice* 12, No. 2 (April 2009), 117–36; Claus Dierksmeier, "Kant on Virtue," *Journal of Business Ethics* 113, No. 4 (April 2013), 597–609.
7 M. Todd Henderson, "The Story of Dodge v. Ford Motor Company: Everything Old is New Again," in *Corporate Law Stories*, ed. Mark J. Ramseyer (New York: Thomson Reuters/Foundation Press, 2009), 56–7.
8 *Dodge v. Ford Motor Co.*, 170 N.W. 668 (Mich. 1919), 671.
9 Henderson, "Story," 62.
10 *Dodge v. Ford*, 683.
11 Kent Greenfield, *The Failure of Corporate Law: Fundamental Flaws and Progressive Possibilities* (Chicago: University of Chicago Press, 2006), 41.
12 Henderson, "Story," 62. He was also improving his own reputation and his company's by extension, avoiding the moniker of robber baron.
13 As Einer Elhauge writes, corporate managers "always had some legal discretion (implicit or explicit) to sacrifice corporate profits in the public interest"; "Sacrificing Corporate Profits in the Public Interest," *New York University Law Review* 80 (2005), 738; David Millon, "Shareholder Primacy in the Classroom after the Financial Crisis," *Journal of Business and Technology Law* 8 (2013); Lynn A. Stout, *The Shareholder Value Myth: How Putting Shareholders First Harms Investors, Corporations, and the Public* (San Francisco: Berrett-Koehler, 2012). Milton Friedman's "The Social Responsibility of Business is to Increase Its Profits," *New York Times Magazine* (13 September 1970) was also influential in sustaining the idea of shareholder primacy.
14 Subpart (b)(2) states that a corporation "[m]ay take into account ethical considerations that are reasonably regarded as appropriate to the responsible conduct of business," while subpart (b)(3) states that a corporation "[m]ay devote a reasonable amount of resources to public welfare, humanitarian, educational and philanthropic purposes." American Law Institute, *Principles of Corporate Governance: Analysis and Recommendations* 1, pt. II, § 2.01 (1992). For a discussion, see Daniel J. Morrissey, "The Riddle of Shareholder Rights and Corporate Social Responsibility," *Brooklyn Law Review* 80 (2015), 371.
15 On state statutes authorizing corporate philanthropy, see Robert A. Katz and Antony Page, "Sustainable Business," *Emory Law Journal* 62 (2013), 884; and Millon, "Shareholder Primacy," 194–5.

16 Clive Crook, "The Good Company," *The Economist* (January 20, 2005). www.economist.com/special-report/2005/01/20/the-good-company.
17 See John M. Conley and Cynthia A. Williams, "Engage, Embed, and Embellish: Theory Versus Practice in the Corporate Social Responsibility Movement," *Journal of Corporate Law* 31 (2005), 24–5.
18 Morrissey, "Riddle"; Kellye Y. Testy, "Linking Progressive Corporate Law with Progressive Social Movements," *Tulane Law Review* 76 (2002), 1239. See also: *A. P. Smith Mfg. Co. v. Barlow*, 98 A.2d 581, 583 (N.J. 1953) and Levitt, *Dangers*, 42.
19 Cherry and Sneirson, "BP Oil Disaster," 986–7.
20 Elhauge's broader argument is that such managerial discretion is "affirmatively desirable because it allows social and moral sanctions to optimize corporate conduct" ("Sacrificing," 868).
21 Ibid., 577.
22 M. Todd Henderson and Anup Malani, "Corporate Philanthropy and the Market for Altruism," *Columbia Law Review* 109 (2009) 575–6; 611–2.
23 Ibid., 581.
24 G.E.M. [Elizabeth] Anscombe, *Intention, second edition* (Oxford: Basil Blackwell, 1957: repr. Cambridge: Harvard University Press, 2000), 24.
25 www.bp.com/en/global/corporate/sustainability/environment.html, accessed 3 November 2018.
26 Conley and Williams, "Theory Versus Practice," 37. Even CSR's most ardent detractors make a similar point, assessing the danger that "the corporation would eventually invest itself with all-embracing duties, obligations, and finally powers" leading to "fascism" (Levitt, *Dangers*, 44–6).
27 Dave Eggers, *The Circle* (New York: Alfred A. Knopf/McSweeney's Books, 2013), hereafter cited in the text parenthetically as *C*.
28 Willfull blindness is the legal doctrine stating that a corporation can be held criminally liable if it deliberately disregards reasonable suspicions of criminal activity. *U.S. v. Bank of New Eng., N.A.*, 821 F.2d 844, 856–57 (1st Cir. 1987). See Blake Weiner, Kimberly Austin, John Lapin, and Mary McCullough, "Corporate Criminal Liability," *American Criminal Law Review* 55 (Fall 2018), 970–1, and William Laufer, "Corporate Bodies and Guilty Minds," *Emory Law Journal* 43 (Spring 1994), 647–730.
29 For a more substantial treatment of the debate over corporate intention in law and literature, see Lisa Siraganian, *Corporate Form: The Meaning of Persons in Legal and Literary Modernism* (Oxford: Oxford University Press, 2020), forthcoming, which argues that the possibility that large collective organizations might mean to do what they do animated an astonishingly diverse set of American writers, artists, and theorists of the corporation in the first half of the twentieth century, stimulating a revolution of thought on intention.

Chapter 4.3

# Remedial fictions

## The novelization of habeas corpus and the history of human rights

*Sarah Winter*

What kinds of political leverage or effects on public opinion can legal fictions produce when they appear in fictional narratives? Are legal persons rendered more fictional, and therefore deprived of their legal implications or force, when they are transformed into characters in a novel? Twentieth-century philosophers Lon L. Fuller and Owen Barfield point out that legal fictions and literary fictions share a common conceptual terrain because both exemplify the role of metaphor in making meaning. In a 1930 article, Fuller observes:

> For every legal word which has been able to disencumber itself of its burden of extra-legal connotation, there are ten words which carry with them into the law a mass of non-juristic associations—frequently with the result that their legal use continues to be felt as fictitious.[1]

For instance, Fuller argues:

> Those who contend that "corporate personality" is and must be a fiction should be reminded that the word "person" originally meant "mask"; that its application to human beings was at first metaphorical. They would not contend that it is a fiction to say that Bill Smith is a person; their contention that "corporate personality" must necessarily involve a fiction must be based ultimately on the notion that the word "person" has reached the legitimate end of its evolution and that it ought to be pinned down where it now is.[2]

More optimistically, in a 1947 essay on "Poetic Diction and Legal Fiction" Barfield hypothesizes:

> [I]f the aptness of a metaphor to mislead varies inversely with the extent to which it continues to be felt and understood as a metaphor and is not taken in a confused way semiliterally, then the contemplation by the mind

> of legal fictions may really be a rather useful exercise. For these are devices of expression, of which the practical expediency can easily be understood, and whose metaphorical nature is not so easily forgotten as they pass into general use.[3]

These accounts suggest that, insofar as they call attention to the metaphorical nature of legal fictions, literary adaptations of legal fictions can cast new light on the historical relationship between the fiction of personhood and the attachment of rights to legal persons.[4] Fuller's and Barfield's philologically informed discussions of legal fictions also suggest that it might not be confusing, but rather illuminating, to interpret legal personifications in imaginative fictions semi-literally in order to remain cognizant of the literal connotations and legal history incorporated into the legal metaphor.

Perhaps no form of legal personhood inherited from the past has haunted crises in the common law to greater political effect than the "corpus" summoned by the writ of habeas corpus. In this chapter, I analyze a set of literary and legal conventions concerning rights to personal liberty in the domains of law, politics, and culture that emerged from British abolitionists' creation of a persuasive narrative about the "human rights" of enslaved Africans as secured through the instrumentality of the writ of habeas corpus, a strategy that gained wide publicity in relation to the *Rex v. Knowles, ex parte Somerset* case of 1771–1772. I then consider whether such legal personifications as the corpus could have a similarly instrumental status when they appear in a novel by exploring how William Godwin's *Things as They Are; or The Adventures of Caleb Williams* incorporates a fictionalized habeas corpus narrative. This reading of the novel arises not simply from its depiction of prisoners, jailers, and courtroom scenes, but also from Godwin's writing it during a period leading up to and coinciding with the suspension by government of the 1679 Habeas Corpus Act from May 1794 to July 1795 as part of a set of measures meant to suppress political dissent in England in the wake of the French Revolution.[5] Godwin had begun composing *Caleb Williams* in February 1793, but his completion of the novel from the early months of 1794 until its publication in May overlapped with the arrest in December 1793, trial in March 1794, and incarceration following conviction of a radical reformer and personal friend, Joseph Gerrald, to whom Godwin affirmed, "You represent us all."[6] I argue that Godwin's novel stages a fictional reinstatement of the political prisoner's "corpus" that had become foreclosed in the legal arena. Contributing Gothic conventions to the fictionalized "corpus," and in this way perpetually reminding the reader that the prisoner's human body has been captured by the law, the novel might also be said to envision a new kind of legal person endowed with "human rights."

A crucial point of intersection between the concurrent forms of political activism pursued by abolitionists and by radicals such as Godwin, and between the public debates and publications they produced, is to be found in their strategic legal uses and fictional adaptations of the forms of action characteristic of habeas corpus jurisprudence, through which they generated a resonant focus on the legal personification of the "corpus." The abolitionists sought political leverage by making a connection between the illegality of enslavement as a violation of natural liberty and fundamental due process protections in the English law against indefinite incarceration. These strategic uses of the habeas corpus process represent a conceptualization of "human rights" via the procedures of the common law, and thus provide a different frame of reference for the history of modern human rights than to locate their origins in the political arguments, promulgated by Thomas Paine and in the American and French Revolutions, that the "rights of man" are inherent in each human being at birth.[7] The conceptualization of "human rights" that I trace here, while not commensurate with post-1948 conceptions of human rights founded in the United Nations Universal Declaration of Human Rights, can also permit new interrogations of their relation to the history of empire and to forms of legal definition and judicial process outside the domain of international law.

In his magisterial history of English habeas corpus jurisprudence, Paul D. Halliday emphasizes that the common-law Great Writ of habeas corpus *ad subjiciendum et recipiendum* ["to undergo and receive"] was "less concerned with moving bodies—many writs did that—than with inspecting the thinking and actions of those who confined bodies."[8] The writ's expression of sovereign prerogative was thus "addressed to the jailer's franchise" as granted by the sovereign.[9] The writ itself was "literally, a scrap of parchment about one or two inches by eight or ten inches in size, directing the jailer to produce the body of the prisoner along with an explanation of the cause of the prisoner's detention," called the return.[10] The judge's ruling on the legality of the cause of the detention stated in the return would result in the prisoner's remand to jail, or release on bail, or, if the detention had been illegal, release and dismissal of charges. In naming habeas corpus cases, the term "ex parte" appears before the name of the person to whom the writ pertains—that is, the prisoner—meaning that the ruling is "on one side only; done by, for, or on the application of one party alone."[11]

Halliday shows that seventeenth- and early eighteenth-century habeas jurisprudence drew on the status of habeas corpus as a common-law writ based in sovereign prerogative to extend the authority of King's Bench into all the territories, jurisdictions, and corporations, including colonial corporations, established by the sovereign. He observes that, until the end of the eighteenth century, "[t]he law concerned with habeas corpus thus marked a huge zone of inclusion, the farthest reaches of a singular subject status, even while other aspects of English law remained immobile."[12] The effects of such inclusiveness can be seen in the cultural politics and specific legal strategies of early British abolitionists. Starting in the 1760s, abolitionists attempted to extract a ruling from the English High Courts on the illegality of slavery in England through legal suits affecting fugitive slaves recaptured by their masters while in England;

several of these suits involved habeas corpus proceedings.[13] These cases were the result of black slaves' courageous attempts to escape from servitude after they had been brought to England from the American colonies and the British possessions in the West Indies.[14] In one of the most famous of these habeas corpus cases brought by abolitionists, *Rex v. Knowles, ex parte Somerset* (also known as *Somerset v. Stewart*), the Chief Justice of King's Bench, William Murray, Lord Mansfield, issued from his chambers a writ of habeas corpus to remove James Somerset (also spelled Sommersett) from the custody of John Knowles, a ship captain who was holding the self-emancipated slave shackled on board his vessel, waiting to be shipped to Jamaica to be sold on the orders of his former master, Charles Stewart. In the return to the writ, which was read aloud in court, Knowles asserted that Somerset was a fugitive slave subject to seizure and resale by his master.[15] After a series of hearings between December 1771 and June 1772 before the Court of King's Bench, Chief Justice Mansfield declared, in brief:

> So high an act of dominion was never in use here; no master ever was allowed here to take a slave by force to be sold abroad, because he had deserted from his service, or for any other reason whatever. We cannot say the cause set forth by this return is allowed or approved of by the laws of this kingdom; therefore, the man must be discharged.[16]

Historians have often interpreted Mansfield's decision as a narrow one, which did not greatly impact the legality of slavery.[17] Yet Mansfield seems to have managed to rule more broadly on the status of fugitive slaves in England, while staying within the remit of the habeas corpus process, by deciding on the return to the writ. In addition, Halliday documents that during the 22-year period when Mansfield presided over King's Bench, the court's rate of release on all writs of habeas corpus was 80 percent.[18] The *Somerset* ruling is therefore also indicative of Mansfield's repeated equitable use of habeas corpus to extend legal jurisdiction and correct abuses of authority.[19]

It was this sort of equitable common-law jurisprudence that the British abolitionists, most prominently Granville Sharp, seem to have counted on. The author of an adulatory 1820 biography of Sharp, who had acted behind the scenes in supporting Somerset's lawyers, reserves some of his most fervent praise for Mansfield's ruling:

> The world had seen, with the most grateful sensations, men of the highest talents and consummate legal knowledge [Somerset's lawyers] gratuitously striving in defence of injured human rights, and united with no other rivalry than to try who should best plead the cause of the helpless. Nor could it contemplate with less respect, a chief magistrate of the first court of English judicature laboriously attentive to arguments which controverted his own

> former proceedings, and, in the end, deliberately establishing a judgment opposite to them—in behalf of humanity.[20]

This conclusion that Mansfield had reversed himself in the *Somerset* decision referred to his rulings in several prior cases, where the chief justice had seemed reluctant to rule on the legality of slavery in England.[21]

In this account by Sharp's biographer, we can also notice how the abolitionists' understanding of the *Somerset* ruling goes beyond a celebration of English jurisprudence and creates a model for identifying slaves' "human rights."[22] Although the term "humanity" could be construed as a moral sentiment indicating humane treatment or benevolence on the part of the judge, I would like to emphasize the legal connotations arising from the entire phrase, "in behalf of humanity." The abolitionists' semi-literal construal of Mansfield's ruling reactivates the metaphorical law Latin meaning of "*ex parte* humanity," thus defining "humanity" as a collective legal person endowed with rights and extrapolated from the individual normally designated in the *ex parte* habeas corpus proceeding. According to this account, Lord Mansfield's decision sided with "humanity." Through this logic, the legal corpus of the unjustly detained slave in turn comes to personify enslaved persons in general, along with their potential rights under English law, and they in turn, through the abolitionists' insistence on their common human status, personify "humanity." The circulation in abolitionist publications of this interpretation of Mansfield's ruling in *Somerset* also indicates how the legal fictions and the prestige of the habeas corpus process could be used for the purposes of anti-slavery political activism.

In treating the *Somerset* case among others as confirmations of enslaved Africans' "human rights," British abolitionists also devised the conventions of a popular habeas corpus narrative about their rescue and emancipation by the writ. For example, in his widely read chronicle, *The History of the Rise, Progress, and Accomplishment of the Abolition of the African Slave-Trade by the British Parliament* (1808), leading abolitionist Thomas Clarkson describes another rescue of a former slave from deportation from England engineered by Sharp prior to the *Somerset* case:

> The vessel on board which a poor African had been dragged and confined had reached the Downs, and had actually got under weigh for the West Indies. In two or three hours she would have been out of sight; but just at this critical moment the writ of *habeas corpus* was carried on board. The officer, who served it on the captain, saw the miserable African chained to the mainmast, bathed in tears, and casting a last mournful look on the land of freedom, which was fast receding from his sight. The captain, on receiving the writ, became outrageous; but, knowing the serious consequences of resisting the law of the land, he gave up his prisoner, whom the officer now carried away safe, but now crying for joy, to the shore.[23]

In Clarkson's account, the writ as legal instrument becomes the protagonist of a sentimental scene of rescue and liberation.[24] All of the human actors in the scene—the officer who carries it, the captain who attempts "outrageously" to resist it, and the slave who is liberated by it—are animated and given their roles by the arrival of the writ with its extension of the English High Courts' powers to restrain violations of individual rights and uphold ancient constitutional liberties.[25] The writ's remedial agency in this scenario, with its power to move bodies by the force of law, seems to absorb and redirect both the fugitive slave's prior acts of resistance and the violence of those who have recaptured him. Its effective action also contrasts strongly with the affective responses of misery, anger, and joy at liberation that it unleashes, suggesting how political agency, and not simply outrage or celebration, could be derived from the legal process through its transformation into and dissemination as a popular narrative construing enslavement as the kind of arbitrary and unlawful detention against which habeas corpus serves as a remedy.

Extrapolating from my account of the *Somerset* case, I identify a group of recurring protagonists of the abolitionists' popular habeas corpus narrative: (1) *the writ itself*, with its attached return; (2) *the advocate* who obtains the writ from the judge on behalf of the prisoner; (3) *the corpus*, understood dually and semi-literally as the physical body of the prisoner that the writ moves from place to place, and as the legal person that appears before the court, accompanied by the writ and return; and (4) *the jailer*, who must supply an account of the cause of the detention inscribed in the return to the writ. In addition, when this judicial process is included in the narrative, another character type often appears which I call the *chastened magistrate*, or the judge who—like Lord Mansfield, according to the abolitionists—overturns his earlier rulings and corrects his unjust prejudices.[26]

Through its novelization, this popular habeas corpus narrative gained new political implications in the aftermath of the French Revolution. Godwin's *Caleb Williams* enhances the fictive status of the "corpus," which in this moment of political crisis takes on the guise of the political prisoner. Rather than adhering to the conventions of sentimental novels as Clarkson does, however, Godwin develops the emotional intensity and political implications of Gothic fiction's focus on internecine violence, or what he calls in the preface "the modes of domestic and unrecorded despotism by which man becomes the destroyer of man" (3).

*Caleb Williams* offers a trenchant critique of various kinds of flawed judicial process in a fictional world where habeas corpus protections, whether in their statutory or common-law forms, seem to be completely absent. The years between 1792 and 1799 saw "an unprecedented amount of repressive legislation" by the British government in reaction to the French Revolution and radical publications such as Thomas Paine's two-part treatise, *Rights of Man* (1791–1792) that defined universal natural rights as the basis for a new political order that would overthrow monarchy and aristocracy.[27] The ministry of

William Pitt the Younger gained the support of Parliament to suspend habeas corpus in May 1794, for the purposes of quickly detaining and prosecuting members of the London Corresponding Society (LCS). LCS "conventions," or large-scale public meetings during the previous months to agitate for annual parliaments and universal (adult male) suffrage, were viewed by government as analogous to the "conventions" of the French National Assembly, and as efforts to overthrow the monarchy and Parliament and install a revolutionary government.[28] *Caleb Williams* was published on 26 May 1794, less than two weeks after habeas corpus had been suspended on 12 May, a measure that had been anticipated by radicals.[29] The suspension of habeas corpus was one among a series of measures for suppressing political dissent passed between 1792 and 1799, including a Royal Proclamation banning "seditious meetings and publications" issued in May 1792, the financing of loyalist publications and associations, the recruitment of spies and informers to gather actionable information on known radicals and republicans, and the authorization of local officials to organize a "Volunteer corps" that could act to repel invasions and also be mobilized "for the suppression of riots and tumults."[30] Pitt's government put the earliest of these measures into action by arresting on charges of high treason and bringing to trial in October through December 1794 leading members of the LCS, including the shoemaker and secretary of the LCS Thomas Hardy, the philologist John Horne Tooke, and the silk merchant and writer John Thelwall. Tooke and Thelwall were Godwin's close friends; Godwin attended their trials, visited them in prison, and contributed to their defense by publishing anonymously in the *Morning Chronicle* a series of articles providing a detailed refutation of Chief Justice Sir James Eyre's formal charge of treason. All three of these men's trials ended in acquittals that were widely believed to have discouraged the government from undertaking many more prosecutions for sedition and treason.[31] Nevertheless, the defendants had been imprisoned under harsh conditions for five months prior to their trials.

Not as fortunate as these men tried in England, LCS members Joseph Gerrald, Thomas Muir, William Skirving, and Maurice Margarot had been convicted by Scotland's supreme criminal court, the High Court of Justiciary, in an earlier set of trials in March 1794. Having been arrested on emergency charges of sedition—as "persons liable to arbitrary punishment"—for making speeches at a "British Convention of the Delegates of the People" in Edinburgh, Gerrald, Skirving, and Margarot received severe sentences of 14 years' transportation and penal servitude at Botany Bay. In a letter prior to Gerrald's trial, Godwin counselled his friend that he should justify his actions as eloquently as possible in order to have the maximum effect on the public, since his right of assembly was protected by the English constitution. But he also warned against mounting a political protest in court: "Truth can never gain by passion, violence, and resentment. … The public want men of this unaltered spirit, whom no persecution can embitter."[32] Yet Gerrald's rhetoric, which included accusing his prosecutors of "tyranny," was not free of provocation: "Surely the experience of all ages should have taught our rulers that persecutions never can efface principles; and that the thunders of the state will prove impotent when wielded against patriotism, innocence, and firmness."[33] The Chief Justice Clerk, Lord Braxfield, head of the criminal judiciary of Scotland and the presiding judge at Gerrald's trial, construed Gerrald's speech as further evidence of sedition, and he warned the jury:

> When you see Mr. Gerrald taking a very active part and making speeches such as you have heard to-day, I look upon him as a very dangerous member of society, FOR I dare say, he has eloquence enough to persuade the people to rise in arms.[34]

After his conviction, Gerrald was detained at the Edinburgh Tolbooth as well as at Newgate and other London prisons for more than a year, before his abrupt transfer on May 2, 1795 to a ship bound for New South Wales, where he died a year later.[35] In an 1832 account of his composition of *Caleb Williams*, Godwin reports that Gerrald received one of the first copies of the novel while he was in jail one evening and "read through the three volumes before he closed his eyes."[36]

While he could not undo Gerrald's conviction, Godwin's novel nevertheless re-imagines and re-litigates Gerrald's trial by staging a very different outcome to his fictional prisoner and first-person narrator Caleb's eloquence before an ad-hoc court. An educated servant to the aristocratic landowner Falkland, Caleb learns of Falkland's secret murder of a neighbor in an affair of honor. After he decides to leave Falkland's service, Caleb is arrested and imprisoned on false charges of theft issued by his master. Following months of detention without access to legal counsel, habeas corpus, or bail, Caleb manages to escape. Rendered by his master's persecution into a fugitive "corpus" lacking access to a writ, in the novel's dénouement, Caleb summons Falkland, both his jailer and master, to court to hold him accountable for his crimes. Caleb's eloquent speech amazes the magistrate and other spectators and wins their sympathy; overpowered by Caleb's sincerity, Falkland embraces him, recognizing Caleb's "heroism" and innocence, and admitting his own "infamy" (335). Falkland appears in the final trial scene as a version of the chastened magistrate, punished by the victim of own injustice and reduced to the "corpse-like" (329) effigy of a man who has been left to waste away while incarcerated. Caleb usurps the magistrate's role by forcing Falkland to provide a narrative, like the jailer's return to the writ, which reveals that his detention and pursuit of Caleb were illegal. Conducted in the novel under an implied state of suspension of the habeas corpus statute, Caleb's makeshift proceeding is necessarily defective, however, and the roles in the judicial process that should have remained distinct become interchangeable. These procedural flaws create a certain illegitimacy, which contributes to Caleb's overpowering feelings of remorse for causing Falkland's death. In fact, Falkland's health has been destroyed by a visit to his plantations in the West Indies (317–8;

329), an explicit indication of the novel's linkage of "domestic despotism" to the violence of slaveholding.

*Caleb Williams* also implies a semi-literal understanding of the habeas corpus process which uncovers, materializes, and turns into a novelistic plot the metaphorical Latin connotations of "you have the body." In the initially drafted ending of the novel that Godwin rejected but that survives in manuscript, Caleb's attempt to expose Falkland's tyranny and criminality fails, as Gerrald's attempts to vindicate himself had done. In this version, Caleb also appears in court to accuse his master of murder, but he speaks with "rapidity, perturbation and vehemence that were absolutely alarming to my hearers" so that the presiding magistrate silences him, demanding, "Do you believe you can overbear and intimidate us? … Never was the dignity of administrative justice in any instance insulted with so bare faced and impudent a forgery!" (342). Caleb's attempt to stage a substitute habeas corpus hearing is unmasked and disqualified, and he descends into madness as the perpetual prisoner of Falkland. Caleb confesses to his journal that "True happiness lies in being like a stone—Nobody can complain of me—all day long I do nothing—am a stone—a GRAVE-STONE!—an obelisk to tell you, HERE LIES WHAT WAS ONCE A MAN!" (346; emphasis in original). Caleb becomes the foreclosed "corpus": permanently incarcerated and silenced, he also represents the monumentalized but suspended writ itself—providing its epitaph. Caleb's petrification, however, still indicates semi-literally the presence of his human body through its deprivation of agency.

It is also possible to draw out a further connection in Godwin's writings between the fictionalized "corpus" in *Caleb Williams* and early abolitionist activism. In the second 1796 edition of his *Enquiry Concerning Political Justice* (1793), a highly influential text among political radicals which brought Godwin his initial fame, he refers to the arguments "from certain deplorable prejudices" in defense of slavery voiced "a few years ago in the English parliament and nation respecting the slave trade." Supporters of slavery asserted the supposed "contentment" of slaves with their condition because "they are not conscious of the evils against which you [abolitionists] exclaim." Godwin interpolates a refutation:

> Are they contented? I am not contented for them. I see in them beings of certain capacities, equal to certain pursuits and enjoyments. It is of no consequence in the question that they do not see this, that they do not know their own interests and happiness. They do not repine? Neither does a stone repine. That which you mention as an alleviation, finishes in my conception the portrait of their calamity. Abridged as they are of independence and enjoyment, they have neither the apprehension nor spirit of men. I cannot bear to see human nature thus degraded. It is my duty, if I can, to make them a thousand times happier than they are, or have any conception of being.[37]

Like Caleb in his guise as the indefinitely incarcerated, petrified "corpus," enslaved persons are systematically dehumanized, reduced to a stone-like existence of endurance. The resonance of the alternative, rejected ending of *Caleb Williams* with Godwin's account of the slaves' deprivation of necessary "independence and enjoyment"—but not of their humanity or "human nature"—shows that the novel's Gothic fictionalization of the "corpus," or the composite legal and physical body of the political prisoner, bears affinities to the abolitionists' understanding of slaves as subjects of "injured human rights."

For those readers of Godwin's novel who were informed about the political trials of English radicals, the published text of *Caleb Williams*, with its substitute habeas corpus proceeding vindicating the prisoner, also summons the "corpus" of Joseph Gerrald and those of the other convicted LCS members before the court of public opinion. As Godwin explained in a published letter responding to a review in the anti-Jacobin journal *British Critic* in 1795, which had attacked Godwin's novel as intended "to throw an odium upon the laws of [his] country," the novel's true "object is of much greater magnitude":

> It is to expose the evils which arise out of the present system of civilised society; and having exposed them to lead the enquiring reader to examine whether they are, or are not, as has commonly been supposed, irremediable; in a word, to disengage the minds of men from prepossession, and launch them upon the sea of moral and political enquiry. ... Your correspondent comes nearer the point when he ... states my object to be: "the laws of this country, and their mode of execution"; or rather, as he ought to have stated, the administration of justice and equity, with its consequences, as it exists in the world at large, and in Great Britain in particular.[38]

Beyond its immediate reference to the political situation in England, Godwin seems to envision a more expansive, world-wide remedial impact of the novel that is also less reliant on an appeal to readers' moral sentiments and more oriented toward a deliberative judgment based in principles of legality and political justice. The novel's attention to the "consequences of the administration of justice" during a period of suspension of the remedial jurisdiction of habeas corpus enlists its readership in a public demand for a return to constitutional forms of political and legal accountability.

*Caleb Williams* captures the legal instrumentality of the "corpus" and shifts it into a political register by endowing it with a further level of fictionality, making it doubly personified, a Gothic literary personification of a legal person who returns to haunt the British public sphere where its actual legal appearance and efficacy have been temporarily nullified. Godwin's novel intensifies the legal personality's fictionality and therefore demonstrates its adaptability to other uses. The novel's version of the habeas corpus remedy is not of an entirely different order from the actual judicial process, however, but differs in exercising its effects for the political education of readers. Although the novel lacks legal authority, the author can nevertheless strive for an influence analogous to that of the judge by crafting a narrative that addresses each reader directly.[39] As Godwin wrote in 1832, looking back on the time of political crisis during which he wrote the novel:

> I said to myself a thousand times, "I will write a tale, that shall constitute an epoch in the mind of the reader, that no one, after he has read it, shall ever be exactly the same man that he was before."[40]

I have argued that the larger historical questions of definition pertaining to "human rights" and habeas corpus in the late eighteenth-century legal and political domains are enhanced in the literary fiction by means of its insistence on the implied human body of the "corpus." The novel's fictional personifications of rights-bearing legal persons are pronouncedly semi-literal, never fully denaturalized and "pinned down" (Fuller) within their legal frame of reference, never completely disembodied or disencumbered of their extra-legal connotations. The "corpus," whether in law or fiction, becomes a particularly powerful proxy for the "human" in "human rights" as a form of embodied legal personhood because the "corpus" can never appear without a body, and when the writ fails to issue and mobilize it, the "injured" human body of the prisoner or the slave, bereft of a remedy for its loss of legal rights, declines and perishes. In this respect, the "corpus" we have studied here may also personify, ahead of its time, a demand for the remedies of modern international human rights—yet to be fully instantiated in law—for violations against the body.

This chapter's account of "human rights" claims within the history of late eighteenth-century British abolitionism and radical politics highlights how activists, lawyers, and novelists applied the habeas corpus judicial process in new ways and within new kinds of political narratives. In these narratives, habeas corpus represents not only a remedy for unlawful arrest and detention, but also a political strategy for bringing the injustices perpetrated by the law and the state before the eyes of the public. These narratives also support the legitimacy of using the ancient legal process of the writ of habeas corpus for the significant purpose of attributing legal personhood and extending common-law protections to the enslaved and to political dissidents deemed dangerous to public safety, and, in this way, ascertaining not simply their legal rights under the constitution but also, more inclusively, their "human rights."

## Notes

1 L.L. Fuller, "Legal Fictions," *Illinois Law Review* 25, No. 4 (December 1930), 380.
2 Ibid., 377.
3 Owen Barfield, "Poetic Diction and Legal Fiction," in *The Importance of Language*, ed. Max Black (Ithaca and London: Cornell University Press, 1962), 69.

4 I have benefitted from Simon Stern's analysis in "Legal and Literary Fictions," in *New Directions in Law and Literature*, ed. Elizabeth Anker and Bernadette Meyler (Oxford University Press, 2016), 313–26.

5 E.P. Thompson, *The Making of the English Working Class* (New York: Vintage, 1963), 128.

6 Godwin, letter to Joseph Gerrald, January 23, 1794, in William Godwin, *Things as They Are, or the Adventures of Caleb Williams*, ed. Maurice Hindle (London: Penguin, 1988), 358; all further references appear in the text. Pamela Clemit charts Godwin's composition of *Caleb Williams* in *The Godwinian Novel: The Rational Fictions of Godwin, Brockden Brown, Mary Shelley* (Oxford: Clarendon Press, 1993), 37.

7 Recent studies linking the history of human rights to the French and American revolutions and the writings of Thomas Paine are Lynn Hunt, *Inventing Human Rights* (New York: Norton, 2007) and Peter de Bolla, *The Architecture of Concepts: The Historical Formation of Human Rights* (New York: Fordham University Press, 2013).

8 Paul D. Halliday, *Habeas Corpus: From England to Empire* (Cambridge, MA: Harvard University Press, 2010), 40–1.

9 Ibid., 42.

10 Ibid., 48.

11 *Ex parte*, definition: http://legal-dictionary.thefreedictionary.com/ex+parte (accessed April 14, 2013).

12 Halliday, *Habeas Corpus*, 265.

13 These cases are discussed in F.O. Shyllon, *Black Slaves in Britain* (London: Oxford University Press, 1974).

14 Douglas A. Lorimer, "Black Slaves and English Liberty, A Re-examination of Racial Slavery in England," *Immigrants and Minorities* 3, No. 2 (1984), 135.

15 Francis Hargrave, one of Somerset's lawyers, reprints the text of the return in his report of the trial, *An Argument in the Case of James Sommersett A Negro Lately Determined in the Court of King's Bench* (London, 1774), 4–6.

16 "Historical Chronicle, *Monday* 22 [June]," *The Gentleman's Magazine* XLII (June 1772), 293–4; emphasis in original. This is an abbreviated text of Mansfield's ruling, of which there are several other extant transcriptions.

17 Among the many publications discussing the *Somerset* decision and its influence, see: James Walvin, *Black and White: The Negro and English Society 1555–1945* (London: Allen Lane/The Penguin Press, 1973), 117–31; Shyllon, *Black Slaves in Britain*, 82–176; James Oldham, "New Light on Mansfield and Slavery," *Journal of British Studies* 27, No. 1 (January 1988), 45–68; David Brion Davis, *The Problem of Slavery in the Age of Revolution 1770–1823* (New York: Oxford University Press, 1999), 469–522; Ruth Paley, "After *Somerset*: Mansfield, Slavery and the Law in England, 1772–1830," in *Law, Crime and English Society, 1660–1830*, ed. Norma Landau (Cambridge: Cambridge University Press, 2002), 165–84; George Van Cleve, "*Somerset's Case* and Its Antecedents in Imperial Context," *Law and History Review* 24, No. 3 (Fall 2006), 601–45; and William M. Wiecek, "Somerset: Lord Mansfield and the Legitimacy of Slavery in the Anglo-American World," *University of Chicago Law Review* 42 (1974–1975), 86–146.

18 Halliday, *Habeas Corpus*, 55.

19 Ibid., 33, 132–3, 174–6, 324–5. Halliday emphasizes: "By issuing the writ, [in Somerset's case], King's Bench fitfully made a new jurisdiction for itself; by its judgment, it began—very slightly—to kill off the jurisdiction of slaveholders over their slaves, just as it had always contained the jurisdiction of all others who held the bodies of the king's subjects." *Habeas Corpus*, 176.

20 Prince Hoare, *Memoirs of Granville Sharp, Esq. composed from his own manuscripts, and other authentic documents in the possession of his family and of the African Institution: with observations on Mr. Sharp's biblical criticisms*, vol. 1. (2 vols., London, 1820), 93–4.
21 Hoare, *Memoirs of Granville Sharp*, 59; Halliday, *Habeas Corpus*, 174–5.
22 On the self-legitimizing cultural and political agendas of British abolitionism, see Christopher Leslie Brown, *Moral Capital: Foundations of British Abolitionism* (Chapel Hill: University of North Carolina Press, 2006).
23 Thomas Clarkson, *The History of the Rise, Progress, and Accomplishment of the Abolition of the African Slave-Trade* (2 vols., London, 1808) Vol. 1, 74–5.
24 For a cogent analysis of the instability and limitations of British abolitionists' sentimental definitions of "humanity," see Lynn Festa, "Humanity Without Feathers," *Humanity: An International Journal of Human Rights, Humanitarianism, and Development* 1, No. 1 (Fall 2010), 3–27.
25 Clarkson most likely refers to the 1771 case of Thomas Lewis, in which Sharp played a central role in obtaining the writ of habeas corpus. The case was tried on appeal to King's Bench before a jury, which did not find sufficient evidence that Lewis was his master's property, so that Lord Mansfield did not rule on the legality of slavery. F.O. Shyllon, *Black Slaves in Britain*, 43–54.
26 For further discussion of the chastened magistrate figure, see Sarah Winter, "The Magistrate, the Camp, and the Novel: J.M. Coetzee and the Subject of Human Rights," *NOVEL: A Forum on Fiction* 47, No. 2 (Summer 2014), 261–83.
27 Boyd Hilton, *A Mad, Bad, and Dangerous People? England 1783–1846* (Oxford: Clarendon Press, 2006), 65–74.
28 Thompson, *Making of the English Working Class*, 144–5.
29 Maurice Hindle, Introduction, *Caleb Williams*, xi; John Barrell, *Imagining the King's Death: Figurative Treason, Fantasies of Regicide* (Oxford: Oxford University Press, 2000), 182.
30 Hilton, *A Mad, Bad, and Dangerous People?*, 71–2.
31 The charges against the other LCS members who had been detained were dropped later in 1794 and 1795 (Barrell 400–1). For a detailed study of these treason trials, see Barrell, *Imagining the King's Death*.
32 William Godwin, letter to Joseph Gerrald, January 23, 1794; in Godwin, *Things as They Are, or the Adventures of Caleb Williams*, ed. Hindle, 356–8.
33 *The Trial of Joseph Gerrald, Delegate from the London Corresponding Society, to the British Convention, Before the High Court of Judiciary, At Edinburgh, on the 3d, 10th, 13th, and 14th March, 1794, For Sedition, Taken in Short-hand by Mr. Ramsey* (Edinburgh: James Robinson, May 3, 1794), 233.
34 Ibid., 240.
35 Thompson, *Making of the English Working Class*, 128; Michael T. Davis, "Gerrald, Joseph (1763–1796)" in *Oxford Dictionary of National Biography*, online ed., ed. Lawrence Goldman (Oxford: Oxford University Press, 2004–2010 (accessed August 22, 2010).
36 From Godwin's Preface to the 1832 Standard Novels edition of *Fleetwood*; in *Caleb Williams*, ed. Hindle, 353–4.
37 William Godwin, *An enquiry concerning political justice, and its influence on general virtue and happiness. The second edition corrected in two volumes*, Vol. 1 (London, 1796), 443–4. *Eighteenth Century Collections Online*. Gale (accessed November 24, 2015).
38 William Godwin, To the Editor of the *British Critic*, London, 7 June 1795, pp. 94–5; quoted in Mark Philp, *Godwin's Political Justice* (Ithaca, NY: Cornell University Press, 1986), 108.

39 According to William St Clair, *Caleb Williams* was by far Godwin's most popular novel: "It was reprinted thirteen times before the end of the [nineteenth] century and twenty-six times in Godwin's lifetime in England, Ireland, the United States, France, Germany, and Switzerland." *The Godwins and the Shelleys* (Baltimore: The Johns Hopkins University Press, 1989), 122.

40 From Godwin's Preface to the 1832 Standard Novels edition of *Fleetwood*; in *Caleb Williams*, ed. Hindle, 350.

Part 5

# Fictional discourse and the law

## A theoretical perspective

Chapter 5.1

# Legal fictions and legal fabrication

*Simon Stern*

Since the inception of the common-law courts, jurists and lawyers have been highly attentive to certain questions about how law manages its own administration, such as rules of pleading, rules of court, and civil procedure more generally, but only in the last two hundred years or so has there been a similar degree of attention to the more abstract issues bearing on the law's operations—what we might call "doctrinal procedure" or "the law of the common law." Conventions governing proof standards and the binding power of precedent, for example, did not become formalized until the nineteenth century,[1] and the same applies to legal fictions. Up that time, they "just grew" like Topsy, with only brief and occasional efforts, by common lawyers, to explain or theorize them. However, in the course of the nineteenth century, as lawyers became increasingly self-conscious about the nature and legitimacy of their activities, all of these phenomena came under the scrutiny of a theorist equipped with the tools of categorization and normative evaluation. Whereas historians of a subject such as contracts or group litigation can study the evolution of the practice in relation to many centuries' worth of commentary on it, scholars interested in these more conceptual issues have a more limited fund of commentary to place against the history of legal practice.

Nevertheless, once they were isolated and theorized, these aspects of doctrinal procedure came into their own as subjects of analysis, and they have generated a significant amount of research over the last century. Scholarship on legal fictions has burgeoned in recent years, fueling work not only by law professors but also literary critics, in which the concept of the legal fiction is assigned a wide range of meanings.[2] In what follows, I consider one of the most influential theories of legal fictions and show why it does not serve the purposes that commentators usually ask of it. Next, I try to explain what gives the legal fiction a distinctive legal function, and the answer I propose is that legal fictions seem, to modern commentators, to do for law what metafiction does for imaginative writing. That analogy, in turn, prompts another question—namely, why is it that a relatively small group of doctrinal propositions (the ones that are repeatedly offered as classic examples of legal fictions) are taken as exhausting the category of devices that self-reflexively expose law's own constructive operations, when many other legal tools also perform the same function?

## 1 Two theories of fictions

Two accounts of legal fictions have played an extremely influential role in recent scholarship: Henry Sumner Maine's account, in *Ancient Law* (1861), and Lon Fuller's account, first published in a trio of articles in the early 1930s and reprinted in book form in 1967.[3] Fuller's account has received a considerable degree of attention in recent scholarship, but Maine's discussion has attracted much less scholarly attention; although many commentators have drawn on it, few have subjected it to critical scrutiny. Consequently, I examine Maine's treatment in more detail below, and consider Fuller's analysis very briefly.

Maine's account of legal fictions remains highly influential even though some of its central tenets have, at least implicitly, been rejected. Contemporary scholars often quote Maine's definition of legal fictions as a preliminary step before focusing their attention on a particular example (such as coverture, civil death, corporate personhood, the "one drop" rule, or the reasonable person).[4] Maine furnishes a genealogical definition that may have answered the needs of his day; today, however, it is invoked with little attention to the constraints it establishes. One of the features that may help to account for its contemporary appeal involves the sense of evasiveness it captures. He asserts that fictions are pervasive in the common law—so pervasive as to be absolutely omnipresent—and although commentators rarely acknowledge the full significance of this claim, they seem to relish its implications.

Here, then, is the account that Maine furnishes:

> I employ the word "fiction" in a sense considerably wider than that in which English lawyers are accustomed to use it, and with a meaning much more extensive than that which belonged to the Roman "fictiones." Fictio, in old Roman law, is properly a term of pleading, and signifies a false averment on the part of the plaintiff which the defendant was not allowed to traverse; such, for example, as an averment that the plaintiff was a Roman citizen, when in truth he was a foreigner. The object of these "fictions" was, of course, to give jurisdiction, and they therefore strongly resembled the allegations in the writs of the English Queen's Bench, and Exchequer, by which those Courts contrived to usurp the jurisdiction of the Common Pleas:—the allegation that the defendant was in custody of the king's marshal, or that the plaintiff was the king's debtor, and could not pay his debt by reason of the defendant's default. But I now employ the expression "Legal Fiction" to signify any assumption which conceals, or affects to conceal, the fact that a rule of law has undergone alteration, its letter remaining unchanged, its operation being modified. The words, therefore, include the instances of fictions which I have cited from the English and Roman law, but they embrace much more, for I should speak both of the English Case-law and of the Roman Responsa Prudentum as resting on

> fictions. ... The *fact* is ... that the law has been wholly changed; the *fiction* is that it remains what it always was.[5]

At first glance, this analysis might seem to exemplify a rhetorical approach to the subject: courts are resorting to fictions on those occasions when, like a bunco artist, they distract readers by talking of stability although in reality they are covertly rearranging things. Hence it might seem to follow that when a court acts openly, it is not relying on a fiction, no matter how bizarre or fanciful its reasoning. A closer look, however, shows that Maine is concerned not with rhetoric but with concepts and institutions.

According to Maine, a fiction arises whenever "[an] assumption ... conceals, or affects to conceal, the fact that a rule of law has undergone alteration, its letter remaining unchanged, its operation being modified." And as Maine shows, in the discussion that follows, such an assumption is at work in every case in which a court changes the law. That is because "the *fiction* ... that [the law] remains what it always was" is, in his view, an institutional fiction that applies to the workings of common-law courts generally. This fiction is expressed by the proposition that courts do not make new law, but only find the law. Consequently, even if a judge were to state, in the course of a decision, that the result was to change the law, that would not dispel the "assumption which conceals" the fact of change, because that assumption does not depend on a particular instance of judicial rhetoric, but rather on a claim about the nature and operation of common-law courts generally.

Maine's definition is genealogical because it makes a doctrine's status as a fiction turn on how the doctrine was developed. Maine places legal fictions in contrast to two other modes of legal change: alteration by equity and by statute. A fiction arises whenever a court changes the law, and a fiction never arises when legal change occurs by way of equity or statute. Equity is the conceptual instrument of change in the common law: "Equity ... differs from ... Fictions ... in that the interference with law is open and avowed."[6] Once again, it may seem that Maine is presenting a rhetorical argument, but on his view, courts must resort to equity in order to change the law, and hence a failure to invoke the court's equitable power necessarily brands the decision as fictional.[7] Legislation differs from both law and equity because of the agent that effects the change:

> [Legislation] differs from Legal Fictions just as Equity differs from them, and it is also distinguished from Equity, as deriving its authority from an external body or person. Its obligatory force is independent of its principles. The legislature, whatever be the actual restraints imposed on it by public opinion, is in theory empowered to impose what obligations it pleases on the members of the community. There is nothing to prevent its legislating in the wantonness of caprice.[8]

Legislative change produces no fiction, because the legislature is not confined by the institutional claim that it does not make law—in fact, that is precisely what legislatures are known to do. And equitable change produces no fiction, because the use of equity is the proper means of change by a court.

Consequently, for one who subscribes to Maine's account, no doctrine can be characterized as fictional until we first determine the doctrine's origin: Was it by a court or a legislature? If by a court, was there any talk of equity? Yet in many contemporary uses, the term is reserved for doctrines that are bizarre, fanciful, strained, or implausible, regardless of the means by which they were produced. Adherence to Maine's account would require that the credentials of any candidate for fictionality must be verified by tracing the doctrine back to its source, and then confirming that in the interim, no court in the same jurisdiction has adopted the result by using equity, and no legislature has done so by statute. Either of these events would terminate the fiction and place the doctrine on a new footing. Taken seriously, Maine's approach would involve highly specific historical claims: a given doctrine was fictional only for a certain time span, until the fictional solution was replaced by some other instrument of legal change. This kind of historical examination is conspicuously absent from most contemporary discussions of legal fictions, which tend to proceed as if fictionality depends on the content of a legal proposition rather than its source or the conditions in which it is posed.

Consequently, to invoke Maine's definition as the basis for explaining the fictionality of corporate personhood or civil death appears misguided for two reasons. First, according to Maine, the number of fictions in the common law is vast—in fact, the great majority of all legal doctrines are fictions, having been generated entirely by courts, or by courts as a way to fill in legislative gaps. (Although Maine emphatically embraces this view, it is rarely mentioned in modern discussions that refer to him.) The comparatively small list of doctrines that appear repeatedly in discussions of the subject would hardly scratch the surface, nor does Maine's account helpfully explain why civil death or corporate personhood *in particular* should count as fictions (since the list is so huge). Second, the fictionality of any given doctrine depends on details (which jurisdiction? which era?) that appear to hold very little interest for most of the scholars who quote Maine.

Taken at face value, Maine's account seems to have little to offer for most commentators—in the fields of both law and literature—who are interested in the classic examples of legal fictions. This area of scholarship is concerned with fictional dimensions of corporate personhood, for instance, that differentiate it from concepts such as "substantial similarity" in intellectual property, or "reasonable discoverability" in the law of limitations (which would both count as fictions, in many jurisdictions, according to Maine). Why, then, does Maine's treatment continue to have so much appeal? I suggest that the answer lies in Maine's talk of "concealment," which hints at an evasive attitude surrounding the establishment of the fiction. In much of the recent research on legal fictions, it is this air of evasiveness, rather than the doctrine's pedigree, that seems to justify the label. Insofar as this change in the application of the term "legal fiction" has gone unacknowledged, one might be tempted to say that the ongoing use of the same label exemplifies precisely the kind of fictionality that Maine's definition itself targets: the term's operation has been modified, its object has shifted, but the continued reference to Maine's account implies that its letter and substance have remained unchanged.

Turning briefly to Fuller's theory of fictions, we may note that its central requirement is falsity. He writes that a legal fiction is "either (1) a statement propounded with complete or partial consciousness of its falsity, or (2) a false statement recognized as having utility."[9] If Maine's definition appears unhelpful because it would require us to verify the source of a given doctrine, Fuller's raises concerns because the language of truth and falsity seems inapposite for many of the doctrines that are normally characterized as fictions (and for legal concepts more generally). Is the standard of the "reasonable person" true or false? It is hardly evident that the standard includes any propositional content that would make this question meaningful. A standard is simply a means of evaluating liability: those who meet or exceed it are not liable, and those who fall short (and cause harm as a result) are liable. To say that someone did not meet the standard, in a given case, involves no assertion about the defendant's personality; it attaches a legal label to the person's acts, just as countless other doctrines do, and hence it is hard to see how falsity could enter into the discussion. Again, is it true or false that a person is "civilly dead"? It is true if we take the doctrine to name a legal result, and false if we can discern, within the formula, a referential claim that designates something besides the person's legal status. These are vexed issues, and I cannot do full justice to them here.[10] Suffice it to say that Fuller's "falsity" comes closer to the nub of the fiction than Maine's "concealment" does, but neither one seems to account satisfactorily for the doctrines that consistently figure in most discussions of the subject.

## II Legal fiction as metafiction

Perhaps the appeal of both Maine's and Fuller's accounts lies in the attitude they convey rather than the framework they delineate. According to Maine, fictions are an instrument of change—but they are the wrong instrument. According to Fuller, they are false, but they do not hide their falsity, and that is what allows them to be productive. Both commentators recognize something about the productive and creative work of fictions that separates them from the other modes of legal invention. I suggest that legal fictions do for law what metafiction does for imaginative writing. By this I mean that modern commentators are interested in a different phenomenon than the one that interested Maine and Fuller: rather than deceit, or falsity, or the instrumental value of a false premise, modern commentators are interested in fabrication, creativity, constructive capacity—and they are especially interested in law's ability to make things up when a legal device calls attention to this ability, rather than concealing it. In the 1960s and 1970s, novelists such as John Fowles, John Barth, and Robert Coover sought out new ways of highlighting the creative capacities of the novelist, by writing fiction in which they called attention to the author's control over the story and the reader's participation in the imaginative enterprise that fosters the experience of narrative coherence. Using techniques now called metafictional, these writers made a point of pulling back the curtain, speculating openly about what might happen next in the plot, or how the reader was experiencing the text, or why characters were made to behave in the way they did.[11] It is precisely this kind of attention to the creative act that commentators on legal fictions mean to register, when they say corporate personhood or coverture is a legal fiction. Far from concealing the law's operations, these doctrines appear—to those commentators—to be highlighting the law's ability to create, or change, or refashion on its own terms. Whereas the metafictions of a Fowles or a Coover are self-conscious efforts on the part of a writer to break the illusion of realism, legal fictions are not deployed by judges who have a penchant for reminding their readers about law's creative capacities; rather, on this account, the doctrine's fictional dimension is in the eye of the beholder, which helps to explain why there is disagreement about which doctrines count as fictions.

There is more to say about the analogy to metafiction than I can elaborate here; I will close by considering the question of why relatively few doctrines are regarded as fictions. Since law is a thoroughly artificial enterprise, we might say that everything in law is a fiction, including estoppels, patent abuse, and the *Rooker-Feldman* doctrine. Although all of these evince law's creative capacities, they evidently are not perceived as highlighting those capacities, for the same reason that relatively few writers of fantasy and science fiction attempt the metafictional gestures of A.S. Byatt, Jennifer Egan, or Jeanette Winterson. Novelists who are busy creating new life forms and revising the laws of physics, or populating a plot with mythical beings, may see little reason to point out how much control they have over the story, since there is no likelihood that a reader will succumb to the illusion of realism to begin with. There must at least be some chance that readers will see an imaginative work as referring generally to the world they experience, if there is to be any point in observing that "this is not a pipe." Most doctrines are so entirely creatures of the law that no one would mistake them for anything else.

Law is often quite open about its creative capacity. On a motion to dismiss, for example, courts invariably begin by stating that, for purposes of the motion, they must assume all allegations pleaded in the complaint to be true.[12] Then, if the court denies the motion, those facts are placed back in the category of conditional assertions that still have to be established according to the canons of evidence law. It would be hard to find a more direct acknowledgement of law's ability to fabricate things than a fact accepted as true in one moment and put aside as requiring proof in the next. Moreover, the grant or denial of a motion to dismiss can have significant extralegal consequences, so one cannot say that the conditional assumption of truth matters only within the legal sphere, and has no effect outside that sphere. Evidently, this example and numerous others that one might furnish belong to the category of legal devices and concepts that are artificial in the same way that fantasy and science fiction novels are artificial: the artifice is at once readily apparent and perfectly mundane.

Those doctrines that are typically regarded as legal fictions, such as corporate personhood and civil death, are doctrines that not only have extralegal effects, but that could be mistaken for having extralegal reference. Perhaps this way of perceiving them reflects a misapprehension about the referential nature of legal language; however, if one accepts that a doctrine's fictional status depends on the eye of the beholder, then the relevant distinction turns not on a correct view of how legal meaning works, but on questions about ordinary language and the law's attribution of technical meanings to terms that are drawn from ordinary language. Legal persons overlap with, and merge into, persons in the vernacular, finding attachments outside the legal domain in ways that estoppels and the *Rooker-Feldman* doctrine cannot. This apparent merging, I suggest, is the effect that corresponds to the literary metafiction, highlighting the law's constructive capacity. Even though artifice plays a vital role in modern law, we seem to need fictions to bring that realization into visibility, and that is their most distinctive feature.

## Notes

1 See e.g. Jim Evans, "Change in the Doctrine of Precedent During the Nineteenth Century," in Laurence Goldstein, ed., *Precedent in Law* (Oxford: Clarendon Press, 1987), 45–65; and Neil Duxbury, *The Nature and Authority of Precedent* (Cambridge: Cambridge University Press, 2008).

2 See e.g. the essays in Maksymilian Del Mar and William Twining, eds., *Legal Fictions in Theory and Practice* (Cham: Springer, 2015); Nancy J. Knauer, "Legal Fictions and Juristic Truth," *St. Thomas Law Review* 23 (2010), 1–49; Karla F.C. Holloway, *Legal Fictions: Constituting Race, Composing Literature* (Durham: Duke University Press, 2014); Trish Ferguson, *Thomas Hardy's Legal Fictions* (Edinburgh: Edinburgh University Press, 2013).

3 Henry Sumner Maine, *Ancient Law: Its Connection with the Early History of Society, and its Relation to Modern Ideas* (London: Murray, 1861); Lon L. Fuller, *Legal Fictions* (Stanford: Stanford University Press, 1967).

4 For some recent examples, see Roy Sorenson, "Lying to Mindless Machines," in Eliot Michaelson and Andreas Stokke, eds., *Lying: Language, Knowledge, Ethics, and Politics* (Oxford: Oxford University Press, 2018), 293; Daniel S. Kleinberger, "Shape Shifting in the Law," *William Mitchell Law Review* 38 (2011), 586–7; Gilbert Leung, "Illegal Fictions," in Benjamin Hutchens, ed., *Jean-Luc Nancy: Justice, Legality and World* (London: Continuum, 2012), 82; Marcus Waithe, "Empson's Legal Fiction," *Essays in Criticism* 62 (2012), 288.

5 Maine (note 3), 25–6.

6 Ibid., 28.

7 At most, we can say that Maine's account is rhetorical in the sense that a failure to invoke the language of equity is the feature that brands the decision as fictional.

8 Maine (note 3), 29.
9 Fuller (note 3), 9.
10 For some discussion of these issues, see Simon Stern, "Literary and Legal Fictions," in Elizabeth S. Anker and Bernadette Meyler, eds., *New Directions in Law and Literature* (Oxford: Oxford University Press, 2017), 313–26; Michael Quinn, "Fuller on Legal Fictions: A Benthamic Perspective," in Del Mar and Twining (note 2), 55–82; Karen Petroski, "Legal Fictions and the Limits of Legal Language," *International Journal of Law in Context* 9 (2013), 485–505; Frederick Schauer, "Is Law a Technical Language?" *San Diego Law Review* 52 (2015), 501–14.
11 For some classic analyses, see Patricia Waugh, *Metafiction: The Theory and Practice of Self-Conscious Fiction* (London: Routledge, 2002); Linda Hutcheon, *Narcissistic Narrative: The Metafictional Paradox* (London: Methuen, 1980).
12 See e.g. *Bell Atlantic Corp. v Twombly*, 550 U.S. 544 (2007).

## References

Del Mar, Maksymilian and William Twining (eds). *Legal Fictions in Theory and Practice.* Cham: Springer, 2015.

Duxbury, Neil. *The Nature and Authority of Precedent.* Cambridge: Cambridge University Press, 2008.

Evans, Jim. "Change in the Doctrine of Precedent During the Nineteenth Century." In: *Precedent in Law.* Edited by Laurence Goldstein, 45–65. Oxford: Clarendon Press, 1987.

Ferguson, Trish, *Thomas Hardy's Legal Fictions.* Edinburgh: Edinburgh University Press, 2013.

Fuller, Lon. *Legal Fictions.* Stanford: Stanford University Press, 1967.

Holloway, Karla F. *Legal Fictions: Constituting Race, Composing Literature.* Durham: Duke University Press, 2014.

Hutcheon, Linda. *Narcissistic Narrative: The Metafictional Paradox.* London: Methuen, 1980.

Kleinberger, Daniel S. "Shape Shifting in the Law." *William Mitchell Law Review* 38 (2011), 586.

Knauer, Nancy J. "Legal Fictions and Juristic Truth." *St. Thomas Law Review* 23 (2010), 1–49.

Leung, Gilbert. "Illegal Fictions," In: *Jean-Luc Nancy: Justice, Legality and World.* Edited by Benjamin Hutchens. London: Continuum, 2012.

Maine, Henry Sumner. *Ancient Law: Its Connection with the Early History of Society, and its Relation to Modern Ideas.* London: Murray, 1861.

Petroski, Karen. "Legal Fictions and the Limits of Legal Language." *International Journal of Law in Context* 9 (2013), 485–505.

Quinn, Michael. "Fuller on Legal Fictions: A Benthamian Perspective." In: *Legal Fictions in Theory and Practice.* Edited by Maksymilian Del Mar and William Twining, 55–82. Cham: Springer, 2015.

Schauer, Frederick. "Is Law a Technical Language?" *San Diego Law Review* 52 (2015), 501–14.

Sorenson, Roy. "Lying to Mindless Machines." In: *Lying: Language, Knowledge, Ethics, and Politics.* Edited by Eliot Michaelson and Andreas Stokke, 285–300. Oxford University Press, 2018.

Stern, Simon. "Legal and Literary Fictions." In: *New Directions in Law and Literature.* Edited by Elizabeth S. Anker and Bernadette Meyler, 313–26. Oxford: Oxford University Press, 2017.

Waithe, Marcus. "Empson's Legal Fiction." *Essays in Criticism* 62 (2012), 291–301.

Waugh, Patricia. *Metafiction: The Theory and Practice of Self-Conscious Fiction.* London: Routledge, 2002.

Chapter 5.2

# Linguistic fictions and legal rule

*Hans J. Lind*

As outlined in Chapter 1 of this volume, since the last heyday of the treatment of legal fictions in the early twentieth century, counterfactuality has generally been understood as a necessary condition of fictionality. This is still the case with those newer theories of legal fictionality that are not bound to an outdated understanding of truth as metaphysical correspondence, but support newer criteria for truth (e.g. truth as consensus, truth as consistence, cf. pp. 15–16), or maintain that truth claims within law are not to be equated with claims in extra-legal discourses (cf. pp. 17, 23). Apart from some notable exceptions, even the critical re-readings of Bentham, Vaihinger, Kelsen and Fuller, which occurred during the last four decades, do not seem to have added much to the picture – at least if one considers the unchanged definitions in major law dictionaries and in a not insubstantial number of more recent essays (see pp. 6–10). My chapter aims to offer an alternative to the classical understanding of legal fictions, using continental European statutory fictions as a paradigm. In the process of revising this chapter, a piece originally written in 2010/2011 for a faculty workshop[1] and subsequently to be published in the group's proceedings,[2] I was surprised to see how valid its claims still are, particularly considering the renewed interest that led to a wave of recent publications on the issue – and the chapter only needed a few additional paragraphs to be brought up to date. This chapter is, however, part of a larger project on a reassessment of fictionality in general – and has to be understood in this context. I am convinced that the early noted merely linguistic nature of statutory fictionality[3] can provide valuable insights for a general definition of fictional discourse that is not bound to the classical true–false dichotomy, the latter still being inherent in the majority of today's approaches to legal fictionality. I am convinced that, by doing so, it might even assist the interdisciplinary endeavour of fictional theory in finding a transdisciplinary criterion of fictionality in general (cf. p. 36).

## I Statutory fictions as an object of inquiry

From a theoretical perspective, statutory fictions are of particular interest as an object of inquiry, since they do not bear the stain of "weakness"[4] and "trickery", or even of "usurpation"[5] and "violence",[6] which is commonly associated with the fictions of judicature (judicial fictions). While judicial fictions have early been regarded as "the stealing [of] legislative power, by and for hands, which could not, or durst not, openly claim it",[7] in contrast, statutory fictions are a deliberate choice of the legislator, "who needs not feign" but "commands".[8] Although some scholars maintain that "legislators should avoid fictions",[9] statutory fictions are even the rule in civil law countries nowadays, due to peculiarities in the construction of legal relationships in many continental codes that I will comment on more extensively later in this chapter. Statutory fictions are not a new phenomenon, however. Since they date back to the heyday of Roman law, as the famous *fictio legis Corneliae* illustrates, statutory fictions have a long history both of use and of theoretical reception,[10] and most of the arguments presently used by scholars were already raised at the latest during the nineteenth or early twentieth century.

Statutory fictions have multiple surface structures when appearing in the contemporary civil codes. While the French *Code Napoléon*, which dates from 1804, often only "presumes,"[11] terminology varies considerably in statutory fictionality. Regarding the legal status and the right to inherit of the unborn (but conceived) child, the German civil code (*BGB*, est. 1898) states that the unborn "counts as born"[12] ("gilt als geboren"). In a comparable provision in the Spanish civil code (est. 1898), the unborn "is held as born" ("tiene por nacido", Art. 29), while § 22 of the Austrian civil code (est. 1812) states that the unborn is "regarded as born" ("wird als geboren angesehen").

Although continental legal scholarship usually qualifies these rules as "legal fictions",[13] in terms of fictionality, the status of such deeming provisions, sometimes referred to as "linguistic fictions",[14] has already been disputed among the early scholarship. A significant number of scholars have objected to this qualification that statutory fictions do not meet the general criteria of fictionality, a claim often based on the presuppositions that counterfactuality is the relevant criterion. While, among the latter, it has been held that statutory "fictions" are not at all a "factual" question,[15] more differentiated views do not categorically exclude deeming provisions, but claim that it makes a difference whether a "legal" or a "natural" fact is "feigned" – thus whether the possible referents alluded to are natural (real) entities, or legal entities, the latter's ontological status being questionable.[16] I will, however, claim both views are equally incorrect: neither can counterfactuality (even in its newer clothing, with truth understood as "consensus", see p. 15) be the decisive criterion for statutory fictions, nor is the question relevant if concepts of natural (ordinary, extra-legal) language are concerned, or specific concepts of legal language use. It is particularly the latter question I will devote most part of this chapter to, for it is connected to another misconception: the newer theory that it is a dissociation of ordinary (natural) language use and legal language use that is constitutive for legal fictionality.[17]

My essential claim is that, in order to explain statutory fictions, no special theory of legal fictional discourse is necessary. Instead, statutory fictions can well be explained (and thus defined) by using a Wittgensteinian understanding of language use in general and a theory of linguistic use as institutionalized practice in particular. I claim that statutory fictions – and maybe fictions in general – are nothing other than overtly marked provisional deviations from a practice of denotative use within a sufficiently institutionalized superordinate framework. Fictionality is then understood to consist in the mere particularity that within a certain institutionalized practice of language use (e.g. the legal use, or the statutory use), a conflicting alternate linguistic practice of use is established, a practice, however, that does not globally replace the previous convention, but only suspends and thereby confirms the latter, creating an overt parallelism of practices that itself can become institutionalized (e.g. as the institute of "legal" or "statutory fiction"). I will claim that this solely relative, but hierarchical, definition (overt and limited deviation from the immediately superordinate practice) has the advantage that fictionality can be talked about and referred to without resorting to any notion of truth, that it can be applied both in realist and nominalist systems, and that it can serve not only as a model both for statutory fictionality in particular and legal fictionality in general, but also as a criterion for a general, transdisciplinary valid minimal definition of fictionality.

## II The form and function of statutory fictions

Early in the renewed treatment of legal fictionality, three distinct approaches on statutory fictions were taken. Regarding the criterion of counterfactuality, statutory fictions were either understood as counterfactual or non-counterfactual forms of legal fictionality. The alternative was that they were claimed to be wrongfully labelled "fictions". In the latter tradition, different strategies to deny deeming provisions the status of fictions were applied. Statutory fictions were excluded from the label "fictions" either for not being counterfactual (Kelsen, Somlò), or they were said to lack a certain imaginative character constitutive for legal fictionality (Ross).[18] In the former tradition, Baker, in his 2001 essay, holds that statutory fictions cannot be fictions, since "rules of law cannot be true or false in the factual sense",[19] and the latter argument was recently revived by Stern,[20] who has investigated the question whether a particular narrative and imaginative engagement was inscribed in legal fictionality. As does Campbell,[21] Stern does not categorically exclude deeming provisions from the category of legal fictions, but assumes that they often do not share the same constraints he understands as constitutive for a fiction.[22]

Functionalist approaches also deprived statutory fictions of a place, e.g. for not being expedient, or, because, as the product of an all-potent lawgiver,[23] these fictions' intention was not to mask the fact that "a rule has undergone alteration".[24] Even Jhering, who defines legal fictionality as a combination of form and function,[25] considers those statutory "fictions", which are merely linguistic, not to truly belong to the category.[26] According to Jhering, only those provisions deserve to be truly called fictions where "an affair is so violently pressed together" that it then fits a legal rule, demanding from the "the legal imagination

[…] to think one and the same thing in a different 'gestalt'".[27] Comparably, Leonhard distinguishes "merely formal 'fictions'" from "real fictions".[28]

Sometimes even an interesting mix of quasi-metaphysical, formalist and functionalist approaches can be found. Instructive here is the often reiterated dictum of Kelsen, that statutory fictions are in fact not fictions in the "true" sense, since, as regulative shortcuts[29] serving the mere aim of legal economy,[30] they do not consist in an "imagining 'as-if'"[31], but in a "treating 'as-well'".[32] Fuller adequately calls these particular statutory fictions "abbrevatory fictions",[33] after de Tourtoulon's (and Savigny's[34]) qualification as legal "shorthand".[35] While rejecting judicial fictions for not being expedient, thus assuming a functional position, Kelsen, when deciding the issue of statutory fictionality, instead resorts to an examination of the performative status of the illocution, later considered characteristic for speech act approaches. Here, the argument of a categorical impossibility of counterfactuality[36] and the question of the illocutionary nature of the provision are furthermore profoundly interlinked: analogously to Sidney's dictum on the poet, Kelsen claims that "the law affirms nothing".[37] Many of Kelsen's contemporaries have assumed a similar viewpoint,[38] presuming counterfactuality to be the key criterion for fictionality in general, and denying the latter to statutory fictions, since, in deeming provisions, an illocutionary act other than an assertion is said to be performed. Two years before Kelsen, Somlò stated in his 1917 monograph:

> Since legal clauses are not assertive, but directive clauses, and […] the realm of fiction are assertive clauses, directives cannot contain fictions in this general, non-legal sense.[39]

Although Kelsen has been understood as particularly opposed to statutory fictionality, it is evident that, in light of fictional theory, a revision of the above assumptions is long overdue. It is relevant here not only that fictional theory can in fact account for non-counterfactual fictions, but also that it has later been maintained by proponents of speech act approaches that fictional illocutions were in fact not assertive (cf. Chapter 1, p. 25–7).

Similar considerations must apply to the question of imaginative engagement as criterion. While Kelsen understands fictionality to be possible in judicial decisions, despite their authoritative nature,[40] he, in the tradition of Demelius, also maintains for statutory fictionality that it would be incorrect to assume the judge being commanded to counterfactually imagine an equality of situations.[41] Instead, statutory fictions are understood to consist in nothing other than the operational shortcut that two situations are equated in terms of their legal consequences (Savigny, Demelius).[42] In Kelsen's essay, it remains unclear, however, if, though the situations are not truly "imagined as equal", some sort of imagining is nevertheless involved.[43] Fictional theory has not without reason long grappled with the question of whether the imaginative engagement in fictionality is a real confusion of the feigned with the real, or consists in a distanced or mixed receptive stance. The latter was, in the context of legal fictionality, examined not only by Demelius, but also by Bülow and Leonhard.[44] While Leonhard assumes that the law in fact "prescribed" that "in every single case of application, a non-existing fact had to be imagined",[45] Bülow, in his 1879 essay, has pointed at statutory fictionality as an instrument that intentionally engages the human imagination by constituting a "command to the judge to imagine".[46] Tourtoulon has also identified a general imaginative in legal fictionality that reigns in the shadows behind the obvious merely operational aim of legal fictionality, understanding legal fictionality to consist both in a functional and psychological dimension, with the latter drawing on "the desire inherent in human nature to evade unpleasant realities, and to evoke pleasant imaginaries."[47] Jhering also assumed an implicit command inherent in statutory fictions addressed to the judge, which required him to "regard — as if".[48] For Jhering, however, only some, but not all, statutory fictions demand "from our imagination [...] to think the factual relation different".[49] More recently, it has also been pointed out that, already for Fuller, the question of a certain "intellectual operation" of pretence distinguishes dead from living fictions, describing "the death of fiction [...] as a result of the operation of the law of economy of effort in the field of mental processes", eliminating a previously existing imaginative dimension characteristically inherent in legal fictionality.[50] Some of Kelsen's contemporaries, though assuming that the lawmaker indeed only commands, have also accounted for forms of legal fictional imagination as part of statutory fictions. Krückmann, though agreeing with Kelsen on the performative nature of statutory fictionality, nevertheless seems to presuppose that the "command to treat 'as if'"[51] is a qualified form of an "imaginative treatment 'as if'".[52]

Within the latter positions, however, differences again exist, e.g. as to whether some statutory fictions have factual contents that allow true fictionality, while others haven't,[53] or as to what exactly a particular provision means. That it is correct to not only consider the surface structures is something Searle has emphasized.[54] The problem is, however, that scholars have extracted very different deep-level structures from the same surface structures of statutory deeming provisions.[55] The fact that in some of the codes presumptions and statutory fictions share the same vocabulary also complicates the matter.[56] In the case of the statutory fictions of the continental codes, the latter problem is furthered by the particularity that scholars commonly not only presume the usual linguistic dichotomy of surface and deep-level structure, but, as will later be shown, need to add another deep-level dimension to the equation: the "inner system" of latent commands, that, in the case of the continental codes, are, however, (re-) presented not as commands, but in a quasi-realistic system of propositions that have an assertive surface structure ("outer system").[57]

The arguments of the above debate also show not only that an agreement is far from being found, but that the debate shares a certain dogmatic circularity – or that it is not fruitful at least to my project (which aims at using legal fictionality to develop a transdisciplinarily valid criterion for fictional discourse in general). Most of the above approaches presuppose to know what "real" fictionality is in general, or at least what legal fictionality consists in – and thus from the start include or exclude statutory fictions from the category of legal fictions, depending on which definition of fictionality is presupposed. By doing so, the debate on statutory fictions in a way mirrors the debate on fictionality in fictional theory – and my suggestion to choose an empirical perspective in the latter case (cf. p. 35) is my justification also to assume an empirical approach to statutory fictions in this essay. Instead of excluding particular statutory fictions or statutory fictions in general from the category "fiction", I will provisionally presume statutory fictions to in fact be a form of fictionality for the sole reason that statutory fictions historically were often labelled "legal fictions",[58] and in fact have even been considered the paradigm of legal fictionality (Jhering).[59] Also, in the case of the continental civil codes, both in terms of their structure and terminology, deeming provisions are genealogically closely linked with the treatment of legal fiction in the Roman legal tradition and the *usus modernus.* To be "seen as", "held as" or "count as" were the vernacular translations of the most common keywords pertaining to Roman legal fictionality debated in early modern continental legal discussion,[60] and since most of the continental codes were drafted in the period between the end of the eighteenth century and the late nineteenth century, lawmakers who chose to include deeming provisions did so with a clear awareness of the terminological and technical origin of these provisions. It can even be assumed that the authors of such provisions were decisively aiming at incorporating "fictions" in their laws and statutes. Furthermore, many of the "new" civil codes had been recognized as a deliberate institutionalization of the Roman legal tradition by contemporaries[61] – and thus, at least in the early application of these codes, lawyers and judges would immediately identify many provisions as classical legal fictions on grounds both of content and terminology, the latter demonstrating a visible connection to legal fictionality as instituted in the legal system prior to the times of codification.

Due to the above-mentioned particularities of my approach (empirical basis, transdisciplinary perspective), it is particularly irrelevant for me whether statutory fictions are "correctly" labelled as legal "fictions". Instead, I will try to extrapolate those characteristics of statutory fictionality that could serve as criteria for a definition of fictionality in general that is not bound to the classical notion of counterfactuality. Since statutory fictions have often been categorized as non-counterfactual, or even non-assertive (Kelsen, Somlò, etc.), this type of legal "fiction" might serve particularly well in providing such a definition. Because this chapter is part of an overall project that aims at involving the legal discussion in the ongoing debate on finding a transdisciplinary definition of fictional discourse as part of fictional theory, it is also necessary for me to ignore those particularities that distinguish legal from literary fiction, and instead focus on the common denominators. It might appear that by doing so, I oppose approaches such as Simon Stern's and Andrei Marmor's in this volume, which concentrate on the *differentia specifica* of literary and legal fictionality. The contrary, however, is actually the case: I think the latter approaches are valuable contributions when it comes to further establishing a taxonomy of sub-types of fictional discourse and differentiating the legal fictional discourse (or even statutory fictionality) from other forms of fictionality. When the aim is to first establish a transdisciplinary category of fictional discourse in general, however, it is inevitable to neglect those particularities and instead focus on the common denominator(s).

## III Legal fictions and the limits of legal language

If understood as an assertion, to deem a child to be "born" before he or she is actually born for the purpose of being able to inherit (§ 1923 II *BGB*) seems to clearly conflict with factual reality. Similarly, to deem fruit that have fallen from a neighbor's tree to be fruit of the land they have fallen on to (§ 911 *BGB*) also appears to involve an act of counterfactual imagination. Especially the former, as an apparently counterfactual assumption, might be the paradigm of statutory fictionality, at least if understood as a proposition in metalanguage. It is also clear, that in these two cases, it could be held that a "natural" or "realist" perspective forced the lawmaker to overtly mark the provision as "counterfactual", using a certain historically or systematically prescribed terminology (e.g. "deemed", "count as", "held as", "is to be regarded as"). Accordingly, it has been strongly maintained that when assessing statutory fictions, it makes a difference whether the feigning pertains to legal or natural concepts, assuming the latter not be comparable in terms of existence.[62] While, in the former case, an extension of the respective legal concept might have sufficed to remedy a problem, in the latter case, realist convictions might have prohibited the lawmaker from simply extending a concept, forcing him to use the detour of an overt fiction instead (or to put it into Abraham Lincoln's famous words, forbade to make a tail a leg). As early as Roman times, it seemed axiomatic that there were "limits to the abuse of words which neither lawyers nor legislators should transgress",[63] and that "not even a statute can so abuse words as to impose false classification".[64] Regarding the unborn, "birth" as a concept seems to allow little conceptual wiggle room; and comparably, since fruit are understood to be part of the plant they originate from, also little conceptual leeway was to be expected in the case of § 911 *BGB*. The same can even be held for Jhering's example that a Jew is feigned to be a Christian, or the old textbook case of a provision pertaining to a communal swimming pool restricted to use by women that stated: "The pool attendant is deemed a woman in terms of the rules of this statute."[65] Consequently, one might assume that also one of the oldest fictions, the Roman feigning of a person to have died a free man at the time of his capture, though having much later died in captivity (the aforementioned *fictio legis Corneliae*), or that a person continues to live despite his or her factual death, fundamentally differs in nature from the newer statutory fiction of § 49 II *BGB*, which treats a dissolved corporate society as if still "existing" until the liquidation has been completed – at least if one upholds the assumption that a corporate person is not comparable to a physical person from a metaphysical or ontological perspective.

The majority of statutory fictions, however, are conceptually less clear. What about those provisions in continental family law that deem a child not to be related to its father (e.g. § 1589 II *BGB*),[66] or those that, on the contrary, deem a person to be the father who is clearly not the biological father? A similar issue is the past treatment of illegitimate children as orphans, or at least as fatherless:[67] was a fiction unavoidable here since it is factually impossible to actually sever the biological relation of a child to its real father? Although the possible result of a child having more than one father has been understood as only beneficial by legal scholars,[68] to correctly categorize these cases is more difficult than the first type of statutory fictions. It is at least debatable whether "related" is a legal or a non-legal concept, and whether it shares the same conceptual reality as "father", which is usually understood to be of a more "natural" nature.[69] The latter, however, is especially problematic, since legal and non-legal terminology are, from a genealogical perspective, irreducibly intertwined, with law having incorporated the majority of pre-legal conceptualizations while legal concepts have invaded the normal language to an extent that they now appear to be "natural". As long as material existence served as a criterion both for truth and fictionality, an *ad-rem* relation allowed the necessary differentiation; however, the consideration of truth and correspondence in the first chapter of this volume (cf. p. 11–25) has definitely weakened such link. Additionally, the conceptually divergent treatment of the same issues in different social and legal orders furthers a certain relativity of standpoint. Similar to archaic German law, where being accepted as part of the family (understood as a rather formal unit not necessarily based on blood ties) was constitutive for being related,[70] it could be claimed that it was considered equally "natural" in Roman law for a daughter to cease to be related to the father once she was married: it might not be a legal fact (only) that emancipation terminates previously existing family relations.[71] It might even be considered equally natural that members of the Roman household, even if unfree, were tied so closely to the latter that they would inherit once they were freed.[72] These particularities, however, already make it difficult to classify an ancient Roman fiction: that blood relatives, who were not part of the household, to be able to inherit, had to be feigned to be related.[73] Correspondingly, legal scholars have questioned the validity of the distinction between natural and legal factuality both in general and as a criterion for fictionality in particular.[74] While Kelsen strictly distinguishes between legal and non-legal use of the same word or concept and highlights the law's authority to determine a certain use (such as the word "father"),[75] Gaius's treatment of constructive theft in context of the Law of the Twelve Tables seems to instead disregard the theoretical distinction between legal and non-legal use:

> [T]he law cannot turn someone who is not a manifest thief into a manifest thief any more than it can turn someone into a thief at all, or take a man who is not an adulterer or a murderer and make him an adulterer or

> murderer. What the law can indeed do is make a man liable to the same penalty just as if he had committed theft or adultery or murder, even though in fact he has committed none of these.[76]

Unfortunately, things do not seem to get easier if one considers fictionality pertaining to purely legal entities. While it is clearly marked as a statutory fiction that § 49 *BGB* deems a corporation to continue to exist despite it having been terminated, it has also long been debated whether corporate personhood itself already is a fiction, with the majority understanding the hypostatization of the concept of the natural person that led to corporate personality being fictitious, whereas others instead claimed corporate personhood to be either a non-physical, but real entity, or a legal "abstraction", merely consisting in a bundle of legal relations.[77] But if the view of the majority that every company is a fictional entity was correct, what would it then exactly mean that § 49 *BGB* subjects such a fictional entity to the additional (now statutory) fiction that it persists to "exist", presupposing that its "existence" in fact already has been terminated? Would the second "fiction" be less "false" than the first one? Similar considerations have been made pertaining to other legal constructions, both more abstract ones (power, obligations, duties, rights, etc., which already Bentham listed as paradigms of fictitious entities),[78] and more particular legal relations (as contracts, wills, declarations of intent, etc.). In contract law, for example, a number of provisions "feign" legal acts or declarations as being made or absent. While it has been claimed that contracts have a factual basis that precedes law, justifying them to be treated as a factual entity,[79] and leading to a distinction between the "real" contract and the "legal" contract in some of the early scholarship,[80] the respective statutory fictions of contract law are often held to differ from the former types not only in degree, but in nature, since they are said not to be "counterfactual", at least not in the literal sense of the word.[81] Alf Ross has commented on this issue,[82] and in a newer essay, Baker maintains that the view "that an implicative contract, or promise" is "something patently untrue" is solely based on false "presuppositions" (e.g. that we imagine a contract to be "something primarily factual").[83] Regarding corporate persons, Baker in fact revived the nineteenth-century discussion[84] on legal personhood:

> It is convenient to use anthropomorphic language – a body having a head and members – and this is sometimes said to be a fiction. But it is not fictitious in the same way that John Doe, or Cinderella, is a fictional human being.[85]

Throughout his essay, Baker insists on the differentiation between "reality", "nature" and "existence" on the one hand, and "creatures of the legal mind" on the other, where there can be "nothing fictitious, in the strict sense of the term".[86] Kelsen already raised a similar claim in his 1911 treatise. Kelsen not only highlighted the fact that fictions need to be distinguished from abstractions and legal constructions, but also that legal entities might even be incorrectly labelled fictions since they do not form a part of the factual world – and that to confuse them with natural entities would be a severe methodical error.[87] During the same era as Kelsen, Tourtoulon also commented on this particular problem.[88]

From a functionalist perspective, the latter statutory fictions share an interesting trait which makes them highly fruitful for my project. While in the case of the unborn (*nasciturus*) it might have been impossible to tackle the problem without a fiction, at least when presupposing a realist perspective, as far as mere legal entities and concepts are concerned, either an alternate provision or a redefinition of the legal concepts could have made a fictional provision superfluous. Instead of deeming that non-responsiveness to an offer is an acceptance in certain cases, the lawmaker could have simply legally redefined "acceptance" to include non-responsiveness in certain cases.[89] When it comes to legal entities or relations, it generally seems to be the case that a sole change in the surface structure could completely eradicate the fictional nature of a provision – a particularity that led to the early claim that statutory fictions were only in a "linguistic" sense fictional (Bierling, Leonhard, Somlò, Fuller)[90] – and that due to the authoritative nature of law, from an ontological perspective, "as if" was in fact equal to "is". Since in these cases the difference between "normal" and deeming provisions seems to only be a matter of form, it is understandable that both functionalists and counterfactualists have claimed that statutory "fictions" were not to be considered as "real" fictions. Unsurprisingly, this merely formal nature of statutory fictionality[91] has been repeatedly noted, and most of the earlier scholarship on fictionality (Bierling, Jhering, Krückmann, etc.) already dealt with the question of how legal fictions could be adequately replaced by nonfictional provisions that have the same effect.[92] In the above-cited essay, Baker states:

> Where a dog is deemed to be a cat or declared to be a cat, there is obviously no intention of defying or subverting nature. [...] But if a deed, unlike a dog, is purely a creature of the legal mind, then it might be redefined without the need for fiction or deeming.[93]

A not insubstantial number of scholars tried to oppose this argument by claiming that even in the legal realm, certain realist necessities sometimes make fictions inevitable. Kuntze in his 1856 monograph[94] understands the legal realm as an organic system, which has its own natural laws, comparable to the natural laws in physics, with the consequence of truth and falseness mirrored equally in this artificial system. Within this system, provisions cannot be arbitrarily stipulated, but instead need to be integrated without contradictions, with fictions being an unfortunate[95] but necessary means to avoid contradictions in this quasi-realist system.[96] Although the idea in this regard shares an overlap with pragmatist approaches, even mirroring Neurath's criterion of truth (cf. p. 16), the legal order is, however, understood not only to possess certain organic treats (as a system that is considered not only to be "grown", but to be an organic whole where everything has its proper place and function), but also as irreducibly tied to the real world. Consequently, both in the case of the *nasciturus* and the *fictio legis Corneliae*, Kuntze claims that a fiction was inevitable, since being considered a legal entity was literally impossible in the lack of a "material substrate" existent in the factual realm.[97] Similarly, in ancient law, the stoic conviction that the unborn does not possess a soul might have precluded a nonfictional approach to the issue, even on the deep-level-structure of the latent norm. During the early twentieth century, such "legal mystification" (Kelsen)[98] has, however, been harshly criticized – for example, by Esser, who condemns the inflationary "systematical confusion between legal and natural concepts" in recent scholarship.[99] Such criticism started early, as Demelius's opposition to Kunze's argument shows.[100] Correspondingly, though not considering statutory fictions to be "real" fictions, Kelsen asserts for legal fictionality in general[101] that the legal realm has its own definition of counterfactuality, regardless of whether legal or natural concepts are used.[102]

## IV Compensatory fictions and the quasi-realist conceptual system of the continental civil codes

It is the functionalist perspective that also provides some interesting insights on the nature of statutory fictionality, and I will provisionally assume a functionalist view, which I will nevertheless later substitute with a purely formalist definition. It has been long held that legal fictionality always serves equity,[103] and this is surely most evident when applied to the case of the unborn. Here, on closer examination, the above-mentioned provisions of the German civil code actually seem to already be based on false premises. § 1923 *BGB* in fact reads:

1 Only someone alive at the time of devolution can inherit.
2 He who does not yet live, but already was conceived, counts[104] as alive at the time of devolution.

It is evident that, at least from a modern scientific understanding, already subsection 1 incorrectly equates birth with being alive, and that the legal fiction ordained in subsection 2 rather serves the truth (or, in the legal realm, equity, by compensating the unjust effects caused by this categorical error). It is not helpful here to discern when such classificatory "wrong" became apparent – obviously, the stoic conception equating birth and animated life was already contested, and led to a contradictory treatment of unborn life in the early republic.[105] What is instead essential here is that this particular statutory fiction has a very different function to the one previously cited: it aims at restituting a conceptual wrong (here a falsity in conceptual classification) that leads to a legal wrong, since equal things are treated as unequal. Fictionality in this regard seems to agree with its old functionalist criterion: legal fictionality understood as a means of adapting the law to new understandings while conserving its past structure and main dogmas (Henry Maine's "its letter remaining unchanged").[106] In the case of the *nasciturus*, the fiction was in fact avoidable, as the treatment of the issue in a different continental civil code shows. In the Swiss civil code, no fiction is needed in order to attribute legal personhood to the *nasciturus*; the unborn is instead simply stipulated to be a person, thus possessing legal capacity. Bouvier's dictum, that the lawmaker does not need to feign, but simply commands,[107] seems to be most appropriate here. The German penal code (*Strafgesetzbuch*) also did not hesitate to change the conceptual classificatory system of the past by adding "unborn life" to the scope of protected life[108] – and thereby effectively modifying the semantic field of "life" without having to resort to a "fiction".

That legal fictions remedy a classificatory (or linguistic) wrong – a wrong in legal terminology or conceptualization, which might otherwise lead to an inadequate (or unjust) legal result – is a provisional functional criterion that merits further investigation. In order to do so, I want to focus more closely on the relation of statutory fictions as serving truth (or equity) with the dissociation between (1) codification (surface structure), (2) latent norm (command) and (3) the particular equation of interests involved that lie at the origin of a particular norm (as the lawmaker's normative decision). I will argue that within the quasi-realistic conceptual systems the continental civil codes have chosen, statutory fictions were not always, but in most cases, an inevitable choice, since the underlying normative considerations of the lawmakers could not be adequately "translated" into the conceptual system the codes use. I will also argue later that the functional viewpoint shows that in fact a purely formal (linguistic) definition can be extrapolated from the examples I will give.

In any given legal culture, a dissociation is possible, between what is called "just" on the one hand, and what is prescribed by the legal system, regardless of whether it is oral or written, on the other. Since every legal norm has a complex network of competing and overlaying interests and considerations at its origin, classical legal philosophy would have understood justice as the correct weighing and balancing of the interests involved – and it has been maintained that there was only one right (thus "just") choice, based on a compelling reference system. Earlier systems assumed a fixed compass (*lex aetherna*, natural law, religion); newer considerations included other perspectives, such as utilitarianism (Bentham, Jhering, Heck).[109] In contrast, the modern understanding of law as positive law, at least when based on the principle of a separation of law and ethics, assumes that legal norms instead are arbitrary, for the weighing of interests that culminates in a codified norm is often a political decision (Larenz),[110] involving a number of different considerations (economical, socio-political, etc.) which can be weighed in very different ways. While positive law has made the dissociation between justice and law to a certain degree irrelevant, the continental civil law system has instead added a new dissociation to the equation: between the normative choices (political decisions) of the legislator, as the latent, deep-level normative decision on the one hand, and the resulting quasi-realistic conceptual system, as the manifest dimension of positive law of the continental codes on the other. The latter problem is a question of mediality, and could in fact be described as an issue of translations: to in a functional sense[111] succeed in adequately translating the underlying normative considerations (the lawmakers decision as to how certain conflicting interests are to be weighed and balanced) not into direct commands, but into a quasi-realist conceptual system instead. These latent,[112] underlying normative decisions of the legislator are not to be confused with the equally latent "norm", defined as the deontic deep-level structures the provisions of the codes provide. The latter is in fact a result of the codes' surface structures, and not its premises, and can be construed by putting together the numerous incomplete and quasi-realist provisions of the civil codes to a complete command.[113] Ideally, the (resulting) norm will secure the legislator's latent intentions (and thus the underlying normative decision as the perlocutionary aim), but there is no guarantee.

My essential claim here is that the purpose of a relevant number of statutory fictions is to serve as a remedy that secures the lawmaker's normative decision (his to a certain degree arbitrary balancing of interests) in light of an inevitable discrepancy between these decisions on the one hand, and, on the other hand, the resulting provisions of the quasi-realistic conceptual system of the continental civil codes, which were chosen as the media to convey these prior decisions. Or to phrase it differently: statutory fictions are necessary since the media chosen (quasi-realist conceptual system) has its limits in conveying the lawmaker's deontic considerations. The gap that needs to be overcome is in fact a difference in nature – and thus a qualitative one: translating deontic decisions into a quasi-metaphysical descriptive system that has an assertive surface structure.

A number of examples are instructive in this context. According to the surface structure of virtually every continental code, minors lack the capacity to contract – they "cannot" contract. What is correctly presented as factual in assertive propositions on law (metalanguage) is, in fact, a deontic one: a minor shall not be able to create obligations that the legal framework will enforce to be fulfilled. In communicating such convictions, not only have different legal systems chosen different ways (e.g. direct commands vs. the quasi-realistic conceptual system of the continental codes), but they also differ considerably in the criteria used to determine capacity. While some cultures purely rely on formal criteria (e.g. in Roman law the Sabinian school relied on the formal attribution of the *toga virilis* to the adolescent),[114] others have chosen a fixed age as the criterion, but again considerably vary in what age is stipulated. Fourteen years was the demarcation line of the Roman Proculian School, and in the Islamic legal tradition, Ibn Umar has suggested 15 years, Abu Hanafi advocated 17 years, while other Islamic schools have concentrated on puberty as a manifest criterion.[115] That all these legal traditions share a common denominator despite the obviously diverging choice of criterion can be shown by excavating the latent deep-level structural content of these legal provisions in context. If the age criterion is regarded in context with other provisions of the respective legal order, it becomes evident that all these cultures have instituted provisions that modify (or, in a certain sense, even rectify) the criteria chosen – and that they in fact implicitly agree that not age but the mental capacity to fully understand one's declarations and actions would be the only adequate criterion. Some of the legal systems have chosen presumptions or fictions[116] to remedy the problem that the formal criterion (age, puberty or clothing) inevitably fails in providing adequate results in every single case. Within some schools of the Shari'a that maintained puberty as the criterion, an irrebuttable presumption that puberty has been reached by the age of 15 has been added to facilitate the application, not surprisingly just around the time when, according to modern science, important cognitive developments have usually taken place that enable the adolescent to assess risk better and reach more reasonable decisions.[117] Regarding the capacity to contract, an additional criterion, "*rushd*" (prudence, economical considerateness)[118] was also introduced, in order to remedy the problematic effects of a strict age demarcation in cases where the mental capacity to understand the effects of one's own declarations and actions was not yet present. Conversely, in Roman law, *impuberes infantia maiores* were treated as if being *puberes* in those cases where a capacity to understand the implications of their actions was already evident prior to reaching the demarcation line.

All these cases, including the latter fiction, share the common trait that a particular "translation problem" existed, which needed to be compensated: the problem that a fixed criterion, as a metaphysical/realist or formal criterion, was not the ideal signifier to convey the practical considerations (and the subsequent normative decisions) involved. The use of different criteria used also shows that at the origin of most of the provisions on legal capacity lies a network of conflicting interests that needed to be balanced. Even if legislations did not assess the interests involved differently, they might nevertheless differ considerably in choosing a means of conveying these decisions (in terms of the surface structures used).

In the case of legal capacity, most legislations see a need to unconditionally protect the minor against his own, possibly unreasonable, decisions. The interests of the other party that might not be aware of the lack of capacity to contract, however, have also found their way into the rules stipulated, choosing criteria for capacity that are also potentially manifest to the other party. In order to better balance the conflicting interests involved, and avoiding the above-mentioned fictions or presumptions of the Roman or Islamic legal tradition, the German civil code has decided against a disjunctive treatment of the topic of capacity, and instituted a third institute, "limited capacity", that is applicable in the case of adolescents, and that need not feign *impuberes infantia maiores* to be *puberes*, but instead simply orders that their actions can have certain (limited) legal effects. Even in this more differentiated system, however, some fictions were inevitable in order to secure just results. One example is the fiction that a contract concluded by a minor is nevertheless deemed valid from the beginning if the minor's parents later agree, or are non-responsive when asked.[119] Another example is that contractual relations of an adult lacking legal capacity are feigned as valid if they are part of insignificant daily-life business paid in cash.[120] Both the French civil code (*CC*)[121] and the Swiss civil code (*ZGB*) have opted for an alternate path instead, avoiding statutory fictions, but nevertheless achieving similar, or, in the case of the Swiss *ZGB*, virtually the same results as the German civil code. Art. 11 *ZGB* simply stipulates that "everybody" possesses legal capacity, the capacity to contract is, however, subsequently limited to those who are "adult and capable of sound judgement" (Art. 13 *ZGB*). Art 17 non-parsimoniously adds a list of those who cannot be considered as the latter: persons of unsound mind, minors under 18 years, and persons under legal guardianship. Art. 19 then orders that these persons, however, can acquire legal claims if they are only beneficial, or part of negligible transactions of daily life. Art. 19 also stipulates that they nevertheless can be liable in case of tort. Art. 19b simply adds a provision that protects the third party for those cases where the person lacking capacity to contract was responsible for falsely appearing to possess capacity.

Although the Swiss civil code clearly illustrates "that the legislator need not feign, he commands" (Bouvier),[122] the Swiss example also shows that, by doing so, fictions could only be avoided at the expense of consistency and parsimony. Though relying on the quasi-realistic tradition, the provisions of the Swiss civil code fail in establishing a quasi-conceptual universe that is systematically concise and free of quasi-metaphysical contradictions, and would have allowed dogmatic/systematic arguments being used as an aid in deciding unclear matters (e.g. by allowing a systematic or dogmatic interpretation of a certain passage). Instead, the Swiss code provides a list of more or less direct commands that fail to form a uniform whole, and needs to be memorized instead of being able to be deduced from a consistently organized system.

That systemic considerations (such as coherence and consistency) might be the true reasons for legal fictions was recognized early on. In his 1930 monograph, Geny writes:

> Il faudrait reconnaître à la fiction une fonction dogmatique [...] Par l'exercice de celle-ci, elle servirait à encadrer les solutions, qui s'y appuient, dans le système du droit positif, considéré comme un ensemble ferme. Grâce à la fiction, ce système acquerrait plus de cohérence et de consistance théorique, en même temps que se développeraient spontanément les résultats pratiques poursuivis.[123]

Similar considerations can also be applied in the seemingly different, at first sight "counterfactual" fiction pertaining to the *nasciturus*. That the unborn was treated in a comparable manner both by Stoics and non-stoic convictions, despite their fundamental disagreement on whether the soul is actually attributed at the moment of birth,[124] could have already served as an indicator that considerations other than metaphysical or religious ones might be the common denominator of these doctrines. Scholars agree that practical considerations in fact played a considerable role, such as the impossibility of determining exactly when a child has been conceived, or the historically high rate of death during pregnancy and birth. But the aims and effects of social and religious conviction were also considerably involved in the genesis of such doctrines, such as the principle in many cultures that infants with genetic defects (the so-called "monsters", including hermaphrodites, and overtly mentally disabled infants) should not be considered as heirs to the parents' estate. In fact, they were often killed after birth,[125] and already therefore should not be able to acquire property or rights. The Swiss civil code is interesting here, since it managed to integrate some of the above considerations (the problem of the historical high rate of death before or at birth) without resorting to a fiction: It simply ordained that the unborn can inherit, but, in order to balance the interests involved, it incorporated a retroactive condition:

> The child can inherit from the moment of his conception, provided that it is later born alive.[126]

Similarly, the French *Code Civil*,[127] the Portuguese *Código Civil*,[128] the Polish *Kodeks Cywilny*[129] and the Italian *Codice Civile*[130] can all avoid a statutory fiction. The Italian Code, however, stretches the system even further, since it allows a person that is not even conceived to be heir.[131] And the terminology used in the French non-parsimonious patchwork provision clearly shows that the question of capacity was once irreducibly tied to presuppositions of existence (equated with birth):

> In order to succeed, one needs to *exist* at the time of devolution, *or* needs to be already *conceived* [...].[132]

While most of the continental civil codes have chosen the path of denying the unborn the status as legal subject and therefore also consider it not to possess legal capacity, but at the same time regard it as being able to inherit and receive gifts (using either a fiction or an exception instituted by law), an alternative to the latter options has been proposed: that the unborn could simply be stipulated to be a legal subject in general, with no further need to additionally comment on dependent matters, such as heredity.[133] Deciding for this option, the Swiss civil code has ordained that the *nasciturus* in fact possesses legal personality (Art. 31 I ZVG), making any inheritance fiction superfluous. But even here a retroactive condition was added in order to balance the considerations of interests involved: "[...] provided that it is later born alive". (Art. 31 II *ZVG*). The Spanish *Código Civil* decided for a compromise instead. Not only the particular question of heredity, but the question of legal personhood in general was regulated by ways of statutory fiction. While Art. 29 decides that only who is born is a person in the legal sense, the unborn is nevertheless "held as born" – but only insofar as it is favorable for him; and the latter is also limited by a number of other provisions. Similar provisions are then repeated for the matter of heredity.

That the quasi-realist system in fact represents nothing other than a lawmaker's decision on how to balance the competing interests involved is most clearly shown by the fact that, in the legal treatment of the *nasciturus*, some legal cultures even had to resort to a hybrid structure, stipulating that the unborn is a legal subject only when beneficial to him. In the rules of the Austrian civil code (*ABGB*) on the unborn (literally a patchwork provision), a bundle of diverging interests which needed to be balanced in fact becomes manifest – and the question of what is ordained by way of fiction seems to be only of relative nature, depending on which interest was chosen to be addressed first: § 22 *ABGB* orders that the unborn is protected by civil law from the moment of his conception (avoiding, however, stipulating that it is a legal subject). The general provision is then altered by a second provision that stipulates that only regarding rights (and not regarding duties) the unborn "is seen as born", creating the ambivalence that, in the context of this provision, the first stipulation could in fact already be a statutory fiction. Then the next fiction is added: that if the child is later not born alive, it is "regarded as if it has never been conceived".[134]

Even the above-mentioned question of who a fallen fruit belongs to seems to involve a balancing of interests, since the statutory fiction of § 911 *BGB* explicitly lists an exception that is not based on metaphysical or ontological considerations, but on considerations of interest: the initial rule is exempted if the neighbor's land is public property. In the case of the already terminated corporation, a similar caveat is added: the corporation is only feigned to continue to exist insofar as this is necessary to achieve the aim of its liquidation.[135]

The above considerations are important for the argument of this chapter.

First, they prove that neither ontological nor metaphysical considerations (e.g. in the case of the unborn: the question debated during the eighteenth century whether human life already "exists" – opposed to mere vegetative life)[136] were, in fact, decisive for the use of legal fictionality in these cases.[137] Instead, the quasi-realist conceptualization only served as a medium to convey a decision on how to balance the interests and considerations involved. For the case of the *nasciturus*, the treatment of unborn life in tort and criminal law can substantiate this purely teleological argument. In Roman law, for example, only the termination of unborn life by non-family members was legally sanctioned,[138] evidencing that the family's economic interests were the primary motivation for the protection of the *nasciturus* here, and during the Third Reich, population politics were in fact the main reason for a protection of the unborn.[139] Consequently, the case of the unborn is not in any way different from the less "natural" cases discussed (capacity, corporate personhood, etc.). That, in the case of the unborn, more "natural" matters of "existence" were concerned is then only accidental – and thus irrelevant both for the legal regulations in general and for the decision for a statutory fiction by some of the legal orders in particular.

Second, the above considerations also clearly show that whether a rule is established in the form of a fiction is purely a relative questions. For example, in the case of the unborn, whether a provision institutes a fiction is only dependent on the obviously arbitrary preceding decision whether the *nasciturus* was initially stipulated by law to be a legal subject, or not, and whether this position was unrestricted, or limited. Often, of course, the initial choice was motivated by the decision to keep the vocabulary and the conceptualizations of the past legal tradition (as, for instance, the German civil code shows with respect to the Pandect tradition).[140] The above considerations also demonstrate that whether a statutory fiction was installed depends greatly on how considerate the lawmaker was regarding keeping the conceptual system concise and free of contradictions.[141]

It thus can be summarized that the "great" continental civil codifications of the nineteenth and early twentieth century, which could deliberately construct a system when they were instituted, demonstrate that statutory fictions were not mere means to adapt past law. Instead, the need for statutory fictions arises when, in the process of translating legislative decisions that evaluate, accommodate and balance the diverging interests in a typical situation into a conceptual system, a conceptual criterion is chosen that is not ideal in representing the complex interests that had to be balanced – with some legal orders in fact choosing statutory fictions as the preferred way of compensate the resulting discontents. Fictionality here also is a merely relative question, depending on certain (arbitrary) premises.

A case in contractual obligations, which has been dominating German legal textbooks since 1899, demonstrates two points very clearly. First, that considering the palimpsest of opposing and overlaying interests, the quasi-realist conceptual system the continental civil codes use is not always suitable to serve as a means to translate what has been decided by the lawmaker as a just accommodation of the particular interests and considerations involved. Second, that the quasi-realistic conceptual system in fact exercises a dangerous (illusionary) realist effect. In the case, a customer (C), entering a room unaware that an auction is taking place, raises his hand in order to signal to a friend. With his "bid" being the highest, the question was if he in fact purchased the item being auctioned. In order to decide the case, the early scholarship analytically dissected the concept "contract" by discerning its properties as if it was a real entity (thereby following a quasi-realist proceeding which Jhering would have renounced as "conceptual jurisprudence").[142] Presupposing that a contract "naturally" consists of two congruent contractual declarations, the scholars tried to discern the true nature of a "declaration", assuming that it necessarily contained two elements: an illocution with an objectively discernible propositional content and (subjective) intent. Since C intentionally had raised his hand, the consequential question for the court then was whether a contractual declaration, as a subcategory, also requires an intent to contract (which was absent since C was not aware that he would enter a business relationship by raising his hand) or if, instead, a mere intent to act (raise his hand) was sufficient. The crux of the problem of this textbook case was that neither of the two conceptual alternatives would have produced just results when applied to contractual relations in general. The textbook problem remained unsolved until the matter was finally decided by the Federal Court of Justice nearly a century later[143] – and it was in fact solved by deviating from the quasi-realistic viewpoint the German civil code prescribes. Instead of pondering on the nature of "acceptance" as a quasi-realist concept, in order to determine what the legal term "acceptance" entailed, the court revisited the interests of the participants involved in such cases (including the legitimate trust established by the other party) and decided that the only just criterion would be to ask if the customer could have prevented his error by applying reasonable prudence. While this decision has generally been understood as "just", it has, however, been strongly criticized by scholars. Critics mainly objected that introducing a criterion of negligence to the question of what an "acceptance" is, a question that needs to comply with basic realist premises, means to introduce a foreign element into the quasi-realist conceptual system of the German civil code. While the court was thus correct in its assessment of the deep-level structures of law (the lawmaker's decision on how to balance the interests involved which lie at the origin of each latent norm of the civil code system), in their decision, the judges failed to adequately conceptually "translate" them, and thus to find a correct way to integrate these latent considerations into to the conceptual "system" (the quasi-realistic system) the lawmaker has chosen to use.

For the purpose of this chapter, the above decision is highly illuminating in two regards. First, it demonstrates that, in the case adjudicated, the quasi-realist system literally failed in translating the chosen evaluation of interests into its conceptual system (code), since it provided only two quasi-realist criteria as options which both seemed "unjust" if generalized, and thus could not serve as a medium to translate the legislator's deep-level considerations. Second, the decision also suggests how the above criticism could have been averted: by the legal fiction that, in case of negligence, contractual intent (though absent) is deemed present, thereby leaving the dogmatic quasi-realistic conceptual system of civil law intact. That the court did not resort to the latter fiction is easily explained. Judicial fictions are not accepted in the current German system of civil law, and this is for the reason already stated above: that in light of positive law, normative decisions are to a certain degree arbitrary, and it is therefore reserved for the legislator to stipulate the result of a concrete evaluation of interests as law. Considering Jhering, a solution, however, might have been at hand. In his monograph, Jhering had already proposed a proceeding to jurisprudence which he considered superior to jurisprudential fiction: "analogical extension" of the norm[144] – and both "operations", legal fiction and analogical extension, in a sense, appear as two sides of the same coin.[145] Some scholars have even noted that certain deeming provisions could in fact be considered as *interpretationes extensivas*.[146] The latter is not surprising, though: Jhering repeatedly points at the kinship of fictional discourse and the extension of a concept:

> A certain similarity exists between fiction and the artificial extension of natural concepts, […] e.g. the extension of the concept "fruit" to the *uti* (*fructus civiles*), of the person to the corporation, of the thing to a complex of things (legal things) etc.[147]

## V Toward a formal definition of fictionality as institutionalized practice

While in the above cases functionalist considerations are helpful in explaining the "why" of statutory fictions, the functional perspective also aids in constructing a purely formal definition of statutory fictions from the surface structure of the above examples, following the insight that the above-noted legal fictions are nothing but linguistic practices which modify a pre-existing meaning. To understand continental statutory fictionality as solely based on the arbitrary choice[148] to install a quasi-realist system for the means of regulating social reality, thus rendering statutory fictions into nothing but compensatory provisions that often could be avoided by adapting or replacing the conceptual system, permits us to see statutory fictionality as a merely relative question that can be captured by an equally relative formal definition based on the idea of institutionalized linguistic practices. Both types of statutory fictions discussed above – those which are usually referred to as counterfactual and those referred to as non-counterfactual – from a formalist perspective have clear common denominators which could well serve as criteria for a general definition of fictionality:

- first, that within a certain practice of language use, a conflicting alternate practice of (denotative) use is established;
- second, that this new practice does not globally replace the previous convention, but only suspends it;
- and third, that it is overt both that the superordinate convention is suspended and that this suspension is limited, with the consequence that by marking the deviation as limited, the subordinate practice at the same time deviates from and reaffirms the conventions of the superordinate discourse.[149]

What legal fictionality as practice therefore presupposes is nothing other than an existing convention of use that is sufficiently institutionalized, and the comparably sufficient institutionalization of a divergent subordinate denotative practice (colloquially called "fiction") within this superordinate practice. Since such definition of fictionality does not require the superordinate practice to be "factual" or "realist", not only is the question of fictionality to be understood as merely relative, but, furthermore, such institution can be meaningfully talked about and referred to without alluding to any notion of existence – and can be applied both in nominalist and realist systems of belief.

The fact that, in such relativism, only the relation to the directly superordinate practice is of relevance as a reference system is also the reason why I disagree with some of the newer definitions, such as Campbell's assumption that legal fictionality "arises from the content of the rule being false when regarded as a question of fact according to non-legal classifications",[150] or with an even newer claim that legal fictions are a "true legal proposition asserted with the conscious recognition that they are inconsistent in meaning or otherwise in semantic conflict with true propositions asserted within some other linguistic system (or elsewhere in law)".[151] Although I strongly agree with the criterion of consciousness, I cannot concur with either the insistence on semantics alone or the claimed irrelevance of the question of which system is the referential system for deviation ("some"). According to the above assessment, the only relevant referential system is always the immediately superior system. I therefore also consider it an error to assume that legal fictionality is based on the fact that legal word meaning can deviate from natural word meaning, as Schauer recently claimed.[152] It is in fact the deviation from a superordinate (conventional) legal use,[153] not from natural, extra-legal use, that is constitutive for statutory fictionality, though often the conventional legal use and the natural language use will coincide. What is true, however, is that fictional discourse is in a way parasitic[154] to the superordinate practice it is a part of – and therefore inevitably presupposes a superordinate practice of use. This superordinate practice can be "realist" or "natural", the latter however being no requirement (contrary to Schauer's belief).

Although being "overt" or "marked" is also a necessary property of this subordinate practice, and in the case of statutory fictions, overtness is usually secured by a certain terminology used ("counts as", "is held as", "is regarded as"), the required markers are not necessarily semantical. As fictionality in general, as an institutionalized practice of use, is a pragmatic issue, it is enough, if, in the context of the superordinate discourse, the "nature" of the practice can be identified. That the subordinate practice is sufficiently institutionalized is thus especially relevant, when clear (semantical) markers are missing. Here, pragmatics will contribute a part by contextualizing a provision as fictional.

The ongoing dispute, as to which particular legal provisions are or at least historically have been "real" fictions, or which legal concepts can be "truly" called "dogmatic fictions" (e.g. as pertaining to the corporate person), is under such a definition also a mere question of form. The above definition is especially useful in this respect, since it also accounts for ambivalences, and is furthermore able to accommodate change in the status of a provision or concept – thus allowing a diachronic perspective, explaining why fictions can cease to be fictions if they are not commonly identified as fictions anymore, and why scholars seem to disagree more strongly nowadays as to whether certain provisions are fictions. A not unsubstantial part of the current disagreement pertains to the question what "to deem" or to "count as" in a statutory context literally means, and Wittgenstein's pragmatic definition of the meaning of a word as being defined by its actual use in language accords well with an institutionalized understanding of statutory fictionality in particular and legal fictionality in general. That, for centuries, legal scholars could identify statutory fictions by a certain vocabulary ("*siremps*", "*perinde ac si*", etc.) was legitimately based on the circularity that, in the context of statutes, these terms were already understood as pertaining to legal fictionality as an institutionalized practice – and were deliberately used both by the lawmaker when installing a fiction, and by the recipient when assessing and applying the norm. The same circularity also applies to judicial fictions: a "*si — esset, tum si — oporteret*" would have been immediately identified as pertaining to a legal fiction both on the side of the producer and the recipient, and fictionality would equally have been evident if *Numerius Negidius* and *Aulus Agerius* (or their modern equivalents John Doe and Richard Roe)[155] appeared as parties in a legal dispute. Especially in the case of statutory fictions, the terminology of fictional makers in the continental codes ("count as", "seen as", "held as") follows long-established traditions, being translations of the Latin keywords later institutionalized as part of *usus modernus pandectarum*, which found themselves respectively incorporated in the continental legal discourse on the *ius commune*, and were – at least during the times of codification – produced and received under the latter presuppositions and in clear conscience of the implications resulting from such use. Although it was early on held by Demelius that one should not rely too much on semantic markers, and while counterfactuality was still the key criterion, even formalist scholars (such as Menochio in his 1594 tractate) needed a second criterion in addition to the above markers to distinguish fictions from presumptions,[156] a legal keyword approach was nevertheless usually considered safe. Even Demelius, despite upholding a definition based not on surface structures but on deep-level structures, had to concede that at least during a certain period, the keyword criterion would lead to the correct identification in practically all cases of legal fictionality.[157] Some forms of literary fictionality in fact share this apparent trait with statutory fictionality: "Once upon a time" as an opening line is often a reliable criterion for a narrative being fictional, and a passage that contains "little did he know" also might often serve as an indicator of its fictionality, though the latter is, of course, less reliable than the former.

The above considerations also explain why the fictional status of statutory fictions is more strongly contested currently than in the past, or why the status of dogmatic fictions (as corporate fictionality) always has been strongly debated. In contrast to statutory fictions, dogmatic fictions are often less explicitly marked as fictions, making the (pragmatic) discursive context (e.g. as constituted by precedent or legal theory) decisive if an overt deviation is present. Also, both in the case of statutory and dogmatic fictions, under the presupposition of a formalist definition, historical changes in the superordinate practice inevitably affect the fictional status of the subordinate practice, e.g. if in the case of statutory fiction, a certain vocabulary loses its marking function (e.g. if certain semantic or pragmatic signposts of statutory fictionality – "to deem", "to count as", etc. – are no longer recognized as belonging to the established tradition of statutory fictionality). From a formalist perspective, a statutory fiction then inevitably ceases to be a fiction, for "forgetting" the fictional status of a practice either changes the superordinate framework of use or is itself based on a change that has already occurred in the superordinate framework, preventing past fictions from being recognized as such. Fuller already hypothesized on what would happen to a certain procedural fiction if the superordinate practice changed:

> A fiction dies when a compensatory change takes places in the meaning of the words or phrases involved, which operates to bridge the gap that previously existed between the fiction and reality. This is a process that is going on all the time.[158]

Fuller also allowed for the fact that prolonged use might lead to a change in the superordinate system:

> When the English Court pretended that the Island of Minorca was a part of the city of London once [...] there was little probability that an isolated pretense would lead to a change of the word "London", that it would embrace a spot in the Mediterranean. But even procedural pretense may lead to the development of word meanings.[159]

Comparably, another already historic change has more recently been noted: that "persona" (originally meaning "mask") was once understood as a fiction even in context of the natural person.[160]

Legal discourse, however, has a particularity here to be aware of: since it does not require a homogenous and parsimonious practice of use, competing (and thus contradictory) practices within a single superordinate practice are possible, as the provisions of the Swiss ZGB on the unborn clearly demonstrate.[161]

There are, of course, difficulties inherent in the above claims – as the question, whose perspective is decisive both for the questions of overtness in general, and in particular in the case of historical change. The possibilities are in fact numerous here: the reasonable recipient, the empirical majority of recipients, the individual (and thus accidental) recipient, the legal scholar, the majority of legal scholars, etc.[162] These difficulties, however, are not generic to legal fictionality, but are also present (and heatedly debated) within fictional theory.[163] The question of perspective might also explain why even in the case of a formalist definition, fiction is sometimes falsely understood as a question of degree: As in the case of literary discourse – and parallel to the formulation of categories (see p. 33–4) – institutionalized practices that have "naturally" developed (thus have developed over time instead of being invented and installed) have less clear boundaries, because either the members of the practice might adhere more or less strict to established rules, or the practice itself might have not been homogeneous from the beginning.

It needs to be further decided if the above criteria can already serve as sufficient criteria for fictionality, or only as necessary criteria, with additional criteria still to be established (e.g. in terms of speech act theory), which, in their generalizations for all types of fictionality, would, for example, allow to better distinguish fictionality from certain forms of non-serious use, the latter, however, not being a problem for the case of statutory fictionality. It is an advantage of a flat minimal approach here, that the such questions, however, need not (yet) be decided for the criteria to be operable, and that above provisional criteria can in fact serve at least as a provisional heuristic instrument of approaching the question of fictionality in general, despite a number of limitations, which need to be further investigated.

## Notes

1 Arbeitstreffen Netzwerk Fiktion der Deutschen Forschungsgemeinschaft, Freie Universität Berlin.
2 See p. 41 note 87.
3 Eduard Hölder, "Die Einheit der Correalobligation und die Bedeutung juristischer Fiktionen", *Archiv für die civilistische Praxis* 69 (1868), 223: "keine Besonderheiten des Rechts, sondern höchstens der Rechtssprache"; Ernst Rudolf Bierling, *Juristische Principienlehre* (Freiburg i.B.: J. C. L. Mohr, 1894), 101; Rudolf Leonhard, *In wie weit gibt es nach den Vorschriften der deutschen Civilprozeßordnung Fictionen?* (Berlin: Ferdinand Dümmler, 1880), 7, 9 (for newer statutory fictions in the German Procedural Code); Felix Somlò, *Juristische Grundlehre* (Leipzig: Felix Meiner, 1917), 527; Lon Fuller, *Legal Fictions* (Stanford: Stanford UP, 1967), 11.
4 John Bouvier, *A Law Dictionary. Adapted to the Constitution and Laws of the United States and the Several States of the American Union; with References to the Civil and other Systems of Foreign Law* (Philadelphia, PA: T. & J.W. Johnson, 1856), 1: 520.
5 Ibid.
6 Bob Cover, "The Bonds of Constitutional Interpretation: Of the Word, the Deed, and the Role", *Georgia Law Review*, 20 (1986), 81920, cited by Aviam Soifer, "Reviewing Legal Fictions", *Georgia Law Review* 20 (1986), 882.
7 Jeremy Bentham, *A Fragment on Government*, ed. J.H. Burns and H.L.A. Hart (Cambridge: Cambridge UP, 1988), 117.
8 Bouvier, *A Law Dictionary*, 1: 520.
9 Pierre Olivier, *Legal Fictions in Practice and Legal Science* (Rotterdam: Rotterdam UP, 1975), 142.
10 Demelius already gives a detailed account of the historical development of legal fiction (Gustav Demelius, *Die Rechtsfiktion in ihrer geschichtlichen und dogmatischen Bedeutung* (Weimar: Hermann Boehlau, 1858). Regarding the English scholarship, the newer essays of Maclean (cf. p. 42 note 104) and Peter Birks ("Fictions ancient and modern", in *The Legal Mind: Essays for Tony Honoré*, ed. Neil MacCormick and Peter Birks (Oxford: Clarendon, 1986), 83–101) are good introductions.
11 That the terminology alone is not decisive has long been maintained by scholars. While normal presumptions are easy to discern, since usually the proof of the contrary is explicitly or implicitly allowed by law, irrebuttable presumptions and

deeming provisions often have similar surface structures – and often even the terminology is interchangeable, as Art. 255 of the Swiss civil code shows. Particular caution needs to be taken when assessing provisions that those codes have developed from the French *Code Civil* (as e.g. the Italian and the Spanish Code), since, in the latter, presumption is in fact the rule. On the categorical difference between presumptions and fictions, cf. supra Chapter 1 note 110.

12 § 1923 *BGB*. The most literal translation would be "is valid for"; "gelten" means "to be valid", "to have a (certain) value" (Jacob Grimm and Wilhelm Grimm, *Deutsches Wörterbuch*. 16. Vol. (Leipzig, 1854–1961), 5:3066), but also "to correspond to something in value" (Friedrich Schmitthenner, *Kurzes deutsches Wörterbuch für Etymologie, Synonymik und Orthographie* (Darmstadt: G. Jonhans, 1837), 177, 250. Etymologically, a notion of reciprocity was early inherent: "gelten" primarily meant "to pay" or "to compensate". However, "als etwas gelten" connotes to accept something as equal which in fact isn't. Brinckmeier lists "to pass as something" as synonymous (Eduard Brinckmeier and Carl Müller, *Allgemeines Deutsch-Fremdwörterbuch und vollständigstes Fremdwörterbuch* (Braunschweig: Verlag von Oehme und Müller, n.d.), 169).

13 "juristische Fiktion" (D), "fiction juridique" (F), "ficción jurídica" (ES), "finzione giuridica" (IT), "ficção jurídica" (PRT), "juridische fictie" (NLD),

14 John Baker, *The Law's Two Bodies: Some Evidential Problems in English Legal History* (Oxford: Oxford UP: 2001), 49; Alf Ross, "Legal Fictions", in *Law, Reason and Justice: Essays in Legal Philosophy*, ed. Graham Hughes (New York: New York UP, 1969), 222–3 ("linguistic expression"). Already within the early scholarship, authors have pointed at the merely linguistic nature of certain fictions, cf. supra note 3.

15 Cf. Kenneth Campbell, "Fuller on Legal Fictions", *Law & Philosophy* 2 (1983), 356.

16 Fuller's observation that "it is more difficult to say that a given statement is false, when it relates purely to legal concepts, than when it relates to extra-legal fact" (Fuller, *Legal Fictions*, 28) might have been an early source of this error.

17 Frederick Schauer (cited by Douglas Lind, "The Pragmatic Value of Legal Fictions", in*: Legal Fictions in Theory and Practice*, ed. Maksymilian Del Mar and William Twining (Cham: Springer, 2015), 99). Another form of the question is whether something is a question of law or a question of fact: here naturalistic fallacies are also common: see Campbell, "Fuller on Fictions", 357

18 Ross ("Legal Fictions", 222), however, also comments on the question of an impossibility of counterfactuality in statutory fictionality (as Kelsen and Somlò do). In *Directives and Norms*, Ross furthermore states: "There is no reason to speak of false assumptions, or anything ficticious" (Alf Ross, *Directives and Norms* (Routledge & Kegan Paul, 1968), 31). That legal fictionality is also tied to questions of metaphor and image is not only mentioned Ross by, but also by Fuller (Fuller, *Legal Fictions*, 15–19), and Stern (Stern, "Legal and Literary Fictions", *SSRN* 4, 11, see p. 8 and p. 41 note 86.).

19 Baker, *Bodies*, 44. Esser has harshly criticized the distinction between "real" and merely linguistic fictions: Josef Esser, *Wert und Bedeutung der Rechtsfiktion* (Frankfurt a.M.: Klostermann, 1940), 17, 26; Ross seems to follow: Alf Ross, "Legal Fictions", in Law, Reason and Justice: Essays in Legal Philosophy, ed. Graham Hughes (New York: New York UP, 1969), 223.

20 Simon Stern, "Legal Fictions and Exclusionary Rules", in: Del Mar and Twining, *Legal Fictions*, 157–73; Simon Stern, "Legal and Literary Fictions", in *New Directions in Law and Literature*, ed. Elizabeth Anker and Bernadette Meyler (Oxford UP, 2017), 313–26. Available at SSRN: https://ssrn.com/abstract=2425999. Please note that the page numbers of the SSRN version are different from the printed book. In order to facilitate access, I will use the SSRN numbering in this chapter.

21 Campbell sees room for statutory fictions (Campbell, "Fuller on Fictions", 366), but assumes that the typical deeming provisions "'q is deemed to be p' usually creates no fiction" (368). Campbell also comments on the question of imaginative engagement as criterion (363).
22 Stern, "Exclusionary Rules", 167–70; Stern, "Legal and Literary Fictions", *SSRN* 12.
23 Fuller, *Legal Fictions*, 90.
24 Henry Maine, *Ancient Law* (Cambridge/New York: Cambridge UP, 2012 [1861]), 26–7; cited by Soifer, "Reviewing Legal Fictions", 876; Savigny also upheld a functionalist criterion in his 1814 monograph defining legal fictionality as conservatism in innovation: Friedrich Carl von Savigny, *Vom Beruf unsrer Zeit für Gesetzgebung und Rechtswissenschaft* (Heidelberg: Mohr und Zimmer, 1814), 32. Fuller has, however, argued that even some statutory fictions could fulfil this criterion: Fuller, *Legal Fictions*, 91.
25 Rudolph von Jhering, *Geist des römischen Rechts auf den verschiedenen Stufen seiner Entwicklung* (Leipzig: Breitkopf und Härtel, 1852–1869), 3: 289: "das Charakteristische ist die Form, in der sie dieselbe vermittelt, und der Zweck, dessentwegen sie dies thut". The function (aim) of a fiction is further explicated in *Geist*, 3: 286–7.
26 Jhering, *Geist*, 3: 289.
27 Jhering, *Geist*, 3: 289.
28 Leonhard, *Fiktionen*, 14. Leonhard also revisits Jhering's example of the Jew as a "fictive Christian" on p. 13.
29 "abbrevierende Ausdrucksweise": Kelsen, "Theorie", 640; "abkürzende Formulierung der Rechtsnorm": Kelsen, "Theorie", 641; Jhering also envoked the idea of a truncated relegation of certain statutory fictions (which Jhering would not qualify as true fictions): "[E]s ist eine abgekürzte Form der Fassung der anzuwendenden Rechtsgrundsätze, eine Verweisung": Jhering, *Geist*, 3: 298. Bülow ("Civilprozessualische Fiktionen und Wahrheiten", *Archiv für die civilistische Praxis* 62 (1879), 4) ("kurze Verweisung") and Bierling ("verweisende Rechtssätze") follow: Somlò, *Grundlehre*, 526 note 1.
30 Kelsen, "Theorie", 639–40.
31 Kelsen, "Theorie", 639 ("Behandeln [...] 'Als-Ob'"), 640 ("Es ist ein Mißverständnis zu glauben, dieser Effekt werde dadurch erzielt, daß der Rechtsanwender zu der Vorstellung gezwungen wird [...]").
32 Kelsen, "Theorie", 639.
33 Fuller, *Legal Fictions*, 81.
34 Savigny, *Beruf*, 32.
35 Fuller, *Legal Fictions*, 81.
36 While Kelsen assumes that a "contradiction to reality" is possible in law, if reality is understood not as the "natural reality" but as the "legal reality" (e.g. in the case of procedural fictions, 648, cf. supra Chapter 1, note 221), Kelsen claims that in the case of statutory fictions, such a contradiction was literally unthinkable: Kelsen, "Theorie", 638. To make clear that statutory fictions are not real fictions, Kelsen usually uses quotation marks in this context.
37 Kelsen, "Theorie", 643.
38 E.g. Krückmann, who understands statutory fictionality as a "command to treat as if": Paul Krückmann, "Wahrheit und Unwahrheit im Recht", *Annalen der Philosophie* 1 (1919), 188.
39 Somlò, *Grundlehre*, 524–5.
40 Kelsen, "Theorie", 646; assuming that a part of cognition is implicitly inherent in every judicial decision.
41 Kelsen, "Theorie", 640, although it remains unclear if a certain imaginative engagement is in fact present other than the imagination of "equality".

42 Following Savigny, Demelius understood "Gleichsetzung" (Equation) as the key principle of legal fictionality, Demelius, *Rechtsfiktion*, 80, 86, 88; Bülow also comments on the issue: Bülow, "Fiktionen", 4.
43 See also: Kelsen, "Fiktionen", 633.
44 Like Demelius, Bülow, however, repeatedly insists on the fact that in statutory fictionality= the judge does not "really" believe the situation or fact feigned, e.g. Bülow, "Fiktionen", 46; Leonhard claims that in the case of the Roman fiction, the statutory fiction was in fact an a demand to fantasize respective the situation adjucated: Leonhard, *Fiktionen*, 11. In contrast to this, the current statutory fictions were to be considered an "'interpretatio extensiva' […] without coercing the judge to feign anything, i.e. to assume something false as true.", Leonhard, *Fiktionen*, 10 (my translation).
45 Leonhard, *Fiktionen*, 11; see, however, supra note 44.
46 Bülow, "Fiktionen", 7.
47 Tourtoulon, *Les Principes philosophiques de L'histoire du Droit* (Lausanne/Paris: Librairie Payot, 1908–1919), 451: "La fiction tout en étant un instrument subtil de technique juridique est aussi nettement l'expression d'un désir inhérent à la nature humaine: effacer les réalités douloureuses, évoquer les bonheurs imaginaires." Tourtoulon even sees this as the basis of the *fictio legis Corneliae* (Tourtoulon, *Principes*, 450).
48 "angesehen", as the German translation of the Latin "videtur", Jhering, *Geist*, 3:287 (for the case of *the fictio legis Corneliae*).
49 Jhering, *Geist*, 3: 290 (my translation).
50 Campbell, "Fuller on Fictions", 365.
51 "befehlsmäßiges Behandeln 'Als-ob'"; Täter": Paul Krückmann, "Fiktionen und Bilder in der Rechtswissenschaft", *Annalen der Philosophie* 3 (1923), 425.
52 Loc. cit.
53 Leonhard, *Fiktionen*, 7, 9 who distinguishes linguistic statutory fictions from "true" fictions; Krückmann, op. cit., also distinguishes linguistic from real fictions. The former are treated on pp. 188–90, whereas "real" or "explicit fictions" (e.g. 119–24 *BGB* a.F.) are assessed on p. 177.
54 John R. Searle, "A Classification of Illocutionary Acts", *Language in Society* 5, No. 1 (April 1976), 13.
55 As already said, Kelsen has understood most of the statutory fictions simply as commands not to treat "as if", but to treat "as well", denying that counterfactual equality is actually imagined: Kelsen, "Theorie", 639–40. Leonhard explicates: "If the law commands the judge to treat the *contumax* as confessive in any single case, then this is only an alternative form for the sentence, that the *contumacia* shall always have the effects of a confession, […] If only the form of a sentence would be relevant when it comes to decide its fictionality […] not the lawyer, but the grammar scholar would need to register this form as a cumbersome form to express simple ideas": Leonhard, *Fiktionen*, 12–13; Jhering also treats this matter (3:286), and Fuller has also commented on the issue, formulating deep-level structures for statutory and non-statutory fictionality: Fuller, *Legal Fictions*, 36–7, 47. Campbell also comments on the issue: Campbell, "Fuller on Fictions", 353–4, 366–8.
56 Art. 255 of the Swiss ZGB, for example, uses "gilt als" ("counts as") and "wird vermutet" ("is presumed") interchangeably in a provision that is clearly a presumption, not a fiction. That presumptions and fictions share the same vocabulary can be traced back to the Roman legal tradition. Cf. Jacopo Menochio, *Commentariorum de praesumptionibus conjecturis, signis et indiciis*, (Lugduni (=Lyon): G. Rovillium, 1588) who lists the same keywords for both types, and distinguishes fiction from presumption in terms of certainty. Kelsen, however, has objected that fictions and

presumptions differ in nature, and not (only) in degree of certainty (Kelsen, "Fiktionen", 640); see supra note 11 and Chapter 1 note 110.

57 Karl Larenz, *Richtiges Recht: Grundzüge einer Rechtsethik* (München: C.H. Beck, 1979), 168f., 437f. However, it has strongly been disputed whether an inner system (understood as the unity of all latent legal norms that rule civil law) exists; cf. Hans-Martin Pawlowski, *Methodenlehre für Juristen. Theorie der Norm und des Gesetzes* (Heidelberg: C.F. Müller, 1999), 86; Larenz, *Richtiges Recht*, 437.

58 Bülow, in his 1879 essay on legal fictionality, considers all statutory fictions to be "real" fictions. Bülow was, however, criticized by his contemporary Leonhard: Leonhard, *Fiktionen*, 9.

59 Jhering, *Geist*, 3:287.

60 Cf. p. 221.

61 The German civil code (*BGB*) was criticized by Gierke as a "compendium of the Pandects now cemented in legal paragraphs": Otto von Gierke, *Der Entwurf eines Bürgerlichen Gesetzbuchs und das deutsche Recht* (Leipzig: Duncker & Humblot, 1889), 3. While also based on the Roman doctrine, the Austrian civil code is said to be more oriented to the tradition of the *Institutiones Gai* (Wendland), like the French *Code Civil.* The Swiss civil code is more complicated in this respect, since a number of different tradition overlap here, including influences from the French *Code Civil*, which itself is an amalgamation that fundamentally includes the Roman tradition (including the *corpus iuris civile*). Cf. Paul Koschaker, *Europa und das Römische Recht* (München/Berlin: C.H. Beck, 1966). The French civil code has successfully disseminated in Europe, also influencing many other continental codifications, such as the codes of Spain and Italy, although the latter also integrated the system of the pandects constitutive of the German codification.

62 E.g. Ross, "Fictions", 223.

63 Birks, "Fictions", 83.

64 Birks, "Fictions", 84.

65 Reinhold Zippelius, *Juristische Methodenlehre* (München: C.H. Beck, 1985), 32.

66 § 1589 II *BGB* is, however, no longer in use.

67 According to Leineweber, Canonic law negated any relations between an illegitimate child and his father: Anke Leineweber, *Die rechtliche Beziehung des nichtehelichen Kindes zu seinem Erzeuger in der Geschichte des Privatrechts* (Königsstein: Hanstein, 1978), 61. And in Medieval Saxon law, illegitimate children were understood to be "unreal" persons that had neither relatives nor rights: Steffen Baumgarten, *Die Entstehung des Unehelichenrechts im Bürgerlichen Gesetzbuch* (Köln/Weimar/Wien: Böhlau, 2017), 40.

68 Krückmann, "Wahrheit", 163.

69 Already Nietzsche doubted that the presuppositions of such categorization were correct: Friedrich Nietzsche, "On Truth and Lying in an Extra-Moral Sense", in: *Friedrich Nietzsche on Rhetoric and Language*, ed. and trans. Sander L. Gilman, Carole Blair and David J. Parent (New York; Oxford: Oxford UP, 1989).

70 Eva Schuhmann, *Die nichteheliche Familie, Reformvorschläge für das Familienrecht mit einer Darstellung der geschichtlichen Entwicklung und unter Berücksichtigung des Völker- und Verfassungsrechts* (München: C.H. Beck, 1998) 3, 15 (cited by: Baumgarten, *Entstehung*, 26).

71 Herbert Hausmaninger and Walter Selb, *Römisches Privatrecht* (Wien: Böhlau, 1989), 142. In the case of the father, Papinianus instead insists on the dichotomy between real/natural and legal fatherhood: Tourtoulon, *Principes*, 456.

72 On the principle of agnation, cf. Maine, *Ancient Law*, 150.

73 Hausmaninger and Selb, *Römisches Privatrecht*, 406–8.

74 Campbell belongs to the latter category, claiming not only that the law recognizes "three categories: questions of law, of fact, and of mixed law and fact", but that "the law is its own determiner of what falls into which category": Campbell, "Fuller on Fictions", 257.

75 Kelsen, "Theorie", 641: "The husband is the 'legal father' of the child conceived in adultery [...] A fiction in the sense of a contradiction to reality would further require the legal concept 'father' to be identified with the natural fact of the likewise labelled male procreator. Such a fiction is however merely false and harmful and utterly uncalled for" (my translation).

76 Birks, "Fictions", 84.

77 In his 1903 monograph, Hold-Ferneck lists three options: a "corporate person" has been understood as a something "real", or as a "fiction", or as an "in-between" (an "abstraction"): Alexander Hold-Ferneck, *Die Rechtswidrigkeit* (Jena: Verlag Gustav Fischer, 1903)). Gierke invokes a "psychological reality" for the corporate person (Gierke, *Bürgerliches Gesetzbuch*, 1: 119, note 29). Jhering also comments on the issue (*Geist*, 3: 290): "For the second relation the term 'fictions' has become common, and I do not want to oppose this general practice of use." Cf. Chapter 1 notes 42 and 214 (and accompanying text).

78 Jeremy Bentham, *The Works of Jeremy Bentham. Published under the Superintendence of his Executor, John Bowring. 11 Volumes* (Edinburgh: William Tait, 1838–1843), 8: 126.

79 Johannes Emil Kuntze, *Die Obligation und Die Singularsuccession des römischen und heutigen Rechts* (Leipzig: Hermann Mendelssohn, 1856), 283: "for me, a contract is in its essence a fact, and only a fact, and we can only ask if [such fact] has legal effects, or instead remains ineffective" (my translation).

80 Cf. Kuntze, *Obligation*, 283 note 8.

81 E.g. by Baker, *Bodies*, 42.

82 Ross, "Fictions", 221.

83 Baker, *Bodies*, 43.

84 See supra note 77 and p. 48 note 214

85 Baker, *Bodies*, 46.

86 Baker, *Bodies*, 47; Kelsen would have agreed, cf. Hans Kelsen, *Hauptprobleme der Staatsrechtslehre, entwickelt aus der Lehre vom Rechtssatze* (Tübingen: Mohr, 1911), 180–1.

87 Ibid.

88 Tourtoulon, *Principes*, 452–3.

89 A number of civil codes (such as the Swiss civil code) have in fact chosen this alternate way of a simple, direct command which does not bother with (quasi-)realist constraints, cf. p. 214.

90 Bierling, *Prinzipienlehre*, 101; Leonhard, Fiktionen 7, 9 (for newer statutory fictions in the German procedural code); Somlò, *Grundlehre*, 526–7; Fuller, *Legal Fictions*, 11, 20. From the more recent scholarship, Ross, "Legal Fictions", 223, also raises this claim.

91 Somlò, *Grundlehre*, 527; Bülow, "Fiktionen", 4–6; Esser, *Rechtsfiktion*, 26.

92 Bierling, *Prinzipienlehre*, 103, 104 note 3; Jhering, *Geist*, 2: 370 and 3: 289; Krückmann, *Wahrheit*, 122–4. Fuller also revisited the topic: Fuller, *Legal Fictions*, 20.

93 Baker, *Bodies*, 46; Larenz (citing Esser) also highlights the fact that, at least regarding some statutory fictions, a mere legal definition of the term would have secured the same effect: Karl Larenz and Claus-Wilhelm Canaris, *Methodenlehre der Rechtswissenschaft* (Berlin/Heidelberg/New York: Springer, 1995), 84.

94 Kuntze, *Die Obligation und Die Singularsuccession des römischen und heutigen Rechts* (Leipzig: Hermann Mendelssohn, 1856).

95 Kuntze, *Obligation*, 89, 272.
96 Kuntze however understands fictions as a means that only superficially complies with the "organic system of law": Kuntze, *Obligation*, 272.
97 Kuntze, *Obligation*, 378 (cf. 380, 384); Kuntze's position was, however, strongly contested by some of his contemporaries such as Demelius.
98 "juristischer Mystizismus": Kelsen, "Theorie", 638.
99 Esser, *Rechtsfiktion*, 124.
100 Demelius, *Rechtsfiktion*, 83–4.
101 Though claiming that for statutory fictionality in particular, a contradiction was impossible.
102 Kelsen does not use the term "counterfactuality "but "contradiction" – and declares that while epistemological fictions (in Vaihinger's sense) require a contradiction to "natural reality" ("Natur-Wirklichkeit"), "true "legal fictions correspondingly require a contradiction to the "legal reality" ("Rechts-Wirklichkeit") the latter being identical with the "legal order" ("Rechtsordnung"); see pp. 23, 40 (note 221–3)
103 "*In fictione juris semper aequitas existit*": Eckhard Kessler and Ian Maclean (eds), *Res et Verba in der Renaissance* (Wiesbaden: Harrassowitz in Kommission 2002), 156. The Roman legal tradition lists "*utilitas*" and "*aequitas*" as legitimate purposes for legal fictions: Ian MacLean, "Legal Fictions and Fictional Entities in Renaissance Jurisprudence", *The Journal of Legal History* 20 (1999), 5.
104 More literal: "is valid for" (c. supra note 12).
105 Cf. Alfred Pernice, *Marcus Antistius Laboe. Das römische Privatrecht im ersten Jahrhundert der Kaiserzeit.* (Halle: Verlag der Buchhandlung des Waisenhauses, 1873), 196–206.
106 Maine, *Ancient Law*, 26.
107 Bouvier, *A Law Dictionary*, 520.
108 Adolf Schönke and Horst Schröder, *Strafgesetzbuch* (München: C.H. Beck, 2010), Vorbem. § 211 ff. Rn. 1.
109 Cf. Philipp Heck, "Gesetzesauslegung und Interessenjurisprudenz", *Archiv für civilrechtliche Praxis* 112 (1914), 1; Rudolf Wiethölter, "Begriffs- oder Interessenjurisprudenz "in *Festschrift Gerhard Kegel*, ed. Hans-Joachim Musielak and Klaus Schurig, (Stuttgart: W. Kohlhammer, 1987), 213–63.
110 Bernd Rüthers, "Hans Brox als Methodenlehrer – Von der Interessen- zur Wertungsjurisprudenz", *Rechtstheorie* 41, No. 2, 141–50.
111 The idea that any translation process in law has its main aim not in transferring the letter or meaning of the law, but in succeeding with the perlocutionary aim of the command: cf. Janny Leung, "Ideology and Political Meaning in Legal Translation", in *Meaning and Power in the Language of Law*, ed. Janny Leung, J. and Allen Durant (Cambridge: Cambridge UP, 2018), 236–58.
112 Larenz and Canaris, *Methodenlehre*, 140.
113 Continental law scholars agree that the provisions of the continental codes are in fact often incomplete and that the resulting command in fact needs to be construed, cf. Larenz and Canaris, *Methodenlehre*, Chapter 2 (especially note 1). Allot instead defines latent norm as "a law which has not yet been articulated, but which provokes what may be considered acts of compliance": Anthony Allott, *The Limits of Law* (London: Butterworth, 1980), 30.
114 Hausmaninger and Selb, *Römisches Privatrecht*, 135.
115 Noel Coulson, *Commercial Law in the Gulf States* (London: Graham & Trotman, 1984), 32–3.
116 On the distinction between presumptions and fictions, see supra notes 11 and 56; Chapter 1 note 110.

117 Cf. *The Oxford Handbook of Developmental Psychology, Vol. 1: Body and Mind*, edited by Philip David Zelazo (Oxford/New York: Oxford UP, 2013), especially "Part 4: Cognitive Development"); see also: Jean Piaget, *Selected Works. Vol. 3: Origins of Intelligence in the Child* (London: Routledge 1997 [1936]).
118 Coulson, *Commercial Law*, 32–3.
119 § 108 *BGB.*
120 § 105a *BGB.*
121 Art. 1145 CC states that every person is able to conclude a contract, as long as no exception is stipulated by law. Art. 1146 CC lists a number of exception, such as non-emancipated minors. Art. 1148 stipulates that even persons who lack the capacity to contract can effect certain minor day-to-day transactions.
122 Bouvier, *A Law Dictionary*, 520.
123 François Geny, *Science et technique en droit privé positif: Nouvelle contribution à la critique de la méthode juridique* (Paris: Sirey, 1913), 376; Geny, however, rejects the idea that fictions are merely linguistic: "En même temps, le résultat s'opère par voie logique, non pas, comme certains l'ont dit, à titre de simple expédient terminologique", 377.
124 Pernice, *Labeo*, 197–8.
125 Cf. Pernice, *Labeo*, 204–5.
126 Art. 544 ZGB, my translation.
127 Cf. Art. 725 CC: "Pour succéder, il faut exister à l'instant de l'ouverture de la succession ou, ayant déjà été conçu [...]."
128 Art. 44 II Código Civil, like the Swiss Code, attributes rights to the unborn under condition that he is later born alive.
129 Art. 927 II KC.
130 According to Art. 1 of the Codice Civile, legal personality starts with birth. A number of provisions, however, allow the unborn to inherit, or to receive gifts: Art. 462 mandates that the capacity to success already starts with conception.
131 Art. 462 CC.
132 Art. 725 CC, my translation, emphasis added.
133 I recall a debate in Poland on the issue during the revision of the *Kodeks cywilny*; as far as I know, the legislator decided against this option.
134 § 22 *ABGB* "Even unborn children can demand, from the moment of their conception on, to be protected by law. Provided only their rights are concerned, and not the rights of a third party, they are regarded as born; a child born dead however will however be regarded as never having been conceived [....]" (my translation).
135 Art. 49 (2) *BGB.*
136 Philipp Eduard Huschke, *Studien des römischen Rechts* (Breslau: Joh. Fried. Korn, 1830), 1: 183 note 21.
137 Art. 29 I of the Spanish civil code; § 22 of the Austrian *ABGB.*
138 Schönke and Schröder, *Strafgesetzbuch*, Vorbem. § 211 ff. Rn. 1.
139 Schönke, loc. cit.
140 Cf. supra note 61.
141 As demonstrated above, the Swiss Code is less concerned with consistency and coherence, see above p. 214.
142 "Begriffsjurisprudenz": Rudolf von Jhering, *Scherz und Ernst in der Jurisprudenz* (Darmstadt: Wissenschaftliche Buchgesellschaft 1992 [1924]), 260.
143 BGHZ 91, 324 (07.06.1984 – IX ZR 66/83).
144 Jhering, *Geist*, 3: 292. On pp. 369–70 of the second volume (Leipzig: Breitkopf und Härtel, 1858), Jhering more closely defines this "operation".
145 Correspondingly, Leonard concedes that many of the deeming provisions of the German procedural code (*Zivilprozessordnung*) are codified forms of such

analogical proceeding: Leonhard, "Fiktionen", 10; Jhering has, however, noted that both practices are in fact complementary: "Instead of extending the legal clause so that the relation can find a place, [in the case of fiction] the relation is violently pressed together so it can fit in. [...] [T]he actual extension of the legal clause is covered up, veiled" (Jhering, *Geist*, 3: 289, my translation).

146 Jhering, *Geist*, 3: 285, citing Gottlieb Korte.

147 Jhering, *Geist*, 2: 408.

148 Of course, in the continental legal systems, such choice need not have been evident, since the European civil law systems have slowly grown out of the Roman legal tradition and the *usus modernus*. At the time of codification, however, to keep such a system was the free choice of the lawmakers, since alternatives were in fact debated. Cf. e.g. Gierke, *Bürgerliches Gesetzbuch*, loc. cit.

149 The latter is not a necessary part of the definition, but rather a consequence that facilitates understanding the hierarchical character of the relation of the two practices at hand.

150 Campbell, "Fuller on Fictions", 359.

151 Lind, "Pragmatic Value", 84.

152 Frederick Schauer, "Legal Fictions Revisited", in: Del Mar and Twining, *Legal Fictions*, 126.

153 As the immediately superordinate practice of use.

154 Searle has already commented on the parasitic nature of fictional discourse (John Searle, "The Logical Status of Fictional Discourse", *New Literary History* 6, No. 2 (1975), 326). His approach is, however, different from mine, since he defines fictionality as pretended assertive speech, cf. supra p. 25–6.

155 Cf. supra Chapter 1 note 8 and accompanying text.

156 Menochio, *Commentariorum*, 10; cf. supra note 56 and Chapter 1, note 110.

157 Demelius, *Rechtsfiktion*, 76.

158 Fuller, *Legal Fictions*, 14. The question of consciousness is, however, complex in Fuller. Not only is a partial consciousness regarded as sufficient (10), but when Fuller treats the case of forgetting, a functional criterion of fictionality is being evoked instead, since Fuller seems to tie this particular death of fiction to the fact that an unconscious fiction "loses its utility" and "becomes dangerous".

159 Fuller, *Legal Fictions*, 18.

160 Maximilian Koessler, "The Person in Imagination or Persona Ficta of the Corporation", *Louisiana Law Review* 9, No. 4 (May 1949), 446; cf. Jeanne Gaakeer "'Sua cuique persona?' A Note on the Fiction of Legal Personhood and a Reflection on Interdisciplinary Consequences", *Law and Literature* 28 (2016), 287–317; Hans Rheinfelder, "Das Wort '*persona*': Geschichte seiner Bedeutungen mit besonderer Berücksichtigung des französischen und italienischen Mittelalters", *Beihefte zur Zeitschrift für romanische Philologie* 77 (1928). For Affolter, 504, the *persona* is not a fiction, but an abstraction: Friedrich Xaver Affolter, *Das römische Institutionensystem: sein Wesen und seine Geschichte* (Berlin: Puttkammer & Mühlbrecht, 1897). Fuller also revisits the topic: Fuller, *Legal Fictions*, 19.

161 That the superordinate practice ceases to be homogeneous (or has never been homogenous in the first place) can be monitored both in the French *Code Civil* or the Swiss *Zivilgesetzbuch*.

162 Cf. Fuller, *Legal Fictions*, 10–11; Lind, *Pragmatic Value*, 94. According to Baker, "most fictional devices were, in origin, collusive" (Baker, *Bodies*, 54).

163 See Chapter 1 note 300 (and accompanying text). The decision much depends on the question of whether fictionality is considered to be a semantic or a pragmatic feature (and thus whether "signposts" of fictionality do exist).

## References


Baker, John. *The Law's Two Bodies: Some Evidential Problems in English Legal History.* Oxford: Oxford UP, 2001.

Ballentine, James. *A Law Dictionary.* Rochester, NY: Lawyers Co-operative Pub. Co, 1969.

Bentham, Jeremy. *A Fragment on Government.* Edited by J.H. Burns and H.L.A. Hart. Cambridge: Cambridge UP, 1988.

Bierling, Rudolf. *Juristische Principienlehre.* Freiburg i.B.: J.C.L. Mohr, 1894.

Birks, Peter. "Fictions ancient and modern". In: *The Legal Mind: Essays for Tony Honoré.* Edited by Neil MacCormick and Peter Birks, 83–101. Oxford: Clarendon, 1986.

Bouvier, John. *A Law Dictionary.* Philadelphia, PA: T. & J.W. Johnson, 1856.

Bülow, Oskar. "Civilprozessualische Fiktionen und Wahrheiten". *Archiv für die civilistische Praxis* 62 (1879), 1–96.

Campbell, Kenneth. "Fuller on Legal Fictions". *Law & Philosophy* 2 (1983), 339–70.

Coulson, Noel. *Commercial Law in the Gulf States.* London: Graham &Trotman, 1984.

Demelius, Gustav. *Die Rechtsfiktion in ihrer geschichtlichen und dogmatischen Bedeutung.* Weimar: Hermann Boehlau, 1858.

Esser, Josef. *Wert und Bedeutung der Rechtsfiktion.* Frankfurt a.M.: Klostermann, 1940.

Fuller, Lon. *Legal Fictions.* Stanford: Stanford UP, 1967.

Gaakeer, Jeanne. "'Sua cuique persona?' A Note on the Fiction of Legal Personhood and a Reflection on Interdisciplinary Consequences". *Law and Literature* 28 (2016), 287–317.

Geny, François. *Science et technique en droit privé positif: Nouvelle contribution à la critique de la méthode juridique.* Paris: Sirey, 1913.

Gierke, Otto von. *Der Entwurf eines Bürgerlichen Gesetzbuchs und das deutsche Recht.* Leipzig: Duncker & Humblot, 1889.

Hausmaninger, Herbert and Walter Selb. *Römisches Privatrecht.* Wien: Böhlau, 1989.

Heck, Philipp. "Gesetzesauslegung und Interessenjurisprudenz". *Archiv civilrechtliche Praxis* 112 (1914), 1.

Huschke, Philipp Eduard. *Studien des römischen Rechts.* Breslau: Joh. Fried. Korn, 1830.

Hold-Ferneck, Alexander. *Die Rechtswidrigkeit.* Jena: Verlag Gustav Fischer, 1903.

Honsell, Heinrich. *Römisches Recht.* Berlin: Springer, 2006.

Jhering, Rudolf. *Geist des römischen Rechts auf den verschiedenen Stufen seiner Entwicklung.* Leipzig: Breitkopf und Härtel, 1852–1869.

Jhering, Rudolf. *Scherz und Ernst in der Jurisprudenz.* Darmstadt: Wiss. Buchges 1992 [1924].

Kelsen, Hans. *Hauptprobleme der Staatsrechtslehre, entwickelt aus der Lehre vom Rechtssatze.* Tübingen: Mohr, 1911.

Kessler, Eckhard and Ian Maclean (eds). *Res et Verba in der Renaissance.* Wiesbaden: Harrassowitz in Kommission, 2002.

Koessler, Maximilian. "The Person in Imagination or Persona Ficta of the Corporation". *Louisiana Law Review* 9, No. 4 (May 1949), 435–49.

Koschaker, Paul. *Europa und das Römische Recht.* München/Berlin: Beck, 1966.

Krückmann, Paul. "Fiktionen und Bilder in der Rechtswissenschaft". *Annalen der Philosophie* 3 (1923), 418–426.

Krückmann, Paul. "Wahrheit und Unwahrheit im Recht". *Annalen der Philosophie* 1 (1919), 114–90.

Kuntze, Johannes Emil. *Die Obligation und Die Singularsuccession des römischen und heutigen Rechts.* Leipzig: Hermann Mendelssohn, 1856.

Larenz, Karl. *Richtiges Recht: Grundzüge einer Rechtsethik.* München: C.H. Beck, 1979.

Lecocq, Lucien. *De la Fiction comme procede juridique.* Paris: Arthur Rousseau, 1914.

Leineweber, Anke. *Die rechtliche Beziehung des nichtehelichen Kindes zu seinem Erzeuger in der Geschichte des Privatrechts.* Königsstein: Hanstein, 1978.

Leonhard, Rudolf. *In wie weit gibt es nach den Vorschriften der deutschen Civilprozeßordnung Fictionen?* Berlin: Ferdinand Dümmler, 1880.

Leung, Janny. "Translation Equivalence as Legal Fiction". *In The Ashgate Handbook of Legal Translation.* Edited by King Kui Sin, Anne Wagner and Lee Cheng, 57–69. Farnham/Burlington, Ashgate, 2014.

Lind, Douglas. "The Pragmatic Value of Legal Fictions". In *Legal Fictions in Theory and Practice.* Edited by Maksymilian Del Mar and William Twining, 83–107. Cham: Springer, 2015.

Maclean, Ian. "Legal Fictions and Fictional Entities in Renaissance Jurisprudence". The Journal of Legal History 20 (1999), 1–24.

Maine, Henry. *Ancient Law.* Cambridge/New York: Cambridge UP, 2012 [1861].

Menochio, Jacopo. *Commentariorum de praesumptionibus conjecturis, signis et indiciis.* Lugduni (=Lyon): G. Rovillium, 1588.

Miller, Sidney. "The reasons for some legal fictions", *Michigan Law Review* 8 (1910): 623–36.

Nietzsche, Friedrich. "On Truth and Lying in an Extra-Moral Sense". In: *Friedrich Nietzsche on Rhetoric and Language.* Edited and translated by Sander L. Gilman, Carole Blair and David J. Parent. New York, Oxford: Oxford UP, 1989.

Olivier, Pierre. *Legal Fictions in Practice and Legal Science.* Rotterdam: Rotterdam UP, 1975.

Pawlowski, Hans-Martin. *Methodenlehre für Juristen. Theorie der Norm und des Gesetzes* Heidelberg: C.F. Müller, 1999.

Pernice, Alfred. *Marcus Antistius Laboe. Das römische Privatrecht im ersten Jahrhundert der Kaiserzeit.* Halle: Verlag der Buchhandlung des Waisenhauses, 1873.

Piaget, Jean. *Selected Works. Vol. 3: Origins of Intelligence in the Child* (London: Routledge 1997 [1936]).

Ross, Alf. "Legal Fictions". In: *Law, Reason and Justice: Essays in Legal Philosophy.* Edited by Graham Hughes, 217–34. New York: New York UP, 1969.

Rüthers, Bernd. "Hans Brox als Methodenlehrer – Von der Interessen- zur Wertungsjurisprudenz". *Rechtstheorie* 41, No. 2, 141–50.

Savigny, Friedrich Carl von. *Vom Beruf unsrer Zeit für Gesetzgebung und Rechtswissenschaft.* Heidelberg: Mohr und Zimmer, 1814.

Schauer, Frederick "Legal Fictions Revisited". In: *Legal Fictions in Theory and Practice.* Edited by Maksymilian Del Mar and William Twining, 112–29. Cham: Springer, 2015.

Schönke, Adolf and Horst Schröder. *Strafgesetzbuch.* München: C.H. Beck, 2010.

Schuhmann, Eva. *Die nichteheliche Familie.* München: C.H. Beck, 1998.

Searle, John. "A Classification of Illocutionary Acts", *Language in Society* 5, No. 1 (April 1976), 1–23.

Searle, John. "The Logical Status of Fictional Discourse". *New Literary History* 6, No. 2 (1975), 319–32.

Soifer, Aviam. "Reviewing Legal Fictions". *Georgia Law Review* 20 (1986), 871–915.

Somlò, Felix. *Juristische Grundlehre.* Leipzig: Felix Meiner, 1917.

Stern, Simon. "Legal and Literary Fictions". In: *New Directions in Law and Literature.* Edited by Elizabeth S. Anker and Bernadette Mayler, 313–26. Oxford: Oxford UP, 2017.

Stern, Simon. "Legal Fictions and Exclusionary Rules", in: *Legal Fictions in Theory and Practice*. Edited by Maksymilian Del Mar and William Twining, 157–73. Cham: Springer, 2015.

Tourtoulon, Pierre de. *Les Principes philosophiques de L'histoire du Droit*. Lausanne/Paris: Librairie Payot, 1908–1919.

Wiethölter, Rudolf. "Begriffs- oder Interessenjurisprudenz". In *Festschrift für Gerhard Kegel*. Edited by Hans-Joachim Musielak and Klaus Schurig, 213–63. Stuttgart: W. Kohlhammer, 1987.

Wolterstorff, Nicholas. "Response to Beardsley on 'Fiction as Representation'". *Synthese* 46, No. 3 (1981), 315–32.

Zelazo, Philip David (ed.). *The Oxford Handbook of Developmental Psychology. Vol. 1: Body and Mind*. Oxford/New York: Oxford UP, 2013.

Chapter 5.3

# Cognitive fictionalizing and legal legitimacy

*Karen Petroski*

August 9, 2014: Just after noon on this sunny Sunday, in a suburb of St. Louis called Ferguson, Missouri, 28-year-old Ferguson police officer Darren Wilson shot and killed 18-year-old Michael Brown in the middle of a street in a residential area. Wilson is white, and Brown was African-American. Bystanders and passers-by immediately began discussing the event and comparing accounts of what they had seen.[1] A crowd of concerned onlookers grew as local police, unused to gatherings of this size, awaited investigators. Brown's body lay face-down in the street, visible to the crowd, until detectives erected screens around it an hour and a half later, and his body remained in the street for two and a half hours after that.[2] Many members of the mostly African-American crowd saw this treatment of Brown's body as callous and disrespectful. Police made little effort to explain their activities to community members and did not reveal the identity of Brown's shooter for six days.

The events of that afternoon touched off months of demonstrations against police brutality and racism in Ferguson and around the United States. In Ferguson, the demonstrations were repeatedly disrupted by violence, looting, and arson. Residents of the already highly segregated St. Louis metropolitan area became more and more anxious about racial conflict, and the absence of any official account of the events of August 9 contributed to widespread feelings of powerlessness and police distrust, as well as to multiple divergent understandings of what occurred during the encounter between Brown and Wilson. Alongside these events, the county prosecutor, Robert McCulloch, opened an investigation into the possible filing of criminal charges against Wilson for causing Brown's death. Unusually, instead of making the decision himself, McCulloch decided to submit the case to a grand jury to decide whether Wilson should be prosecuted for wrongful homicide.[3]

The presentation of the case to the grand jury took three months and more than 70 hours.[4] McCulloch finally announced the grand jury's decision not to indict Wilson on the evening of the Monday before Thanksgiving, November 24, 2014, in a 20-minute-long speech that seemed carefully scripted but was widely perceived as inept and counterproductive. This speech, and the reaction to it, are the focus of this essay. About one-third of the way through the speech, just before formally announcing the grand jury's decision, McCulloch declared, "The duty of the grand jury is to separate fact from fiction."[5] With this sentence, he invoked a familiar dichotomy that has structured discussions of law by the public and by scholars for the past century. The dichotomy identifies "fact" with the true, the objective, and the legitimate, and fact's opposite—"fiction"—with the false, the subjective, and the illegitimate. The dichotomy implies that the job of legal professionals is to purge fiction from the legal system and to help produce decisions based on fact. Journalists and academics responding to McCulloch's statements rejected much of what he communicated in the speech as disingenuous, but these critics did not question the validity of this basic dichotomy. Instead, criticism of the speech mostly focused on McCulloch's failure to investigate or represent the facts of the Darren Wilson case honestly. Critics accused McCulloch of misleadingly presenting his own carefully engineered narrative as neutrally factual. In making this criticism, however, the commentators themselves depended on something very much like fiction: an imagined alternative course of events that McCulloch did not pursue.

Academic lawyers and scholars interested in fictional discourse are comfortable with the idea that lawyers and judges are always, in a sense, telling stories or constructing narratives. While there is some tension between this notion and the fact–fiction dichotomy described above, the two positions are not necessarily inconsistent, since not all narratives are fictional. The idea that legal practice might inevitably involve another kind of fictionalizing is not nearly so familiar. The phenomenon that this chapter begins to investigate, called a form of fiction-making here, has been described in a number of other ways in various disciplines: as hypothetical or conjectural reasoning, as supposition, as the generation of counterfactual and not-quite-factual possibilities. This essay will refer to the phenomenon as "cognitive fictionalizing," in order to stress, first, its importance to legal decision-making and justification and, second, its kinship to our understanding and description of the kinds of imaginary states of affairs that are more traditionally the subject of fictional statements. It will use McCulloch's address to explore the fundamental role of the imagination of alternative possible courses of events in legal practice. It will suggest the possibility that counterfactual thinking and its presentation in legal explanation are basic ways that legal actors conventionally pursue some of the values usually associated with "fact," including trustworthiness and objectivity. This account does not reject the goal of factual accuracy in legal decision-making. Instead, it describes a kind of fiction as crucial to attaining that goal.

The first of the sections that follow describes McCulloch's address and the critical reactions to it, explaining the roles played by narrative and cognitive fictionalizing in both the speech and the responses. The three sections following consider more broadly the function of cognitive fictionalizing generally and its function in legal practice and offer some tentative explanations for the relative scholarly neglect of the latter issue. A brief concluding section summarizes some of the main arguments made in this chapter. This section suggests more forthright acknowledgment of the ways in which legal legitimacy is not threatened by cognitive fictionalizing, but rather depends on such fictionalizing.

## I Fact versus (two kinds of) fiction

McCulloch drew his contrast between fact and fiction about one-third of the way into a press conference that one critic called a "bizarre self-justifying ramble."[6] Not just a simple announcement, the address was more like a string of narratives. McCulloch began with a critical reference to the proliferation of competing witness accounts of Brown's death, then launched into a detailed description of the process McCulloch's office had used to present the case to the grand jury. After discussing this process for roughly ten minutes, McCulloch announced the grand jury's fact-finding duty, then finally revealed the grand jury's decision not to charge Wilson.[7] By prefacing this key announcement as he did, McCulloch set up the about-to-be-announced grand jury decision as a matter of fact, rather than fiction. His sequencing suggested that the jurors had successfully managed to identify the objective reality amid the conflicting accounts of Brown's death that McCulloch had spent the first several minutes of his address criticizing, and therefore that the grand jury's decision was unassailably legitimate.

Journalists and legal commentators were uniformly critical of the announcement's content and presentation. Criticism focused in particular on the unusual methods McCulloch described his office as using in presenting the case to the grand jury. The process followed was unusual in several ways. First, McCulloch and the assistant prosecutors who presented the case "inundated the grand jury with 'every scrap of evidence [they] could find,'"[8] instead of following the normal procedure of offering the evidence that would support a finding of probable cause.[9] Second, although grand jury proceedings are not adversarial (the potential indictee is not represented by defense counsel), the prosecutors in the Wilson case presented some of the evidence as it would have been presented in an adversarial proceeding (e.g. by pointing out contradictions between the physical evidence and some eyewitnesses' accounts).[10] Third, again in a departure from normal practice, the prosecutors did not recommend a charge to the grand jury, but offered the jurors a menu of potential charges from which to select.[11]

Commentators saw these approaches as both predetermining the grand jury's conclusion and allowing McCulloch to dodge responsibility for it. On this widely shared view, McCulloch constructed a self-serving story about the activities of his office in connection with the case. The story selectively omitted important information and misleadingly framed other details in order to deemphasize McCulloch's control over the course of events and the outcome. McCulloch's speech does indeed contain multiple stories, including not only those mentioned above, but also a story describing how the grand jury deliberated, and, at the very end of the address, an account of what happened on August 9 during the encounter between Brown and Wilson. As he recounted these stories in his address, McCulloch did consistently deny his role in their creation. In his account, neither McCulloch nor his assistants told any particular story to the grand jury; the grand jury just received "all the evidence."[12] McCulloch was aligned with his critics, however, in his general suspicion of storytelling. In particular, his speech describes (non-narrative) physical and forensic evidence as more dependable than the narrative accounts of eyewitnesses:

> The physical evidence does not change because of public pressure or personal agenda. Physical evidence does not look away as events unfold nor does it blackout [sic] or add to memory. It remains constant and is a solid foundation upon which cases are built.[13]

Even though McCulloch's address was a resounding failure as a rhetorical performance, his critics mostly seemed to agree with this apparent vision of law as, ideally, a story-free enterprise, or at least an enterprise in which storytelling is subject to severe constraints. This position underlies more specific criticisms of McCulloch that might otherwise seem inconsistent. One theme in the criticism of McCulloch, as suggested above, was that he constructed the stories he told in the address for the purpose of avoiding personal responsibility.[14] On this view, McCulloch's mistake was not that he told a story, but that he did not include himself in the story as an active agent; he did not reveal the bias inherent in the story. Another prominent critical theme, however, was that there was no way for McCulloch to have handled the case properly, because his personal history prevented him from approaching it impartially.[15] On this view, the address was flawed not just because of the way McCulloch presented the information, but more basically because of the nature of the underlying information: McCulloch could not have told a defensible story about the grand jury process because his background made him incapable of pursuing truth in this case. Like McCulloch's own denigration of witness testimony, this perspective identifies the legal process with truth-seeking and suspects the contaminating influence of any arguably subjective agent in that process. McCulloch and his critics thus seem to share a notion of stories—at least in this case—as inevitably subjective, distorted, and inappropriate to legal decision-making, a notion McCulloch himself summed up as a contrast between fact-tracking law and illegitimate fiction.[16]

All of McCulloch's critics, however, either implicitly or explicitly compared the approach he took to the case with another approach that he did not take. The view of McCulloch's address as brazenly denying his own role in predetermining the grand jury's decision presupposes that if McCulloch's office had presented the case to the grand jury differently, the grand jurors might have reached a different conclusion. The view of McCulloch as personally biased presupposes that if he had stepped aside from the prosecution, and someone lacking his background had prosecuted the case, the process might have led to a more factually accurate, legitimate, and acceptable result. Both perspectives imply the possibility of an alternative to what is understood to have actually taken place. Critics holding these views made their points by inviting their audiences to imagine how such alternative courses of events would have unfolded.[17] Although McCulloch's critics disparage fiction in one sense, then, in this other sense they make use of something like fiction, something involving the imagination and description of non-actual states of affairs.

McCulloch's critics did not draw attention to their use of this kind of reasoning, nor did they address whether it is consistent with a vision of law as a fact-oriented enterprise. But journalists' professional role does not ordinarily oblige them to examine and defend their own logic in this way. It is not clear that the same can be said of lawyers like McCulloch. As will be discussed further below, in legal settings, consideration of hypothetical alternatives and their implications is neither new nor unusual. Such consideration is, in fact, sometimes explicitly required by legal rules.[18] McCulloch's public statements about the Wilson case went beyond a (perhaps excusable) lack of self-awareness about the prevalence of such considerations in legal practice. During and after the address, McCulloch deviated from standard legal practice more basically by appearing positively allergic to admitting the possibility of alternatives to the course he followed. He closed his announcement, for example, with what sounded like a call for civic reflection and social change: "I urge everyone who was engaged in the conversation, who was engaged in the demonstrations, to keep that going. … And to do it in … [a] way that we can benefit from this, by changing the structure … by solving the issues that lead to these sorts of things."[19] When a reporter present at the address asked what changes to "the structure" McCulloch would propose, however, McCulloch responded, "There's just no way to answer a question like that."[20] The following month, discussing the timing of his announcement with another reporter, McCulloch insisted "that he did not believe events [such as the arson that evening in Ferguson] would have been different had he chosen to wait until daylight to reveal the grand jury's conclusion."[21]

McCulloch's persistent refusals to consider alternatives to the course he followed are consistent with the commitment to fact he expressed in his speech. It would have been a challenge for him to present the narratives he offered as factual and yet as just a few of several possible sets of stories that could have been told about the events of August 9, the presentation of evidence to the grand jury, and the grand jury's deliberations. McCulloch's aversion to alternative accounts might even be an understandable, if not excusable, side-effect of his professional identity as a prosecutor.[22] But the critical reaction to his speech and conduct suggest a widespread sense that his refusal to consider alternative possibilities was deeply inconsistent with his professional obligations. In other words, the problem with McCulloch's speech was not that, or not only that, it included several stories, or that those stories were constructed from a particular perspective. The address could have included factual narratives.[23] The more basic problem with the address was that it failed to tell an acceptable story because of McCulloch's persistent failure to consider how things might have been different—revealed through his persistent refusal to acknowledge any such considerations. To tell an acceptable story, McCulloch would have had to describe himself as open to possibility, including the possibility that Wilson might have acted wrongfully.

Viewed this way, McCulloch's address and the responses to it reveal a more complex set of links among fact, fiction, and law than the traditional dichotomy suggests. McCulloch and his critics agree that legitimate legal decisions are based on fact and are objective, rather than subjective (a synonym, in this context, for biased or self-serving). They also seem to agree that perceiving a legal decision as legitimate often involves perceiving it in the context of several stories, or narratives. Although they do not necessarily conflict, these two points are still in some tension. Most narratives imply the endorsement of some perspective and are vulnerable to criticism on that basis.[24] Such subjective accounts of events, unchecked by testing against others' accounts and other information, are the kinds of "fiction" that both McCulloch and his critics reject as legally inappropriate. But not all narratives are fictional, and—less familiarly—not all departures from fact are so tightly perspective-bound. Indeed, one of the ways of determining whether a particular narrative is sufficiently anchored in fact is to explore alternative possible sequences of events or run mental simulations—to generate fictions.[25] These sorts of fictions are endemic in legal discourse and decision and are considered acceptable and legitimate, even though they are very rarely explicitly discussed.[26] The next sections of this chapter will further explore some of the ways in which the entertainment of possibilities involves a kind of fictionalizing and suggests some possible explanations for the general repression of legal awareness of this phenomenon.

## II Counterfactual reasoning as cognitive fictionalizing

As Nicholas Rescher has pointed out, the use of hypothetical and counterfactual reasoning is a venerable practice,[27] and scholars have been actively interested in explaining the pervasiveness of such reasoning, as well as its structure and operation, since at least the early twentieth century. The most ambitious such account probably remains Hans Vaihinger's *The Philosophy of "As If"* (1911).[28] Over the past several decades, academic interest in this phenomenon has spread outside philosophy to influence and even transform some areas of inquiry, including some closely related to law.[29] Full exploration of these scholarly developments is impossible in the space available here. This chapter will just outline a few major themes of this work and explore some of the senses in which its subject is a kind of "fictionalizing."

Hypothetical or counterfactual propositions are propositions that we know are possibly (in the case of hypotheticals) or certainly (in the case of counterfactuals) not consistent with states of affairs in the actual world. They are thus not factual propositions. However, they can help us understand states of affairs in the actual world; they help us understand facts. Such propositions are necessary components of the scientific method.[30] The generation of scientific hypotheses for testing involves the imagination and, usually, the communication of non-actual states of affairs before they can have been factually tested. This practice, too, thus involves fictionalizing in a sense, yet most would agree that it aims at truth determination, not away from it. As shown above, criticism of a course of action also depends on at least the implication of such possibilities, if not their explicit statement. In addition, the positing of counterfactual sequences is now widely considered to be a necessary part of causal explanation.[31]

In the mid-twentieth century, philosophers seeking an understanding of the general structure of such reasoning began describing it as involving the postulation of alternative "possible worlds."[32] The American philosophers Robert Stalnaker and David Lewis started to explore this way of analyzing counterfactual statements in the late 1960s and early 1970s, focusing on the inferences implicit in different kinds of "if-then" statements, such as "If you drop the glass, it will break" or "If I had been born in France, I would speak French better than I actually do." Statements taking these forms had been puzzling to philosophers because of their peculiar truth status. We intuitively evaluate some statements of this kind as true. But in the case of counterfactuals like "If I had been born in France …," we know that the antecedent, or premise, is false. (I was born in the United States.) According to traditional logic, since the premise is false, it would seem that the conclusion inferred from it, and thus the entire proposition communicated by the sentence, must also be false. As Stalnaker put it, "A conditional sentence expresses a proposition which is a function of two other propositions, yet not one which is a truth-function of those propositions."[33] To explain our contrary intuition, Stalnaker and Lewis followed earlier philosophers in suggesting that we think of conditional statements as referring not to facts about the actual world, but to possible facts, or facts about a possible world. This suggestion does not completely solve the puzzle, however, since it is not clear how we could check whether references to "possible" things are referring properly and therefore whether the statements containing them are communicating true propositions.

Counterfactual statements share many of their peculiarities with statements referring to nonexistent or fictional entities, like unicorns or Sherlock Holmes. Most would agree that Sherlock Holmes does not exist in the actual world, but also that some statements about him seem intuitively true, such as the statement that he lived in London. In the context of already written-about fictional characters, in contrast to counterfactual conditionals, there is an easy way to check our intuitions about truth; we can check the truth of at least some statements about Holmes by consulting the fictional narratives describing him.[34] Such narratives also provide a model for thinking about the possible worlds that operate in the counterfactual-conditional context. They help justify the use of the label "fiction" to refer to these other, counterfactual and hypothetical, possible worlds; we engage with and reason from such unwritten-about possibilities in ways resembling our engagement with narrative fiction. Much of the psychological research on counterfactual reasoning depends on this analogy; it studies the cognitive processing of hypotheticals by asking experimental subjects to read miniature fictional narratives, then draws more general conclusions about the cognitive handling of possible (unwritten-about) states of affairs from the subjects' behavior and self-reports.[35]

This understanding of the relationships between fiction and fact challenges the familiar fact–fiction dichotomy relied on by McCulloch and many of his critics. From the perspective described here, the key distinction is not that between fact and fiction, but that between the actual world and possible worlds. In assessing the propriety or truth of a statement, the important question to ask is not whether it is a factual or fictional statement, but whether it is referring to the actual world or to an appropriate or inappropriate possible world. An appropriate possible world would, perhaps, be one whose relationship to the actual world is such that multiple people can agree on the truth of statements about that possible world. Although such a possible world is imaginary, it can in this way also be a basis for objective assessments. A statement or a story may thus refer to a possible world and yet be objective and legitimate. As the next section will explain, lawyers routinely depend on this possibility.

## III Cognitive fictionalizing in U.S. legal education and culture

Law students in the United States are asked to imagine alternatives from the very beginning of their education. On the first day of their first class, their professors will as likely as not pose hypothetical questions to students based on the day's reading or on other students' responses to the professor's questions. Hypotheticals "help define the boundaries between those situations where the rules apply and those where they do not"[36] and thus help students understand how a legal rule works, as well as what it says. Similarly, law school examinations and bar examinations do not ask examinees simply to recite rules but typically require written legal analysis of hypothetical scenarios.[37] This approach tests students' skills in "problem identification and definition" as well as information retention and problem-solving. These approaches to instruction and examination have been central to American legal education since at least the early twentieth century,[38] and they would have been part of McCulloch's legal education at Saint Louis University. Despite their consistent use, however, and the frustration they cause many novice law students, they have received very little direct academic scrutiny.[39]

Law professors' classroom use of hypothetical questions makes sense. It is not just that hypothetical questions help students understand legal rules; students benefit in other ways from developing comfort in analyzing imagined or supposed scenarios. Practicing lawyers need to imagine alternative possible courses of events in many different settings, including client advising ("If you breach contract X, the result might be Y; it's also possible, but less likely, that Z could happen") and the development of legal strategy ("If we file motion X, our adversary is likely to respond with cross-motion Y; it's also possible, but less likely, that our adversary will do Z").[40] Much legal doctrine also requires analysis or argument in explicitly hypothetical form. Legal attributions of causal effect are based on counterfactual reasoning, as are legal determinations of monetary relief.[41] Many other doctrines, especially but not only procedural doctrines, similarly involve the juggling and assessment of possibilities. McCulloch's arguments for dismissal of an anonymous grand juror's lawsuit against him relied heavily on several of these doctrines, including those of standing, ripeness, and failure to state a plausible claim. Each of these doctrines allows a court to decline to adjudicate an action when the plaintiff has not brought the "possible world" described in his or her complaint close enough to the actual world as perceived by the judge and other parties to the action.[42]

Few would deny that the provision of advice to clients, the development of legal strategy, and the identification of causes responsible for particular effects can be undertaken in acceptable, legitimate, and even objective ways. Suppose, for example, that McCulloch had described the grand jury's decision as a consequence of his office's presentation of the evidence. This description would involve an acknowledgment that the grand jury's conclusion could have been otherwise, had the evidence been presented otherwise. But the description seems more, rather than less, objective and legitimate than the description McCulloch actually gave. On this analysis, McCulloch's mistake seems to have been less a matter of disrespect for facts than a matter of using the wrong kind of fiction. Instead of using narratives denying the presence of fiction in the stories he recounted, McCulloch could, and maybe should, have established his freedom from bias by expressing a commitment to hypothetical thinking.

The last part of this chapter suggests that a world in which McCulloch did so is in some ways not too distant from our own. Before that, however, it will explore some possible explanations for legal academics' silence regarding cognitive fictionalizing.[43] This silence is curious, given the large amount of work on the topic outside law, legal scholars' willingness otherwise to borrow from disciplines such as philosophy and economics, the key role that hypothetical and counterfactual reasoning plays in legal education and culture, legal scholars' interest in generating additional counterfactual scenarios outside the classroom,[44] and legal academics' extensive attention to narrative fictionalizing.

## IV Explaining the legal repression of cognitive fictionalizing

Why have lawyers and legal academics not acknowledged the links between fiction and hypothetical reasoning that philosophers and psychologists have recognized? This section sketches two possible ways to understand the peculiar legal position on the scope of the term "fiction." The first explanation looks to the twentieth-century development of American ways of thinking and writing about law, fact, objectivity, and fiction. The second explanation, which is not an alternative to the first but a supplement to it, considers the social-psychological functions served by legal processes, especially criminal prosecution, and by discourse about them.

In the 1920s and 1930s, the American Legal Realists began to insist on acknowledging (and, if possible, closing) the gap between law and action, or between legal discourse and the world on which that discourse claims to act.[45] One way to close the gap, pursued by many post-Realists, is to seek more accurate information about the actual world and to use that information to inform decision-making. The empirical legal scholarship of the late twentieth and early twenty-first centuries follows this approach.[46] Because the approach requires that law and legal decisions be based on fact, it suggests that legitimate legal decision-making cannot involve fiction. If what we want is a closer link between law and the actual world, it might seem to be a foregone conclusion that law cannot incorporate fiction, since fiction does not refer to the actual world.[47] McCulloch's speech participates in this tradition in its blunt contrast between fact and fiction.

McCulloch's contrast between fallible testimony and infallible physical evidence, or fiction-prone and factual forms of evidence, participates in a related tradition, the demand for legal objectivity. This demand is another response to the perception of a gap between law and the actual world.[48] The law depends on human agents, but each of these agents will view the world and the law from a particular individual perspective, and this variability could cause legal rules and decisions to drift away from experiences outside the law, as well as to differ unacceptably from case to case. One way to respond to these risks, once they are perceived, is to describe or assert the objectivity of legal processes and decisions. McCulloch used several techniques of this kind in his address. He stressed the availability of evidence uncontaminated by human agency, and he presented the grand jury as a quasi-expert body. These techniques for communicating objectivity are analogous to those used in other disciplines.[49] In this kind of rhetoric, the opposition between objective and subjective maps on to the opposition between fact and fiction. As this chapter has sought to explain, the two oppositions are not identical. A subjective narrative is not necessarily fictional, and a non-factual or non-actual hypothesis or narrative may be objective. Nevertheless, if we must associate fiction with either objectivity or subjectivity, the latter association may seem more natural, since both fiction and subjectivity apparently concern the contents and functioning of individuals' minds, rather than the world outside them.

We can also explain the features of McCulloch's failed presentation in another way. This explanation focuses on McCulloch's resistance to acknowledging any alternatives to the course he pursued. As the previous section explained, cognitive fictionalizing pervades lawyers' thinking and speech, but this kind of thinking and talking is seldom recognized as pervasive, and even less often considered to be a kind of fictionalizing. Instead, legal writers tend to apply the label "fiction" to narratives that are unreliable or that conflict with acknowledged fact. Drawing an absolute distinction between law and fiction in this way allows legal decision-makers and popularizers to present legal conclusions as certain; this presentation helps assuage Realist-style anxieties about law's responsiveness to the actual world and about the legitimacy that would presumably flow from that responsiveness. The distinction probably also addresses other psychological needs. Tom Tyler and his colleagues have argued that legal professionals and members of the public have a strong "psychological desire" to "achieve closure" in the resolution of legal disputes, especially criminal matters.[50] Since we can almost always learn more about what actually happened in any given case, the goal of closure is not necessarily compatible with actual certainty about the "facts," but it may be approximated or at least superficially addressed by declarations of certainty about the facts.[51]

Prosecutors might feel the pressure to address this goal of certainty more acutely than many other legal professionals do. A number of observers have noted that prosecutors often succumb to a kind of "tunnel vision": an inability to entertain alternative factual accounts of a putative crime.[52] Perhaps especially among prosecutors of McCulloch's generation, occupational pressure encouraging tunnel vision has been reinforced by popular-culture representations of criminal justice as involving the confident and accurate revelation of culpability.[53] This phenomenon does not usually operate exactly as it did in the Wilson case. More commonly, prosecutors with tunnel vision ignore evidence suggesting innocence, rather than evidence that might support a conviction. But it might be that we seldom see prosecutorial tunnel vision operating to defendants' benefit simply because most prosecutorial decisions not to charge are invisible to the public.[54] Indeed, we can summarize many criticisms of McCulloch's use of the grand jury in the Wilson case as charging McCulloch with tunnel vision: He had concluded that Wilson was not guilty and therefore encouraged his assistant prosecutors to present the case to the grand jury in a way that would lead the grand jurors to the same conclusion.

On the account presented here, McCulloch's most basic mistake was not that he substituted fiction for fact, misrepresented the facts, or created a story to confirm his own personal bias, although he might have done each of these things. Before doing any of these things, he failed to do something else: consider various alternative possibilities, without drawing any firm conclusions about their actuality, and test them against the perceptions of others. McCulloch's presentation of his conclusions to the public revealed this error, but describing it accurately is challenging, due to the peculiar role that legal discourse and discourse about the law have assigned to the term and concept "fiction." Nevertheless, the widespread condemnation of McCulloch's handling of the Wilson case suggests an equally widespread tacit acceptance of the dependence of legal legitimacy on cognitive fictionalizing.

## V Law as a set of possible worlds

Although narrative accounts carry the risk of bias, most of us would accept that we need narratives to make sense of what happens in the actual world. We would have a hard time assigning responsibility for actions, for example, on the basis of forensic evidence alone, without generating a narrative to explain the evidence. We also know that not all narratives are fictions. When lawyers and members of the public say they want legal processes and decisions to track "fact," they are after narratives that accurately describe the actual world, as it is perceived by as many other people as possible. (In this context, a "fictional" narrative would describe a possible world conjured up by its author, who might also be its narrator, and communicated to others without regard for those others' first-person perceptions of the world.) Thus McCulloch's use of narrative in his speech was not necessarily inconsistent with his dismissal of fiction. But his dismissal of fiction was based on an oversimplified conception of "fiction," one apparently shared by many of his critics. In this conception, while not all narratives are fictional, all fiction takes narrative form, and such narratives are inappropriate to legal practice (making many if not all narratives presumptively suspect in a legal setting). The goal of this chapter has been to suggest that legal practice in fact requires a type of thinking and talking that is very closely related to the kind of thinking involved in generating and understanding fictional narratives—not because they are narrative in form, but because they concern possible worlds. In law, this type of thinking does not result in extended narratives; it serves other purposes, such as creating premises for planning and reasoning, or allowing practitioners to certify their objectivity by laying open their assumptions and considerations for scrutiny by clients, colleagues, and other interlocutors.

We could describe the generation of alternative possibilities, and micro-narratives based on them, as a kind of folk remedy developed by legal practitioners and educators to combat cognitive bias, tunnel vision, our tendency to be overconfident about the accuracy of our own perceptions. Generating alternative accounts allows the generator, or her interlocutor, to identify those possibilities that are more aligned with the experiences of others. Thus, this sort of fictionalizing enables agreement and objectivity, even though it begins in an act of subjective creativity. Unfortunately, the widespread use of these practices has not been matched by widespread acknowledgment or discussion of them. Use of these practices has remained unnamable, due to at least two phenomena: first, the widespread equation of fiction with extended narratives presented for purposes of entertainment or self-indulgence,[55] and second, the concern, shared by legal practitioners and the public, that law and legal activity deal with real-world events, or "fact," as much as possible as those events are perceived by the people affected, and do not operate in a separate "law-world" accessible only to insiders. The unfortunate result of this state of affairs is that lawyers and legal popularizers have been prevented from discussing some of the ways in which quintessentially legal activity—hypothetical reasoning and the consideration of alternatives—is not all that different from everyday imaginative activity.

## Notes

1 This account is based primarily on the interview and evidence summaries in U.S. Department of Justice, Report Regarding the Criminal Investigation into the Shooting Death of Michael Brown by Ferguson, Missouri Police Officer Darren Wilson (March 4, 2015).

2 Descriptions of the events following Brown's death are based on U.S. Department of Justice, Office of Community Oriented Policing Services, After-Action Assessment of the Police Response to the August 2014 Demonstrations in Ferguson, Missouri (2015), 5–11.
3 See e.g. Noam Scheiber, "St. Louis Prosecutor Bob McCulloch Abused the Grand Jury Process,' *New Republic*, November 25, 2014.
4 See Julie Bosman et al., "Amid Conflicting Accounts, Trusting Darren Wilson," *New York Times*, November 25, 2014.
5 Jeremy Kohler, "Statement of St. Louis County Prosecuting Attorney Robert P. McCulloch," *St. Louis Post-Dispatch*, November 24, 2015.
6 David Feigen, "The Independent Grand Jury That Wasn't," *Slate*, November 25, 2014.
7 Kohler, "Statement."
8 Scheiber, "St. Louis Prosecutor."
9 See Benjamin Weiser, "Mixed Motives Seen in Prosecutor's Decision to Release Ferguson Grand Jury Materials," *New York Times*, November 25, 2014.
10 See e.g. Scheiber, "St. Louis Prosecutor" ("McCulloch's team essentially cherry-picked evidence establishing Wilson's innocence … [T]hey accepted Wilson's account at face value, even leading him toward exculpatory statements through their questioning, while going out of their way to pinpoint flaws and contradictions in alternative accounts from other witnesses."). See also Feigen, "The Independent Grand Jury That Wasn't" ("[J]ust like in every other case, McCulloch had used his role as 'legal adviser' to the grand jury to structure evidence and frame the presentation in such a way as to yield the very conclusions suspicious residents of Ferguson always feared."); Monica Davey et al., "Raised Hands, and the Doubts of a Grand Jury," *New York Times*, November 29, 2014 ("[T]he prosecutors, and sometimes the jurors, often treated Officer Wilson's account as the truth, leaving questions about it unasked."); Complaint, Grand Juror Doe v. McCulloch, No. 4:15-cv -6-RWS, filed January 1, 2015.
11 See Dana Millbank, "Bob McCulloch's Pathetic Prosecution of Darren Wilson," *Washington Post*, November 25, 2014 ("[H]is decision not to recommend a specific charge to the grand jury essentially guaranteed there would be no indictment.").
12 Kohler, "Statement."
13 Kohler, "Statement."
14 See Feige, "The Independent Grand Jury That Wasn't."
15 See e.g. Frances Robles, "St. Louis County Prosecutor Defends Objectivity," *New York Times*, August 20, 2014; Kimberly Kindy, "Q&A with Robert McCulloch," *Washington Post*, September 25, 2014; Millbank, "Bob McCulloch's Pathetic Prosecution."
16 See e.g. Bennett L. Gershman, "The Prosecutor's Duty to Truth," *Georgetown Journal of Legal Ethics* 14 (2001), 309.
17 See e.g. Scheiber, "St. Louis Prosecutor"; Toobin, "How Not to Use a Grand Jury."
18 See e.g. Nicholas Rescher, *Hypothetical Reasoning* (Amsterdam: North-Holland, 1964), 5–7 (describing uses of hypothetical reasoning in assessing causation, value, and significance).
19 Kohler, "Statement."
20 Millbank, "Bob McCulloch's Pathetic Prosecution."
21 Monica Davey, "St. Louis County Prosecutor Says Actions on Ferguson Were Correct," *New York Times*, December 19, 2014.
22 See the discussion below, notes 54–56 and accompanying text.
23 See e.g. Peter Goldie, *The Mess Inside: Narrative, Emotion, and the Mind* (Oxford: Clarendon Press, 2012): 152.

24 See Goldie, *The Mess Inside*, 152–61.
25 See Daniel Kahneman and Amos Tversky, "The Simulation Heuristic," in Daniel Kahneman, Paul Slovic, and Amos Tversky, eds., *Judgment Under Uncertainty: Heuristics and Biases* (Cambridge: Cambridge University Press, 1982), 201.
26 See Robert N. Strassfeld, "If ...: Counterfactuals in the Law," *George Washington Law Review* 60 (1992), 339.
27 See Rescher, *Hypothetical Reasoning*, 68–70.
28 Hans Vaihinger, *The Philosophy of "As If": A System of the Theoretical, Practical, and Religious Fictions of Mankind*, C.K. Ogden, trans. (1911; Indianapolis: Bobbs-Merrill, 1924).
29 These include economics, history, political science, literary theory, and psychology. Cf. Chapter 1, pp. 20, 24, 47 n. 190–6.
30 See generally the account of scientific and objective knowledge and truth-approximation in Karl Popper, *Objective Knowledge: An Evolutionary Approach* (Oxford: Clarendon Press, 1972).
31 See e.g. H.L.A. Hart and Tony Honoré, *Causation and the Law*, 2nd ed. (1959; Oxford: Oxford University Press, 1985), lviii, 15; J.L. Mackie, *The Cement of the Universe: A Study of Causation* (Oxford: Clarendon Press, 1974): 68.
32 For an overview, see Christopher Menzel, "Possible Worlds," *Stanford Encyclopedia of Philosophy*, October 21, 2013, accessed January 3, 2020, at http://plato.stanford.edu/entries/possible-worlds.
33 Robert Stalnaker, "A Theory of Conditionals," in *Ifs: Conditionals, Belief, Decision, Chance, and Time*, Robert Stalnaker, William Harper and Glenn Pearce, eds. (London: Springer, 1981), 41.
34 See especially David Lewis, "Truth in Fiction," *American Philosophical Quarterly* 15:1 (1978), 37; see also David Lewis, *Counterfactuals* (Oxford: Basil Blackwell, 1973); David Lewis, "Counterfactual Dependence and Time's Arrow," *Noûs* 13 (1979), 455.
35 See the experiments described in Ruth M.J. Byrne, *The Rational Imagination: How People Create Alternatives to Reality* (Cambridge: MIT Press, 2007), and Neal J. Roese and James M. Olson, eds., *What Might Have Been: The Social Psychology of Counterfactual Thinking* (Mahwah: Lawrence Erlbaum, 1995).
36 Susan M. Williams, "Putting Case-Based Instruction into Context: Examples from Legal and Medical Education," *Journal of the Learning Sciences* 2, No. 4 (1992), 367, 383.
37 Williams, "Putting Case-Based Instruction into Context," 389.
38 See e.g. Karl N. Llewellyn, *The Bramble Bush: On Our Law and Its Study* (Dobbs Ferry: Oceana, 1930); Karl N. Llewellyn, "On the Problem of Teaching 'Private' Law," *Harvard Law Review* 54 (1941), 775.
39 For an exception proving the rule, see e.g. Paul Gewirtz, "The Jurisprudence of Hypotheticals," *Journal of Legal Education* 32 (1982), 120.
40 See Bernard Jackson, *Law, Fact, and Narrative Coherence* (Liverpool: Deborah Charles Pubs., 1988).
41 See Strassfeld, "If"; see also Hart and Honoré, *Causation in the Law*.
42 See Memorandum in Support of Defendant McCulloch's Motion to Dismiss, Grand Juror Doe v. McCulloch, Case No. 4:15-cv-6-RWS, filed January 1, 2015, Federal District Court for the Eastern District of Missouri.
43 Only two American legal academics have studied the operation of hypothetical reasoning in any detail: Strassfeld, "If"; Mitchell, "Case Studies, Counterfactuals, and Causal Explanations," *University of Pennsylvania Law Review* 152 (2004), 1517.
44 See e.g. Jack M. Balkin, ed., *What* Brown v. Board of Education *Should Have Said: The Nation's Top Legal Experts Rewrite America's Landmark Civil Rights Decision*

(New York: NYU Press, 2001); James Ming Chen, "The Sound of Legal Thunder: The Chaotic Consequences of Crushing Constitutional Butterflies," *Constitutional Commentary* 16 (1999), 483.

45 See especially Roscoe Pound, "Law in Books and Law in Action," *American Law Review* 44 (1910), 12; Karl N. Llewellyn, "A Realistic Jurisprudence: The Next Step," *Columbia Law Review* 30 (1930), 431.

46 See John Henry Schlegel, *American Legal Realism and Empirical Social Science* (Chapel Hill: University of North Carolina Press, 1995).

47 See Lon Fuller, *Legal Fictions* (Palo Alto: Stanford University Press, 1967); Karen Petroski, "Legal Fictions and the Limits of Legal Language," *International Journal of Law in Context* 9, No. 4 (2013), 485.

48 Important landmarks in this development were Oliver Wendell Holmes, Jr., "The Theory of Legal Interpretation," *Harvard Law Review* 12 (1899), 417; Joseph C. Hutcheson, Jr., "The Judgment Intuitive: The Function of the 'Hunch' in Judicial Decision," *Cornell Law Review* 14 (1929), 274; Jerome Frank, *Law and the Modern Mind* (New York: Brentano, 1930).

49 See Lorraine J. Daston and Peter Galison, *Objectivity* (New York: Zone Books, 2010).

50 See especially Tom R. Tyler, "Viewing *CSI* and the Threshold of Guilt: Managing Truth and Justice in Reality and Fiction," *Yale Law Journal* 115 (2006), 1050.

51 See Tyler, "Viewing *CSI*," 1067.

52 See e.g. Daniel S. Medwed, "The Prosecutor as Minister of Justice: Preaching to the Unconverted from the Post-Conviction Pulpit," *Washington Law Review* 84 (2009), 35, 37; Susan Bandes, "Loyalty to One's Convictions: The Prosecutor and Tunnel Vision," *Howard Law Journal* 49 (2006), 475; Keith A. Findley and Michael S. Scott, "The Multiple Dimensions of Tunnel Vision in Criminal Cases," *Wisconsin Law Review* 2006 (2006), 291.

53 See e.g. Michael M. Epstein, "For and Against the People: Television's Prosecutor Image and the Cultural Power of the Legal Profession," *University of Toledo Law Review* 34 (2003), 817.

54 See e.g. Angela J. Davis, "The American Prosecutor: Independence, Power, and the Threat of Tyranny," *Iowa Law Review* 86 (2001), 393.

55 On the historical origins of these connotations for "fiction," see Peter Lamarque and Stein Haugom Olsen, *Truth, Fiction, and Literature: A Philosophical Perspective* (Oxford: Clarendon Press, 1994), 269–76.

## Bibliography

Balkin, Jack M., ed. *What* Brown v. Board of Education *Should Have Said: The Nation's Top Legal Experts Rewrite America's Landmark Civil Rights Decision* (New York: NYU Press, 2001).

Bandes, Susan. "Loyalty to One's Convictions: The Prosecutor and Tunnel Vision," *Howard Law Journal* 49 (2006): 475.

Bosman, Julie, et al. "Amid Conflicting Accounts, Trusting Darren Wilson," *New York Times*, November 26, 2014.

Byrne, Ruth M.J. *The Rational Imagination: How People Create Alternatives to Reality.* Cambridge: MIT Press, 2007.

Carnap, Rudolf. *Meaning and Necessity.* Chicago: University of Chicago Press, 1947.

Daston, Lorraine J. and Peter Galison. *Objectivity.* New York: Zone Books, 2010.

Davey, Monica. "St. Louis County Prosecutor Says Actions on Ferguson Were Correct," *New York Times*, December 19, 2014.

Davey, Monica and Alan Blinder. "After Disputed Verdict, Reckoning for Ferguson," *New York Times*, November 26, 2014.
Davey, Monica, et al. "Raised Hands, and the Doubts of a Grand Jury," *New York Times*, November 29, 2014.
Davis, Angela J. "The American Prosecutor: Independence, Power, and the Threat of Tyranny," *Iowa Law Review* 86 (2001), 393.
Eligon, John and Manny Fernandez, "In Protests from Midwest to Both Coasts, Fury Boils Over," *New York Times*, November 24, 2014.
Epstein, Michael M. "For and Against the People: Television's Prosecutor Image and the Cultural Power of the Legal Profession," *University of Toledo Law Review* 34 (2003), 817.
Feigen, David. "The Independent Grand Jury That Wasn't," *Slate*, November 25, 2014.
Findley, Keith A. and Michael S. Scott. "The Multiple Dimensions of Tunnel Vision in Criminal Cases," *Wisconsin Law Review* 2006 (2006), 291.
Frank, Jerome. *Law and the Modern Mind*. New York: Brentano, 1930.
Fuller, Lon. *Legal Fictions*. Palo Alto: Stanford University Press, 1967.
Gershman, Bennett L. "The Prosecutor's Duty to Truth," *Georgetown Journal of Legal Ethics* 14 (2001), 309.
Gewirtz, Paul. "The Jurisprudence of Hypotheticals," *Journal of Legal Education* 32 (1982), 120.
Goldie, Peter. *The Mess Inside: Narrative, Emotion, and the Mind*. Oxford: Clarendon Press, 2012.
Goodman, Nelson. *Fact, Fiction and Forecast*, 3rd ed. Indianapolis: Bobbs-Merrill, 1973 [1955].
Hart, H.L.A. and Tony Honoré. *Causation and the Law*, 2nd ed. Oxford: Oxford University Press, 1985 [1959].
Holmes, Jr., Oliver Wendell. "The Theory of Legal Interpretation," *Harvard Law Review* 12 (1899), 417.
Hutcheson, Jr., Joseph C. "The Judgment Intuitive: The Function of the 'Hunch' in Judicial Decision," *Cornell Law Review* 14 (1929), 274.
Jackson, Bernard. *Law, Fact, and Narrative Coherence*. Liverpool: Deborah Charles Pubs., 1988.
Kindy, Kimberly. "Q&A with Robert McCulloch," *Washington Post*, September 25, 2014.
Kohler, Jeremy. "Statement of St. Louis County Prosecuting Attorney Robert P. McCulloch," *St. Louis Post-Dispatch*, November 24, 2015.
Lamarque, Peter and Stein Haugom Olsen, *Truth, Fiction, and Literature: A Philosophical Perspective*. Oxford: Clarendon Press, 1994.
Lewis, David. *Counterfactuals*. Oxford: Basil Blackwell, 1973.
Lewis, David. "Truth in Fiction," *American Philosophical Quarterly* 15, No. 1 (1978), 37.
Lewis, David. "Counterfactual Dependence and Time's Arrow," *Noûs* 13 (1979), 455.
Llewellyn, Karl N. *The Bramble Bush: On Our Law and Its Study*. Dobbs Ferry: Oceana, 1930.
Llewellyn, Karl N. "A Realistic Jurisprudence: The Next Step," *Columbia Law Review* 30 (1930), 431.
Llewellyn, Karl N. "On the Problem of Teaching 'Private' Law," *Harvard Law Review* 54 (1941), 775.
Mackie, J.L. *The Cement of the Universe: A Study of Causation*. Oxford: Clarendon Press, 1974.

McDonald, Soraya Nadia. "Protesters Across the Country React to Grand Jury's Decision Not to Indict Darren Wilson," *Washington Post*, November 25, 2014.

"The Meaning of the Ferguson Riots," *New York Times*, November 25, 2014.

Medwed, Daniel S. "The Prosecutor as Minister of Justice: Preaching to the Unconverted from the Post-Conviction Pulpit," *Washington Law Review* 84 (2009), 35.

Menzel, Christopher. "Possible Worlds," *Stanford Encyclopedia of Philosophy*, October 21, 2013, accessed January 3, 2020, http://plato.stanford.edu/entries/possible-worlds.

Millbank, Dana. "Bob McCulloch's Pathetic Prosecution of Darren Wilson," *Washington Post*, November 25, 2014.

Mitchell, Geoffrey "Case Studies, Counterfactuals, and Causal Explanations," *University of Pennsylvania Law Review* 152 (2004), 1517.

Petroski, Karen. "Legal Fictions and the Limits of Legal Language," *International Journal of Law in Context* 9, No. 4 (2013), 485.

Popper, Karl. *Objective Knowledge: An Evolutionary Approach*. Oxford: Clarendon Press, 1972.

Pound, Roscoe. "Law in Books and Law in Action," *American Law Review* 44 (1910), 12.

Rescher, Nicholas. *Hypothetical Reasoning*. Amsterdam: North-Holland, 1964.

Robles, Frances. "St. Louis County Prosecutor Defends Objectivity," *New York Times*, August 20, 2014.

Roese, Neal J. and James M. Olson, eds. *What Might Have Been: The Social Psychology of Counterfactual Thinking*. Mahwah: Lawrence Erlbaum, 1995.

Scheiber, Noam. "St. Louis Prosecutor Bob McCulloch Abused the Grand Jury Process," *New Republic*, November 25, 2014.

Chen, James Ming. "The Sound of Legal Thunder: The Chaotic Consequences of Crushing Constitutional Butterflies," *Constitutional Commentary* 16 (1999), 483.

Stalnaker, Robert. "A Theory of Conditionals," in *Ifs: Conditionals, Belief, Decision, Chance, and Time*, Robert Stalnaker, William Harper and Glenn Pearce, eds. London: Springer, 1981.

Strassfeld, Robert N. "If ...: Counterfactuals in the Law," *George Washington Law Review* 60 (1992), 339.

Toobin, Jeffrey. "How Not to Use a Grand Jury," *The New Yorker*, November 25, 2014.

Tyler, Tom R. "Viewing *CSI* and the Threshold of Guilt: Managing Truth and Justice in Reality and Fiction," *Yale Law Journal* 115 (2006), 1050.

United States Department of Justice, Report Regarding the Criminal Investigation Into the Shooting Death of Michael Brown by Ferguson, Missouri Police Officer Darren Wilson, March 4, 2014.

United States Department of Justice, Office of Community Oriented Policing Services, *After-Action Assessment of the Police Response to the August 2014 Demonstrations in Ferguson, Missouri*. Washington, DC: Department of Justice, 2015.

Vaihinger, Hans. *The Philosophy of "As If": A System of the Theoretical, Practical, and Religious Fictions of Mankind*, C.K. Ogden, trans. Indianapolis: Bobbs-Merrill, 1924 [1911].

Weiser, Benjamin. "Mixed Motives Seen in Prosecutor's Decision to Release Ferguson Grand Jury Materials," *New York Times*, November 25, 2014.

Williams, Susan M. "Putting Case-Based Instruction Into Context: Examples from Legal and Medical Education," *Journal of the Learning Sciences* 2, No. 4 (1992), 367.

Chapter 5.4

# Law as authoritative fiction[1]

*Andrei Marmor*

## 1 Law and fiction as closed prefixed contexts

When we talk about the law, we may be talking about very different things. In this chapter I am interested in the law as normative content that can form a premise in a practical argument. Part of what we mean by the spacio-temporal aspect of law is that statements about any particular legal contents are necessarily prefixed by an implicit formula "According to the law in legal system S at time t ...".[2] Kelsen noticed this a long time ago, suggesting that norms can be legally valid only as part of a legal order, unified, Kelsen claimed, by derivation from a single *basic norm*.[3] As Raz pointed out, Kelsen's assumption that legal systems are unified by derivation from a single *basic norm* is empirically questionable.[4] But Raz understood and developed Kelsen's main insight here to mean that statements about the content of any given law can only be made and articulated from the vantage point of some particular legal order. When I say, for example, that you have a legal obligation to φ in context C, what I must mean is that from the point of view of the relevant legal order, you ought to φ in C. You may not have this obligation from a different normative vantage point, such as morality or religion, and you may not have this obligation in a different jurisdiction or according to a different legal system. Furthermore, as Raz famously argued, a speaker who asserts a legal proposition from the vantage point of a given legal order need not endorse that vantage point, normatively speaking; one can make "detached" statements about what the law in S requires or permits without necessarily seeing oneself committed to the normative force of S.[5]

Now the formula "According to *F* ..." is prevalent in other contexts as well, and, in itself, is sometimes quite meaningless. We can say, for example, that "according to the laws of nature it is the case that X", but in this case, X would be true, if it is, regardless of the prefix "according to *F*". The prefix here makes no difference to the truth value of the statement. But in the legal case it does. To see when and how the prefix "according to *F*" (or "In *F*") makes a logical difference, we should dwell for a moment on David Lewis's analysis of truth in fiction.[6] Lewis starts with an example of how mixing different points of view in an argument may result in a fallacy. So here is Lewis's famous example:

Sherlock Holmes, we are told in the Arthur Conan Doyle mysteries, lived at 221B Baker Street in London. Let us assume, therefore, that there is some sense in which (1) is true:

(1) Sherlock Holmes lived at 221B Baker Street, London

It turns out, however, that the building at 221B Baker Street in London at the time was a bank. Let us therefore assume that at the relevant times, (2) is true:

(2) The building at 221B Baker Street, London, is a bank.

The inference from (1) and (2) would seem to be:

(3) Sherlock Holmes lived in a bank.

But, of course, (3) is clearly false. What has gone wrong here? Lewis tells us that we made the mistake of moving from a *prefixed* to an *un-prefixed* context. (1) is true only if it is prefixed by an operator such as "In the fiction *F* ..."; whereas (2) is true only if taken as un-prefixed (in the real world, as it were). Thus, unless (2) is prefixed by the same operator "in fiction *F* ...", you cannot conclude that (3) is true in the fiction; and because (1) is true only if it is prefixed, you cannot conclude that (3) is true in an un-prefixed sense. Surely, this is quite right, and I will refer to this problem as the *Lewis fallacy*.

Now, the Lewis fallacy requires some refinement, even in the case of fiction. Consider the following inference:

(4) Sherlock Holmes lived in London.
(5) London is a city in the United Kingdom
(6) Sherlock Holmes lived in the United Kingdom.

We have the same structure here as in (1) to (3), but a very different result. (4) is clearly prefixed by "In the fiction *F*...", whereas (5) seems to be un-prefixed; it is just a fact in the real world that London is in the UK. But there is no fallacy here. Any sensible reader of the Conan Doyle mysteries would have assumed, and rightly so, that Sherlock Holmes's escapades take place in the UK. And, crucially, this would be the case even if the United Kingdom (or England, or Great Britain) is never explicitly mentioned in the text. So what is it that makes the inference of (4) to (6) valid, as opposed to (1) to (3) which is not?

The solution has to be this: Although (5) seems to be an un-prefixed proposition, in the context of this inference it is not; (5) is incorporated into the fiction by implication. The assumption here is that fictions typically incorporate by implication an indefinite, though limited, number of facts (or factual assumptions) about the world, at least those that are relevant, and can be assumed to be salient and well known to potential readers. A reasonable reader of the Sherlock Holmes mysteries can be expected to know that London is a city in the UK, and thus, even if the text does not mention this explicitly, it can be regarded as incorporating it by implication. (Assuming, of course, that there is nothing in the text to suggest otherwise.) Thus we avoid the Lewis fallacy; the entire inference of (4) to (6) should be regarded as contained within the prefixed context. Similarly, even if the mysteries never refer to Sherlock Holmes's nose, we can assume that he had one (and only one), in virtue of the stated fictional fact that he is a man. These kind of unmentioned facts can be said to be incorporated in the fiction by implication and thus, for inferential purposes, they can be regarded as prefixed statements. The conditions and limits of implicitly incorporated assumptions in fiction are problematic, of course, and sometimes indeterminate.

As we mentioned above, there are prefixes which create a Lewis-type fallacy, and others which don't. Let me call them *closed* and *open* prefixes, respectively. Open prefixes are such that they can occur in arguments with un-prefixed statements to yield valid conclusions. For example, prefixes such as "According to the laws of nature (or, according to science; or according to the laws of thermodynamics) …"; or "According to modal logic …". So what is it about closed prefixes that they create the Lewis fallacy? One suggestion might be to look at the semantics of the prefix. It is probably implicit in the semantics of scientific prefixes that they range over un-prefixed statements to yield valid conclusions. In other words, it is probably part of what it means to prefix a statement by "according to science" that the statement following the prefix is meant to apply unconditionally.[7] Whereas it is part of the meaning of a prefix such as "according to fiction *F* …" that it ties the truth value of the statement to be contained within a world demarcated by the prefix – that is, the world of fiction *F*. This is probably true, but it may not be enough. Still, you may wonder, what makes it the case that some prefixes are closed? The suggestion that I will endorse and try to support throughout this chapter is that some prefixes are such that they designate a *constitutive relation* to the truth-values of the statements prefixed by them. A statement is true in a fiction, if it is, because the fiction states it. The saying so makes it true, so to speak. It doesn't mean that there are no limits here; even fiction cannot make it the case that X is true in the fiction if X is something that we cannot possibly imagine or otherwise entertain in your minds (such as a "square circle" or even, perhaps, "a delightful torture of an innocent child".) What those limits are and how to account for them is an interesting question, but we need not try to resolve it here.[8]

In short, closed prefixes are those in which a constitutive relation obtains between certain essential features of the world/context designated by the prefix, and the truths of the statements expressed in that world/context. Now you might wonder what other prefixes are closed, besides fiction, that is? Law, I will argue shortly, is a closed prefix, but there are many others. Structured games, for example, constitute closed prefixed contexts. When the umpire in a soccer game orders a player "out", it is true, in the game of soccer, that the player has to leave the field. The game is a closed prefixed context. It is only according to the rules and conventions of the game that if the umpire orders the player "out", then the player, in the game, from the game's perspective, as it were, is to leave. The rules and conventions of the game constitute the context that determines certain statements about that context to be true or false.[9]

Why is the law, however, a closed prefix? A good starting point is to see that the truth value of any statement about the content of a legal premise depends on the specific jurisdictional prefix. Take any statement expressing some legal premise, such as (7) "A ought (legally) to φ in C", and you will immediately realize that whether (7) is true or false depends on the specific prefix. According to the law in $S_1$ at t, (7) can be true, and according to the law in $S_2$ at t it may not be, and the same goes for the time variant. It may have been true until last week but no longer is. Some legal philosophers may doubt that this is necessarily the case. Perhaps there are some universal truths about legal contents that are not prefix-variant. What I have in mind here are very general principles, such as the idea that wrongs need to be rectified, criminals need to be punished, or agreements need to be kept, and things like that. There is a sense in which it might be true that all legal systems must instantiate some such principles, and therefore there might be a sense in which such abstract and general precepts are universally legal, as it were, un-prefixed. I doubt that there is a serious sense in which such principles are legal, but it doesn't matter much for our purposes. After all, actual laws can deviate from such principles; not all wrongs are legally rectified and not all promises are binding contracts, etc. So there might be some general principles that law purports, perhaps even necessarily, to instantiate; but it is the instantiation that legally matters, not the guiding ideals.

Be this as it may, suffice it for our purposes if you agree that, by and large, the truth value of legal statements is prefix-dependent. But still, you might think that this is not enough to make the legal context a closed prefix. After all, we don't seem to get the Lewis fallacy by mixing legal statements with un-prefixed statements of non-legal facts. On the contrary, almost every legal syllogism seems to do just that, reach a legal conclusion from statements about the law and statements about non-legal facts. Consider this example:

(8) According to the law in S at t, anyone who is an X ought to φ in circumstances C.
(9) John is an X (in S at t)
(10) Therefore, John ought, legally, to φ in C.

Clearly (8) is a prefixed statement and it would seem that (9) is not; it is just a fact in the world, so to speak, that John happens to have feature X in the relevant time and circumstances. And yet, despite the fact that we seem to mix a prefixed premise (8) with an un-prefixed premise (9), we get a valid conclusion in (10). But this is an illusion. The legal conclusion in (10) follows only if (9) is incorporated into the legal prefix by implication, presupposition, or stipulation. It has to be the case that according to the law in S at t, John is an X. Factual premises must be incorporated, explicitly or implicitly, into the legal framework to make legal syllogisms valid.[10]

Consider a simple case. Suppose it is the law (here and now) that accepting an offer under specified conditions amounts to the formation of a legally valid contract. Suppose you offer to sell me your car for a certain amount of money, and I reply by saying "Yes, I accept the offer". May we conclude that we just formed a legally valid contract? Not so fast. It depends on whether our relevant expressions in the particular context *count as* an offer and an acceptance in the eyes of the law; there has to be an explicit or implicit legal finding that they do. And notice that these kind of findings can always be legally challenged and debated. Events in the world need to be internalized into a legal framework; they need to be legally recognized as relevant or established facts, to form premises in legal arguments. Without such incorporation to the prefixed context, we do get the Lewis fallacy.

Lawyers often talk about something similar but in a way that is potentially confusing. Lawyers acknowledge the "finding of fact(s)" as an essential aspect of any legal argument, but the expression is ambiguous. In one sense it can mean exactly what I suggest here – that the relevant facts need to be incorporated into the legal framework – but in another, perhaps more common sense, it can simply mean the authoritative ascertainment of what really happened. In litigation contexts, therefore, the finding of facts is a two-stage affair: courts may need to ascertain what really happened, whether A really said that X or whether B really intended to kill his victim, things like that; and then when the event in the world has been found, authoritatively, to have occurred, there is a finding, as it were, though often implicit, that the way things happened counts as the legally incorporated fact or event. It may be worth keeping in mind that, quite generally, the assumptions about what counts as a legally relevant fact inevitably guides the findings of fact in the factual sense. After all, events and actions in the world allow for an indefinite number of descriptions and levels of specification. Which ones we pick out to ascertain for purposes of formulating premises in a legal argument depends on what counts, legally speaking, as the relevant kind of fact. Therefore, when we include a factual assumption in a legal argument, that is, when we rely on a certain non-legal fact as a premise in the argument, we thereby implicitly incorporate it into the legal prefix. By stating that *this fact* matters, legally, we make that fact, as it were, part of the legal framework; we implicitly assume that it is the kind of fact that counts, legally, as the relevant kind.

To put this in a formal way, any legal syllogism involving premises about legal content and non-legal facts, must conform to this form:

(1) According to the law in S at t, if X then legal result Y
(2) $E_x$ [an event in the world of X type]

(3) $E_x$ *legally counts as* X in S at t.
(4) Therefore according to S at t, X
(5) Therefore [legal result] Y in S at t.

Unlike in fiction, however, it would seem that there are no antecedent conditions attached to the kinds of facts law can incorporate into its prefixed context. In the fictional context we would think that factual assumptions can be incorporated within a given fictional story only under certain conditions, such as common knowledge of the relevant facts, relative salience, relevance to the story, lack of contrary indication in the text, etc. In the legal case, however, it seems that there is no room for such constraints; in principle, any non-legal fact or event in the world can be incorporated into the legal context if the law applies to it. And the law can apply to almost anything. Now this, I think, is true but only up to a point or, to be more precise, with an important caveat. The law does not necessarily incorporate into its prefixed context every true factual assumption that follows, logically and empirically, from facts it relies upon, explicitly or implicitly. In other words, non-legal facts are not automatically incorporated into the legal context even if they are true and potentially relevant; incorporation of facts to the prefixed world of a legal context often requires authoritative finding, and sometimes the actual authoritative finding defies empirical truth, and even logical consistency.

Suppose, for example, that the law in S at t is –

(11) "Anyone in possession of an object with feature X ought to $\varphi$ in context Z".

Now suppose that people would normally assume that objects of type A, B, and C are objects with feature X; so they would assume that in context Z, anyone who possesses A, B, or C ought to $\varphi$, according to this law. But now suppose it also happens to be the case, though not widely known, that objects of type D, perhaps not sharing any conspicuous features with objects of type A, B, and C, also happen to have feature X. Does (11) apply to objects of type D as well? The legal answer is not obvious, and cases in which a court might decide otherwise are not unheard of. A nice case in point is *Nix v Hedden*[11] where the Court held that tomatoes are to be classified as vegetables and not fruit for the purposes of the tariff regulation in question, even though, as the Court acknowledged, tomatoes are, actually, fruit. Or *Yates v U.S.*,[12] where the Court decided that fishes are not "tangible objects" for the purposes of the Federal law in question. True factual assumptions are not necessarily incorporated into the law, even when they are clearly relevant. And the same goes for logical consistency; the law often tolerates, and sometimes for good reasons, a certain level of incoherence.[13]

## II Saying so makes it so

At least part of what explains the fact that law, like fiction, is a closed prefixed context stems from the fact that in both cases, of law and of fiction, the domain is one of those in which the *saying so makes it so*. John Searle remarked once that you cannot fry an egg just by saying that "I hereby fry an egg", but if you are a minister you can marry a couple by saying that "I hereby declare you husband and wife"; and anyone can make a promise by saying "I hereby promise you to φ".[14] Speech act theorists have called these examples *performative* speech acts, whereby by uttering an expression the speaker can accomplish a certain action beyond the act of stating or affirming a proposition. But the category of performative speech acts is very wide, and there are good reasons to think that there are several different kinds of performatives.[15]

Some speech acts gain their performative aspect in virtue of rules or conventions at the background which stipulate that A's saying "S" counts as doing Y in context C. The rules constituting the legality of marriage, for example, stipulate that a minister's declaration, in the appropriate circumstances, counts as marrying a couple. Or the rules of an institution may stipulate that the chair of a committee can officially adjourn a meeting by declaring that the meeting is adjourned. In such cases the saying so makes it so only because rules or conventions make it the case that the saying so counts as doing a certain kind of act. Elsewhere I called this type of cases *institutional performatives*.[16] Other types of performatives, however, perhaps most, actually, may not require any rules or conventions to enable the performative aspect of the speech act. As Strawson demonstrated a long time ago, one can perform an act of warning simply by saying, under appropriate circumstances, "The ice over there is very thin!"[17] In saying this one performs an action, beyond that of asserting a proposition, of course, by way of expressing an intention that the hearer can grasp as the intention it is, namely, of warning you that the ice is thin and you'd better be careful. According to Bach and Harnish, most performatives operate in this way because most of them express a statement about the attitude of the speaker, and the performative succeeds as such when the hearer recognizes the relevant attitude or intention expressed.[18] Let me call these types of cases *general performatives*. Finally, there are performatives which are not statements at all; they are not truth-apt expressions, but count as actions of certain types by way of making recognizable moves in a conventional practice, such as greeting or thanking. I called them conventional performatives, because these are the kind of expressions that gain their literal meaning as recognizable moves in some conventional social practice or other.[19]

In short, there are several types of performatives and their felicity conditions might be quite different. However, the types of cases in which the saying so makes it so that I'm interested in here is closely related, but different. I want to focus on cases in which the saying that "S" in a given context makes it the case that S is true in that context. Now, there is a considerable overlap between performative speech acts and cases in which a statement is rendered true by its expression alone.[20] By saying to your friend that she is invited to your dinner party, for example, you make it true that she is now invited to the party, and this is true only because you have expressed the invitation. Similarly, by expressing a promise to someone you have made it true that you promise, and you made it true by virtue of saying so. And if you tell your employee, for example, that he is fired, then you make it true that the employee is fired, and it's true by virtue of your saying so.[21] In short, there are countless performatives that express a statement which is rendered true by its expression alone, under the appropriate conditions, of course.

Now consider truth in fiction. Generally speaking, something is true in a given fiction because the fictional text says so. If a fictional text says that "the moon is green", then it is true, in that fiction, that the moon is green, and it's true because the fiction says so. (Unless, of course, the fiction also says something else that would make you doubt that it really asserts that the moon is green.) As we noted above, the saying need not be explicit; some content can be incorporated into a fiction by implication. But even incorporated content is a function of saying so; content incorporated into a fiction has to follow from, or be presupposed by, what the fiction says.

Let's take a step back. There is no fictional story unless the story has been told by someone. Even a myth or a legend has had to be told by someone at some point; sentences in some natural language have to be expressed, whether written down or voiced. Fiction is an artifact; it has to be *created* by humans. And it is an artifact created by saying things.[22] Let me call these cases *expressive artifacts* – that is, artifacts created by sayings or, more generally, by use of expressive means of symbolism or communication. To paraphrase Searle again, although you cannot create a chair by saying "I hereby make a chair", you can create a story by simply telling it. Generally speaking, intangible artifacts, such as fiction, poetry, music, myths, religion, etc., are created by means of communication; they are constituted by sayings. Intangible artifacts, quite generally, tend to be expressive artifacts, constituted by means of expression.

There is a complex web of connections here, so let me recap briefly. The starting point is to bear in mind that there are countless types of action we can perform by a speech act, beyond the act of asserting a proposition. Some of these actions are made possible by rules or conventions in the background which stipulate that saying "S" in context C counts as doing Y in that context. Other performative speech acts do not rely on any particular conventions or rules in the background (that is, beyond the rules and conventions of the relevant language, of course). Most performative speech acts also exhibit the feature that something is rendered true by saying it. It is often the case that a statement S is rendered true by uttering S in the normal, appropriate, circumstances. Finally, and most importantly for our purposes, there are expressive intangible artifacts created by performative speech acts. Expressive artifacts belong to domains in which the saying so makes it so in the relevant domain. Both law and fiction, I will argue, are expressive artifacts in this sense. And I will argue that expressive artifacts, at least those in which truth-aptness applies to some degree, are closely tied to the idea of closed prefixed contexts.

## III Law as expressive artifact

Before we proceed with the argument, there are a few things I need to say about the nature of artifacts. An artifact is an object created by humans for some purpose. There are many kinds of artifact in the world we inhabit. There are chairs, cars, computers, houses, and countless other objects deliberately created to serve some function or purpose in our lives. We can use them for their intended purpose or for other purposes, perhaps not intended; we can modify their uses in various ways. It is generally thought that artifacts are objects deliberately created for some purpose, with that purpose in somebody's mind, as it were. And that is surely correct about most ordinary artifacts we use in our daily lives. But deliberate creation for a purpose is not necessary for an artifact to come into existence as such. Some artifacts may have been created by chance, or later significantly modified by repeated use, without any deliberate design. What is essential for an object to be an artifact, I will assume here, is that it has been created by humans and that it is used by humans for some typical or designated purpose or other.

Not all artifacts are objects in the physical sense. Many of the artifacts we have are intangible: novels, poems, legends, gods and, generally, narratives, would be prime examples. Stories are created by human beings. They have authors, even if, sometimes, the authors are not known and difficult to individualize (as with the coming into existence of a legend or a myth). What makes stories artifacts is the fact that they are created by humans, with their particular properties or content, if you will. I hope we can proceed by assuming that the intentions with which an object is created are not necessarily constitutive of what that object is. We can certainly grant that artifacts, tangible and intangible, come into existence intentionally. They are intentionally created as objects of a certain kind. But it is not always the intention of the original creator of an object that makes it an artifact of a certain kind. Something that was created or otherwise came about as an X may become a Y-artifact by repeated and widespread Y-uses of it. Creation is sometimes no more than recurrent and widespread intentional use.

Generally speaking, although exceptions are possible, artifacts exist, and persist, when there is a population or a community that treats them as such.

Many of the artifacts we encounter are compound, by which I mean that they are artifacts within artifacts. Think about a painting or a sculpture exhibited in an art museum. The painting is an artifact, of course, but so is the museum. Thus a painting exhibited in a museum is an artifact within an artifact, but not only in a spatial sense. An art museum is an institution with certain features created by humans for certain purposes, serving various functions. When a painting is exhibited in a museum, the exhibition, in the context of a museum, gives the painting certain meaning and function that it might not otherwise have. In some cases, the differences are subtle, in others, quite profound. A Rembrandt painting might not be affected all that much by being exhibited in the *Frick* collection, but the exhibit of a mirror stuck in a pile of sand in an art gallery may contribute to the artistic nature of the object a great deal.[23] It may not even be a work of art without the institutional support it gets by being positioned where it is. Putting an artifact in another artifactual context often changes the quality of the artifact.

There is a particular kind of compound artifact, however, that is relevant to both fiction and law. There are many instances in which social conventions shape the ways of creating artifacts of a certain kind. There are conventions, for example, about what counts as a realistic novel, or as epic poetry, and those conventions would shape and guide ways in which authors create a novel or write an epic poem and of course, the ways in which we read them. There are conventions about symbolism that would shape the ways in which directions in space are indicated, and thus signs made, etc. In previous work I argued that there are conventions about what counts as a competitive game, and they would shape ways in which we invent and play structured competitive games, how we react to them, etc.[24] If conventions are also artifacts, as I think they are, then these would all be examples of compound artifacts. A novel, for example, would instantiate both original creation by the author, which would make it a paradigmatic example of an intangible artifact, but also some conventional norms and guidance in the background, contributing something, perhaps tacitly, to what the novel as an artifact is. And this makes, essentially, every novel a compound artifact. Novels, in this respect, are very much like paintings in an art museum, obviously in a more intangible manner.

I am assuming that there is not much I need to say by way of establishing that conventions are (intangible) artifacts. Conventions meet all the conditions about artifacts we mentioned above; they are created by humans for particular purposes, their persistence and contents depend on the ways in which they are actually used, and, metaphysically speaking, their existence is a function of what users make of them.[25] Now it is true, of course, that conventions are rarely created in a deliberate manner to serve as conventions; conventions tend to emerge in an organic, often slow and invisible manner, evolving in ways that are difficult to retrace with any great accuracy, even in retrospect. But as I mentioned before, this is often true about artifacts, even tangible ones.

I hope we said enough here to show that law, like fiction, and perhaps art in general, is a compound artifact. But let's take the analogies a step further, or, rather, back to the point we started with, to see how law and fiction are created by expressive means. They are both compound *expressive* artifacts. And that is so, because in both cases, as in some others, the saying so makes it so. Fiction is created by telling a story – that is, by expressing sentences in a natural language. And notice that the story told is constitutive of the truths in it. And so is the law. Law is created by performative speech acts, mostly of the institutional kind. And those speech acts constitute what the law is; they constitute what is true in the law. There are limits to this, of course; just as there are ways in which one can fail to tell a story, say, by asking us to envisage the unimaginable, authorities can fail to make law in various ways. Furthermore, I do not mean to exclude the possibility that there may be other things that contribute to legal contents, even moral considerations, if you insist. But that is true of fiction as well; many things can contribute to ways in which we interpret a fiction, besides what the fiction says or implicates. In both cases, however, the story has to have been told by someone for there to be a story that we can think of and interpret in various ways.

Law is created in myriad ways at different levels. Legal rights, obligations and powers can be created, modified and abolished at individual levels, at group levels and generally, at the level that applies across an entire jurisdiction. In all these cases, the creation or modification of the law is done by speech acts. In previous work I argued, at some length, that the enactment of a law, by democratic institutions or otherwise, is a collective speech act, and I will not repeat the argument here.[26] We can add to it, however, by noticing the multitude of ways in which institutional performative speech acts modify the law. Judicial decisions can create or modify the law by the court's holding that the law is this or that; contractual obligations are formed by speech acts – that is, by one making an offer and the other accepting it; official acts with legal ramifications are carried out by regulations and instructions, and so on and so forth. All over the spectrum we create and modify the law by performative speech acts. And most of these performative speech acts, including enactment of laws, are of the institutional kind; there are rules or conventions in the background stipulating that A's saying "S" in context C counts as doing Y. Which is, of course, what makes the law a compound artifact, and a rather complex one at that.

One possible exception that comes to mind here is customary law. It is sometimes the case, perhaps more so in the international domain, that laws are created, as it were, by long-standing custom – that is, by some general and consistent conformity with a presumed norm over a long period of time. Now the question of how to reconcile customary law with the idea that laws have to be created in some deliberate manner, is an old chestnut. My purpose here is not to defend any particular version of good old legal positivism. Suffice it to see that law is very much like fiction in this respect as well. Most fiction is created by an author deliberately telling a story, in writing or by some other expressive means. But we have quite a lot of fiction stemming from myths and legends, the origins of which are often obscure and intractable. As I mentioned above, artifacts, quite generally, often come into existence in obscure ways, and what determines their existence as an artifact of a certain kind is mostly a matter of repeated widespread use for some purpose or other. And that is true of expressive artifacts as well. They must have been created by some speech acts at some point, but their original creation sometimes matters little to ways in which we use them now, and ways in which we understand their contents.

You may still press the question of whether customary law is an exception to the idea that law is generally created and modified by performative speech acts. I may not have a clear answer to that, but it doesn't matter much. Even if there are some exceptions, the law is created, by and large, by speech acts. And the kind of speech acts in question are typically institutional performatives, namely, enabled by rules or conventions at the background determining that by saying "S" in context C, one performs Y – that is, one creates or modifies something that is legally significant. Generally speaking, however, in the legal context, very much like in fiction, the saying so makes it so; it makes it true, in the context, that it is the law.

Law, like fiction, is an expressive artifact, and that has a lot to do with the fact that both are closed prefixed contexts. Like fiction, the law does not describe how things are, irrespective of its own creation, as it were; it creates a world in itself by stipulating that the relevant legal world is so and so. And this, I hope you can see, is what makes the legal domain a closed prefix. If the law purported to describe how things are in the world outside it, then, of course, it would be an open prefix, but the law is not in the business of telling us how things are. It is in the business of telling us how they ought to be, or what we ought to do, *from a legal point of view*. And in actual legal systems, those who make the law make it true, in the law, that it is what they say it is, because law, like fiction and like other expressive artifacts, is one of those domains in which the saying so makes it so.[27] And hence it is a closed prefix.

Now, of course, the creation of law is much more complex than fiction; as I mentioned earlier, in every jurisdiction there are countless people and institutions who can contribute to what the law is on this or that, from legislatures and courts, to administrative agencies, bureaucrats, corporations, and even private individuals in their everyday transactions. But these complexities do not change the essential picture. All these creations and modifications of law are performative speech acts given their legal significance by a complex web of rules and conventions (many of which are themselves previously enacted legal rules).

Generally speaking, then, I submit that expressive artifacts are closed prefixes; enacting a law gets you only as far as enacting a law, something that is true in a particular legal order, and only from a legal point of view. Stories and laws, by themselves, don't make anything true outside the story or the legal world, so to speak. Now, of course, a good story is one that you can learn something from, and it should reveal to you truths or insights of various kinds beyond it. And that is true of law as well. There is a lot we can learn from the law, about the human condition and human relations, about morality and politics and whatnot. But you don't learn these things by way of accepting their truths in virtue of the law's saying so. What is true in a fictional story is one thing; what you can learn from it is another. Similarly, what is true in the law, or what the law is, is one thing, and what you can learn from it is another.

Furthermore, we should keep in mind that with respect to both fiction and law, as with respect to other closed prefixed contexts, statements can be made from the vantage point of the prefixed context as well as externally, about things in that context. Not everything we say about a fiction has to be said from the point of view of the fiction in question; we can express statements about it, externally, as it were. A great deal of literary theory and literary discourse is external, in this sense.[28] It makes statements about various aspects of the prefixed context, but from the outside, as it were. For example, saying that "Sherlock Holmes is a detective" is an internal statement, rendered true or false by what the story says or implicates. But saying that "The character of Sherlock Holmes exhibits stereotypes of chauvinism typical of Victorian England" is not prefixed. It is a statement about certain aspects of the prefixed context, not within it. And, of course, the same goes for statements about the law. When we say that the law requires this or that, we would normally make the statement as prefixed by the relevant legal order, but we can also make many statements about aspects or elements of the legal order that are external, not prefixed. Which is essentially what we do, for example, when we subject laws to moral scrutiny or other kinds of critique.[29]

## IV Law's spacio-temporal aspect

In one conspicuous sense, however, the law is very much unlike fiction and most other expressive artifacts: it is authoritative. And it is authority backed by force, closely tied to actual political sovereignty. It is precisely because the law is authoritative that the legal prefix is jurisdictional. Practical authorities, in general – whether backed by force or not – are authorities only relative to their jurisdiction. Jurisdiction is something that defines the scope of an authority's normative powers, answering the question of what are the issues on which an authority gets to decide and with respect to whom (and both are relative to a time frame, of course). There is no practical authority without some jurisdictional boundaries. Now, this is not the place to develop a theory of practical authority to substantiate these claims, I have done that elsewhere.[30] But I need to recap some of the main points I made in developing an institutional conception of authority to help us see the relevant connections here. The main argument is that the answer to the question of what it is to have a practical authority is a three-stage affair. To have practical authority is to have normative power in some systematic sense; power, in this systemic sense, must be granted or constituted by norms – that is, some rules or conventions; and such power-conferring norms are essentially institutional – that is, they form part of some institution or social practice. Notice that these three conditions only pertain to what it is to have authority. They do not bear directly on any question of moral legitimacy or moral reasons to comply with any putative authority's directives.

Normative power is not necessarily systematic in the sense in which authorities have power. Practical authorities, however, have much more complex normative powers. To be a practical authority is to have powers to choose from a range of options whether and how to introduce changes in the normative landscape that prevails in the area of one's authority, and this kind of power is complex: it typically includes choices about how to introduce a change, who is subject to it, how to monitor non-compliance and how to respond to it, how to modify the directives if need arises, etc., etc. In other words, authoritative powers are inevitably complex, constituted by a set of interlocking norms, defining who gets to have the power, the content and scope of the power, ways in which it can be exercised, ways in which it can be enforced, and other auxiliary matters. And these kinds of things can only be constituted by rules or conventions.

In previous work I argued that the only kind of rules or norms that can confer these kinds of powers on authorities are social or institutional rules. Practical authorities must operate within some social practice or an institution that grants them the kind of normative powers they have.[31] However, even if you doubt that this is necessarily the case, I hope you would see it as unproblematic to concede that the de facto authority of law is entirely practice-dependent, at least in this limited sense. Namely, in the sense that there is no legal authority without it forming part of a complex social practice in which it operates and which grants it the normative powers that it has. And I hope we can also see that it is precisely this practice dependence of authorities that grounds the idea of jurisdiction. Authorities can only obligate those who belong to the practice or institution that grants them the powers they have. Practical authorities' normative powers are always limited to the particular jurisdiction in which they have those powers.

Necessarily one can only have jurisdiction at any given time relative to some population. Authoritative powers are always relative to those who are subject to the normative powers in question, which is to say, confined to the people who participate, voluntarily or not, in the social practice that grants the authority the powers it has.[32] But in the legal case, normative powers meet brute power; legal authority is the kind of authority that is backed by force – brute force, I mean – and that tends to make legal authority territorial. The exercise of brute power over people, especially on a larger scale and over some extended period of time, tends to be very closely associated with control over territory. Which is to say that legal jurisdiction is, practically speaking, almost invariably territorial.

I don't think that I made any philosophical news here. Nor would it be surprising to hear that none of this territorial stuff applies to other expressive artifacts, like fiction. Fiction has nothing to do with practical authority, and it certainly has nothing to do with brute force. Fiction has no jurisdictional aspects. But other intangible artifacts do have some jurisdictional elements. Structured competitive games tend to have clearly demarcated jurisdictions; they have boundaries. The boundaries typically demarcate terms of participation; they draw the line between participants and observers, and things like that. And then, of course, many religions have jurisdictional elements, partly because they purport to be authoritative, and partly due to legalistic or quasi-legalistic aspects of the religion. In short, I don't think that the jurisdictional aspect of law is all that unique to it; other expressive artifacts may exhibit similar aspects. What is unique to law, however, as an expressive artifact that purports to exercise practical authority over people, is its close connection to, or even dependence on, brute force. Law is the kind of expressive artifact, maybe the only kind, that is forced on us by brute power.

Law and political sovereignty are difficult to separate. And this makes the law not just authoritative fiction; it makes it fiction backed by force. A strange thing this is, but the law is a strange kind of artifact and, in some respects, rather unique.

## Notes

1 This essay has been redacted by the editor with the author's permission.
2 I do not intend to exclude various domains of international law from this generalization, though obviously the individuation of the relevant system may be a bit more complicated.
3 See e.g. Hans Kelsen, *General Theory of Law and State*, transl. Anders Wedberg (New York: Russell & Russell, 1961), 42.
4 Joseph Raz, *The Authority of Law* (Oxford: Clarendon Press, 1979), chapter 7.
5 Ibid. H.L.A. Hart disagreed with certain aspects of Raz's analysis, arguing that the relevant difference here pertains to different types of obligation; legal obligation is not like a moral obligation from a certain point of view. (H.L.A. Hart, *Essays on Bentham* (Oxford: Oxford UP, 1982),161). Yet, of course, Hart has never denied that legal obligations are indexed to particular legal orders, presupposing a particular legal point of view, as Kelsen and Raz have suggested.
6 David Lewis, *Philosophical Papers. Vol. 1* (New York, NY and Oxford: Oxford UP, 1983), 262. See also Amie Thomasson, *Fiction and Metaphysics* (Cambridge: Cambridge UP, 1999), 107, and Andrei Marmor, *The Language of Law* (Oxford: Oxford UP, 2014), chapter 3.
7 Not necessarily, of course; pragmatics is always relevant. In some contexts of conversation or in some populations, "according to science" may be used to express what the speaker takes to be a closed prefix. Consider, for example, someone from a fundamentalist evangelical community saying, "Well, according to science it is the case that X ...". Such a speaker may mean quite the opposite of what we mean, suggesting that X is not really true; it's only true from a "scientific" perspective, one the speaker does not quite share, as it were.
8 See e.g. Nils-Hennes Stear, "Imaginative and Fictionality Failure: A Normative Approach", *Philosopher's Imprint* 15 (2015), 1–18.
9 See Andrei Marmor, *Social Conventions* (Princeton, NJ: Princeton UP, 2009), 59–61. Of course, not all statements about things that happen in a game are prefix-dependent. We can say, for example, that "*A* ran to catch the ball", which is true or false regardless of the game context.
10 See also Marmor, *The Language of Law*, 81–4.
11 149 U.S. 304 (1893).
12 674 U.S. (2015)
13 See Andrei Marmor, "The Rule of Law and its Limits", *Law & Philosophy* 23 (2004), 1–43.
14 John Searle, "How Performatives Work", *Linguistics and Philosophy* 12 (1989), 535–58.
15 I am partly relying here on more detailed arguments I presented in my *Social Conventions*, chapter 5.
16 See my *Social Conventions*, chapter 5.
17 Strawson's essay "Intention and Convention in Speech Acts" in: Strawson, Peter. *Logico-Linguistics Papers* (London: Methuen & Co, 1971).
18 Kent Bach and Robert M. Harnish, *Linguistic Communication and Speech Acts* (Cambridge, MA: MIT Press, 1979) and Kent Bach and Robert M. Harnish, "How Performatives Really Work", *Linguistics and Philosophy* 15, (1992), 93–110.

19 Marmor, *Social Conventions*, 127–9.
20 See E.J. Lemmon, "On Sentences Verifiable by their Use", *Analysis* 22 (1962), 86–9. According to Bach and Harnish ("How Performatives Really Work"), all performatives are such that their expression, under appropriate circumstances, renders them true, because they are all expressions of the speaker's attitude. Elsewhere I raised some doubts about this generalization; at the very least, their analysis cannot be applied to conventional performatives where the expression is not truth-apt. See Marmor, *Social Conventions*, chapter 5.
21 I use examples in which the sentence expressed employs an explicit performative verb, such as "promise", "fired", "adjourned", etc. Most of these performatives can be accomplished without using the explicit performative verb. Also notice, however, that an unambiguous sentence can use a performative verb literally without it being used as a performative.
22 See Thomasson, *Fiction and Metaphysics*, chapter 3.
23 Robert Smithson's "Leaning Mirror" (1969), currently exhibited in Dia:Beacon, New York, is exactly that: a double-sided mirror stuck in a pile of sand.
24 See Marmor, *Social Conventions*, 59–61.
25 This is not meant to be a general statement about the ontology of artifacts. In the metaphysical debates about the ontological status of artifacts I try to stay above the fray. Thomasson (*Fiction and Metaphysics*) rightly explains, I think, that the ontological debates should focus on the question of how to understand metaphysical dependence relations and the principle of parsimony. Cf. Peter van Inwagen, *Material Beings* (Ithaca, NY: Cornell UP, 1990), chapter 13.
26 See Marmor, *The Language of Law*, chapter 1.
27 See Marmor, *Philosophy of Law*, chapters 1–4.
28 See Thomasson, *Fiction and Metaphysics*, at 105–6.
29 See Marmor, *Philosophy of Law*, at 53–5.
30 See Andrei Marmor, "An Institutional Conception of Authority", *Philosophy & Public Affairs* 39, No. 3 (2011), 238–61.
31 See Marmor, "An Institutional Conception of Authority", 246–7.
32 As I explained elsewhere in some detail (Marmor, "An Institutional Conception of Authority", 248–52), the question of whether participation is voluntary or not, and to what extent, has a crucial bearing on the conditions of the legitimacy of practical authorities.

## References

Bach, Kent and Robert M. Harnish. *Linguistic Communication and Speech Acts*. Cambridge, MA: MIT Press, 1979.

Bach, Kent and Robert M. Harnish. "How Performatives Really Work". *Linguistics and Philosophy* 15, (1992), 93–110.

Byrne, Alex. "Truth in Fiction: The Story Continued". *Australian Journal of Philosophy* 71 (1993), 24–35.

Finnis, John. *Natural Law and Natural Rights*. Oxford: Oxford UP, 1980.

Hart, H.L.A. *The Concept of Law*. Oxford: Clarendon Press, 1994 [1961].

Hart, H.L.A. *Essays on Bentham*. Oxford: Oxford UP, 1982.

Kelsen, Hans. *General Theory of Law and State*. Translated by Anders Wedberg. New York: Russell & Russell, 1961.

Lemmon, E.J., "On Sentences Verifiable by Their Use". *Analysis* 22 (1962), 86–9.

Lewis, David. *Philosophical Papers. Vol. 1*. New York, NY and Oxford: Oxford UP, 1983.

Marmor, Andrei. *The Language of Law*. Oxford: Oxford UP, 2014.
Marmor, Andrei. *Philosophy of Law*. Princeton, NJ: Princeton UP, 2011.
Marmor, Andrei. *Social Conventions*. Princeton, NJ: Princeton UP, 2009.
Marmor, Andrei. *Interpretation and Legal Theory*. Oxford and Portland, OR: Hart Publishing, 2005.
Marmor, Andrei. "An Institutional Conception of Authority". *Philosophy & Public Affairs* 39, No. 3 (2011), 238–61.
Marmor, Andrei. "The Rule of Law and its Limits". *Law & Philosophy* 23 (2004), 1–43.
Stear, Nils-Hennes. "Imaginative and Fictionality Failure: A Normative Approach", *Philosopher's Imprint* 15 (2015), 1–18.
Raz, Joseph. *The Authority of Law*. Oxford: Clarendon Press, 1979.
Searle, John. "How Performatives Work". *Linguistics and Philosophy* 12 (1989), 535–58.
Strawson, Peter. *Logico-Linguistics Papers*. London: Methuen & Co, 1971.
Thomasson, Amie. *Fiction and Metaphysics*. Cambridge: Cambridge UP, 1999.
Inwagen, Peter van. *Material Beings*. Ithaca, NY: Cornell UP, 1990.
Walton, Kendall. *Mimesis as Make-Believe*. Cambridge, MA: Harvard UP, 1990.

This essay by A. Marmor appeared first in *Law and Philosophy 37* (Springer Nature). We are grateful for the permission to include the essay in this volume.

# Index

Abolitionism: American 98; British 176–7
Aboriginal rights: substantive test 138–40; evidentiary burden 138–40
Aboriginal title *see* Aboriginal rights
abortion: informed consent to 74–6; privacy doctrine and 70, 73–4; ultrasound regulations 76–7
adultery 84–7; in Arthurian legend 87–90; as English origins story 87, 90; penal function of 85–7; status of child conceived 228n75; as tort 84–5
apparatus 17, 30
archival practices 147–9
Aristotle 14, 20
Arthurian legend 87–90
assertion 23, 25, 29–30, 126, 253–255
authority: in law 23, 30, 160, 201, 252; (J. Raz) 265; of literature 31, 258; normative power 264–5; *see also* command
autonomy 70, 73–4; as basis of constitutional privacy 70–1, 73–5; narrative model of 72, 75–7; spatialization of 70–1, 73

Barfield, O. 175–6
Baudry, J.L. 30
Beardsley, M. 26
Ben Shahar, O. 113
Bentham, J.: criticism of legal fiction 5; language as fiction 11, 15; truth and fiction 7, 9, 14, 28
Blackstone, W. 4–5
Blackstone, W. 84–6
boilerplate 105–11
Braddon, M. E. 155–6
Bradley, F. H. 15
Brown, M. 235–7

capacity to contract 212–14
causation 22, 24, 168, 241–3
choice 105–07, 110–11
Clarkson, T. 179–80
Cohn, D. 27
Collins, W. 156, 157, 159–161
command:in fiction 30–1; in law 203–4, 211–12; in legal fiction 203–4
Comstock laws 68–9
confession *see* evidence
Conrad, J. 212–3
consent 74–6, 106, 108, 112
constraint 106
constructive possession 6
contract 105–11, 171, 208, 212–19, 255–6, 262
Cook, J. 144–46
corporate person *see* person
corporate social responsibility 164
criminal conversation 86
Currie, G. 25, 27, 29

De Tourtoulon, P. 7, 13, 21, 48n205, 204, 209
deconstruction *see* Derrida, J.
deeming provisions 201
deep-level structures 204, 221
Demelius, G. 8, 203–4, 210, 221
Derrida, J. 16, 45n156, 106–08, 110, 112
Dewey, J. 15
directive *see* command
dispositif *see* apparatus
divorce 85–6
Driver, F. 146

Eco, U. 20, 127
Eggert, D. 169–72
Einstein, A. 42n119
ejectment 6
English Revolution 85
equality: dignity of states and 97; among sovereign states 99–100
estoppel 24, 196
evidence: confession 117–23, 125–6, 130; estoppel 24; exploration accounts as 138–50; factual fiction 9; hearsay 119, 140–41; and history 94; and narrative 100–2, 140–1, 237–45; rap lyrics as 124–37; reliability in admission of evidence 140–1; and boilerplate 109–10; weight of evidence 140, 143
Explorer Record 138, 142–4, 148

family resemblance 33–6
Feinberg, J. 70
fiction of survival 4, 6, 206
fictional character *see* fictional entities
fictional entities: in general 11–11, 18–23; Bentham 11, 15; legal entities 22, 48n205, 49n221, 196, 208–10; Lewis fallacy 253; in literature 18–23; reference 18, 20; *see also* Sherlock Holmes
Fifth Amendment 68
Filmer, R. 85
Finch, H. 7
First Amendment 72, 75
Fitzgerald, F.S. 163–5
Foucault, M. 16–17, 71, 73–4, 159
Fourth Amendment 67–8
free choice *see* choice
free will 105
Freedom 68–69, 95, 99–100, 105, 111, 243
Fuller, Lon.: definition of legal fiction 8–10, 195; on the fiction of corporate personhood 175; on metaphor 175; persuasive function of fiction 6; relative nature of fiction 9, 12–13, 16, 21; statutory fiction 203

Gabriel, G. 19, 26
Genette, G. 27–8, 34
Gerrig, R. 31
Ginsburg, R.B. 100–02
Glendon, M.A. 71
Godwin, W. 176; *Enquiry Concerning Political Justice* by 183–4; *Things as They Are, or Caleb Williams* by 176; on slavery 183–4
Goethe, J.W.v. 15, 44n139
Goldberg, J. 85
Goodman, N. 19, 26
Gray, J. 4

habeas corpus 176
Habermas, J. 15
Halliday, P. D. 177–8
Hamburger, K. 27
human rights 176
hypotheticals 24, 236, 239–43

illocutionary act *see* speech act theory
imagination: law 22, 202–4, 236, 239, 242; fiction 31
institutional theories: art and institution 260–1; Henry Maine 193; human behaviour and social institutions 146; institutional performatives 258, 261–3; institutional concept of authority 264–5; language as institutionalized practice 32; law as institution 93, 155–61, 261–2; legal fiction as institutionalized practice 32, 200, 202, 219–22; literary fiction as institutionalized practice 30–2; and memory 97; and subject 71, 74
Iser, W. 31–2

James, W. 15
Jauß, H.R. 31–32
Jhering, R. von: definition of legal fiction 10; command and legal fiction 204; criticism of legal fiction 5; relative nature of fiction 9; statutory fictions 202, 205
judicial archivization 148–9

Kayser, W. 27
Kelsen, H.: legal fiction in general 4, 8, 22–3; statutory fictions 22, 40n64, 205; referential system 22; legal reality 22, 49n221–3; legal person (corporate person) 38n42, 48n214, 208–10; basic norm (Grundnorm) 252
kingship 85–90
Kroller, E.M. 145–6

Lacan, J. 70–1
Lacey, N. 158
Lecocq, L. 8, 21, 40n62, 48n205
legal capacity *see* person
Legal Realism, American 244
Lewis, D. 20–2, 28–9, 241, 252–4
linguistic fiction *see* statutory fiction
literariness 3, 127–8
Locke, J. 71
Luhmann, N. 25

Maine, H. 4–5, 9, 192–5
marital fidelity 87–8
McLaren, I.S. 146
Meinongianism 20
memory: artificiality 15, 92; collective memory and law 92, 97; of eyewitness 238; and narrative 93–4 (Ricoeur); of the Voting Rights Act 98
metafiction 24, 28, 153, 191
Metz, C. 30
Murray, W., Lord Mansfield 178–80

narrative *see* narratology
narratology 17, 27, 93–101,126–9, 236–41, 243–6
*nasciturus see* unborn
Nedelsky, J. 71
Nelson, D. 69–70, 73, 78n8
Nesmith, T. 148–9
Neurath, O. 16

objectivity 236, 240, 242–4, 236
original public meaning 6, 39n44

panfictionality 17, 21, 48n205, 196
Parsons, T. 20
Pavel, T. 26
performative approaches *see* speech act theory
person 48n205, 223; civil identity 156; corporate person 6, 22, 164–6, 175–6, 197, 206, 208, 228n77; intentions of corporate persons 163–74; Kelsen on 38n42, 48n214, 208–10; legal person 6, 70, 38n42, 48n214, 164, 175–6, 184–5, 206, 211–16; persona 127, 175; *see also* fictional entity; physical person 22, 206, 208; unborn 201, 206, 210–11, 214–17, 228n75
Pierce, C.S. 15
possibilism 20
possible worlds 20, 24, 241–2, 245–6
Pound, R. 4
pragmatics 32, 54n300; *see also* speech act theory
pragmatism 15; *see also* Vaihinger, H.
presumption 201, 204; definition opposed to fiction 11, 42n110, 221, 223n11
privacy 67; constitutional right to 67–8, 70–5; domestic 67–70; fictions of 67–71; linguistic subject of 71, 72, 77–8; reproductive rights and 73–8; spatialization of 67–71
prosecutor, role of 239, 243, 245
prototype semantics 33–5

Radin, M. 113
Rakoff, T. 113
Rancière, J. 158
reader–response theory 31–32
reference 18–23, 130, 195–7, 201, 241, 252–7
remedy: fictional 175; legal 180
Repeat player 109
reproductive rights: abortion 73–8; contraception 67–9; struggle for 68–9
Rescher, N. 16, 240
Ricoeur, P. 17, 93–4, 96, 102
Roberts, J.G. Jr. 96–100
Rorty, R. 16, 26
Routley, R. 20
Rubenfeld, J. 72, 80n45

Sanger, C. 76–7, 82n94
Sanger, M. 69, 77
scientific method 240–1
Searle, J. 19, 26–7, 34, 258
self-authoring 68–9, 72, 75
sensation fiction 155–62
Sharp, G. 178–79
Sherlock Holmes 47n199, 241, 253–4, 264
Sidney, P. 28
signification 107, 113
slavery 96–102, 105, 177–83; *see also* Abolitionism
speech act theory 25–30, 126–31, 203, 257–9
Stalnaker, R. 241
standard terms 106, 110
standardization 107–9

Stanley, A. D. 111
statutory fiction 22, 35, 40n64, 200–34
Stephen, F. 157
Suchman, M. 113
system: science 16; law 8, 204, 209–19

Tanovich, D. 140
Tennyson, A. 87–90
treason 85–7
truth: fictions and/as falseness 6–17; fictions and/as truth 8–9, 17–22, 259; narratology and *see* narratology; no–assertion–view 19, 23, 25–30; *see also* pragmatism; statutory fiction and 200–10; theories of 11–17; truth and speech–act theory 25–30, 258–59; Lewis on 20–2, 241, 254–7; and possible worlds 241–2
Tyler, T 245

unborn *see* person

Vaihinger, H. 13, 21–2, 240
Vibert, E. 146
Victorian literature 6, 155–61
voting: Fifteenth Amendment and 95, 98; racial discrimination and 95–7, 99–101; Voting Rights Act of 1965 94–5, 97–8, 100

Walton, K. 27, 32, 54n300
Warren, E. 95
White, H. 17, 94
Williams, S. 70, 72, 75
Wilson, D. 235–7, 239–40, 245
Wittgenstein, L. 33–4, 201, 221
Wolterstorff, N. 26, 51n269
women: expressive rights 68–9; reproductive rights 68–9, 73–8; self–authoring 68–9, 73–6
Woo, G.L.X. 148
Wood, M. 146

Zipursky, B. 85

For Product Safety Concerns and Information please contact our EU
representative GPSR@taylorandfrancis.com
Taylor & Francis Verlag GmbH, Kaufingerstraße 24, 80331 München, Germany

www.ingramcontent.com/pod-product-compliance
Ingram Content Group UK Ltd.
Pitfield, Milton Keynes, MK11 3LW, UK
UKHW010957180926
475701UK00004B/407

*9781032236681*